14.50

D0845735

A HISTORY OF ACCOUNTING THOUGHT

REVISED EDITION

MICHAEL CHATFIELD, D.B.A., C.P.A.

PROFESSOR OF ACCOUNTING
CALIFORNIA STATE UNIVERSITY, HAYWARD

ROBERT E. KRIEGER PUBLISHING COMPANY
HUNTINGTON, NEW YORK
1977

Original Edition 1974
Revised Edition 1977

Printed and Published by
ROBERT E. KRIEGER PUBLISHING CO. INC.
645 NEW YORK AVENUE
HUNTINGTON, NEW YORK 11743

Printed in the United States of America

Library of Congress Cataloging in Publication Data

Chatfield, Michael.
    A history of accounting thought.

    Reprint, with updated bibliography, of the ed.
published by the Dryden Press, Hinsdale, Ill.
    Bibliography: p.
    Includes index.
    1. Accounting—History.   I. Title.
HF5605.C49   1977   657'.09   76-49566
ISBN 0-88275-469-6

Preface

With the trend toward graduate business education in American universities, accounting history is receiving attention both as a seminar subject and as a starting point for topical research efforts. However, its essential materials are scattered through a dozen books and many periodical articles. At present only an institution with an extensive library can offer an adequate course in the subject. This book is designed to draw the basic elements of accounting history together into one volume, to show their relevance to current accounting issues, and to give the reader a general perspective on the development of accounting thought.

Directed toward accounting majors, it provides both a review in depth of familiar concepts and a logical framework within which the materials of specialized seminars in theory, auditing, cost, and international accounting can be introduced and traced forward to the present. It might also be appended to a first course in accounting for graduate students who wish to avoid the routine of a fundamentals course but lack the background to be comfortable in a theory seminar. No technical knowledge above the elementary accounting level is required of the reader.

Since it is clearly not possible to cover every facet of the subject in one volume, several limiting assumptions were necessary. As its title suggests, this book is mainly a history of ideas rather than a chronicle of events or a factual summary. Relevance to contemporary problems was a primary test for inclusion. Accordingly, recent events receive most attention in proportion to the historical time periods covered. Compared to earlier works on accounting history, less space is given to the development of double entry bookkeeping and more to the eighteenth and early nineteenth centuries, when modern accounting technique and theory began to emerge. Each era is seen largely as the story of the economically dominant nation of the time. During the Renaissance this is nearly always Italy; from the seventeenth through the nineteenth centuries it is usually England; in the twentieth century it is most often the United States. Of course no claim is made that the accounting methods used by these societies were broadly representative. Merely than in general they were the leaders and innovators and that, like warfare, accounting history is most easily understood from the viewpoint of the dominant countries in each historical period.

The book itself is divided into three sections. The first seven chapters comprise a roughly chronological history of bookkeeping from Babylonian times to the present. Part II describes the rationalization of accounting which followed the Industrial Revolution: scientific management, systematic costing, auditing, budgetary control, modern taxation, and the rise of the accounting profession. Part III is a "history of theory," tracing and analyzing the evolution of accounting principles.

A list of background and topical readings is provided at the end of each chapter. A more complete, annotated bibliography of writings in the accounting history area may be found in R. H. Parker's *Management Accounting: An Historical Perspective* (New York: Augustus M. Kelley, 1969), and in my *Contemporary Studies in the Evolution of Accounting Thought* (Belmont, California: Dickenson Publishing Company, 1968).

The major change in this revised edition is the inclusion of expanded end-of-chapter bibliographical citations, permitting research in depth on nearly every major topic considered in the book.

The author gratefully acknowledges the comments and suggestions for revision of the manuscript of this book made by Professors Richard P. Brief (New York University), John W. Buckley (UCLA), Richard Homburger (Wichita State University), Chris J. Luneski (University of Oregon), and Maurice Moonitz (University of California, Berkeley).

Hayward, California   Michael Chatfield
December, 1976

Contents

Part I

DEVELOPMENT OF BASIC
ACCOUNTING METHODS

Chapter 1

ACCOUNTING IN THE ANCIENT WORLD

ACCOUNTING AND SOCIAL DEVELOPMENT

Whether the progress of ideology governs the development of social institutions or *vice versa,* there are obvious connections between ideas and the conditions under which people live. A study of their evolution suggests that accounting processes are reactive, that they develop mainly in response to business needs at any given time, and that their growth is relative to economic progress generally. In general, the higher the level of civilization, the more elaborate the bookkeeping methods. And as record keeping needs multiply, the ability of accounting data to promote or hinder economic development also increases.

Sometimes new accounting methods transform the very environment which called them forth. Double entry bookkeeping facilitates large scale business organization, and during the Renaissance certain German city-states where it was adopted progressed markedly faster than nearby cities which continued to use traditional single entry methods.[1] In this century the enhanced status of American public accountants and their increasing control over the contents of financial statements roughly coincided with a corporate shift from debt to equity financing, whose success depended on investor confidence in published reports.

The view of accountancy as a mirror of socioeconomic development has analytical implications. Much of what is known about the daily life of ancient societies has come down to us through their account books. In Edward Gibbon's opinion, our greatest loss of potential knowledge about the Romans resulted from the destruction of the budget presented by Emperor Augustus to the Senate.[2] Partly because of their objectivity and partly because they describe in detail things no chronicler would consider worth mentioning, old lists of receipts and payments have often proved more revealing than the most skillfully written narratives. Conversely, one way to test the validity, or at least the appropriateness, of the doctrines and methods now in use is to follow along their historical trails, especially when they developed for reasons different from those used to justify their retention in modern practice.

The crucial event in accounting history was the emergence of double entry bookkeeping. The "Method of Venice" described by Pacioli in 1494 included most elements of hand bookkeeping as it is practiced today. But it was so different from anything known previously that accounting history divides into two distinct parts, one comprising the 5000 years before the appearance of double entry and the other the 500 years since. Between these two eras there occurs a sharp break in continuity, events of the earlier period seeming at first glance to have a certain historical interest but very little relevance to current accounting issues.

In fact the record keeping, control, and verification problems encountered in the ancient world were in many ways like our own. There seem to be certain perennial demands which every developed society makes on its accounting records. No government could afford not to keep an accurate record of receipts and disbursements. Tax collections in particular were always closely controlled. The accumulation of private wealth led to some kind of stewardship accounting, both to assure the physical protection of assets and to prove that those who administered them had done their job properly. The need for a check on the honesty and reliability of employees made internal control a central feature of all ancient bookkeeping systems. And there was always some kind of audit procedure to expose losses due to dishonesty or negligence. These were the essentials, and ancient accounting was seldom luxurious. Even at the high points of its pre-Christian development—in Babylonia, Egypt, China, Greece, and Rome—bookkeepers faced the problem of holding people accountable in societies where the vast majority were illiterate, where writing materials were relatively costly and numeration was difficult, and where in most cases money did not exist as a common denominator of value. The resulting data had to be of considerable importance to justify the trouble and expense of producing it.

BABYLONIA AND ASSYRIA

From obscure beginnings more than 7000 years ago, the Chaldean-Babylonian, Assyrian, and Sumerian civilizations produced what may have been the first organized government in the world, several of the oldest written languages, and the oldest surviving business records.[3] Periodic floodings made the valley between the Tigris and Euphrates Rivers a particularly rich farming area. Various types of service businesses and small industries were established in the towns, and an extensive trade grew up within and outside the Mesopotamian Valley. There were at least two banking firms, and notations exist of "money current with the merchant" comprising standard measures of gold and silver. The principle of credit was understood. It was common practice for drafts to be drawn on one place and payable in another. The cities of Babylon and Ninevah were known as the "queens of commerce," and Babylonian became the language of business and politics throughout the Near East. Record keeping is thought to have begun about 4000 B.C., though the oldest known commercial documents date from 3500 B.C.[4]

By all descriptions the Babylonians were obsessive bookkeepers, with a passion for organization.[5] They lived in a densely populated river valley whose fertility depended on an intricate system of irrigation canals. Sumeria was a theocracy whose early rulers were considered "bailiffs of the gods," and in this capacity possessed most of the land and herds. Both they and their subjects had to render detailed stewardship accounts to their supernatural masters.[6] Formal legal codes provided even stronger incentives for recording business events. The best known is the Code of Hammurabi, king of the first dynasty of Babylonia (2285–2242 B.C.). It required that an agent selling goods for a merchant give the merchant a sealed memorandum quoting prices; if this was not done, a contested agreement was legally unenforceable. It was customary for every business transaction, even the smallest, to be put in writing and signed by the contracting parties and witnesses. Such was the national temperament that it seems doubtful whether many transactions or commodity movements of any kind went unrecorded.

In these nations whose kings sometimes boasted of their ability to read and write, the scribe was absolutely indispensible to commerce and public administration. He has been called the predecessor of today's accountant,[7] and his functions were similar, but even more extensive. It was his duty not only to put business transactions in writing but to see that legal provisions were complied with in drawing up commercial agreements. Such a "public" scribe might be found sitting near the city gates. The contracting parties would arrive, reach an understanding, and explain to him the nature of their transaction. Using as pencil a wooden rod with a blunt, triangular end, the scribe then recorded their agreement on a small lump of moist clay, enumerating the names of the parties, the items paid or received, promises made, and any other pertinant details. The inconvenience of mass illiteracy was circumvented by having each man carry his signature around his neck in the form of a stone amulet engraved with its owner's mark (and buried with him when he died). Each party to the transaction, and the witnesses, affixed their signatures by impressing these seals into the clay tablet, and the scribe completed the record by writing out their names.[8] The more important commercial tablets were kiln-dried; the rest were allowed to dry in the sunlight.

After an agreement had been written and signed, the scribe sometimes took in hand a new piece of clay and, flattening it to the thickness of a piecrust, wrapped it completely around the original tablet. Like a modern envelope, this outer covering might merely be inscribed with the names and seal impressions of the contracting parties, to identify the inner contents and insure their privacy. But if the purpose was to prevent alteration of a tablet, the whole transaction would be rewritten and signed again on this outer surface, providing in effect a carbon copy. Since the inner and outer messages were supposed to be identical, any tampering with this envelope could immediately be detected by comparing it to the original inscription. Nor could anyone alter the original tablet without first cracking off and destroying the outer shell. Effective forgery would require a complete rewriting and rewitnessing of both tablet and envelope.

The temples and the central and provincial governments of Babylonia employed hundreds of scribes as administrators. Surviving temple accounts on "a great mass of tablets" describe a variety of receipts and disbursements, wage payments, rental income, interest on loans, and real estate transactions.[9] Both the temples and the royal treasury sent scribes to distant parts of the Empire as collectors of sacrifices and taxes. These men incurred travelling expenses for which they were later reimbursed, and the allowance tablets which were prepared are equivalent to modern expense accounts. Tithes and property taxes were normally paid in kind. Cereals, cattle, and other farm commodities were received daily at storehouses throughout the country. If not quickly disposed of, they would have overloaded the facilities and caused losses due to spoilage. Scribes recorded the types and quantities of goods as they arrived and supervised their segregation for sale, use, or accumulation. Periodically tl ey prepared inventories of assets on hand and charge-and-discharge type summaries of commodities received and paid out. There are evidences of royal examination and audit.[10]

EGYPT

Government accounting in Egypt had a generally similar development, though the introduction of papyrus as a writing surface made records less cumbersome and permitted a wider use of supporting documents. As in Babylonia, national cohesion depended on the organization of royal finance, whereby storehouses in each district received taxes paid in kind and forwarded the less perishable items to a central treasury. In such an empire, held together by record keeping, scribes were again the "pivots on which the whole machinery of the treasury and other departments turned."[11] With minute care the bookkeepers attached to each storehouse recorded all that was received and the details of its use. Nothing left the treasury without a written order. Additional security was provided by an elaborate internal control system which required that the records of one official agree with those of another. Accuracy was advisable,

because accounts were audited by the storehouse superintendents, gross irregu-
larities being punishable even by mutilation or death.

The importance given such records contrasts curiously with their lack of
sophistication. Egyptian and Babylonian bookkeeping developed rapidly during the early progress of those civilizations and then virtually stagnated for
several thousand years. Their receipt and disbursement records remained essentially lists which cannot be considered accounts at all in the modern sense
of data accumulation categories. It has been argued[12] that better methods were
not needed because these nations changed so little after an initial period of
development, but this only begs the question. The options of a largely illiterate
society which lacks a uniform medium of exchange will always be limited.
They never had coined money, that is, lumps of metal stamped to identify their
purity and weight, and intended for use as currency.[13] Their accounting described commodity movements, treating measures of gold and silver not as
units of value but merely as articles of exchange. The inability to express all
these goods in terms of a single substance made cumulation and summation
very difficult, and an integrated accounting *system* virtually impossible. The
cultural constraints imposed by barter may have been even more inhibiting.
One is reminded of the Andaman Islander, carrying his surplus possession to
the marketplace and waiting there, sometimes for days, in hope of finding
another trader who wanted his goods and had something of equal value which
he in turn wished to have.

We might expect that men who understood the monetary concept could do
better than this even if they lacked money itself. In many ways the economy
of colonial America was more backward than that of ancient Egypt. Commerce was more localized, the inland transportation system was less developed, much of the land was less fertile, and agricultural methods were only
marginally better. The British would not let the colonists coin money, which
was extremely scarce, and until the 1820s trade was carried on largely without
it. As a substitute for cash they evolved a system of "bookkeeping barter"—
barter with a time lag.[14] For example, a dairyman might deliver milk on credit
to a tailor each day, and be paid with a new suit at year end. This required
literacy and the ability of both parties to keep books in terms of an identical
medium of exchange. In other respects the system could be as primitive as
some found in the ancient world. It needed just a record, or at most a balance,
never a summary of all accounts. Ledgers consisted mainly of charges and
credits to men's names. No attempt was made to isolate income, success being
measured in terms of asset increases. Though known, double entry bookkeeping was rarely used.

CHINA

Accounting seems to have developed more slowly but over a longer period in

China than it did in the Near East. During the Chao Dynasty (1122–256 B.C.), government accounting reached a peak of sophistication which was hardly improved on till the introduction of double entry techniques during the nineteenth century. This third and longest dynasty in Chinese history was a period of territorial expansion and a literary and philosophical golden age, producing Mencius, Lao Tse, and Confucius (who is said to have been a government record keeper). The Chaos inherited and built on concepts of financial administration and accountability which originated during the Hsia (2206–1766 B.C.) and Shang (1766–1122 B.C.) Dynasties. They used coined money, and their Bureau of Currency and Produce Exchange acted as a central bank in making loans and buying unsalable goods to stabilize commodity markets. In the procedural areas of internal control, budgeting, and audit, the Chaos probably had no peers in the ancient world.[15]

Perhaps more than any other pre-Christian nation, the Chinese reduced their public finance to a civil service routine in which accounting was used chiefly to evaluate the success of government programs and the efficiency of personnel. The heart of Chao's financial operations was the Grand Treasury, which received revenues, allocated them to other government agencies for their daily use, authorized all expenditures, and prepared summaries of receipts and payments at the end of each fiscal year. Administrative control was facilitated by channeling resources into an elaborate system of funds. In modern terminology these included a *general revenue fund,* where the ceiling for tax rates was established; *welfare funds,* made up of items confiscated by the customs houses at ports of entry; *relief funds,* consisting of surpluses from the state graneries; *reserve funds,* which absorbed the surplus from all other funds and were intended to cover any deficits in budgeted expenditures and to meet unbudgeted needs. There were also a multitude of *special revenue funds.* Public works, maintenance of the royal household, diplomatic missions, payrolls, even public relations were periodically budgeted and funded. It was an impressive arrangement, not only because certain sums were reserved for specified purposes, but because each such fund had its source in a particular kind of taxation or tribute.

The Prime Minister had overall responsibility for the budgetary process and for on-site audits of government departments, but the details of both functions were delegated to the Office of the Comptroller General. As a first step in the budget cycle, data on population, harvest conditions, and productive processes were submitted by the various operating departments. Current census figures were particularly important. The Office of the Superintendent of Records furnished compilations of receipts and disbursements, maps, tabulations of the number of workers in each occupation, kinds and quantities of production tools, and estimates of natural resources. The Office of the Keeper of Government Granaries submitted a report mainly concerning harvest expectations, which in this agricultural empire governed the permissible rate of taxation in kind, and in general the expansion or contraction of government programs. With all this information in hand, the Prime Minister made the major decisions about national financial affairs. This was evidently done in a month's time, because in the first month before the budget year began, the Prime Minister had to deliver a policy speech before princes of the feudal states and government officials. Once general policy was set, the Comptroller General's office fixed the amounts of tributes and worked out the details of collecting revenues and maintaining general revenue funds. The completed budget was entirely an executive document, there being no legislative branch.

The Chinese used a lunar calendar, dividing the year into twelve months of twenty-nine or thirty days, and each month into three ten-day periods called *hsun.* Accordingly, ten-day, monthly, and annual reports were prepared throughout the budget cycle. The ten-day reports were current and descriptive, and evidently were audited on a random sample basis by the Comptroller General's office, while the monthly and annual summaries were audited in detail. In addition, every government agency prepared an annual report on its accomplishments, and these were also audited by the Office of the Comptroller General. Such examinations always emphasized the performance of officehold-ers and were considered preliminary to the triannual examination of officials by the Assistant Minister, which determined who was to be promoted and honored and who was to be demoted, degraded, and publicly humiliated. Being responsible for budget preparation as well as audit, the Comptroller General's office was in the delicate position of passing on its own actions and those of the Grand Treasury, its parent body. The Chaos compensated for this by giving the Comptroller General a higher rank than his nominal superior, the Grand Treasurer. Supported by this novel form of independence, the Comp-troller General could impartially and without fear examine the officials respon-sible for financial operations and the custody of funds.

GREECE

The Athenians of the fifth century B.C. had a public administration different from any discussed previously, in that the citizens possessed real authority over government finance and the official bureaucracy. Expenditure levels were fixed by law. Acting largely through a Council with delegated powers, members of the popular Assembly sponsored financial legislation and controlled the receipt and disbursement of public money. Ten state accountants, chosen by lot, recorded revenues as they came in and compiled lists of government debtors. Acknowledgement of popular sovereignty by even the highest officials made financial disclosure an important concept for the first time in history. To ensure maximum publicity, certain accounts were even engraved in stone and placed on public view. Despite this, fraud seems to have been common, and the records of every officeholder were examined by government auditors at the expiration of his term. "No person who had not rendered his account could go abroad, consecrate his property to a god, or even dedicate a sacred offering; nor could he make a will, or be adopted from one family into another."[16]

Just as in Babylonia, where production and commerce were concentrated in the temples, much of Athenian public wealth was represented by "the property of the gods" as accumulated in the Parthenon and other sacred buildings. But the finances of Greek temple-treasuries were controlled by the state, not by the priests. It was convenient to build up an untouchable reserve for public emergencies by putting surplus funds in the hands of the gods. But whether it was making deposits or borrowing from the deities, the Athenian *polis* was the real creditor as well as the debtor, and the transfers back and forth were essentially bookkeeping transactions.[17] The Assembly appointed the sacred as well as the public treasurers, and annual inventories were made of temple property prior to the installation of new officers. Fairly efficient in controlling such locally derived sources of income, the Athenian system of public finance worked less well in administering an overseas empire. The privilege of collecting tributes from dependent cities was sold to tax farmers on a bid basis.[18]

The most important Greek contribution to accountancy was the invention of coined money "not much earlier than about 630 B.C."[19] It would seem logical that when records were kept in monetary terms bookkeeping would become more specialized, and that this would be especially true of commercial accounts. But De Ste. Croix insists that private accounts were hardly better kept than public ones.[20] The use of coins spread slowly in the Greek world, and its impact on accounting was also gradual. The humble were still illiterate. Business tended to be done in person and settled on the spot; the ordinary Greek found little need for bookkeeping beyond a record of debts owed and owing. Though the Greeks and later the Romans usually recorded all their possessions and transactions in terms of a common monetary denominator, often they did not. Property might be represented in physical quantities and monetary assets in money terms, or coins of different city-states might be mixed together in the accounts. It does seem that banking was more highly developed in Greece than in any earlier society. All bankers kept account books, which might have to be produced as evidence in court. They changed and loaned money, accepted deposits, acted as intermediaries and trustees, and arranged cash transfers for clients through correspondents in distant cities.[21]

The thousand-odd inscribed rolls of the Zenon papyri comprise by far the largest body of surviving accounts from the Greco-Roman world. In 256 B.C., when Egypt was a Greek province, Zenon became manager of the great private estate of Apollonius, finance minister of Ptolemy II, and introduced a meticulous system of responsibility accounting. Each area of the estate—vineyards, farms, grain stores, herds, household, and administrative units—was put in charge of a supervisor who had to render account daily or at frequent intervals. Every transaction was documented, and the resulting records were organized systematically, with similar items grouped in paragraphs and only the total amounts extended. Each had to be approved by Zenon or one of his assistants, after which it was tagged and filed. Departmental vouchers were periodically summarized in a number of ledger-like money and commodity accounts. In some of these, asset acquisitions and disposals were added and deducted as they occurred, permitting a running balance to be kept. Monthly, annual, and even triannual summaries were prepared. All accounts were audited. Managerial control was facilitated by the relative cheapness of papyrus, which allowed preparation of extensive supporting memoranda. Zenon's accounts were much more detailed than the oldest known double entry ledgers, especially as regards originating documents and subsidiary records.[22]

The Zenon archive exemplifies a system of accounting used in Greece from the fifth century B.C., which spread throughout the eastern Mediterranean and the Middle East, and was later adopted and modified by the Romans.[23] Zenon was an exceptionally able administrator, and there is evidence that his accounts were among the best of their kind. In any case their modern aspects should not be allowed to obscure their limitations, especially since these were largely self-imposed. Zenon kept records not so that he could report to outsiders, or calculate taxes due, or help maximize or even determine estate income, but simply to expose losses due to theft, fraud, or inefficiency on the part of his master's servants and others with whom he dealt. His essential aim was the protection of property through control of people. He achieved it by recording and auditing the most minute details of receipts and expenditures, literally down to the price of used nails. The principles of stewardship and conservatism were reflected in such accounts, but never the doctrine of materiality. The usual Greek accounts of this period took the form of a rambling narrative, with receipts and payments often intermingled. A modern reader would be struck by the absence of classification and the infrequency of tabulations. There was elaborate detail, but hardly any attempt to cumulate data, and it is doubtful whether a truly integrated accounting system existed anywhere in the ancient world.[24] A banker, merchant, or estate manager might keep records of his dealings with particular persons, but each would be handled independently, and a transaction with any one would not require entries in his other accounts.

But their failure to produce unified accounts was certainly less damaging to the Greeks and Romans than their inability to use accounting as an aid to decision making. They had nothing like cost accounting.[25] Estate records were considered worthless in valuing a property prior to sale. The landowner had no ready means of judging the alternative costs or profits of raising different crops, because his estate accounts did not allow for separate costing by product lines. Since they made no distinction between capital and revenue expenditures, Zenon's records could not help him estimate the profitability of making capital investments. Neither did they isolate the cost of labor, or enable him to calculate the effect on income of assigning more or fewer workers to a particular crop. Of course, such implicit comparisons with modern practice are not entirely fair to accountants whose main interest was asset protection rather than financial measurement. But in a larger sense the economic shortcomings of both societies must have been aggravated by their inability to allocate resources systematically. It seems likely that poor accounting technique was not the only cause of this situation, since little better use was made of estate accounts until the Industrial Revolution.[26]

ROME

Roman government and bankers' accounts began as elaborations of the records traditionally kept by the heads of families. These latter involved the daily entry of household receipts and payments in an *adversaria* or daybook, and monthly postings to a *codex accepti et expensi* which was in effect a cashbook. Household accounts were important because the law required taxpayers to prepare statements of all their property and outstanding debts, and also because a citizen's civil rights depended to some extent on the amount of property he declared.[27] Moreover, a binding contract could be made between two parties simply by recording it in the account books of each, and the old system of listing receipts and disbursements was gradually extended to include the acknowledgement of debts as well as actual cash payments.[28]

The Roman senate, acting in the name of the people, controlled coinage and public finance under the Republic. The power to order payments was at first delegated to the consuls, but in 443 B.C. was transferred to the censors, who thereby assumed overall charge of the nation's financial administration. Receipts and disbursements were made the responsibility of a small group of quaestors, who managed the treasury, paid the army, and supervised the government's bookkeeping. Under their direction treasury scribes kept daybooks comparable to the family *adversaria,* which were summarized each month in a register resembling the *codex.* They also maintained a *calendarium* or register of debts. An intricate system of checks and counterchecks was established among the various financial officers. Written authorization and a formal order supported by documents was required before money could be paid out by the treasury, and the right to authorize such expenditures was normally withheld from officials whose duties included cash handling. Public accounts were examined by an audit staff supervised by the treasurer. On leaving office the quaestors had to render account both to the senate and to their successors.[29]

The financial arrangements of a city-state, with authority shared among the senate, the censors, and the quaestors, proved inadequate to control the fiscal operations of a vast empire or to pay for its almost continuous wars of conquest.[30] Indeed, the transition from republic to empire was partly a response to the need for centralized control over public finance. Behind a facade of republicanism the legislative authority was eroded and financial as well as political power became concentrated in the executive. Julius Caesar exercised personal supervision over the treasury, and Augustus completely revamped its operations. Perhaps his most significant reform was the introduction of an annual budget, aimed at coordinating the Empire's fiscal activities, limiting expenditures to the amount of estimated revenues, and achieving a more proportional distribution of taxes according to ability to pay. In 292 A.D. Diocletian divided the Empire into twelve dioceses, each of which included a number of adjacent provinces. The governor of each province was responsible to the governor of his diocese for tax collections, and the latter was in turn responsible to one of four praetorian prefects, the emperor's personal financial representatives. After the emperor had fixed the amount to be raised by each praetorian prefect, the prefect issued an order which divided the required amount among the various dioceses; each subordinate official then subdivided this sum among his subordinates. Though local accounting records were used as a check on the amount of collections, the Romans never really solved their internal control problem. This system, as amended by Constantine and his successors, lasted until the fall of the Western Empire in 476 A.D.[31]

Among the most highly developed Roman business accounts were those kept by bankers and stewards, containing as they did tantalizing hints of bilateral form. Bankers maintained three books: an *adversaria*, in which transactions were noted as they occurred; a *codex accepti et expensi* or cashbook; and a *liber rationum*, literally personal ledger or book of accounts, where data from the *adversaria* were classified. We know little about the exact form of these accounts because the entries were usually written on wooden tablets coated with wax. It is known that Roman bankers opened an individual account in the name of each customer, and that these were periodically balanced.[32] If a banker had many loans outstanding, and if a depositor also borrowed, or if a borrower repaid in installments, there would be reason for still more elaborate organization of the *liber rationum*. The need to find a client's balance quickly, and the natural duality involved in loaning money and accepting repayments could have fostered a system in which each payment or receipt was entered twice, to the credit of one account and the debit of another, and in which the *liber rationum* was arranged to show each customer's debits and credits on opposite pages. To support this thesis, Kats maintains that Roman bankers knew how to extend and summarize an account, how to carry its balance forward, how to cancel an entry by means of a contra-entry, and how to transfer the balance of a debt from the account of one client to another.[33] But there is no evidence of duality of entry, or of accounts as data accumulation categories which were increased or decreased by debits and credits.[34]

Another intimation of bilateral form may have appeared in stewards' accounts. Wealthy Romans appointed managers to invest their surplus funds, and special account books were kept by these *curators calendarii,* who were often educated slaves. Kats suggests that the duty of rendering account for stewardship in such cases led naturally to a system of bookkeeping which would allow the owner to see at a glance how his affairs stood, and to check their agreement with a summary "master's account."[35] On receiving money for investment, the *curator* would make a debit entry in the cashbook and credit the master's account. When he loaned money at interest, he debited the borrower's account in the *liber calendarii* and credited cash in the *codex expensi.* When a loan was repaid these entries would be reversed. Cash would be credited and the master's account debited for any payments made to the owner. Thus, a running account of stewardship could be achieved by means of balanced books in which the master's account was the reciprocal and summary of all others, rather like a modern trustee's account. This, if actually done, would have introduced an element of duality into record keeping, but it would not have involved a formal accounting equation, or a balancing of assets and debts, or the cumulation of operating results in a profit and loss account, but simply the keeping of a duplicate record so that a summary could easily be made.[36]

De Ste. Croix counters these speculations by asserting that no important improvements in bookkeeping method can be traced to the Roman era.[37] The Romans introduced techniques for summarizing petty expenses and for cross-referencing from one account to another. There is evidence of bilateral form in one surviving set of records.[38] But the typical Roman account was a continuous narrative, without tabulation of figures or even separation of receipts and payments. They had no concept of debits and credits, and in general they never progressed to the point of separating what we would call debit and credit entries by putting the figures in two parallel columns, let alone on opposite sides of an account.[39] They never developed the system of interlocking real and nominal accounts which is the essence of double entry, nor did they achieve a unified single entry system. None of this was needed, because the Romans' motives for keeping books were hardly more ambitious than those of the Babylonians. Their primary purpose was to detect losses caused by fraud and inefficiency.

ANCIENT AND MODERN BOOKKEEPING

The contrast between ancient and modern accounting can be expressed in terms of a complex but primitive Roman economy which never developed to a point where double entry bookkeeping would have been useful. Why then did double entry first appear in the city-states of Northern Italy, nearly a thousand years after the fall of a society which was organized on so much larger a scale? Double entry imposes a framework in which accounting data can be arranged and cumulated. Yet its orderliness and comprehensiveness do not seem to have been its main attractions to those who first adopted it. Nor was it at first used to find total profits, or as a primary aid in decision making, or to facilitate statement preparation. Its early users seem to have valued it chiefly as a memory aid,[40] a merit the Romans would also have appreciated. There is no reason to think the medieval merchant more ingenious than his earlier counterparts, and in some ways his activities were more restricted. There must have been other differences between the accounting environment of the ancient world and that of the Renaissance.

In *Accounting Evolution to 1900,* A. C. Littleton lists seven preconditions for the emergence of systematic bookkeeping:

> The *Art of Writing,* since bookkeeping is first of all a record; *Arithmetic,* since the mechanical aspect of bookkeeping consists of a sequence of simple computations; *Private Property,* since bookkeeping is concerned only with recording the facts about property and property rights; *Money* (i.e., a money economy), since bookkeeping is unnecessary except as it reduces all transactions in properties or property rights to this common denominator; *Credit* (i.e., incompleted transactions), since there would be little impulse to make any record whatever if all exchanges were completed on the spot; *Commerce,* since a merely local trade would never have created enough pressure (volume of business) to stimulate men to coordinate diverse ideas into a system; *Capital,* since without capital commerce would be trivial and credit would be inconceivable.[41]

Each of these prerequisites to bookkeeping development was present in some form in the ancient world, yet even the most advanced of those civilizations failed to produce a double entry system or anything like it. The potentialities of a written language were always diluted by mass illiteracy. A money economy never fully existed. Greece and Rome were in this sense transitional societies in which monetary assets were usually accounted for in monetary terms, while inventories and other resources were often recorded in physical units. Every ancient society had arithmetic, but none developed a simple way of making calculations. A basic reason for the backwardness of Greco-Roman accounting can be found in their systems of numerical notation.[42] These were inferior parly because of the large variety of symbols used for numbers (the Greeks had twenty-eight), and partly because the Greeks and Romans never learned to express a number's value merely by its position in relation to other numbers. This lack of place value meant that there was little incentive to arrange figures in columns, since they could not be added down like Arabic numerals. And without a columnar separation of receipts and payments, giving rise to the notions of debit and credit, there could of course be no double entry bookkeeping.

Property rights certainly existed in the ancient world, but property acquired by conquest or produced by slave labor was not apt to be used productively.[43] Stewardship of such assets gave rise to inventories and to lists of receipts and payments, but rarely to income measurement. Wealth existed in plenty, but there was no clearly understood concept of capital as a factor in production, nor any felt need for that type of accounting which considers the costs and benefits resulting from alternative uses of assets. Neither was ancient world commerce of a kind to produce double entry. Most pre-Christian societies were agricultural and largely self-sufficient. The ordinary people had little purchasing power, the supply of trade goods was small, and transportation facilities were often poor. Barter, the normal method of exchange, required no bookkeeping because transactions were settled immediately. There were some credit dealings, but not of a kind that offered much incentive for systematic record keeping. Borrowing was more often for consumption than for production or trade. Loans tended to be secured by pledged valuables, and in such cases the banker, like a modern pawnbroker, could be indifferent as to whether the money was ever repaid.[44]

Taken as a whole, the Roman accounting legacy to the Middle Ages was tenacious but of doubtful value. The preference for Roman numerals continued among bookkeepers until the sixteenth century, hundreds of years after the introduction of Arabic numbers. Ironically, a few methods which had failed the Romans proved more suitable for their feudal, small-scale successors. But the economic developments in Western Europe from the eleventh to the fourteenth centuries were in many ways quite different from anything known previously, and seemed to call for a fresh approach in record keeping. An increasing volume of trade helped to create a fund of productive capital and to stimulate an expanded use of credit. Commodity as well as monetary transactions began to be recorded in money terms. Double entry bookkeeping made its appearance in the thirteenth century, but even before this there was a definite tendency to group and classify entries, and in some surviving single entry records, receipts and expenditures are posted in columns side by side. There were also improvements in nonfinancial accounting during this period, and though these did not lead directly to new accounting forms, they nonetheless helped set the stage for their appearance.

FOOTNOTES

1. Walter Eucken, *The Foundations of Economics: History and Theory in the Analysis of Economic Reality* (Chicago: University of Chicago Press, 1951), 283.
2. Edward Gibbon, *A History of the Decline and Fall of the Roman Empire,* E. M. Bury, ed. (New York: The Macmillan Company, 1909-1914), vol. 1, 158.
3. Richard Brown, ed., *A History of Accounting and Accountants* (Edinburgh: Jack, 1905), 16.
4. A.H. Woolf, *A Short History of Accountants and Accountancy* (London: Gee, 1912), 15.
5. Tom B. Jones, "Bookkeeping in Ancient Sumer," *Archaeology* 9 (1956), 17.
6. *Ibid.*
7. Orville R. Keister, "The Mechanics of Mesopotamian Record-Keeping," *The National Association of Accountants Bulletin* 46 (February, 1965), 24.
8. Edward Chiera, *They Wrote on Clay* (Chicago: University of Chicago Press, 1938), 67-69.
9. Brown, *op. cit.,* 19.
10. Orville R. Keister, "Commercial Record-Keeping in Ancient Mesopotamia," *Accounting Review* 38 (April, 1963), 371-76.
11. Woolf, *op. cit.,* 6.
12. Keister, "Commercial Record-Keeping in Ancient Mesopotamia," *op. cit.,* 372.

13. G.E.M. De Ste. Croix, "Greek and Roman Accounting," in A.C. Littleton and B.S. Yamey, ed., *Studies in the History of Accounting* (Homewood, Ill.: Richard D. Irwin, 1956), 22.
14. W.T. Baxter, "Accounting in Colonial America," in A.C. Littleton and B.S. Yamey, ed., *Studies in the History of Accounting* (Homewood, Ill.: Richard D. Irwin, 1956), 272-87.
15. Phillip Fu, "Governmental Accounting in China during the Chao Dynasty (1122 B.C.– 256 B.C.)," *Journal of Accounting Research* 9 (Spring, 1971), 40-51.
16. Quoted in Brown, *op. cit.*, 24.
17. De Ste. Croix, *op. cit.*, 26-27.
18. Woolf, *op. cit.*, 30-31.
19. De Ste. Croix, *op. cit.*, 22.
20. *Ibid.*, 29.
21. Woolf, *op. cit.*, 34-35.
22. H.P. Hain, "Accounting Control in the Zenon Papyri," *Accounting Review* 41 (October, 1966), 700-2.
23. *Ibid.*, 699.
24. De Ste. Croix, *op. cit.*, 32.
25. S. Paul Garner, *Evolution of Cost Accounting to 1925* (Alabama: University of Alabama Press, 1954), 2, 3, 25, 26.
26. Gunnar Mickwitz, "Economic Rationalism in Graeco-Roman Agriculture," *English Historical Review* 52 (1937), 580.
27. B. Penndorf, "The Relation of Taxation to the History of the Balance Sheet," *Accounting Review* 5 (December, 1930), 244.
28. A.C. Littleton, *Accounting Evolution to 1900* (New York: American Institute Publishing Company, 1933), 30.
29. Brown, *op. cit.*, 30-32; Woolf, *op. cit.*, 38.
30. Brown, *op. cit.*, 32-33.
31. *Ibid.*, 32-39.
32. Penndorf, *op. cit.*, 244.
33. P. Kats, "A Surmise Regarding the Origins of Bookkeeping by Double Entry," *Accounting Review* 5 (December, 1930), 313.
34. Littleton, *op. cit.*, 29-32.
35. Kats, *op. cit.*, 316.
36. Littleton, *op. cit.*, 32-33.
37. De Ste. Croix, *op. cit.*, 33.
38. *Ibid.*, 34-37.
39. *Ibid.*, 14.
40. See Chapter Three.
41. Littleton, *op. cit.*, 12.
42. De Ste. Croix, *op. cit.*, 50-61.
43. Littleton, *op. cit.*, 14.
44. *Ibid.*, 14-15.

SELECTED BIBLIOGRAPHY

Brown, Richard, ed. *A History of Accounting and Accountants.* Edinburgh: Jack, 1905. Reprinted by B. Franklin, New York, 1966, chaps. one and two.
Buckmaster, D. "The Indian Quipu and the Jacobsen Hypothesis." *Journal of Accounting Research* 12 (Spring, 1974), 178-181.
Calhoun, George M. *The Business Life of Ancient Athens.* Chicago: University of Chicago Press, 1926.
Chiera, Edward. *They Wrote on Clay.* Chicago: University of Chicago Press, 1938, chap. six.
_____. *Selected Temple Accounts from Telloch, Yokha and Drehem.* Philadelphia: University of Pennsylvania Press, 1921.
Costouros, George J. *Accounting in the Golden Age of Greece.* Unpublished Ph.D. Dissertation, University of Santa Clara, 1972. University Microfilms, Ann Arbor, Michigan.
_____. "Development of Banking and Related Bookkeeping Techniques in Ancient Greece (400-300 B.C.)." *International Journal of Accounting* 8 (Spring, 1973), 75-81.

_____. "Early Greek Accounting on Estates (Fourth Century B.C.)." *Academy of Accounting Historians Working Paper No. 7.* University, Alabama: Academy of Accounting Historians, 1974.

Delmouzou-Peppa, D. *The Institution of Public Accountants in Ancient Greece.* Athens: Institute of Certified Public Accountants of Greece, 1963.

De Ste. Croix, G.E.M. "Greek and Roman Accounting." In A.C. Littleton and B.S. Yamey, ed., *Studies in the History of Accounting.* Homewood, Ill.: Richard D. Irwin, 1956, 14-74.

_____. "Ancient Greek and Roman Maritime Loans." In Harold Edey and B.S. Yamey, eds. *Debits, Credits, Finance and Profits.* London: Sweet and Maxwell, 1974, 41-59.

Forrester, D.A.R. "Incan Contribution to Double Entry Accounting." *Journal of Accounting Research* 6 (Autumn, 1968), 283.

Fu, Phillip. "Governmental Accounting in China during the Chou Dynasty (1122 B.C.– 256 B.C.)." *Journal of Accounting Research* 9 (Spring, 1971), 40-51.

Glautier, M.W.E. "Roman Accounting: the Influence of Socioeconomic Factors on the Development of Accounting Concepts." *International Journal of Accounting* 8 (Spring, 1973), 59-74.

Green, Wilmer L. *History and Survey of Accountancy.* Brooklyn: Standard Text Press, 1930. Reprinted by Nihon Shoseki, Osaka, 1974. Chapters one and two.

Grier, Elizabeth. *Accounting in the Zenon Papyri.* New York: Columbia University Press, 1934.

Hain, H.P. "Accounting Control in the Zenon Papyri." *Accounting Review* 41 (October, 1966), 699-703.

Herskowitz, Herrmann. "The Roman Literal Contract and Double-entry Bookkeeping." *Journal of Accountancy* 49 (May, 1930), 350-353.

Jacobsen, Lyle E. "The Ancient Inca Empire of Peru and the Double Entry Accounting Concept." *Journal of Accounting Research* 2 (Autumn, 1964), 221-28.

Jones, Tom B. "Bookkeeping in Ancient Sumer." *Archaeology* 9 (1956), 16-21.

Kats, P. "A Surmise Regarding the Origins of Bookkeeping by Double Entry." *Accounting Review* 5 (December, 1930), 311-316.

Keister, Orville R. "Commercial Record-Keeping in Ancient Mesopotamia." *Accounting Review* 38 (April, 1963), 371-76.

_____. "The Incan Quipu." *Accounting Review* 39 (April, 1964), 414-16.

_____. "The Influence of Mesopotamian Record-Keeping." *Abacus* 6 (December, 1970), 169-181.

_____ "The Mechanics of Mesopotamian Record-Keeping." *National Association of Accountants Bulletin* 46 (February, 1965), 18-24.

Littleton, A.C. *Accounting Evolution to 1900.* New York: American Institute Publishing Company, 1933. Reprinted by Russell and Russell, New York, 1966, chap. two.

Melis, F. *Storia della Ragioneria.* Bologna: Dott. Cesare Zuffi, 1950.

Merritt, B.D. *Athenian Financial Documents of the Fifth Century.* Ann Arbor: University of Michigan Press, 1932.

Mickwitz, Gunnar. "Economic Rationalism in Graeco-Roman Agriculture," *English Historical Review* 52 (1937), 577-89.

Most, Kenneth S. "The Accounts of Ancient Rome." *Academy of Accounting Historians Working Paper No. 3.* University, Alabama: Academy of Accounting Historians, 1974.

_____. "Accounting by the Ancients." *Accountant* 160 (May 9, 1959), 563-566.

_____. "How Wrong was Sombart?" *Accounting Historian* 3 (Spring, 1976), 1, 6.

Murray, D. *Chapters in the History of Bookkeeping, Accountancy, and Commercial Arithmetic.* Glascow: Jackson, Wylie, 1930, 125-38.

Penndorf, B. "The Relation of Taxation to the History of the Balance Sheet." *Accounting Review* 5 (December, 1930), 243-51.

Robert, R. "Roman Accounting." *Accountant* 137 (August 10, 1957), 157-158.

Smith, C.A. "Speculation on Roman Influence on the Theory of Double Entry Bookkeeping." *Accounting Research* 5 (1954), 337-339.

Stone, Williard E. "Antecedents of the Accounting Profession." *Accounting Review* 44 (April, 1969), 284-291.

Ten, Have, O. *The History of Accountancy.* Palo Alto: Bay Books, 1976, 22-29.

Woolf, A.H. *A Short History of Accountants and Accountancy.* London: Gee, 1912. Reprinted by Nihon Shoseki, Osaka, 1974. First four chapters.

Chapter 2

MEDIEVAL ACCOUNT KEEPING

Bookkeeping during the Middle Ages evolved in several distinct directions. The development in northern Italy of venture partnerships and overseas trading led to the double entry system used today, and it is tempting to make accounting history the history of double entry record keeping by passing quickly over the thousand years between the fall of Rome and the publication of Pacioli's *Summa.* Being out of the mainstream of events leading to double entry bookkeeping, the details of medieval practice outside Italy tend to be neglected or allowed a merely historical interest.

English accounting techniques of this period deserve attention for several reasons. Early government tax rolls and manorial account books are among the oldest surviving documents in the English language, and the approaches that were made to particular problems in these areas find obvious parallels in modern practice. Medieval agency accounting laid the foundations for our doctrines of stewardship and conservatism. It helped create the conditions for the rapid advance in accounting technology which occurred during the Renaissance. Beyond this, the pervasiveness and durability of these systems suggest that double entry bookkeeping is not a uniquely efficient way to organize financial data—that in many cases, simpler methods can yield equally useful results.

THE FEUDAL BACKGROUND

In contrast to the codified accounting procedures of the Roman Empire, medieval record keeping tended to be localized and centered around a number of specialized institutions. While it is difficult to isolate the Roman influence, in both periods accounts were kept mainly because employers needed to monitor subordinates who were acting as their agents. The closest parallel to Roman bookkeeping method is found in the receipt and disbursement accounting of the Catholic Church, which for hundreds of years levied and collected taxes throughout Europe. As early as the sixth century, deacons were appointed to administer church properties and report on their revenues. Agents of the papal treasury were located in the provinces and made responsible for forwarding receipts to Rome.

The value of accounting as an aid to systematic estate management was recognized early. In the ninth century Charlemagne produced the *Capitulare de Villis,* a series of detailed instructions to his steward on supervision of the royal lands and reporting to the soverign. Though methods of calculation were primitive and accounting periods irregular, "Charlemagne stressed the need for orderliness, for gathering together like topics under a single heading and going through the probable sources of revenue in order."[1] An annual inventory was taken of the royal estates and chattels. Payments and receipts were recorded in separate books, with any balance remitted to the king.

In pre-Norman England literacy was so rare, even among the nobility, that a written system of accounts would hardly have justified its cost. Until the eleventh century, financial data was nearly always communicated and verified orally, written documents being merely supplementary to the more important spoken word.[2] At that time, introduction of the abacus and other improvements in arithmetic technique roughly coincided with a rebirth of interest in the written language. A system of written records gradually formalized an earlier, essentially oral accounting tradition.

Feudal society is often pictured as a multilayered pyramid, with individuals at each lower level guaranteed certain rights in exchange for certain duties. Such a structure required many delegations of authority and the transfer of land rights from nominal owners to actual possessors and users. The characteristic accounting problem was one of vertical communication and verification between principal and agent. In English estate accounting this gave rise to the charge and discharge statement made on behalf of a manorial steward for his lord, while in royal finance it led to the proffer system of recording and verifying tax collections.

GOVERNMENT ACCOUNTING

The English authorities shared with earlier governments a need to regulate the levying and collecting of taxes. After his invasion of England, William the Conqueror took title to all property in the name of the crown, and in 1086 had a survey made which included all real properties and the taxes due on them.

The *Domesday Book* is remembered mainly as a census, but it also served as a register of land values on which crown assessments could be based.

The oldest surviving accounting record in English is the Pipe Roll, or "Great Roll of the Exchequer," compiled annually from valuations in the *Domesday Book* and from statements of account by sheriffs and others bringing payments to the treasury. Beginning in 1130 A.D., the Pipe Roll provides a 700-year narrative description of rents, fines, taxes and other fixed levies due the king, together with a summary of payments made on these debts and expenses incurred in collecting them.

In its feudal context the Exchequer was more than a department of state charged with responsibility for royal revenues. Its legitimacy resulted from a delegation of crown authority. The essential relationship was still between the king and his subjects and depended on his power to tax and on their obligation to pay. Interaction between the Court of Exchequer's two divisions further illustrates this agency aspect of medieval bookkeeping. The Treasurer's Department, or Lower Exchequer, received money and payments in kind and assayed coins to see that they were "of the prescribed goodness." But the Pipe Roll was the record of the Upper Exchequer, or King's Council, which also had authority to audit the lower council, authorize allowances, settle legal questions arising from the accounts, and give the tax collectors their quittance.

While certain payments could be made directly to the treasury, in most cases an intermediary was needed between crown and citizens. The sheriff was the king's representative in both civil and military affairs and usually occupied the principal castle in the county. He was collector of the king's revenues and bailiff of his country estates, which were farmed out for a fixed rent. He administered justice in the county court, collected rents for the use of roads, forests, and fields, collected import and export duties, tributes from the towns, fines, penalties, and other taxes. He was the main individual accountable at the Exchequer.

THE PROFFER SYSTEM

Twice yearly, at Easter and Michaelmas (September 29), the sheriff of each county was summoned to attend the Exchequer sessions at Westminster. At Easter he brought with him and paid into the Lower Exchequer about half the total assessments for which his county was liable. Any collections of arrears from prior years were checked against the Roll, but no entries were made for deposits of the current year's collections. Instead, the treasurer, having accepted the sheriff's proffer, or payment on account, gave orders for a wooden tally to be cut.

The tally stick as evidence of payment predates even the Pipe Roll. In the twelfth century it was usually a narrow hazelwood stick, eight or nine inches long, notched to indicate the amount received. An incision the width of a man's palm represented a thousand pounds; a hundred pounds was a thumbs-width cut; twenty pounds the width of a little finger; a pound "the thickness of a grain of ripe barley"; a shilling just a notch; a penny a simple cut with no wood removed; and a half-penny a punched hole.[3] After the amount of the sheriff's proffer had been carved, a diagonal cross cut was made an inch or two from the thicker end of the tally, and the whole stick was split down the middle into two identically notched parts of unequal length. The flat sides of both pieces were inscribed in Latin to show that they related to the same debt, and as additional protection, the cross cuts were made at various angles on different tallies, so that no "foil" or shorter piece could possibly be fitted to any "stock" but its own. The sheriff then departed with the stock as his receipt for payments rendered, and the foil was kept by the treasurer for the Exchequer archives.

At Michaelmas the sheriff returns, pays over the rest of the crown revenues, and submits to audit. This is his final accounting. Though he has paid half his county's debt at Easter, the Michaelmas summons is not for the balance, but for the whole year's revenues, and the Receipt Roll is compiled. The treasurer begins by formally asking the sheriff if he is ready to account. If so, the treasurer reads the amount due from his copy of the Pipe Roll. He asks if the sheriff's customary expenses are the same as in the year before. The sheriff must produce writs warranting any extraordinary expenditures. These are read aloud and checked against duplicates from the Exchequer, then recorded in the Roll. Such expenses as repairs to castles are vouched both by writ and by two of the king's surveyors who certify the performance and the cost of the work. There follow a list of accounts which include any arrears of "farm" rents, "conventiones" or voluntary payments to gain the king's favor, murder fines imposed on the county in cases where the murderers cannot be found, aids and "gifts" of cities and boroughs, and the goods of felons and fugitives.[4]

Final settlement takes place across a table laid with the checkered cloth after which the Exchequer is named. On one side is the sheriff and his collections, his tally, and his disbursement vouchers. The treasurer reads from the Exactory Roll on which the current year "farms" of all the counties are written. Across the table from the sheriff an official called the calculator sets out on the checkered squares counters representing the whole year's payments due the crown. This total being agreed to by both parties, the calculator lays out another row of counters showing the amounts paid by the sheriff at Easter. The sheriff's tally stock and the Exchequer's foil are fitted together to verify that the notches and cuttings correspond. As the treasurer calls the amounts due, the sheriff's Michaelmas collections are set out in the squares on his side of the calculating board and "blanched" by the accountant, who has assayed the coin and now subtracts the necessary number of pence in the pound. A new tally will be made for the adjusted amount. Crown vouchers for the sheriff's allowances and expenses are placed on the board as further deductions from the amount due. When all the crown's counters are balanced by payments, tallies, and allowance vouchers, the sheriff is quit. He swears to the marshall

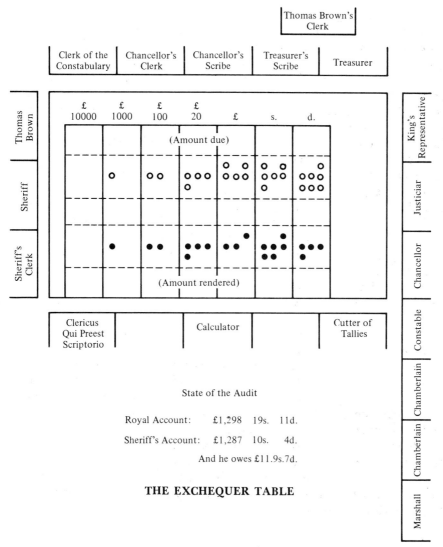

THE EXCHEQUER TABLE

of the Exchequer that he has made his lawful account according to his conscience, and is dismissed.[5]

EVOLUTION OF EXCHEQUER ACCOUNTING

The relevance for us of this essentially visual and oral system is perhaps that
accounting functions may be performed efficiently with very limited means.
Paper was a novelty in England until the sixteenth century, yet without printed
schedules or forms, taxes were routinely collected and delivered intact to the
treasury. The notched stick or its equivalent was a necessary part of taxation

in a society where most debtors were illiterates to whom a parchment receipt meant nothing. Protection against fraud was always a keystone of feudal bookkeeping, and the proffer system proved an ingenious way to assist and control revenue collectors who often had to count with the help of their fingers.

The Exchequer's chief shortcomings were those of a body which pursues immediately useful lines of development while disregarding others which would ultimately complement them. The use of Roman numerals made arithmetic cumbersome and errors hard to find. Worse, it perpetuated a narrative form of account in which no real attempt was made to bring receipts and expenditures face to face in parallel columns. Books of original entry predominated; in the absence of a coordinated ledger-journal system, account classifications were inconsistent and the record of individual receipts was often difficult to trace. Lines of authority and responsibility were often badly defined. Revenue was sometimes intercepted by members of the king's household on its way to the treasury, with the result that a debt appeared on the Pipe Roll but no payment was ever recorded on the Receipt Roll.

Exchequer accounting became more sophisticated as new sources of royal revenue developed. While continuing to serve as receipts, tallies in later years were also used as notes payable, tax anticipation warrants, postdated checks and bills of exchange.[6] A private debt might be acknowledged by a tally cut for the amount owed and given to the creditor, who at the proper time presented it for payment. Resorting to deficit financing, the Plantagenet and Tudor kings first occasionally and then routinely raised money on the security of tallies which gave a lender the right to receive future tax revenues, or even, in the Roman fashion, to collect certain taxes himself. Still later, tallies were assigned and circulated as negotiable instruments, reducing the inflow and outflow of coined money at the Exchequer and complicating the recording of the Receipt Roll. As the volume of Exchequer tally transactions increased, they came to be regarded as a speculative form of investment in government securities, and were discounted by the Goldsmith Bankers. During the eighteenth century they were gradually replaced by Exchequer bills, and were finally abolished in 1826.

MANORIAL ACCOUNTING

Until the late Middle Ages human labor was the most dynamic productive factor, and feudal social systems were designed to keep labor on the land. Manors—the estates of the nobility—were the farms and workshops of medieval Britain. English manorial accounting described the receipts and payments of a self-contained economic entity; the results of dealings with outsiders were designated "foreign" in the accounts. Another characteristic of manorial life was administration by proxy. The manorial duke or earl often depended for his living on the productivity of large landholdings and the efforts of hundreds of people whom he could not personally supervise. Day to day management was normally left to a hierarchy of officials and department heads. The lord's incentive for keeping accounts arose from his need to check on the integrity and reliability of these stewards, to prevent loss and theft, and generally to encourage efficiency. From the steward's viewpoint, accounting records provided evidence that he had discharged his duties honestly and well.

Manorial self-sufficiency and the agency relationship are keys to understanding differences between estate accounts and those of today. Economic independence and the absence of reports to outsiders meant that little of what we call financial accounting was needed. Credit sales were rare. Assets were inventoried but balance sheets were seldom made. The lord's implements might be counted together with the personal property of his tenants, and cash values were sometimes combined with physical quantities of goods in statements of manorial assets. No clear distinction was made between capital and revenue expenditures, the cost of a horse being recorded in much the same way as the cost of the hay it consumed. Expenses might be allocated to various activities in detail, to show the results of each, but overall profit and loss was normally of little interest. Sometimes an account narrative was interrupted to make room for estimates of what might have been earned if a different course of action had been taken.

Manorial officers kept accounts not for the sake of the business entity, as they would today, but for their own protection. On large estates a "surveyor" assembled a book of land rentals and fees due, which was used by the receiver-general who actually collected these revenues and recorded them by sources. Still other officials paid and kept account of wages and expenses. Auditors periodically examined and summarized all these accounts, which were essentially records of the individuals involved, not of the manor. Since their purpose was only to show that duties had been properly performed, there was a natural tendency for each steward to record just the items for which he was responsible and to show each type of receipt in opposition to payments.

The charge and discharge statement is often incorrectly assumed to have originated in executory accounting. In fact it was developed in fifteenth-century Scotland by government accountants, adopted by English manorial stewards, and not widely used by executors until 300 years later. The statement itself was the report of an agent on the assumption and discharge of his responsibilities. It was typically headed with the name of the manor and included the names of the stewards, sometimes those of the auditors, the place and date of the audit, and the period under review. It often contained a money account, with rents and other receipts subdivided by types, and a corn and stock account, with separate categories for grains, cattle, and various types of produce. Beginning balances for each item were shown, then the steward "charged" himself for manorial and foreign receipts and natural increases in flocks, and "discharged" himself by deducting his cash payments, losses, and other uses of these resources.

The manor was more comparable to a modern business in its use of internal control procedures. Like a corporate executive, the manorial overseer was expected to use accounting data to control operations and plan for the future. His duties included frequent unannounced inspection tours of work areas and reports to the lord on good and bad performance. It was considered sound practice to record every transaction and to separate the functions of record keeping and cash handling. Receipts from sales of wood, meat, and hay might be analyzed in comparison with expenses. The sowing of various kinds of grain was often recorded in great detail.[7] It was usual to estimate for a year in advance the need for food, fuel, cloth, and other goods, and to schedule formally the dates on which cash could be released to stewards according to their anticipated needs.

An internal audit system verified the accounts kept in each manorial work area. On one estate the ushers supervising meal service made records of the food served, to be compared with the issue records kept in the kitchen, which could in turn be matched against the lists of incoming provisions and food on hand. The records of pantler and baker were expected to agree as to bread delivered and used. The brewer and butler crosschecked as to beer; the slaughterman checked against the glover as to hides, against the larderer for meat, and against the "chaundler" as to tallow for candles.[8]

Production standards reinforced internal checks. Baker, brewer, and larderer were expected to produce a certain amount of bread, beer, and meat from a given amount of material received. Supply purchases were recorded at the time of delivery, and supplies were locked up when not in use. Frequent physical inventories allowed the stewards to see how closely procurement and issue conformed to the budgeted levels. Clerks in the kitchen, spicery, granary, and other work areas made monthly expense summaries and inventories under supervision of the comptroller's clerks, and the countinghouse clerks assembled these reports into a total of expenses and a "bill of remainders" showing inventories for the whole estate.

Exchequer and manorial bookkeeping techniques were used in keeping manorial household accounts.[9] The royal establishment's almost military organization of duties was a model for the households of the nobility, some of which provided for hundreds of permanent residents and guests. Here also the intention was to exercise control by accounting for every item of expenditure, and again the accountant's main purpose was not to determine income or show that the household was self-supporting, but to obtain his own discharge. Household expenses were commonly set out in the same format as those for the manor as a whole, and for statement purposes might be combined with the annual summaries of other manorial accounts.

MANORIAL AUDIT

The accounts of most larger manors were examined annually by the lord and his domestic council, and often by a specially appointed audit official.[10] An estate sometimes included a number of manors, which might be audited as a group; or auditors might travel from farm to farm. The audit was again basically a check on steward's accountability. It facilitated internal control, allowed more reliance to be placed on financial statements, and provided final discharge for those officers and department heads who handled money. Of all medieval accounting functions, the audit was probably most like its modern counterpart, and most directly influential on modern practice.

At midyear the auditors often made a preliminary examination or "view," which included an assessment of managerial efficiency:

> They would examine the fields and see how much was sown and whether it was well done; examine the stock and the increase and investigate deaths and barrenness; inventory the grange; examine the equipment; assess any expenditure needed and any incidental business; and reckon the interim account of each official. . . .[11]

The view of account thus became a subtle contest between auditor and steward. The latter wished to render accounts profitably for himself by estimating losses generously and revenues and natural increase conservatively. In contrast, the auditor's charge was that the lord must suffer no loss from fraud, negligence, or bad judgment. At Michaelmas on many estates, the auditor told each steward the amount for which he stood charged for the year. The steward produced bills and acquittances showing his expenses and monies paid to the receiver. If allowed by the auditor, these were entered in the account and deducted from the charge; the remainder was then paid by the steward to the auditor, who gave a *quietus* or discharge and turned the cash over to the receiver. Finally, the auditor combined these individual accounts into a charge and discharge statement for the whole estate, sometimes initialing subtotals and writing below the final balance a phrase signifying attestation, such as "Heard by the auditors undersigned."

A final step was the annual Declaration of Audit. The charge and discharge statement as verified by the auditor was read in the presence of the lord and the assembly of stewards whose discharge of duties was under scrutiny. Each might be called on to answer questions and substantiate facts from his personal knowledge. One reason for an oral summary of accounts is obvious: the manor, like the Exchequer, had to be attuned to the realities of a largely illiterate society. But a public hearing (the word audit means "to hear") also offered special protection against fraud, since the facts were being laid simultaneously before all those qualified to recognize omissions and mistakes. In this sense manorial audit was the culmination of a general policy of management by inquiry.

TOWARD ACCOUNTING UNIFORMITY

Like the Romans before them, the British prepared instruction manuals for auditors. These described in detail methods for checking accounts and indicated the types of errors and deception that might be encountered. Treatises on estate management sometimes included model forms for drawing up charge and discharge statements. A farming boom during the thirteenth century created such shortages of manorial clerks and auditors that manorial accounting began to be taught as part of the curriculum at Oxford. This formal training, like the written instructions for auditors, tended to standardize estate accounting practices.

We might expect even more diversity in medieval bookkeeping than was the case. The modern reasons for accounting consistency and comparability scarcely existed. But it does seem that the feudal environment, like any other, favored particular techniques. City governments, monastic and lay estates, households and craft guilds, the "worshipful companies" shared a tradition of charge and discharge bookkeeping and accountability audits. Accounts of all types were synchronized with the farming seasons, Michaelmas signaling the harvest and the end of their natural business year. Single entry bookkeeping in feudal Japan followed a similar pattern of decentralized record keeping, visual numeration by abacus, emphasis on control and the personal discharge of accounting officers.[12]

THE MANOR AND THE WORLD

The manor's self-sufficiency placed limits on its development as an institution. England had been cut off geographically from the Near East trade of the Renaissance, but following the discovery of America found itself in a more favorable position. During the seventeenth century, towns began to replace manors as centers of economic life, and independent manufacturers came into competition with closely regulated guild tradesmen. Expanding overseas trade created new markets and sources of supply. Emphasis shifted from stewardship of manorial assets to protection of corporate investors and questions of income finding and dividend payment. Agency accounting remained, but began to assume the sophisticated form it had taken centuries earlier in northern Italy, where the accumulation of capital and the distances over which trading was carried on lent themselves to branch operations, credit arrangements, and consignment transactions.

We can hardly blame manorial accountants for failing to produce data they did not need. The typical medieval executive "did practically no writing and very little reading."[13] Exchequer and manorial accounts were normally kept on the assumption that king or baron would never look at them. Accounting therefore tended to cease at the point where a department head had enough information for his own use.

Such men were unlikely to develop an accounting method which opposed assets and equities, because they had no real concept of capital.[14] The manor was their capital. Land was seldom bought and sold; they could only value it in terms of some multiple of annual net produce. With production and consumption so interwoven there was little incentive for determining total income.

Nor was systematic cost accounting necessary, since most manors had a repetitive and not easily altered pattern of receipts and expenditures.

But in the areas of internal control and audit, manorial practice was far ahead of Pacioli's "Method of Venice." It demonstrated how accounts kept mainly to strike an annual balance could be adapted to help management run a business from day to day. The doctrine of conservatism was a form of self-protection for the manorial steward facing audit; the same tendency to underestimate is central to modern corporate accounting. Executors and trustees continue to use the charge and discharge statement in accounting for their management of assets held in trust. Even our system of weights and measures, with all of their faults, comes down to us from that era when a yard was the distance from the king's nose to the end of his outstretched arm. If many things have changed, enough similarities remain to make our accounting heritage from the Middle Ages rich in forms, techniques, and ideas.

FOOTNOTES

1. S.M. Jack, "An Historical Defence of Single Entry Book-keeping," *Abacus* 2 (December, 1966), 144.
2. *Ibid.*, 140.
3. Rudolph Robert, "A Short History of Tallies," in A.C. Littleton and B.S. Yamey, eds., *Studies in the History of Accounting* (Homewood, Ill.: Richard D. Irwin, 1956), 76.
4. D.M. Stenton, ed., *The Great Roll of the Pipe for the Second Year of the Reign of King Richard the First*, 39 (London: Publications of the Pipe Roll Society, 1925), Introduction, xiii, xiv.
5. *Ibid.*, xv-xvii.
6. Robert, *op. cit.*, 79-85.
7. N.S.B. Gras and E.C. Gras, *The Economic and Social History of an English Village (Crawley, Hampshire) A.D. 909-1928* (Cambridge, Mass.: Harvard University Press, 1930), 16.
8. A.C. Littleton, "Old and New in Management and Accounting," *The Accounting Review* 29 (April, 1954), 196-200.
9. E.M. Myatt-Price, "Cromwell Household Accounts, 1417-1476," in A.C. Littleton and B.S. Yamey, eds., *Studies in the History of Accounting* (Homewood, Ill.: Richard D. Irwin, 1956), 97-108.
10. A.C. Littleton, *Accounting Evolution to 1900* (New York: American Institute Publishing Company, 1933), 260-264.
11. Quoted in Jack, *op. cit.*, 154.
12. K. Nishikawa, "The Early History of Double-Entry Book-Keeping in Japan," in A.C. Littleton and B.S. Yamey, eds., *Studies in the History of Accounting* (Homewood, Ill.: Richard D. Irwin, 1956), 380-81.
13. H. Jenkinson and D.M. Broome, "An Exchequer Statement of Receipts and Issues 1339-1340," *English Historical Review* 58 (1943), 210.
14. Jack, *op. cit.*, 155-57.

SELECTED BIBLIOGRAPHY

Brown, Richard, ed. *A History of Accounting and Accountants*. Edinburgh: Jack, 1905. Reprinted by B. Franklin, New York, 1966, chaps. three and four.
Chen, Rosita. "Social and Financial Stewardship." *Accounting Review* 50 (July, 1975), 533-543.

Chrimes, S.B. *An Introduction to the Administrative History of Medieval England*. New York: Barnes and Noble, Inc., 1966.
Colvin, H.M., ed. *Building Accounts of King Henry III*. Oxford, England: Clarendon Press, 1971.
Crossley, D.W., ed. *Sydney Ironworks Accounts 1541-1573*. London: Royal Historical Society, Camden Fourth Series, Vol. 15, 1975.
Davies, R.R. "Baronial Accounts, Incomes and Arrears in the Late Middle Ages." *Economic History Review*, 2nd Series, 21 (August, 1968), 211-229.
Finn, R.W. *An Introduction to the Domesday Book*. New York: Barnes and Noble, 1963.
Gras, N.S.B. and Gras, E.C. *The Economic and Social History of an English Village (Crawley, Hampshire) A.D. 909-1928*. Cambridge, Mass.: Harvard University Press, 1930, 13-18.
Hanham, Alison. "'Make a Careful Examination'—Some Fraudulent Accounts in the Cely Papers.' *Speculum* 98 (April, 1973), 313-324.
Harvey, P.D.A. "Agricultural Treatises and Manorial Accounting in Medieval England." *Agricultural History Review* 20 (1972), 170-182.
_____. "The Pipe Rolls and the Adoption of Demesne Farming in England." *Economic History Review*, 2nd Series, 27 (August, 1974), 345-359.
Jack, S.M. "An Historical Defence of Single Entry Book-keeping." *Abacus* 2 (December, 1966), 137-58.
_____. "A Note on F.P. Barnard: The Casting Counter and the Counting Board." *Abacus* 3 (August, 1967), 80-82.
Jenkinson, H., and Broome, D.M. "An Exchequer Statement of Receipts and Issues 1339-1340." *English Historical Review* 58 (1943), 210-16.
Levett, A.E. "The Financial Organization of the Manor." *Economic History Review*, 1st Series, 1 (1927), 65-86.
Littleton, A.C. *Accounting Evolution to 1900*. New York: American Institute Publishing Company, 1933. Reprinted by Russell and Russell, New York, 1966, chap. sixteen.
_____. "Old and New in Management and Accounting." *Accounting Review* 29 (April, 1954), 196-200.
Lyon, Bryce, and Verhulst, A. *Medieval Finance: A Comparison of Financial Institutions in Northwestern Europe*. Providence, R.I.: Brown University Press, 1967.
Maitland, F.W. *Domesday Book and Beyond*. New York: W.W. Norton and Company, Inc., 1966, first article.
Mills, M.H. "Experiments in the Exchequer Procedure (1200-1232)." In R.W. Southern, *Essays in Medieval History*. New York: St. Martin's Press, 1968, 129-45.
Most, Kenneth S. "New Light on Mediaeval Manorial Accounts." *Accountant* 160 (January 25, 1969), 119-121.
Murray, Athol L. "The Comptroller, 1425-1488." *Scottish Historical Review* 52 (April, 1973), 1-29.
Murray, David. *Chapters in the History of Bookkeeping, Accountancy, and Commercial Arithmetic*. Glascow: Jackson, Wylie, 1930, 128-53.
Myatt-Price, E.M. "Cromwell Household Accounts, 1417-1476." In A.C. Littleton and B.S. Yamey, eds. *Studies in the History of Accounting*. Homewood, Ill.: Richard D. Irwin, 1956, 99-113.
_____. "The Twelve at Tattershall." *Accounting Review* 35 (October, 1960), 680-85.
_____. "Examples of Techniques in Medieval Building Accounts." *Abacus* 2 (December, 1966), 41-48.
Oschinsky, D. "Medieval Treatises on Estate Accounting." In A.C. Littleton and B.S. Yamey, eds. *Studies in the History of Accounting*. Homewood, Ill.: Richard D. Irwin, 1956, 91-98.
_____. *Walter of Henley and other Treatises on Estate Management and Accounting*. Oxford, England: Clarendon Press, 1971.
_____. "Notes on the Editing and Interpretation of Estate Accounts." *Archives* 9 (1969 and 1970), 84-89, 142-152.
Poole, R.L. *The Exchequer in the Twelfth Century*. Oxford at the Clarendon Press, 1922.
Postan, M.M., *Medieval Trade and Finance*. Cambridge, England: University Press, 1973.
Richard, Son of Nigel. *The Course of the Exchequer (Dialogus de Scaccario)*. C. Johnson, ed. London: Thomas Nelson and Sons, Ltd., 1950, Introduction.

Robert, Rudolph. "A Short History of Tallies." In A.C. Littleton and B.S. Yamey, eds. *Studies in the History of Accounting*. Homewood, Ill.: Richard D. Irwin, 1956, 75-85.

Ross, Barbara. "The Accounts of the Stewards of the Talbot Household at Blakemere: an Example of Medieval Accounting Practice." *Abacus* 4 (August, 1968), 51-72.

Simpson, A. "Encounters with Accounts." In *The Wealth of the Gentry, 1540-1660*. Chicago: University of Chicago Press, 1961, 1-21.

Stenton, D.M., ed. *The Great Roll of the Pipe for the Second Year of the Reign of King Richard the First*, Vol. 39. London: Publications of the Pipe Roll Society, 1925, Introduction.

Stone, Williard E. "The Tally: An Ancient Accounting Instrument." *Abacus* 9 (June, 1975), 49-57.

Wren, M.C. "The Chamber of the City of London." *Accounting Review* 24 (April, 1949), 191-98.

Chapter 3

THE PRAGMATIC DEVELOPMENT OF DOUBLE ENTRY BOOKKEEPING

Though the exact origins of double entry bookkeeping are unknown, there is substantial agreement on many aspects of its early history. Bilateral accounts developed in northern Italy between 1250 and 1440 in response to increasing trade complexities and to business needs not satisfied by existing accounting systems. They were not a product of any earlier civilization and were not later invented anywhere outside Italy. It now seems likely that double entry originated independently in several Italian city-states where it was applied to similar trading conditions at about the same time. Major innovations were made by merchant-bankers who gradually extended their practice of making dual entries for certain credit transactions. In this way double entry evolved by trial and error, improvements being imitated from one business and city to another. The new system survived because of its inherent advantages over competing methods. For this reason a study of its early "spontaneous" development provides an excellent basis for judging its intrinsic merits.

Because double entry's evolution was determined mainly by the business needs it had to satisfy, descriptions of account methodology and technical developments are perhaps less important than an understanding of the commercial requirements which caused them. This in turn requires some knowledge of medieval trade and Italian commercial practice.

THE ITALIAN COMMERCIAL WORLD

Double entry bookkeeping came into being with the rise of Mediterranean commerce during and just after the crusades (1096–1291). Besides requiring ships and provisions, the crusaders brought back silks, spices, and other Eastern products, stimulating demand for such items and for the production of European exchange goods. New trade contacts gave impetus to a 300-year commercial revolution which foreshadowed the Industrial Revolution of the eighteenth century. Genoa and Venice quickly established themselves as intermediaries in trade relations between Europe and the Near East. Italians not only became the leading merchants of the Middle Ages but nearly monopolized international banking. They regularly put trade competitors out of business and limited others, such as the English, to a local sphere of influence.

Their success resulted particularly from superior business organization. Besides double entry bookkeeping, they invented the bill of exchange in draft form, experimented with marine insurance, mastered the techniques of creating credit money and evolved a body of codified mercantile law which forms the basis of commercial law today. Operating on a scale never before known, they found that bookkeeping methods which worked in a small company broke down when a merchant began trading though a network of factors and international partnerships. Unsystematic records limited the size of such businesses, and beyond a certain point of growth and dispersion caused so much disorder that owners lost control of distant operations.

The Italians had always paid attention to accounting and their tendency to standardize and codify the better practices was an important factor in the development of double entry bookkeeping. As early as the eleventh century Genoese maritime law required scribes to render an account of goods shipped. Milanese accountants compiled registers of taxable land and revised the accounts kept in building a cathedral. Members of the Florentine banker's guild were required to keep accounts and open them to surprise audits by guild agents. Genoese bank bookkeepers had to be licensed notaries and their records had the same formal status as deeds. The first society of accountants was formed in Venice in 1581 and, gaining a virtual monopoly over practice, prescribed a six-year apprenticeship and an oral examination for candidates.[1]

In thirteenth century Italy Littleton's seven "antecedents" for systematic bookkeeping were present in dynamic form. Literacy was widespread among the Italian commercial class and writing was facilitated by the invention of paper. Through their North African trade contacts the Italians became the first Europeans to acquire Arabic numerals which, within a generation after their exposition by Leonardo of Pisa (1202), were widely used by Italian merchants. The existence of a sophisticated money economy and the most stable coinage since Roman times allowed transactions to be reduced to the common denominator necessary for double entry bookkeeping. Property rights were extended to a much larger part of the population than was usual in the ancient world. Capital accumulated from trading was reinvested. Money shortages were a perennial problem during the Middle Ages, and foreignors marvelled at the Italians' ability to do business without cash. But the wide use of credit required written records of amounts owed and owing. The need for a grouping of all items concerning the same person to form a running balance was probably the earliest motive for creating bilateral accounts with opposing debits and credits.[2]

The partnership and agency aspects of Italian commerce also encouraged accounting development. Most large firms were partnerships. To divide profits fairly they needed an accounting system in which all transactions were recorded. The formation of long-lasting partnerships led to a recognition that such businesses were entities in their own right, and that capital and income represented claims of the owners. A system which produced automatic profit and capital balances had obvious attractions for them.

The Italian practice of trading through overseas agents was an important factor in the emergence of double entry bookkeeping. The taxation to which strangers were subject in many trading ports could be avoided by taking a local merchant as consignment agent. Such consignees were expected to remit sales proceeds to owners, and needed accounting records which showed at all times the details of sales, expenses, and indebtedness to their principals. Duality was implied in two parties being at interest in selling the same goods, and in the fact that both made entries for shipments, sales, and amounts due. Each party in effect recorded the same transactions from an opposite viewpoint. Agency bookkeeping may also explain the appearance of inventory accounts, since factors needed an accurate count of goods entrusted to them by different firms, with details of quantities received and sold.

THE NEW SYSTEM'S UNIQUENESS

Though claims are made for an earlier invention of double entry in other places —Greece, Rome, ancient India, Peru, Spain—in fact the Italian system was from the beginning essentially different from any which preceded it. (1) Each transaction was recorded twice, once as a debit and once as a credit, so that total debits had to equal total credits; (2) All accounts were kept in the same monetary unit, and (3) the integration of real and nominal accounts allowed profit and equity figures to emerge as remainders. Even when single and double entry accounts had certain similarities of form they differed widely in scope and purpose. Indeed, single entry *systems* probably developed out of double entry.[3] Single entry records took many forms, including diaries, lists, memoranda, and uncoordinated journals. Often only credit transactions were recorded, and when settlement was made the entries were simply crossed out. There were no nominal accounts. The only requirement for a bookkeeper in such a system might be the ability to read and write.

Littleton points out that double entry bookkeeping seems to hinge on the duality of entries and the equilibrium of debits and credits.[4] Three kinds of duality are evident: of books, between the journal and ledger; of account form, with debit and credit pages opposite; and in the double posting of each transaction. Since trade rests on an exchange of goods and services, this dual aspect is not just a formality but corresponds to a basic reciprocity between buyer and seller, giver and receiver, debtor and creditor. Even so, recording each transaction twice is a necessary but not sufficient condition for double entry. Roman debt accounts are said to have been recorded twice, with payment entries canceling liabilities. Papal records of receipts and payments were often recorded twice by different officials to prove their correctness. The evolution of double entry was not basically the result of a search for arithmetic accuracy. Such an effort could never have produced nominal accounts.

Equilibrium is another essential feature of any double entry ststem. Balancing the positive and negative elements in each account facilitates arithmetic check and ultimately produces capital and income figures. Yet equilibrium alone does not make double entry and its absence—for instance, in modern computer systems—does not prevent complete, coordinated record keeping. Nor does it ensure that all transactions will be recorded. Accounts kept by Roman slaves and medieval factors were maintained in balance without including all transactions.

Littleton and Zimmerman maintain that the essence of double entry is not duality or equilibrium but category integration. "The significance of the ... integration of real and nominal accounts far surpasses every other aspect of accounting development."[5] It is this articulation of accounts and the resulting profit and equity remainders which make double entry a superior analytical tool. Every transaction is drawn into the accounts and can be judged according to its effect on total profit and loss. Only when bookkeeping is thus called on to serve the whole business is the full potential of bilateral accounts realized.

ACCOUNTS OF TRADERS AND BANKERS

How and why did uncoordinated single entry accounts develop into complete, systematic double entry bookkeeping? Since comparatively few records survive, the answers must be speculative. Differences in form and technique between double entry accounts in different parts of Italy suggest that it originated independently in several trading centers. The most important of these were Genoa, Venice, and Florence, and for simplicity's sake the discussion will be centered around them. The first two are coastal cities whose commerce consisted largely of venture trading with the Near East, though they also sent ships to England and Flanders. Florence, located inland, replaced Siena as Europe's leading banking city, developed overland trade routes, and built up wool and silk manufacturing industries.

GENOA AND VENICE

The *Massari* accounts of the City of Genoa (1340) are the oldest surviving records definitely having all the characteristics of double entry. The city accounted for its finances in two ledgers, one kept by two *Massari* (city treasury officials), and a duplicate ledger kept by two *Maestri Razionali,* whose job it was to check the *Massari's* work. The accounts reflect a fully developed double entry form, indicating that the system must have been in use for a number of years before 1340. Probably it dates back at least to 1327, when because of "many frauds" it was decreed that ledgers were to be kept "after the manner of banks."[6] The surviving ledger contains 478 pages. All entries are recorded twice, with debits and credits placed side by side on the left and right sides of each open folio. The date, nature of each transaction, parties involved, the amount, and a cross reference to other ledger accounts affected all are contained in one narrative paragraph. Though it cannot be called typical proprietorship bookkeeping, the *Massari* ledger includes, besides the accounts of city officials, inventory accounts like those of merchants. To raise funds the city government speculated in pepper, silk, wax, and sugar, which it bought on credit and sold immediately at a lower price.

In *The Merchant of Venice,* Shylock pictures a trader who has:

> . . . an argosy bound to Tripolis, another to the Indies; I understand, moreover, upon the Rialto, he hath a third at Mexico, a fourth for England —and other ventures he hath, squandered abroad.

Seaborne venture trading through consignment agents and short-term partnerships was the central influence on the Venetian and Genoese styles of double entry bookkeeping. An investing partner *(commendator)* might trust his goods to an active merchant *(tractador),* who risked the sea voyage, did the actual trading, and on his return made a detailed accounting. In Venice such partnership contracts took two principal forms: the *commenda*, financed entirely by the investing partner, who got three-fourths of the profits, and the *societas maris*, in which the traveling partner usually invested a third of the capital and shared profits equally.

Venture traders operating through commission merchants abroad needed a running balance of goods shipped and received and amounts owed to and by agents. Voyage (consignment out) accounts were charged with the value of goods shipped and credited with sales proceeds as detailed in agents' reports. Returns were made from the Levant trade in Eastern goods for which the agent received credit. The shipper then opened a merchandise account, which was not closed until the goods got in trade were completely sold. Venture profit could be determined just by closing the balances of the voyage and merchandise accounts into profit and loss after each voyage. The simplicity of this system avoided most of the problems faced by modern accountants, especially those resulting from a need to balance the books periodically, find overall income, and prepare financial statements.

The oldest known Venetian accounts are contained in two ledgers of Donaldo Soranzo and Brothers, merchants. One of these (1410–1418) employs a partial double entry system in which every debit has a credit and merchandise accounts are closed to profit and loss, but profit and loss accounts are not combined and transferred to capital. A complete double entry system is used in the second ledger. But both grapple rather unsuccessfully with the problem of coordinating home office and overseas venture accounts. The four Soranzo brothers imported cotton, one brother in Syria acting as commission agent both for the partnership and for various other Venetian merchants. To complete their ledger the Soranzos had to combine Venetian records with those kept in Syria. But they almost entirely lacked unified chronological journals on which to base ledger postings. There were too many books of original entry. Comparison of the Soranzo and later Venetian accounts suggests the following stages of development for the journal. At first ledger postings came from incomplete expense books, daybooks, rentbooks, memoranda, and agents' reports. Later all ledger entries involving cash were posted from a single chronological record called a journal but really a cashbook. The Barbarigo accounts illustrate a third phase, when nearly all ledger postings came from journals but a few were still drawn from the reports of agents. Finally the journal was sharply distinguished from the cashbook with the realization that its main purpose was to serve as a foundation for the ledger.[7]

Andrea Barbarigo was a sedentary merchant who employed the Soranzos as his Syrian agents. His account books (1431–1449) afford the earliest Venetian example of mature venture bookkeeping. Pacioli's *Summa* describes a system essentially like Barbarigo's. Journal and ledger are now mutually indispensible. Ledger accounts are cross referenced, and opposite each journal entry are page references to ledger postings. Debits and credits are distinguished by the words "Per" and "a" respectively. Money values are placed in a crude column at the right. Barbarigo entered in the same cotton account all shipments from a particular agent even if they were spread over several years. For more frequent imports, such as English cloth, he opened new accounts for each lot received and left them open until the lot was sold. Since his business was not continuous in the modern sense, and different voyages had very different chances of success, he determined profits separately for each such venture and rarely had reason to close his books. He drew up trial balances in 1431, 1435, and 1440, then let the accounts run till his death in 1449. His son Nicolo kept a ledger from 1456 to 1482 but struck a formal balance only once, in 1482 when the ledger was full.

The "Method of Venice" was incomplete by modern standards. And it was really many different methods, reflecting wide variations in practice. Because accounts were kept solely for the owner's use there was little reason for uniformity. Yet it was from Venice that double entry bookkeeping went out to the world, and the Venetian style had at least three advantages.[8] (1) Venice was a center of the book trade, the first books on double entry were published there, and the invention of movable type roughly coincided with the perfecting of bilateral accounts. (2) Venetian teachers of bookkeeping had refined the arrangement and wording of entries in ways conducive to clarity, cross reference, and easy arithmetic calculation. (3) Though designed for the overseas merchant, venture double entry was extremely flexible and could easily be adapted to show annual operating results for a whole business and even to include a manufacturer's cost accounts.

FLORENCE

Like their Venetian counterparts, Florentine merchants were basically opportunists. It was natural for a rich trader who wished to settle debts without transferring bullion to add banking to his activities. Florence had eighty banks in 1338 and over a hundred by the end of the century.[9] The distinctive feature of Florentine business organization came to be large merchant-banking partnerships which, like holding companies, controlled a network of foreign branches and subpartnerships.

The earliest bankers' accounts were simply debt memoranda. A banker needed written records which showed how he stood at any moment with respect to borrowers and depositors. Loans and repayments, deposits and withdrawals seemingly created natural opposites in the accounts which encouraged bilateral classifications. But such records were at first quite crude. The oldest surviving Florentine account book (1211) merely contains a series of unconnected notes relating to transactions with bank clients in which an aid to memory was needed. Some early bank records set aside pages for particular customers. In other cases a depositor's account was debited on one page and credited on another. There were no accounts other than for individuals and there was no balancing, hence no systematic way to detect errors and omissions.[10]

Bankers had several reasons to extend these rudimentary personal accounts into a complete double entry system including tangible assets, expenses, and equities. Nominal accounts may have been added when early bankers added trading operations to finance and needed a record system which produced capital and income figures. Also, because of the difficulty and risk of transferring cash, much of the banker's business consisted of acting as intermediary in settling debts. Merchants deposited money in order to make payments by means of bank transfers. The bank simply debited one client and credited another, but this tended toward an integration of accounts. A third motive for creating an articulated Florentine accounting system resulted from the need to keep records, not just for the trader's private use as in Genoa and Venice, but for submission to others. When banker-traders set up permanent foreign branches, the physical separation of owners and managers made necessary indirect supervision and the periodic reporting of summarized accounting data to the home office.

The abundance of early Florentine accounts makes it easier to trace the evolution of double entry there than in either Venice or Genoa. Among the oldest surviving double entry records are those of Rinerio and Baldo Fini

(1296–1305). They contain receivables and payables, expenses (including interest charges), and operating results. Each ledger entry is cross referenced to its corresponding debit or credit. Missing are only owner's equity and accounts showing the composition of tangible assets. The ledger of the Farolfi Company (1299–1300) includes many entries with similar cross-references, some even to a profit and loss account. Prepaid rent is correctly treated as a deferred expense.

Between 1300 and 1345 the most powerful Florentine merchant-banking houses were the Bardi, the Peruzzi, and the Acciaiuoli. The Bardi was the largest of these "Pillars of Christendom" but only fragments of its records survive. In 1336 the Peruzzi, the second largest, had fifteen branches in Western Europe and the Levant, and a staff of ninety agents. The Peruzzi books stand partway between single and double entry. Like the Soranzo records, they included a great many poorly integrated journals. Each ledger entry was cross-referenced, but the two sides of each account were not yet placed next to each other. Instead, debits were entered in the front half of a ledger and credits in the rear half. Though income and expense accounts were used, no arithmetic proof of equality was made, and profits were found, not by closing the ledger, but by inventorying assets and deducting them from total liabilities and capital.

In the 1340s all three companies failed due to overextension of credit and defaults on loans to monarchs. The Alberti del Giudice of Florence was then chosen to collect the papal revenues and became important until it split into several rival firms because of family quarrels. The Alberti books also contain elements of double entry but no complete system. Not all transactions are recorded twice, there is no trace of the expense or profit and loss accounts which would have permitted complete arithmetic check, and again, profits were found without balancing. Of the surviving records, the most extensive is the *libro segreto,* secret account book, containing data on partners' capital from 1302 to 1339, together with twelve financial statements drawn up at irregular intervals to determine income. As in many Florentine companies, from one to five years passed between such settlements, at which time the books were closed, assets and debts were inventoried, and the partnership agreement was renewed or extended. In the meantime partners could not withdraw from the firm and no new partner could join.

Francesco de Marco Datini (1335–1410) made in his own lifetime the transition from a local business using single entry bookkeeping to large-scale branch operations employing a complete double entry system. He was retailer, importer, banker, commission agent, and manufacturer, seeing in diversification a hedge against the risks which had bankrupted others who grew too rapidly. He expanded by opening more than twenty branches, establishing bookkeeping control over his foreign overseers, who he ruled with an iron hand. The Datini ledgers run continuously from 1366 to 1410. After 1390 a fully developed double entry system complete with balance sheets was used in his foreign branches and at his main office in Florence. But the greatest innovation in these ledgers is the conversion from vertical to bilateral account form. Traditionally the debit and credit sections of Florentine ledger accounts had been placed one above the other instead of on opposite pages as in Venice. For example, when a debt was recorded at the top of a particular page, a blank space was left below for the payment entry. Placing of debits and credits simply on the basis of page position was impossible and the Florentine system never could have led to the "shorthand" ledger entries used today. After the introduction of bilateral accounts from Venice, no further important changes occurred in Florentine bookkeeping technique, evidence that both systems were basically alike.[11]

The Medici Bank was founded in 1397 and lasted nearly a hundred years, though it operated only in Western Europe and never attained the size of the Bardi or Peruzzi. The Medici accounts are interesting because of their use of double entry technique for essentially modern purposes—management and control, audit, even income tax calculation. Every year on March 24, books of the branches were closed and copies of their balance sheets were sent to Florence. These listed separately the balance of each customer's account. Thus some Medici balance sheets contained more than 200 items, and since bad debts were the chief threat to a medieval banker's solvency, audit by the general manager and his assistants consisted of examining these statements to prevent granting of excess credit and to pick out doubtful or past due accounts. A thorough check also required the presence of branch managers. They were called to Florence once a year if residing in Italy and at least once every other year if living abroad. The weakness of this internal audit system was that, while balance sheets were checked, branches were not regularly visited by traveling auditors. The bank incurred huge losses because of uncontrolled and insubordinate branch managers and a general lack of coordination. Even its power as papal banker to obtain the excommunication of anyone failing to pay church revenues could not save the Medici Bank, and it failed in 1494.

Industrial cost accounting, like commercial double entry, originated in Renaissance Italy. The Medici industrial partnerships—they controlled two woolen shops and a silk factory in Florence—made an indirect contribution to the evolution of double entry, in that the need to control industrial processes stimulated demand for precise, complete accounting records. To some extent the Medici merged industrial records and double entry bookkeeping, but there is no evidence that cost accounts were kept in double entry form or were part of an integrated double entry system. Since manufacturing was done by outworkers who owned their own tools, the Medici's main concern was to prevent theft and waste. There was little demand for cost finding in the modern sense, nor any urgent need to tie production and sales together in the accounts. The intricacies of medieval coinage also made it hard to extend double entry into industrial accounting. Manufacturers bought raw materials with gold florins but paid workers in silver; thus two sets of records had to be kept. Not till the nineteenth century would double entry bookkeeping be used to show asset transformations within manufacturing companies.

DOUBLE ENTRY BOOKKEEPING BEFORE PACIOLI

Richard Brown suggests that while double entry bookkeeping was fully developed and operational long before Pacioli's *Summa* appeared in 1494, its inventors used it badly.[12] Few merchants relied on their accounts to keep a regular, accurate check on capital and profits. Many regarded the double entry balancing process simply as a way to prove that all transactions had got into the ledger. Little progress was made in accounting control through financial statement analysis. To these faults was added a shortage of capable accountants. Even the better bookkeepers of the time had trouble balancing and were inclined to "plug" differences. It is wrong, as Sombart does,[13] to read great economic significance into the advent of double entry bookkkeeping. Its early users were the progressive minority of firms and at first it did little to methodize business life.

Double entry offered immediate but limited advantages over earlier methods. It provided an aid to the merchant's memory on debts receivable and payable, and a basis for regulating credit and controlling assets. Double entry accounts were comprehensive, systematic, and orderly. Every transaction was recorded and duality of entries gave a check on the accuracy and completeness of the ledger. Bilateral accounts helped proprietors measure the effectiveness of their business decisions and allowed partnerships to divide profits more equitably. Financial statements could be compiled directly from the ledger. Some of these benefits could be achieved by simpler systems, and double entry's success was doubtless also due to the comparative prestige of those who first felt the need for it, and the natural tendency of others to imitate them.

The new system's ability to measure *total* operating results and financial condition was less valued by these early users than its ability to shed light on *particular* events. Most commerce was of the venture type with income calculated piecemeal. Even firms organized for longer periods tended to be small, owners were usually in personal contact with their affairs and kept accounts almost solely for their own use.

Double entry's enduring advantage was that it was appropriate to a much more sophisticated environment than it was designed to serve. Its comprehensiveness and its focus on the sources of profits and capital made it the first bookkeeping methodology with theoretical potential. The integration of expense and equity accounts provided a means of quantifying the distinction between capital and income. Double entry also promoted the concept of the business firm as a separate entity whose purpose was profit maximization. Finally, it contributed to the doctrine of objectivity by restricting account data to the transactions of the firm and by expressing all transactions in terms of a single monetary unit.

Though medieval merchant-bankers could hardly have anticipated all this, fifteenth century business practice was far in advance of the rather simple system described by early writers. Pacioli's *Summa* was a text for the untutored, omitting most refinements just as a book on accounting fundamentals would today. Thus he not only wrote long after double entry was established, but failed to mention things that were good practice 100 years earlier. Pacioli's single journal, wastebook and ledger would hardly have served the Peruzzi, who in 1339 alone opened eleven new journals. The Datini accounts of 1410 include accruals, depreciation, lower of cost or market inventory valuation, and foreign exchange accounts, not one of which was adequately discussed by Pacioli. He did not even mention subsidiary ledgers, controlling or reciprocal accounts, equity reserves, cost accounting or the audit of financial statements. Contemporary records show constant use of these devices. His discussion of the "Method of Venice" also omitted details of developments elsewhere, particularly Florentine balance sheets. If there were two sources of double entry, one pragmatic, the other scholarly, it is certain that practice set the stage for Pacioli's *Summa*. His influence and deserved importance were those due to the disseminator of a basic new idea.

FOOTNOTES

1. Richard Brown, ed., *A History of Accounting and Accountants* (Edinburgh: Jack, 1905), 177.
2. Raymond De Roover, "The Development of Accounting prior to Luca Pacioli according to the Account-Books of Medieval Merchants," in A.C. Littleton and B.S. Yamey, eds., *Studies in the History of Accounting* (Homewood, Ill.: Richard D. Irwin, 1956), 116.
3. Basil S. Yamey, "Notes on the Origin of Double-Entry Bookkeeping." *The Accounting Review* 22 (July, 1947), 264.
4. A.C. Littleton, *Accounting Evolution to 1900* (New York: American Institute Publishing Company, 1933), 27.
5. A.C. Littleton and V.K. Zimmerman, *Accounting Theory: Continuity and Change* (Englewood Cliffs, N.J.: Prentice Hall, 1962), 47.
6. Edward Peragallo, *Origin and Evolution of Double Entry Bookkeeping, A Study of Italian Practice from the Fourteenth Century* (New York: American Institute Publishing Company, 1938), 3.
7. F.C. Lane, *Andrea Barbarigo, Merchant of Venice, 1418-1449* (Baltimore: Johns Hopkins University Studies in Historical and Political Science, vol. 62, No. 1, 1944), 159-63.
8. F.C. Lane, "Venture Accounting in Medieval Business Management," *Bulletin of the Business Historical Society* 19 (1945), 172.
9. Littleton, *op. cit.*, 34.
10. Brown, *op. cit.*, 94.
11. Peragallo, *op. cit.*, 24-30.
12. Brown, *op. cit.*, 107.
13. See Basil S. Yamey, "Scientific Bookkeeping and the Rise of Capitalism," in W. T. Baxter, ed., *Studies in Accounting* (London: Sweet and Maxwell, 1950), 13-30.

SELECTED BIBLIOGRAPHY

Brown, Richard, ed. *A History of Accounting and Accountants.* Edinburgh: Jack, 1905. Reprinted by B. Franklin, New York, 1966, chap. five.
Brun, Robert. "A Fourteenth Century Merchant of Italy: Francesco Datini of Prato." *Journal of Economic Business History* 2 (May, 1930), 451-466.

DeRoover, Florence Edler, "Partnership Accounts in Twelfth Century Genoa." In A.C. Littleton and B.S. Yamey, eds. *Studies in the History of Accounting*. Homewood, Ill.: Richard D. Irwin, 1956, 86-90.
_____. "Francesco Sassetti and the Downfall of the Medici Banking House." *Bulletin of the Business Historical Society* 17 (1943), 65-72.
DeRoover, Raymond. "Andrea Barbarigo's Trial Balance." *Accounting Review* 21 (January, 1946), 98-99.
_____. *Business, Banking, and Economic Thought in Late Medieval and Early Modern Europe* (ed., Julius Kirshner). Chicago: University of Chicago Press, 1974.
_____. "Characteristics of Bookkeeping Before Paciolo." *Accounting Review* 13 (June, 1938), 144-149.
_____. "The Commercial Revolution of the Thirteenth Century." *Bulletin of the Business Historical Society* 16 (1942), 34-39. Reprinted in F.C. Lance and J.C. Riemersma, eds., *Enterprise and Secular Change*. Homewood, Ill.: Richard D. Irwin, 1953, 80-85.
_____. "The Development of Accounting prior to Luca Pacioli according to the Account-Books of Medieval Merchants." In A.C. Littleton and B.S. Yamey, eds. *Studies in the History of Accounting*. Homewood, Ill.: Richard D. Irwin, 1956, 114-174.
_____. "Early Accounting Problems of Foreign Exchange." *Accounting Review* 19 (October, 1944), 381-407.
_____. "A Florentine Firm of Cloth Manufacturers: Management and Organization of a Sixteenth-Century Business." *Speculum* 16 (1941), 3-33. Reprinted in *Business, Banking, and Economic Thought in Late Medieval and Early Modern Europe* (ed., Julius Kirshner). Chicago: University of Chicago Press, 1974, 85-118.
_____. "Lingering Influences of Medieval Practice." *Accounting Review* 18 (April, 1943), 148-51.
_____. "New Perspectives on the History of Accounting." *Accounting Review* 30 (July, 1955), 405-20.
_____. *The Rise and Decline of the Medici Bank, 1397-1494*. Cambridge: Harvard University Press, 1963; paperback edition: New York: W.W. Norton, 1966.
_____. "The Story of the Alberti Company of Florence, 1302-1348, as Revealed in its Account Books." *Business History Review* 32 (1958), 14-59. Reprinted in *Business, Banking, and Economic Thought in Late Medieval and Early Modern Europe* (ed., Julius Kirshner. Chicago: University of Chicago Press, 1974, 39-84.
Lane, F.C. *Andrea Barbarigo, Merchant of Venice, 1418-1449*. Baltimore: Johns Hopkins University, Studies in Historical and Political Science, vol. 62, No. 1 (1944), 153-81.
_____. "Venture Accounting in Medieval Business Management." *Bulletin of the Business Historical Society* 19 (1945), 164-73.
Lee, Geoffrey A. "The Development of Italian Bookkeeping, 1211-1300." *Abacus* 9 (December, 1973), 137-155.
_____. "The Florentine Bank Ledger Fragments of 1211: Some New Insights." *Journal of Accounting Research* 11 (Spring, 1973), 47-61.
_____. "The Oldest European Account Book: a Florentine Bank Ledger of 1211." *Nottingham Mediaeval Studies* 16 (1972), 28-60.
Littleton, A.C. *Accounting Evolution to 1900*. New York: American Institute Publishing Company, 1933. Reprinted by Russell and Russell, New York, 1966, chaps. two and three.
Littleton, A.C. and Zimmerman, V.K. *Accounting Theory: Continuity and Change*. Englewood Cliffs, N.J.: Prentice-Hall, 1962, chap. two.
Lopez, R.S. and Raymond, I.W. *Medieval Trade in the Mediterranean World*. New York: Columbia University Press, 1955, chap. twenty-two.
Martinelli, Alvaro. *The Origination and Evolution of Double Entry Bookkeeping to 1440*. Unpublished Ph.D. dissertation, North Texas State University, 1974. University Microfilms, Ann Arbor, Michigan.
Melis, F. *Storia della Ragioneria*. Bologna: Dott. Cesare Zuffi, 1950.
Molho, Anthony. *Florentine Public Finances in the Early Renaissance 1400-33*. Cambridge: Harvard University Press, 1971.
Peragallo, Edward. *Origin and Evolution of Double Entry Bookkeeping, A Study of Italian Practice from the Fourteenth Century*. New York: American Institute Publishing Company, 1938. Reprinted by Nihon Shoseki, Osaka, 1974.
Ten Have, O. *The History of Accountancy*. Palo Alto: Bay Books, 1976, 30-39.
Yamey, Basil S. "The Functional Development of Double Entry Bookkeeping." *Aecountant* 103 (November, 1940), 333-42.
_____. "Introduction." In A.C. Littleton and B.S. Yamey eds., *Studies in the History of Accounting*. Homewood, Ill.: Richard D. Irwin, 1956, 1-13.
_____. "Notes on the Origin of Double-Entry Bookkeeping." *Accounting Review* 22 (July, 1947), 263-72.

Chapter 4

PACIOLI AND THE "METHOD OF VENICE"

Moderns do not always realize to what extent the Renaissance was an anti-intellectual movement. In the Middle Ages it was the custom to prove things; the Renaissance invented the habit of observing them.
Bertrand Russell, "On Catholic and Protestant Sceptics."[1]

BIOGRAPHICAL

Luca Pacioli was born about 1445 at Borgo San Sepulcro, Tuscany. He received a general education and religious training from the Franciscan friars in the town. At age twenty he went to Venice and became tutor to three sons of a rich merchant, remaining six years. Besides teaching and studying mathematics he gained an intimate knowledge of commerce and bookkeeping, for as he says, "On account of this merchant I travelled in ships carrying goods."[1]

By 1470, when he left Venice, he had completed his first mathematical treatise. From 1475 he was for six years lecturer in mathematics at Perugia and wrote another book on the subject. He then went to Zara in Dalmatia where in 1481 he finished his third book. In 1482 he lectured on mathematics in Rome. Like many young men seeking preferment as teachers he became a Franciscan friar. After travelling throughout Italy and completing his university education with the equivalent of a doctorate, he returned to Perugia in 1486. During the next eight years he gave public lectures at Rome and Venice and taught mathematics at Naples, Padua, Pisa, Assisi, Venice, and finally Urbino. He was thus about fifty years old in 1494 when he returned to Venice for the publication of his fifth book, *Summa de Arithmetica, Geometria, Proportioni et Proportionalita* (Everything about Arithmetic, Geometry and Proportion).

The last third of Pacioli's life followed a similar pattern of teaching, writing, and travel. From 1496 to 1499 he was the first occupant of a professor's chair at the court of Duke Lodovico Sforza in Milan. His friend Leonardo da Vinci helped prepare the drawings for Pacioli's *Divina Proportione* (1497); Pacioli in turn is said to have calculated the amount of bronze needed for Leonardo's huge statue of the Duke. From 1500 to 1505 he was Professor at the University of Pisa, after which he lived in Rome at the court of the Vice Chancellor. He had made a Latin translation of Euclid's works, and returned to Venice in 1508 to revise this treatise, which was printed the following year. In 1510 he became head of the Monastery of San Sepulcro in the town of his birth. Four years later he was appointed by Pope Leo X to teach mathematics at the Academy in Rome. He was still alive in 1523 when the second edition of the *Summa* was published.

It is usual to view the *Summa* mainly as a response to business needs. Pacioli never claimed to have invented any of the procedures he described, and he almost certainly drew on contemporary bookkeeping manuals. De Roover considers that the *Summa* is probably "a more or less reworked version of a manuscript which circulated among teachers and pupils of the Venetian *scuole di abbaco* or schools of commerce and arithmetic."[2] Carried far enough, this view makes Pacioli a mere transcriber. It fails to explain why the *Summa* as exposition remained unsurpassed for 100 years even by imitators who wrote with Pacioli's text in hand. This first printed description of double entry bookkeeping owes a great deal to its author's abilities and to the particular time in which he lived.

Pacioli was most remarkable for his possession of qualities which are common enough in themselves but are hardly ever found together in the same mind. Living at a time when there were few clear dividing lines between professions and sciences, he acquired an amazing knowledge of diverse technical subjects. The tutor who had learned bookkeeping in the house of a merchant was at the same time friar and courtier, administrator and student of military science, the author of mathematics texts and of a book on games. The interests of the commercial man were blended with the talents of a mathematician and scholar.

Pacioli believed with his time in the interrelatedness of disciplines and in the special importance of those exhibiting a "natural" harmony and balance.[3] He was drawn to Alberti, Leonardo, and other painters in whose work the ideas of perspective, proportion, and symmetry found practical expression. Throughout his life he approached mathematics by way of subjects we would scarcely consider related. In 1508, lecturing in Venice on the Fifth Book of Euclid, he began by showing the connection between geometry and religion, medicine, architecture, painting, sculpture, music, law, and grammar.[4] In the *Summa* he describes commercial accounting practice in such minute detail that a novice can understand and apply it, yet he never ceases to emphasize the duality, integrating tendencies, and balancing features underlying double entry procedure.

CONTENTS OF THE SUMMA

The *Summa* was written as a digest and a general guide to existing mathematical knowledge. It covers five topics: (1) algebra and arithmetic, (2) their use in business, (3) bookkeeping, (4) money and exchange, and (5) pure and applied geometry. The thirty-six short chapters on bookkeeping, called *"De Computis et Scripturis"* (Of Reckonings and Writings) were added "To give the trader without delay information as to his assets and liabilities."[5]

Pacioli begins *De Computis* by saying the successful merchant needs three things: sufficient cash or credit, good bookkeepers, and an accounting system which allows him to view his affairs at a glance. Before starting business the trader should prepare an inventory comprising all his business and personal assets and debts. Items should be arranged according to their mobility and value, with cash and valuables listed first because they are most easily lost. The inventory must be completed in one day and assets should be valued at current market prices.

Pacioli's accounting system is based on three books: the memorandum, journal and ledger. The memorandum is the book of original entry and as transactions occur they are recorded chronologically with complete details. These "daybook" entries are essentially a simple narrative in which no attention need be given to form. Though Pacioli admits that some firms kept only the journal and ledger, the memorandum was useful to Renaissance merchants in several ways. To some extent it took the place of printed documents which accompany modern purchases and sales. And, since a number of Italian city-states issued their own money, merchants received many different types of coins. Transactions could be entered in the memorandum in any monetary unit and converted at leisure to the common denominator necessary for double entry bookkeeping. Each day's entries were then recorded in the journal in good form, and a diagonal line was drawn through the memorandum entries.

While various clerks might make daybook entries, the journal was a merchant's private account book, and Pacioli suggests that to preserve secrecy all inventory items should be entered there directly. Journal entries consist of a narrative debit, credit, and explanation in one continuous paragraph. The date appears in the center of the page above each entry; a debit follows preceded by the word "Per"; then two diagonal lines separating debit and credit; then the credit denoted by the word "a"; finally the explanation, which summarizes the memorandum entry. The amount of each transaction is recorded once on the right side of the page. Thus Pacioli's journal had only one column, which was not totalled. There were no compound entries. In *Chapter Twelve* Pacioli opens the journal, first distinguishing between cash and capital, showing how each is journalized, and noting that cash should never have a credit balance. Each successive inventory and memorandum item is then journalized.

The next four chapters of *De Computis* describe the ledger, which of Pacioli's three books is most like its modern counterpart. He favored the keeping of an alphabetical index or "finding key" containing the name of each ledger account and the page number on which it appeared. Since ruled books were not available ready-made, Pacioli next gave instructions for arranging the money and date columns, which are almost identical to those in modern ledgers. Entries take the form of brief paragraphs, with account titles at the top of each page, debits posted to the left side of a double page, labeled *deve dare,* and credits posted to the right, labeled *deve avere.* After numbering the pages and entering the year date in Roman numerals at the top right, the bookkeeper posts Cash in Hand as a debit on page one, just as it was entered first in the journal. As ledger postings are made, he draws two diagonal lines through each journal entry, one from left to right when the debit is posted, the other from right to left when the credit is posted. Both journal and ledger entries include posting references, but while those in the journal indicate the ledger pages to which each entry was posted, the ledger references refer, not to the journal, but to the other half of the ledger entry. Thus it was easy to trace a transaction forward, but in tracing back from ledger to journal the date was the only guide.

Having established this basic framework of books and accounts, Pacioli devotes his next ten chapters to specialized problems and types of transactions commonly encountered by merchants. In *Chapter Seventeen* he gives the entries for bank deposits and withdrawals, advising that care is needed in dealing with banks since they often change bookkeepers, and that a receipt should be obtained when deposits are made. *Chapter Eighteen* discusses accounting for merchandise purchases through brokers. In *Chapter Nineteen* Pacioli shows the correct handling of drafts (notes) payable. *Chapter Twenty* describes the entries for barter transactions, which should be recorded at the current value of the trader's goods.

Chapter Twenty-One lays down principles and entries for joint venture trading. Pacioli explains the use of dual capital accounts and the recording of partners' capital contributions. A proprietorship may mix business and personal assets but a partnership must strictly segregate them, and should close its books annually.

In *Chapter Twenty-Two* Pacioli describes entries for expense disbursements. He suggests that extraordinary expenses and losses be set apart from operating expenses, that a miscellaneous expense account be established, and also a petty cash account, "because we cannot enter every little thing in the account of the merchandise that you sell or buy."

Chapter Twenty-Three describes accounting procedures for a branch store, which is treated essentially like an account receivable. In *Chapter Twenty-Four* Pacioli gives directions for the negotiation and payment of bills of exchange. *Chapter Twenty-Five* explains that some bookkeepers maintain a special account for income and expenditures, and balance it each year. Others keep a subsidiary book and incorporate the results into their general balances.

Chapter Twenty-Six describes the accounting methods to be followed when a merchant or his agent goes on a business trip. If the trader goes himself he is advised to take a small journal and ledger and combine accounts when he returns. If he trusts goods to someone else he should debit this agent's account for money advanced and merchandise taken, and on the agent's return, credit his account for cash remitted and unsold goods.

Chapters Twenty-Seven to *Thirty-Four* deal mainly with the process of closing and balancing the books. Under the Venetian system, when a venture was concluded, the accounts relating to it were ruled and the balances transferred to profit and loss, which at longer intervals was balanced and closed to the capital account. Another peculiarity was that these closing entries originated in the ledger rather than being posted from the journal.

Though he never mentions financial statements or periodic income finding, Pacioli recommends annual balancing. He also assumes that a new ledger will be opened each time such a balance is struck, even if the old book is not full. The piecemeal nature of venture trading made the main purpose of annual balancing the detection of errors, not statement preparation. Before the old ledger is closed its correctness must be proved. This Pacioli does in two steps —by comparison and then by taking a trial balance. He carefully explains the method of comparing journal and ledger entries by "calling over" the accounts. The journal is given to an assistant while the proprietor takes the ledger. The assistant reads each journal entry aloud and checks it off, and the owner finds and ticks off the corresponding ledger entries. If all amounts are correct and no unticked items remain in either book when this calling over is finished, the old ledger can be closed and the new one opened. All asset and liability accounts are ruled and their balances transferred to the new book. Expense and revenue accounts are closed to profit and loss, and its balance to capital, which is then ruled and its balance carried forward. This process must be completed in one day and no new entries are to be made in the meantime.

Pacioli's accounting cycle ends with the trial balance *(summa summarium)*. The bookkeeper lists all debit amounts from the *old* ledger on the left side of a sheet of paper and all credits on the right. If their two "Grand Totals" are equal, the old ledger is finally considered correct. If they fail to balance "that would indicate a mistake in your Ledger, which mistake you will have to look for diligently with the industry and intelligence God gave you and with the help of what you have learned."

IMMEDIATE INFLUENCE AND MODERN RELEVANCE

The *Summa's* influence may be judged according to: (1) the extent to which, by publicizing the better methods of his time, Pacioli improved accounting practice, (2) his effect on teaching and on written bookkeeping methodology, and (3) his influence on accountancy today.

Pacioli's effect on sixteenth century practice is perhaps the hardest of the three to evaluate because it complemented the influence of merchants who were already using the methods he described. That the *Summa* was highly regarded may be seen from the fact that it was published only a few years after the invention of movable type, when printed books were still rare and expensive to produce.[6] Quite arbitrary details described by Pacioli—posting indications, the placing of dates, and the ruling of ledgers and journals—were followed minutely for hundreds of years. The very formalized journal which is still required by law in many European and South American countries owes much to the Renaissance tradition of using that book to put memorandum entries into proper form.

Pacioli's influence on instructional literature is easier to trace. By publishing the essentials of Venetian practice he made accessible accounting knowledge which before had been transmitted mainly through apprenticeship and by the accident of employees changing jobs. In the first 100 years after its appearance the *Summa* was translated into five languages, and books by Italian, English, Dutch, and German authors presented descriptions of double entry bookkeeping based on *De Computis,* spreading knowledge of the "Italian Method" throughout Europe.

Those who consider the *Summa* a dividing line between ancient and modern record keeping remind us that most of today's accounting practices date back to the Renaissance and that near its beginning double entry bookkeeping was explained in a form which approximated its final development. Pacioli's text shows how little bookkeeping has changed in 475 years. The sequence of events in his accounting cycle is familiar, as are most of the special procedures described in the *Summa's* middle chapters. The theory underlying Pacioli's work is even more contemporary. Though his purpose was practical, he constantly emphasized the proprietor and proprietorship, and the advantages of bilateral accounts, particularly in gathering profit and loss totals. In making explicit the mathematical logic underlying double entry, he touched the roots of modern accounting theory.

Most changes in Pacioli's method have been of degree rather than of kind; that is, they are refinements growing out of the larger scale of modern business operations. Pacioli had a great advantage in describing a system used by small merchants who were in daily contact with their businesses. For them his "fundamentals" book covered nearly the whole course of study. The small proprietorships he used as examples required no specialized journals or subsidiary ledgers, no controlling accounts or posting of columnar totals, no formal systems of audit, cost accounting, or budgeting. With fixed assets an unimportant part of capital, depreciation and overhead allocation were unnecessary. At a time when accounting data was almost never made public, financial statements were not usually needed, nor were periodic closings, a careful apportionment of costs and revenues between successive time periods, or the organization of accounts into uniform current and long-term categories. Certain omissions, such as his failure to mention accruals and deferrals, may have occurred because Pacioli considered them too complex for beginners. But most later improvements, and such doctrines as consistency, conservatism, continuity, and the separation of business and personal assets simply would not have been useful to the typical fifteenth century merchant. The "Method of Venice" was the most practical and convenient for his needs.

FOOTNOTES

1. R. Emmett Taylor, "Luca Pacioli," in A.C. Littleton and B.S. Yamey, eds., *Studies in the History of Accounting* (Homewood, Ill.: Richard D. Irwin, 1956), 176.
2. Raymond DeRoover, "New Perspectives on the History of Accounting," *Accounting Review* 30 (July, 1955), 418.
3. See Arthur Koestler, *The Sleepwalkers* (London: Penguin Books, 1964).
4. R. Emmett Taylor, *No Royal Road: Luca Pacioli and his Times* (Chapel Hill: University of North Carolina Press, 1942), 322-26.
5. All quotations are from the translation of Pacioli's text by J.B. Geijsbeek, *Ancient Double Entry Bookkeeping: Lucas Pacioli's Treatise* (Denver: University of Colorado, 1914).
6. Pacioli's was the first *printed* treatise on double entry bookkeeping. In 1458, thirty-six years before the *Summa* appeared, Benedetto Cotrugli wrote *Delia Mercatura et del Mercante Perfetto* (Of Trading and the Perfect Trader), but it was not published until 1573. This work contains a short chapter describing double entry bookkeeping. Cotrugli also wrote in Italian and used the same three books as Pacioli. Though his system had no profit and loss account, closing entries going directly to capital, he recommended preparation of a trial balance. Pacioli knew this manuscript and even attributed the "invention" of double entry bookkeeping to Cotrugli.

SELECTED BIBLIOGRAPHY

Brown, Richard, ed. *A History of Accounting and Accountants*. London: Jack, 1905; Reprinted by B. Franklin, New York, 1966, chap. five.

Brown, R.G., and Johnston, K.S. *Paciolo on Accounting*. New York: McGraw-Hill, 1963.

Burckhardt, Jakob C. *The Civilization of the Renaissance in Italy*. New York: Harper, 1958.

Crivelli, Pietro. *An Original Translation of the Treatise on Double-Entry Book-keeping by Frater Lucas Pacioli*. London: Institute of Bookkeepers, 1924. Reprinted by Nihon Shoseki, Osaka, 1974.

De Roover, Raymond. "New Perspectives on the History of Accounting." *Accounting Review* 30 (July, 1955), 405-420.

Geijsbeek, John Bart. *Ancient Double-Entry Bookkeeping: Lucas Pacioli's Treatise*. Denver: University of Colorado, 1914. Reprinted by Scholar's Book Company, Houston, 1974; and by Nihon Shoseki, Osaka, 1975.

Green, Wilmer L. *History and Survey of Accountancy*. Brooklyn: Standard Text Press, 1930, 88-105. Reprinted by Nihon Shoseki, Osaka, 1974.

Littleton, A.C. *Accounting Evolution to 1900*. New York: American Institute Publishing Company, 1933; reprinted by Russell and Russell, New York, 1966. Chapter five is a summary of Geijsbeek's translation.

Marsland, P.W. "In Pursuit of Pacioli, From Venice to London." *Accountants Digest* 16 (December, 1975), 84-86.

Peragallo, Edward. *Origin and Evolution of Double Entry Bookkeeping, A Study of Italian Practice from the Fourteenth Century*. New York: American Institute Publishing Company, 1938. Reprinted by Nihon Shoseki, Osaka, 1974.

————. "Origin of the Trial Balance." In A.C. Littleton and B.S. Yamey, eds. *Studies in the History of Accounting*. Homewood, Ill.: Richard D. Irwin, 1956, 215-22.

Taylor, R. Emmett. "Luca Pacioli." In A.C. Littleton and B.S. Yamey, eds. *Studies in the History of Accounting*. Homewood, Ill.: Richard D. Irwin, 1956, 175-84.

————. *No Royal Road: Luca Pacioli and his Times*. Chapel Hill: University of North Carolina Press, 1942.

Ten Have, O. *The History of Accountancy*. Palo Alto: Bay Books, 1976, 39-45.

Yamey, B.S. "Fifteenth and Sixteenth Century Manuscripts on the Art of Bookkeeping." *Journal of Accounting Research* 5 (Spring, 1967), 51-76.

Chapter 5

DOUBLE ENTRY BOOKKEEPING AFTER PACIOLI

The 300 years between publication of Pacioli's *Summa* and the scientific accounting of the nineteenth century has been called accountancy's Age of Stagnation.[1] In fact this was a period of refinement and diffusion of bookkeeping methods, during which the logic of double entry remained unchanged but the simple procedures described by Pacioli were elaborated in practice. The memorial and journal were merged into a single book of original entry. Subsidiary records were added, the practice of annual balancing gained popularity, and accrual accounting and financial statements came into wider use. Chapter Six describes the evolution of account books and financial statements during this period. This chapter focuses on the development of accounting technique as revealed by early textbooks and surviving accounting records.

EARLY TREATISES ON DOUBLE ENTRY BOOKKEEPING

Besides becoming a standard reference work for aspiring bookkeepers, *De Computis* was the model for dozens of textbooks, many of them hardly more than unacknowledged translations. Through Pacioli's influence the method of Venice took on a "canonical authority in matters of detail"[2] which lingered until the mechanization of bookkeeping in the twentieth century. Accounting manuals written by merchants, bookkeepers, and teachers described essentially the same system, usually covered the same topics, and used similar examples.

They provide the most complete record of bookkeeping innovations between the fifteenth and nineteenth centuries.

ITALY

Edward Peragallo divides Italian bookkeeping development into three "cycles."[3] During the first, from 1458 to 1558, business practices were more sophisticated than textbooks, and Cotrugli, Pacioli, and their successors only tried to set forth bookkeeping mechanics as developed by merchants. None of them theorized about accounting and none went beyond the record keeping needs of the mercantile firm. Their contribution was not original thought but the spread of bookkeeping knowledge throughout Europe.

The first important work after Pacioli's was a treatise by Domenico Manzoni in 1534. While his exposition of double entry bookkeeping closely followed *De Computis,* he added illustrations of journal and ledger columns. Manzoni's innovations included subordinating the memorial to the journal and ledger, using ledger posting references to journal entries, and journalizing transfers of nominal accounts to profit and loss.

Alvise Casanova's treatise (Venice, 1558) was also mainly a copy of Pacioli's. Casanova was the first author to omit the memorial and use only a journal and ledger. But his main contribution was a more systematic ledger closing procedure. He introduced the practice of journalizing not only closing entries but also transfers of open account balances to new ledgers. His voyage accounts were closed, not as was usual at the completion of each venture, but only at year end. All open balances were then transferred to a balance account, after which the ledger was closed and the contents of the balance account were posted to a new ledger.

During the second cycle of Italian bookkeeping (1559-1795) major improvements were made in Pacioli's model and theoretical research on bookkeeping began. Double entry was adapted to large firms and to monasteries and government accounts. In 1586 Don Angelo Pietra, a Benedictine monk, published the first printed book on accounting for nonprofit organizations. Pietra thought monastery accounts could best be reviewed by examination of detached financial statements. Though statements had been used in practice since the fourteenth century, this was the first time an author had mentioned them. Pietra was also the first writer to consider an enterprise as separate and distinct from its owners, and his advocacy of a balance sheet, income statement and detailed statement of monastery capital resulted from his desire to account for all changes in the entity's financial status, not just changes in owner's equity. In 1633 Ludovico Flori, a Jesuit of Palermo, wrote another text on monastery accounting which elaborated Pietra's ideas. Flori also stressed the importance of financial statements, and was the first author to mention the placing of transactions in their proper fiscal periods. He used a trial balance not only to prove the ledger's correctness but to facilitate its closing. Peragallo calls Flori's the clearest exposition of Italian bookkeeping until the nineteenth century.[4]

Pacioli wrote near the end of an era. Following the discovery of America and the opening of trade routes to the Orient, political and commercial supremacy passed from the Mediterranean to the nations on the North Atlantic coast. A number of concurrent changes hastened the spread of double entry bookkeeping throughout Europe. The founding of nation-states led to more uniform coinage; Arabic numbers replaced Roman; paper came into wide use, and Gutenburg's invention of movable type made printed books widely accessible. For several centuries the progress of double entry bookkeeping was measured more by the extension of its use than by new technical developments.

Accounting improvements usually but not always paralleled rapid increases in a nation's commercial activity and strength. In the fifteenth century Spain was the most important country in Europe, but it lagged behind in bookkeeping knowledge, serving mainly as a transmission belt for ideas between Italy and England. France played a smaller part in early accounting development than might be expected, partly because legislation intended to prevent fraud had the effect of hindering bookkeeping innovations. Important refinements occurred in Germany, Holland and England, and here again, the spread of double entry techniques from Italy to Northern Europe after 1500 was accelerated by the appearance of textbooks describing the new system and its advantages.

GERMANY

German treatises are interesting because of the way in which Italian accounting interacted with an older system of agency bookkeeping. The earliest German texts, by Henrich Schreiber (Erfurt, 1523) and Johann Gottlieb (Nuremberg, 1531) contained elements of double entry but included neither profit and loss nor expense accounts. Both retained the three traditional German account books: journal, ledger, and goods book. It was not until 1549 that Venetian accounting was introduced into Germany in a translation of Manzoni's work by Wolfgang Schweiker. In 1550 Valentin Mennher Von Kempten, a German mathematics teacher, published at Antwerp a more original text, which set out to describe agency accounting but was clearly influenced by Italian double entry. Though using the German system of account books, Von Kempten illustrated compound journal entries for the first time. In a more ambitious text of 1565 he described full double entry bookkeeping, including a profit and loss account and a balance account. Until this time German ledgers had been clumsily arranged, with account titles placed at the start of every line. In 1594 Passchier-Goessens, a Huguenot refugee from Belgium teaching in Hamburg, systematized the ledger by placing account titles at the top of each folio. A later text on double entry by Nicolaus Wolff

(Nuremberg, 1610) kept the old goods book, showing that the Italian method had not entirely replaced traditional German practice. Only in the seventeenth century did German writers adopt completely the system described by Pacioli.

HOLLAND

The first Flemish work on bookkeeping was "Nieuwe Instructie," published in 1543 by Jan Ympyn Christoffels, an Antwerp merchant who had travelled widely and lived twelve years in Venice. He was influenced by Pacioli, and his journal and ledger formats closely follow Manzoni's, but he introduced the trial balance into Holland, and was the first author to price as well as list the opening inventory of assets and liabilities. Nicolaus Petri's text (Amsterdam, 1588) also demonstrated a periodic trial balance. In a move toward establishing specialized books of original entry, he introduced an "expenses book" which summarized cash totals to be posted in the journal.

Like Pacioli, Simon Stevin (1548-1620) was a man of general learning and wide interests who believed in finding practical applications for his ideas. His position as tutor and advisor to the Prince of Orange led to the publication in 1605-1608 of *"Hyponmemata Mathematica"* (Mathematical Traditions), an encyclopedia of mathematics, mechanics, and astronomy. The bookkeeping portion "Account-Keeping for Princes, according to the Italian Method" took the form of a series of questions and answers between Stevin and his royal pupil. Besides arguing rather unsuccessfully for applying double entry to the administration of the royal estates and the army, Stevin gave a ten-chapter exposition of mercantile accounting. Unlike most earlier writers, he based his innovations on a concern for efficiency and a desire to minimize clerical work.[5] He gave an early demonstration of compound entries, introduced the practice of keeping cash and expense accounts in subsidiary books, and where practical, of posting daily and monthly columnar totals rather than individual items. A religious skeptic, he was one of the first to dispense with the custom of prefacing account books with pious invocations.

In his summarizing procedures also Stevin helped bridge the gap between Renaissance and modern accounting. He not only insisted on annual balancing, but contrary to the current practice of authors, his summary listing of assets and liabilities was made outside the ledger. He recommended the owner draw up a "staet" or sheet listing all assets and liabilities. Periodic profit could then be found by comparing net assets with corresponding figures produced at the previous closing. Double entry bookkeeping came to sixteenth century Britain largely by way of the Low Countries, and Stevin was a major influence on English accountants. One authority suggests that the development of accounting theory before the nineteenth century was based on the writings of Pacioli and Stevin.[6] His pioneering work in the development of financial statements will be discussed in the next chapter.

ENGLAND

In England as in Germany, the Method of Venice was influenced by the older bookkeeping system it replaced. Cash basis charge and discharge accounting was appropriate to a feudal society where commerce and money exchange were less important than the operations of self-sufficient landed estates. In contrast, Italian bookkeeping began with the need of merchant-bankers for debt records. The vital interests of these men lay in the future and they emphasized this in their words of accountability ("shall give, shall have"). But in accounting for his master's property the English steward was never primarily a debtor with future responsibilities. His obligation was as much social as financial. Even after adopting double entry bookkeeping, the English in analyzing transactions stressed current rather than future events. "Debit" was equated with "charge" and "credit" with "discharge." And since a charge was something received, the rule became: debit what is received, credit what is paid.[7]

The first English tract on bookkeeping was "A Profitable Treatyce" written in 1543 by Hugh Oldcastle, a draper and teacher of arithmetic and bookkeeping in London. No copy survives, and we know Oldcastle's work only through the 1588 reprint, "A Breife Instruction, etc." by John Mellis, who acknowledged derivation from Oldcastle. Both texts were almost literal translations of Pacioli's, with a few added examples of little value. Mellis omitted eleven chapters of *De Computis,* including those relating to bank accounting, since no bank had yet been established in England.

James Peele, teacher and clerk at Christ's Hospital, wrote the oldest English bookkeeping texts which survive intact. The first, "The Maner and forme how to kepe a perfecte Reconyng, etc." (1553) was in the tradition of Pacioli, though Peele added instructions for keeping ledger accounts and used more illustrative entries. "The Pathe-way to perfectness" (1569), a larger work in the form of a diologue between teacher and student, included detailed instructions for ledger closings.

Peele's second book and John Weddington's "Breffe Instruction" (1567) contain the first English departures from the Italian tradition of double entry. Weddington in particular was influenced by Dutch practice, borrowed very little from earlier manuals, and introduced some real novelties into British accounting literature. To permit division of clerical labor and relieve the ledger of detail, he split the memorandum into separate books covering specific types of transactions: inventory, cash receipts and payments, purchases and sales, exchange, and three books for agency and partnership entries. Each book was a direct source of ledger postings, and the journal was eliminated. While having little immediate effect on practice, this was a radical departure from earlier writings. Weddington's was also the first English text which used Arabic numerals throughout, the first containing compound journal entries, the first to illustrate accruals and deferrals, the first to distinguish between current and long-term debt accounts, and the first in which inventory accounts in the ledger had separate columns for quantities shipped and received.

The early seventeenth century marked the peak of Dutch influence on English bookkeeping texts. John Carpenter, an East India Company employee, in 1632 wrote "A Most Excellent Instruction, etc." whose chief merit was its author's insistence that all ledger entries must first pass through the journal. Even in those times Carpenter was notorious for his borrowings, and most of his book was lifted without acknowledgement from Pacioli, Manzoni, Peele, Oldcastle, and especially from Ralph Handson's translation of Henry Waninghen's text. Handson's 1633 broadside, "Analysis of Merchant's Accompts," was a single printed sheet listing various transactions and giving the double entry accounts to be debited and credited in each case. This compact guide to proper journalizing was a forerunner of bookkeeping texts based on rote teaching. Richard Dafforne, accountant and teacher in London, published in 1636 "The Merchants' Mirrour," in which he used Stevin's method of platonic dialogue and acknowledged his debt to Dutch accounting technique, but rejected such Dutch methods as subsidiary journals and ledgers and compound entries. However, his was the first English text to describe a complete double entry system, and the first to go into several editions.

After the work of Dafforne and his immediate successors, it becomes hard to trace foreign influences on English bookkeeping manuals.[8] Though they often lagged behind practice, later treatises were based essentially on the English experience. They also became more accessible. Before 1600 books on accounting appeared infrequently; by 1800, over 100 had been published in England, and commonly in multiple editions.

Another measure of double entry's acceptance was the failure of its critics. The best known of these was Edward Thomas Jones, who in "Jones' English System of Bookkeeping by Single or Double Entry," (1796) claimed to have invented a system different in principle from double entry, which would save time, facilitate balancing, detect fraud, and make posting to wrong accounts impossible.[9] The English System used only a memorial and ledger, with no subsidiary books. The memorial had three columns. A bookkeeper first entered transactions in the center column, then at his leisure posted debits and credits to the left and right sides. Besides the usual two money columns, Jones' ledger had four extra columns on each side where debits and credits for each quarter of the year were posted. This allowed a quarterly check between ledger totals and memorial balances. Jones omitted all ledger accounts except those for cash, receivables, payables, and capital. His critics pointed out that with no running account of purchases and sales, income had to be found by side calculations and inventory by physical count, and that since neither memorial nor ledger was in full double entry, his claimed check on accuracy was lacking.

But in trying to combine the simplicity of single entry with the comprehensiveness of Italian bookkeeping, Jones was on the right track. Though his English System was never widely used in England (or anywhere), and was later repudiated by its author, the popularity of his book led to examination and criticism of traditional accounting procedures. Jones in his later writings advocated the use of tabular account books, subsidiary ledgers, control accounts, and other labor-saving devices which upset adherence to the details of Pacioli's method, and in the larger sense furthered the tendency of bookkeeping to become statistical rather than descriptive.

Textbooks played a major role in standardizing accounting practice. By the eighteenth century Italian bookkeeping had become dominant and fairly uniform throughout Western Europe. Sometimes this standardization went beyond the similarity of the events being described, and doubtless the influence of textbooks caused double entry to be adopted by merchants who could have managed as well with a simpler, cheaper system. Most of the methods described in early accounting treatises were like those used today. But record keeping was emphasized rather than analysis, and description rather than tabulation. The important topics in modern books—asset valuation, income finding, financial statements—took up very little space in most texts written before 1850.[10] Cost accounting was hardly mentioned; double entry bookkeeping was considered almost entirely from the viewpoint of mercantile traders.

ENGLISH DOUBLE ENTRY PRACTICE, 1436-1800

The commercial life of Tudor England was much like that of Renaissance Venice, and the British were fortunate that the Venetian style of double entry, with its venture accounts and irregular balancing, set the pattern for Italian bookkeeping throughout Europe. English businesses were small, trading tended to be sporadic, and profits were calculated separately for individual voyages or commodities. Most firms kept single entry records which amounted to little more than lists of payments and receipts. But even double entry systems could be very crude. Most were hybrids, using some dual entries but without profit and loss or capital accounts. The typical sixteenth century ledger was a single book containing all a firm's accounts, with little attempt as classification. When one ledger page was filled, the balance was simply carried forward to the next empty page, with the result that cash and other commonly used accounts reappeared at intervals throughout the ledger. Even 100 years later many books contained only receivables and payables, and the same customer's account might handle both. Business and personal affairs were mixed together. Not till the eighteenth century was there a general awareness of double entry's ability to summarize as well as record.[11]

Those merchants who used double entry and those who did not had similar motives for keeping accounts. At a minimum they had to keep track of credit dealings, inventories, and partners' capital. The authors of bookkeeping texts stressed that double entry's main advantage was its ability to make such records orderly and complete. That is, little data was provided that could not be got by simpler means, but ledger balances afforded a classified record of past operations for ready reference. And the descriptive style of journal and ledger entries made it easy for merchants to review particular transactions in detail. Though there was often a desire to calculate profits, automatic profit finding was never built into surviving sixteenth century account books, and does not seem to have been a dominant motive for adopting double entry. Nor were historical accounting results typically used in choosing among alternatives or allocating resources. The opportunistic nature of trading made past operations an uncertain guide to the future, and most merchants apparently did not rely on venture accounts for decision making data—experience was considered less important than fresh news.[12]

Under such conditions the closing process furnished an arithmetic check and, by clearing the ledger of nominal accounts, facilitated the opening of new books. It might incidentally provide the owner with financial statements. While texts often mentioned statements, the greater importance in practice of narrow bookkeeping goals is shown by (1) the irregularity and infrequency of balancing, (2) the failure to correct errors, (3) the limited use made of the profit and loss account, and (4) the variety of asset valuation methods employed.

The striking difference between seventeenth century and modern bookkeeping technique was the failure to balance and close the books regularly. The closing process was tied to random events: the end of a voyage, the filling of a ledger, the sale of a business, the dissolving of a partnership, a merchant's bankruptcy or death. There was no concept of periodic reckoning. Many early texts recommended closing ledgers only when they were full, and eighteenth century authors who demonstrated annual balancing implied that it was optional.[13]

The infrequency of balancing made it a difficult process, and the great test of "accountantship" was the ability to get a correct trial balance. Yet in many cases no attempt was made to correct books which were out of balance. With no responsibility to outsiders, merchants could please themselves, and close contact with their affairs may also have reduced the need for periodic checks of ledger accuracy. The result was a sliding scale of care within the double entry system, in which the accounts of customers, suppliers, and partners were kept current and accurate, but no great effort was made to verify total operating results.

The lack of accrual accounting and periodic balancing, and the mixing of personal and business affairs in the ledger, are all evidence of a disinterest in calculating total income.[14] Venture account balances showed the profitability of particular goods and voyages. Total profit was usually thought of as the change in value of all a merchant's possessions from all causes between two balancing dates or "rests."[15] Its determination was not a task in itself, but a by-product of the closing process. Profit and loss tended to become simply a clearing account. Realized and unrealized income and losses, business and personal items, capital and revenue expenditures, venture accounts, capital contributions and drawings, asset revaluations—all were cleared through or entered directly to profit and loss. It also became a receptacle for items which did not seem to belong anywhere else and a contra entry for debits which appeared to have no credit, and *vice versa.* Even if the resulting net profit figure had been thought important, it could not have revealed comparative firm progress or isolated the business reasons for capital changes.

Feeling no need to find total profits, bookkeepers could value assets as they pleased, without worrying about the affects on income of changing balance sheet values. The main goal of asset accounting was the maintenance of comprehensive ledger records for owners' reference.[16] The merchant could review his financial affairs simply by scanning his ledger accounts. In doing so, he relied more on descriptions of the items than on valuation figures. Even a balance sheet, if one was made, was less a statement of values than an inventory of the fixed asset accounts commonly included both the asset's cost and current payments and receipts arising from its use. Differences between such receipts and payments might or might not be transferred to profit and loss. Similarly, holding gains might be taken up immediately or deferred until the asset was sold. There was no standard practice; several valuation bases were often used for different assets of the same firm, or even for the same asset at different times.[17] Venture accounting did not require depreciation, and systematic asset writedowns were almost unknown.

Accounting for current assets was also dominated by the need for comprehensive records rather than by profit considerations. Accruals and deferrals were handled inconsistently. Bad debts were sometimes written off to profit and loss, but often were transferred to a special asset account such as "desperate debtors." This treatment overstated income but maintained a record of all debts owed the firm, regardless of quality. Rents and interest were sometimes anticipated by accruals but were more commonly recorded in full when payment came due.[18] In inventory accounting also the intention was not to find the correct transfer to cost of goods sold, but to segregate the results of trading in different goods, mainly for accounting control. Both texts and surviving records show separate inventory accounts for different types of goods, and often these had quantity columns next to the money columns so that perpetual inventory records could be maintained. Not until the nineteenth century did it become common for a ledger to contain only a single inventory account.

CONCLUSIONS

Its absence of enforced consistency makes the Age of Stagnation an excellent test period for the idea that accounting techniques are essentially reactive and evolve in response to changing social needs and business conditions. In Italy, Germany, Holland, England and even Japan,[19] double entry bookkeeping was known long before it was widely used. In each of these countries Italian bookkeeping replaced crude agency accounting at the same stage of social development—as a society that had been feudal became predominantly commercial.

But what of the reverse proposition? How much did the spread of double entry bookkeeping affect the European economic expansion which followed the close of the Middle Ages? Walter Eucken has said:

> The knowledge of double entry bookkeeping was a precondition for the south German expansion of the beginning of the sixteenth century. Where this knowledge was lacking or slow to penetrate, as in the Hansa towns, economic development was delayed. It would seem that the conclusion must be that, as the methods of economic calculation improved, a complete transformation occurred in men's attitude to economic life.[20]

Yet it does seem that Italian bookkeeping was more acted upon than acting. The best proof of its limited influence was the very limited way in which it was used by early practitioners. The main technical improvement between the sixteenth and nineteenth centuries was the more frequent use in later accounts of double entry's summarizing ability. "Double entry brought the concept of capital into the accounting records."[21] But the eighteenth century merchant still valued it chiefly for its ability to bring order to his accounts. Most problems we associate with profit finding and asset valuation concerned him hardly at all. Without the paraphenelia of accruals, matching, or periodic reckonings, his venture accounts measured the results of particular operations, while paging through the ledger gave him some idea of overall activity. But he developed neither a clear concept of income nor systematic procedures for judging the success or failure of his business over a period of time. Public investment in firms was rare, a tradition of accountability to outsiders was lacking, and financial statements were of minor importance. It was the Industrial Revolution, not the bookkeeping innovations preceding it, which drew out accountancy's analytical potential. The adoption of double entry bookkeeping by a majority of businesses came only after 1850, with the manufacturing corporation, the income tax, and the emerging accounting profession as major stimulants.[22]

FOOTNOTES

1. Raymond DeRoover, "New Perspectives on the History of Accounting," *Accounting Review* 30 (July, 1955), 409.
2. David Solomons, "The Maner and Fourme how to keepe a Perfecte Reconyng," *Lloyds Bank Review*, no. 43 (1957), 44.
3. Edward Peragallo, *Origin and Evolution of Double Entry Bookkeeping, A Study of Italian Practice from the Fourteenth Century* (New York: American Institute Publishing Co., 1938), 54.
4. *Ibid.*, 89.
5. O. ten Have, "Simon Stevin of Bruges," in A.C. Littleton and B.S. Yamey, eds., *Studies in the History of Accounting* (Homewood, Ill.: Richard D. Irwin, 1956), 243.
6. P.G.A. de Waal, *De leer van het boekhouden in de Nederlander tijdens de zestiende eeuw* (Roermond, 1927), 289.
7. A.C. Littleton, "Anglicizing Italian Terms," in *Essays in Accountancy* (Urbana: University of Illinois Press, 1961), 34-38.
8. B.S. Yamey, H.C. Edey, and H.W. Thomson, *Accounting in England and Scotland: 1543-1800* (London: Sweet and Maxwell, 1963), 170.
9. B.S. Yamey, "Edward Jones and the Reform of Bookkeeping, 1795-1810," in A.C. Littleton and B.S. Yamey, eds., *op. cit.*, 315.
10. Yamey, Edey, and Thomson, *op. cit.*, 191.

11. James Winjum, "Accounting in its Age of Stagnation," *Accounting Review* 45 (October, 1970), 756 ff.
12. S.W. Bruchey, *Robert Oliver, Merchant of Baltimore, 1783-1819* (Baltimore: Johns Hopkins University Studies in Historical and Political Science, vol. 74, no. 1, 1956), 135-41.
13. Winjum, *op. cit.*, 750.
14. Solomons, *op. cit.*, 41.
15. B.S. Yamey, "The Functional Development of Double-Entry Bookkeeping," *Accountant* 103 (November 2, 1940), 339.
16. B.S. Yamey, "Scientific Bookkeeping and the Rise of Capitalism," in W.T. Baxter ed., *Studies in Accounting* (London: Sweet and Maxwell, 1950), 24.
17. Yamey, Edey and Thomson, *op. cit.*, 197.
18. *Ibid.*, 193.
19. K. Nishikawa, "The Early History of Double-Entry Bookkeeping in Japan," in A.C. Littleton and B.S. Yamey, eds., *op. cit.*, 380.
20. Walter Eucken, *The Foundations of Economics: History and Theory in the Analysis of Economic Reality* (Chicago: University of Chicago Press, 1951), 283.
21. Winjum, *op. cit.*, 747.
22. B.S. Yamey, "Some Topics in the History of Financial Accounting in England, 1500-1900," in W.T. Baxter and Sidney Davidson, eds., *Studies in Accounting Theory* (Homewood, Ill.: Richard D. Irwin, 1962), 25.

SELECTED BIBLIOGRAPHY

Baxter, W.T. "Credits, Bills and Bookkeeping in a Simple Economy." *Accounting Review* 21 (1946), 154-66. Reprinted in W.T. Baxter, ed. *Studies in Accounting*. London: Sweet and Maxwell, 1950, 31-48.
_____. "Accounting in Colonial America." In A.C. Littleton and B.S. Yamey, eds. *Studies in the History of Accounting*. Homewood, Ill.: Richard D. Irwin, 1956, 272-287.
Brown, Richard, ed. *A History of Accounting and Accountants*. London: Jack, 1905. Reprinted by B. Franklin, New York, 1966, chaps. five and six.
Bruchey, S.W. *Robert Oliver and Mercantile Bookkeeping in the Early Nineteenth Century.* Johns Hopkins University, M.A. Essay, May, 1946. Reprinted by Arno Press, New York, 1976.
Coleman, A.R., Shenkir, W.B., and Stone, W.E. "Accounting in Colonial Virginia." *Journal of Accountancy* 138 (July, 1974), 32-43.
Coomber, R.R. "Hugh Oldcastle and John Mellis." In A.C. Littleton and B.S. Yamey, eds., *op. cit.*, 206-14.
_____. "Early Accounting Books—and Early Books of Account." *Accountancy* 68 (October, 1957), 433-435.
De Roover, Raymond. "New Perspectives on the History of Accounting." *Accounting Review* 30 (July, 1955), 405-20.
Eucken, Walter. *The Foundations of Economics: History and Theory in the Analysis of Economic Reality*. Chicago: University of Chicago Press, 1951.
Gordon, Cosmo. "The First English Books on Book-keeping." In A.C. Littleton and B.S. Yamey, eds., *op. cit.*, 202-5.
Hartsough, Mildred, "A New Treatise on Bookkeeping under the Fuggers." *Journal of Econimics and Business History* 4 (1931-1932), 539-551.
Hatfield, Henry Rand. "An Historical Defense of Bookkeeping." In M. Chatfield, ed. *Contemporary Studies in the Evolution of Accounting Thought*. Belmont, Cal.: Dickenson Publishing Company, 1968, 1-11.
Kats, P. "Double Entry Book-keeping in England Before Hugh Oldcastle." *Accountant* 74 (January 16, 1926), 91-98.
_____. "Hugh Oldcastle and John Mellis." *Accountant* 74 (1926), 483-487, 641-648.
_____. "James Peele's 'Maner and Form'." *Accountant* 82 (January 11, 1930), 41-44, 88-91, 119-122.
_____. "The 'Novelle Instruction' of Jehan Ympyn Christophle." *Accountant* 77 (1927), 261-269, 287-296.
Kellenbenz, Herman. "The State of Bookkeeping in Upper Germany at the time of the Fuggers and Welsers." *Academy of Accounting Historians Working Paper No. 7*. University, Alabama: Academy of Accounting Historians, 1974.
Kojima, Osamu. "The Synthesis and Division of the Merchandise Account." In *Studies in the Industrial Economics*. Kyoto: Daigakudo Shoten, 1976, 123-134.
_____ ed. *Historical Studies of Double-Entry Bookkeeping*. Kyoto: Diagakudo Shoten, 1975, 252-305.
Kreiser, Larry. "Early American Accounting." *Journal of Accountancy* 142 (July, 1976), 77-80.
Littleton, A.C. *Accounting Evolution to 1900*. New York: American Institute Publishing Company, 1933. Reprinted by Russell and Russell, New York, 1966, chaps. four and six.

Littleton, A.C., and Zimmerman, V.K. *Accounting Theory: Continuity and Change*. Englewood Cliffs, N.J.: Prentice-Hall, 1962, chaps. two and three.
Nishikawa, K. "The Early History of Double-entry Book-keeping in Japan." In A.C. Littleton and B.S. Yamey, eds. *op. cit.*, 380-87.
Parker, R.H. "The First Scottish Book on Accounting: Robert Colinson's *Idea Rationaria* (1683)." *Accountant's Magazine* 78 (September, 1974), 358-361.
Peragallo, Edward. "A Commentary on Vigano's Historical Development of Ledger Balancing Procedures, Adjustments, and Financial Statements During the Fifteenth, Sixteenth, and Seventeenth Centuries." *Accounting Review* 46 (July, 1971), 531-34.
————. *Origin and Evolution of Double Entry Bookkeeping, A Study of Italian Practice from the Fourteenth Century*. New York: American Institute Publishing Company, 1938. Reprinted by Nihon Shoseki, Osaka, 1974.
Previts, Gary J. "Origins of American Accounting." *C.P.A. Journal* 46 (May, 1976), 13-17.
Ramsey, Peter. "Some Tudor Merchants' Accounts." In A.C. Littleton and B.S. Yamey, eds., *op. cit.*, 185-201.
Riley, E.M. "William Prentiss and Co.: Business Success in Eighteenth Century Williamsburg." *Financial Executive* 36 (1968), 35-38, 40-41.
Solomons, David. "The Maner and Fourme how to keepe a Perfect Reconyng." *Lloyds Bank Review*, No. 43 (1957), 34-46.
Sutherland, Paul. "Hugh Oldcastle and the 'Profitable Treatyce' of 1543." *Accountant* 102 (March 23, 1940), 334-336.
Ten Have, O. "Simon Stevin of Bruges." In A.C. Littleton and B.S. Yamey, eds., *op. cit.*, Homewood, Ill.: Richard D. Irwin, 1956, 236-46.
————. *The History of Accountancy*. Palo Alto: Bay Books, 1976, 56-75.
Thomson, H.W. "The Institute's Literary Treasures: How the 'Method of Venice' Came to England." *Accountant* 143 (October 15, 1960), 469-472.
Thomson, H.W., and Yamey, B.S. "Bibliography of Bookkeeping and Accounts—1494 to 1650." *Accounting Research* 9 (1958), 239-57.
Vanes, J., ed. *The Ledger of John Smythe, 1538-1550*. London: Royal Commission on Historical Manuscripts, JP 19, HMSO, 1974.
————. "Sixteenth Century Accounting. The Ledger of John Smyth, Merchant of Bristol." *Accountant* 157 (September 16, 1957), 357-361.
Winjum, James. "Accounting in its Age of Stagnation." *Accounting Review* 45 (October, 1970), 743-71.
————. "The Journal of Thomas Gresham." *Accounting Review* 46 (January, 1971), 149-155.
————. *The Role of Accounting in the Economic Development of England: 1500-1750*. Urbana: Center for International Education and Research in Accounting, 1972.
Yamey, B.S. "Early Books on Accounting: Carpenter's *Most Excellent Instruction* (1632) and Other Works." *Accountant* 137 (December 14, 1957), 683-4.
————. "Edward Jones and the Reform of Bookkeeping, 1795-1810." In A.C. Littleton and B.S. Yamey, eds., *op. cit.*, 313-24.
————. "The Functional Development of Double-Entry Bookkeeping." *Accountant* 103 (November 2, 1940), 332-42.
————. "Handson's *Analysis of Merchants' Accompts*—An Unrecorded Broadside, 1669." *Accounting Research* 8 (1957), 299-304.
————. "Pious Inscriptions; Confused Accounts; Classification of Accounts: Three Historical Notes." In Harold Edey and B.S. Yamey, eds. *Debits, Credits, Finance and Profits*. London: Sweet and Maxwell, 1974, 143-160.
————. "Scientific Bookkeeping and the Rise of Capitalism." in W.T. Baxter, ed. *Studies in Accounting*. London: Sweet and Maxwell, 1950, 13-30.
————. "A Seventeenth Century Double-Entry Journal." *Accountancy* 71 (November, 1960), 639-641.
————. "Some Seventeenth and Eighteenth Century Double-Entry Ledgers." *Accounting Review* 34 (October, 1959), 534-536.
————. "Some Topics in the History of Financial Accounting in England, 1500-1900." In W.T. Baxter and S. Davidson, eds. *Studies in Accounting Theory*. Homewood, Ill.: Richard D. Irwin, 1962, 14-43.
————. "Stephen Monteage, A Seventeenth Century Accountant." *Accountancy* 70 (November, 1959), 594-95.
————. "Weddington's *A Breffe Instruction*, 1567." *Accounting Research* 9 (1958), 124-33.
————, Edey, H.C., and Thomson, H.W. *Accounting in England and Scotland: 1543-1800*. London: Sweet and Maxwell, 1963.
Ympyn, Jan. *A Notable and very Excellente Woorke*. Edited by O. Kojima and B.S. Yamey. Kyoto: Daigakudo Shoten, 1975.

Chapter 6

EVOLUTION OF ACCOUNT BOOKS AND FINANCIAL STATEMENTS

More than most accounting tools, financial statements are the result of cumulative historical influences. Before the Industrial Revolution they were usually prepared as arithmetic checks of ledger balances. Afterward the roles were reversed and it was account books which were reorganized to facilitate statement preparation. As statements became communication devices rather than simple bookkeeping summaries, the journal and ledger evolved from narratives to tabulations of figures from which balances could easily be taken. Beginning in the nineteenth century periodic financial reporting, first to creditors and later mainly to stockholders, led to the subdivision of accounts into current and fixed categories, to refinements of ledger data through accruals and deferrals, and to government regulation of published statements.

THE JOURNAL AND LEDGER, 1500–1900

Most early descriptions of double entry bookkeeping assumed the use of three account books—memorial, journal, and ledger. The memorial was both a diary for recording business events as they occurred and a place where similar transactions could be grouped. Anyone handling a piece of business might make a memorandum notation, entering money amounts in whatever coinage was used. From time to time the bookkeeper transferred these entries in proper double entry form to the journal. Finally the ledger was posted, and here the process usually stopped. Data was obtained not from financial statements but by paging through the ledger. In the fourteenth century one ledger, supplemented by several daybooks, comprised the usual set of accounting records. Later the journal was added as an intermediate record to convert memorial entries into ledger form. As such it was at first less important than the ledger, but by the sixteenth century more uniform coinage and the increasing use of written receipts made the memorandum less necessary. When it went out of use the journal replaced it as the book of original entry.

THE DOUBLE ENTRY JOURNAL

A. C. Littleton identifies two distinct types of early journal entries.[1] The Venetian style, which flourished from about 1430 to 1550, produced a technical, abbreviated form of entry which served as a bridge between the memorandum and ledger, and may have grown out of the wording of ledger entries. The example given in Pacioli's *Summa* is typical:

> *Per* Zuan Antonio of the Messina: *a* cash, paid to him for part of the above mentioned sugar according to the terms of the agreement . xxx

This may be called the "By A - - - , to B - - " form, with *per* (by) coming first and indicating the debtor, followed by *a* (to) for the creditor. Understanding depended on knowledge of these key words which had a technical meaning different from their meaning in common speech.

Simultaneously a very different type of entry developed, probably in Florentine practice. Because it expressed a complete thought and was understandable from the words alone, it may have grown out of memorial records of personal account transactions. Pacioli's sample entry, recast in this form, might read:

> I make debtor Zuan Antonio of Messina and creditor Cash for money paid to him for part of the above mentioned sugar account according to the terms of the agreement xxx

There were three common variations in the wording of this second type: "A is debtor, B is creditor," "A is debtor to B," and "A owes B."[2] It proved to be the successful variant, driving the Venetian style from use and becoming the forerunner of modern journal entries.

After 1600 the journal entry evolved from a style that was narrative and personal to one that became abbreviated and statistical. The eighteenth century journal was a seminarrative, usually indicating debit and credit entries to be posted rather than personified "debtors" and "creditors":

> Charges Zuan Antonio of Messina to cash paid to him for part of the above mentioned sugar xxx

By the mid-nineteenth century descriptive entries had given way almost entirely to a "technology of position" in which debits and credits were indicated by indentations and by the location of figures in columns:

Bills Payable Dr.	xxx	
to Cash		xxx

The terms signifying position had already become irrelevant and were later dropped, leaving the modern journal as a statistical sorting device designed to facilitate posting accuracy.

CHANGING LEDGER FORMATS

The double entry ledger also evolved from a personal to a statistical format. Since the earliest ledger entries were essentially memory aids, it was natural that they should be written in complete descriptive sentences, expressing complete thoughts in a form easily understandable by laymen, and that they should refer specifically to both the debit and credit sides of each transaction. Each half of a ledger entry was in fact a complete journal entry written in the ledger account, making this kind of ledger less a compilation of figures than a narrative grouping of whole transactions.[3]

But personification, not the narrative form, was the essence of early ledger entries. They were always written from the viewpoint of an owner or owners dealing with outsiders. Double entry bookkeeping began with such personal accounts and the earliest ledgers contained nothing else. Even after ledgers were expanded to include tangible assets and equities the personal influence remained, affecting the phrasing of entries and the words of accountability used.

Since the Italian ledger was used particularly to formalize verbal debt agreements, entries described future events. Though terminology varied, all contained formal words of accountability which looked to the future. *Debet dare* (should give), that is, return to proprietor, was a typical debit notation, while *debet habere* (should have) indicated a credit, that is, a receipt from the proprietor. Thus the debit side was the "give" side and the credit side the "have" side.

March 7, 1340	March 12, 1340
Debit eighty 100-lb. lots of pepper and credit, on page 9, Venciguerre Imperiali; pepper priced at 24 libbre and 5 soldi per 100-lb. lot. Libbre 1, 940 Government broker Luchas Domatus.	Credit pepper and debit, on page 3, Cristiani Lomellini for pepper sold him for the account of Joanne de Franco of Florence, at the price of 22 libbre, 14 soldi, 6 denari per 100-lb. lot. Libbre 227, soldi 5.

This classical Italian ledger entry changed little between the early fourteenth and the mid-sixteenth centuries. It was in paragraph form, a four part narrative describing a giver, a receiver, a thing given, and a thing received. This example is from the Pepper Account of the Genoa Commune ledger.[4]

In the early seventeenth century the narrative form of ledger account gave way to entries in which position, not wording, distinguished debits from credits. Popularized by Simon Stevin and his English imitators, this style lasted nearly 300 years without basic changes:

Notes Debet			Year 1600			Notes Credit		Year 1600		
0	Jan.	Per capital fol. 3	144	0	0	30	May	Per Peter DeWitt fol. 10	334	16	0
28	Mar.	Per David Roels fol. 15	95	4	0	4	Aug.	Per Pepper fol. 16	610	0	0

As this example from *Hypomnemata Mathematica* shows, the essence of Stevin's style was brevity. The full sentences have been shortened, details of transactions have been dropped, and the account title and debit and credit labels are separated from the body of the entry and have become parts of the heading. The ledger account is now basically a tabulation of values.

Two minor improvements were made early in the eighteenth century. Ledger accounts had traditionally been written on opposite pages of the open book, with account titles as page headings on each side. The account title was now dropped from the heading of the credit folio and the phrase "per contra" took its place. Also the words "debit" and "credit," derived from the Latin *debet dare* and *debet habere* were further shortened to "dr." and "cr.". The resulting format lasted nearly 100 years in English practice.

By the mid-nineteenth century both sides of a ledger account were drawn up on a single page under a single title. Accounts were now treated as tabulations of facts relating to the heading. Details in the body of an account were explanations of amounts rather than cross references to contra-accounts:

Dr.			Bills Receivable					Cr.	
1847 May 10	6	to Wm. Johnson	150	00	1847 Nov. 10	12	By Cash	150	00

The manual ledger of today is different only in the absence of the "Dr." and "Cr." in the titles and the "to" and "by" references in the explanation columns. By 1900 these last vestiges of the complete thought entry had disappeared from most ledgers, whose purpose had become simply the tabulation of account balances for easy statement preparation.

FINANCIAL STATEMENTS

THE TRIAL BALANCE

The earliest writers on double entry bookkeeping emphasized that it provided a built-in check on the correctness and completeness of ledger postings. But while Pacioli understood the purpose and construction of the trial balance,[5] neither of the summarizing statements recommended by him were trial balances in the modern sense. The *Balancio del Libro* (Balance of the Ledger) was to be drawn up first, after the nominal accounts had been closed to capital, and like a post-closing trial balance, it simply verified the equality of remaining debit and credit balances. The *Summa Summarium* (Sum of Sums) was prepared as a final proof of closed accounts whose balances had been transferred to the new ledger. All debit entries from the *old* ledger were listed on the left side of a piece of paper and all credit entries on the right side; the proof was their equality. Peragallo calls this a futile procedure, which "proved" only that all the ledger accounts had been closed.[6] The closed ledger was sure to balance even if it contained errors, because both sides of each account had been equalized when their balancing figure was entered before transfer to the new ledger. The trial balance was in general use by the end of the fifteenth century, but the *Summa Summarium* had a short life and may never have been widely used.

THE BALANCE ACCOUNT

The next step toward financial statements came by way of the balance account. This was a single account which listed all the debit and credit balances in the ledger. It not only tested the accuracy of ledger closings, but gathered asset and equity balances into a summary convenient for transfer to a new ledger. Its emergence as a standard bookkeeping procedure also increased awareness of the interrelationship between real and nominal accounts. For example, Gottlieb in 1546 calculated profit in the balance account as the sum of changes in assets, liabilities, and start of period capital. But there is no evidence in early texts that the balance account was meant to be reproduced outside the ledger.[7] Like the profit and loss account, its main use was as a clearing and transfer medium.

RENAISSANCE BALANCE SHEETS

How did the balance account evolve into a balance sheet? There were a number of causes. During the Middle Ages, Italian city-states and German municipalities levied property taxes which required the preparation of financial statements. A French ordinance of 1673 required merchants to make an "inventory" every two years "of all their fixed and movable properties and of their debts receivable and payable."[8] The intention was to aid possible bankruptcy proceedings by preserving an overview of each firm up to the latest statement date. From the earliest Florentine *Balancio* in the fourteenth century, partnership profits had been calculated as the difference between the net assets of two successive accounting periods. The admission or withdrawal of partners legally dissolved such businesses and made a calculation of capitals necessary. Merely closing partnership books might not suffice, for then only the bookkeeping partner would preserve a record of the situation at that moment. The need for asset revaluations at the time of ownership changes also called for a separate schedule of resources and debts.[9]

Above all, as companies grew larger, more people had an interest in their operations, and separate statements were needed because direct access to the ledger became impossible for all who wanted information. Following the appearance of joint stock companies in the seventeenth century, demands for separate statements became urgent as creditors and shareholders sought data about their investments.

Early statements were made either by copying the accounts as they appeared in the ledger, or by working from trial balance figures to produce columnar reports. In his 1635 text Dafforne illustrated a six-column statement in which the first pair of columns showed a trial balance of totals, the middle pair a trial balance of balances, and the right hand columns a balance sheet containing the remaining assets and equities. Later writers added profit and loss columns and entered inventory counts to adjust beginning figures, creating what we would call a worksheet. In time these unwieldy columnar statements dropped out of textbooks, to be replaced by "account" and "report" form balance sheets showing final figures but not their derivation.

Throughout this period the balance sheet was by far the most important financial statement, and often the only one prepared. Users wanted data about assets and capital; expenses and revenues were considered incidental. Simon Stevin's *Hypomnemata Mathematica* broke this pattern by stressing the equal importance of nominal accounts. In presenting his most famous illustrative example, Stevin explained that the "Estate" (balance sheet) of Derrick Roose was so called because it included only such items as "make up the estate on a certain day" and excluded all other accounts which "indicate increase or decrease of capital."[10] His balance sheet was typical for its time, with assets opposite liabilities and income shown as the net change in capital during an accounting period:

The Estate of Derrick Roose
made up on the last day of December 1600

Estate of Capital debit		Estate of Capital credit	
	£ s d		£ s d
(list of liabilities) 51-8-0		(list of assets) 3191-17-1	
Balance debit, to close			
the statement 3140-9-1			
Total 3191-17-1		Total 3191-17-1	

The remainder (Capital) at year end is 3140-9-1
At the beginning of the year it was 2153-3-8

Increase during the year 987-5-5

But Stevin did not stop there. "In order to make certain that the account is correct, I collect all remainders of accounts increasing or decreasing capital," and including all remainders of accounts omitted from the balance sheet "because they do not represent actual things."[11] But this "Proof of the Estate" was more than the traditional test of ledger equality. It not only confirmed the profit figure shown on the balance sheet but described how it was earned, detailing the expenses and revenues which caused the net capital change represented by income:

Proof of the Estate

Estate of Capital debit		Estate of Capital credit	
	£ s d		£ s d
Trading expenses	57-7-0	Profit on cloves.	75-4-7
Household expenses . . .	107-10-1	Profit on nuts	109-7-2
Total	164-17-0	Profit on pepper	18-19-0
		Profit on ginger.	41-8-4
Profit, agreeing with		Profit and Loss	907-3-4
the above statement. . . .	987-5-5	(prior credit bals.)	
	1152-2-5		1152-2-5

THE BRITISH BALANCE SHEET

The form of modern financial statements was determined chiefly by the nineteenth century English experience. A more complete background to the companies acts is given in Chapters Seven and Nine. Briefly, during the eighteenth century bookkeeping began to be adapted to corporate needs. Its purpose was no longer simply to aid management, but also to inform investor decisions and, in a broader sense, to help allocate resources and maintain a money market in an economy which was becoming industrialized. The collapse of the South Sea Company speculations, accompanied by large investor losses, led to the Bubble Act of 1720, which for 100 years restricted the formation of new joint stock companies. It was not until 1844 that the Joint Stock Companies Act again made the corporate form available for general use.

In framing the companies acts, Parliament was probably more influenced by the English tradition of responsibility accounting than by Italian double entry bookkeeping.[12] Incorporation was granted as a privilege in return for which joint stock companies incurred specific public duties. Promoters and company officers were considered stewards placed in charge of investors' capital; as such, they had a duty to publicize their use of these assets. Acting on this premise, the British pioneered legislation to protect investors. The Companies Act of

1844 required the distribution to stockholders of audited balance sheets. The 1856 Act abandoned earlier accounting and audit requirements, but included a model balance sheet which reflected the English view of corporate responsibility.

Like the charge and discharge statement, this model report grouped related balance sheet items into subtotals and placed obligations and their discharge opposite one another. These were improvements in themselves, representing an interpretive arrangement of data in place of a simple sequence of ledger balances. Since management's initial responsibility was created by the sale of stock, the top section of the 1856 model balance sheet contrasted permanent capital from stock sales and the permanent assets bought with the proceeds. The distinction made by English classical economists between fixed and circulating capital may have persuaded legislators to separate current from fixed assets and liabilities.[13] The last two items of stewardship were the reserve for contingencies and retained earnings available for dividends; contrasted to these were the cash and operating assets which funded them:

Dr.   BALANCE SHEET of the____Co. made up to____1856   Cr.

Capital and Liabilities   *Property and Assets*

  I. *Capital from stock sales*   III. *Property*
     a. Shares outstanding   a. Immovable
     b. Price per share   b. Movable

 II. *Debts and Liabilities*   IV. *Debts owing to the firm*
     a. Long-term liabilities   a. Notes Receivable
     b. Short-term debts   b. Accounts Receivable
                             c. Bad debts

 VI. *Reserve for Contingencies*   V. *Cash and Investments*
VII. *Profit available for div'ds.*

Contingent Liabilities

This model format, with assets on the right, equities on the left, and permanent capital at the top, is almost a complete reversal of the modern American balance sheet. It was also a departure from classical Italian practice, and this has been attributed to several causes. Some point to Simon Stevin's influence on English textbook presentations (see page 69). Also, the balance account showed such a reversed order after an old ledger had been closed but before the new one had been opened And several early English corporations produced statements in this form. Earlier British legislation was another influence on these model statements.[14] English accounting texts written between 1721 and 1858 showed balance sheets with assets on the left, but after 1858 this order was reversed. The assets-on-the-right arrangement was recommended by the Companies Act of 1862. The Regulation of Railways Act of 1868 not only made it mandatory but also required a horizontal division of the data in terms of "opposites."

Once statement preparation became the main purpose of bookkeeping, ledger figures began to be refined to more closely approximate current market prices. The need for periodic reporting made asset valuation a major issue for the first time and stimulated interest in percentage depreciation. Techniques for accruing rent and interest had been used in practice since the fourteenth century, but there had never before been urgent reason to apply them widely or systematically. Similarly with inventory valuation. Jacques Savary in 1712 had shown understanding of lower of cost or market, obsolescence write-downs, and net realizable value, but it was not until the late nineteenth century and the wide use of financial statements that standardized inventory pricing began to develop. Before then there had existed a great variety of acceptable valuation methods, with little or no tendency toward uniformity. The new importance of financial reporting created a need for consistency and compara-bility of data, which in turn strengthened arguments in favor of historical cost accounting and realization at the point of sale.

AMERICAN FINANCIAL REPORTING

In America as in England the balance sheet was the primary statement—but for different reasons. The British balance sheet developed as a report to stock-holders on management's stewardship of contributed funds. Nineteenth cen-tury American corporations had no comparable history of large losses from stock speculation and were not as closely regulated, nor was incorporation considered a privilege which created reciprocal disclosure obligations. American corporations were usually small and drew most of their capital, not from stock sales, but from short-term bank loans. Their balance sheets were directed mainly toward bankers, whose conventional wisdom was that a borrower's ability to repay maturing loans was related more to the conversion of in-ventory into cash than to earning power.[15] This focus on liquidity rather than earnings caused current assets and liabilities to be placed at the top of the American balance sheet. And it is likely that the absence of government reg-ulation encouraged statement formats which simply followed the ledger balances, placing assets on the left, equities on the right.

The bankers' "liquidity doctrine" was severely tested during the inventory depression of 1920–21, when American wholesale prices fell 40 percent, caus-ing a billion dollar inventory shrinkage.[16] Current sales from inventories had to be made much below historical cost, reducing cash inflows and making loan repayments difficult. As credit dried up, bankers saw the limitations of a loan policy based solely on liquidity, and corporate borrowers realized their vulner-ability during recessions if they depended for financing on short-term loans. They accordingly sought funds from sources less sensitive to changes in their current cash position. During the 1920s mass marketing of stock issues became a popular way to finance corporate expansion, since the resulting equity in-crease put no immediate pressure on working capital.

When stock sales became the chief external source of funds, and stockholders the primary statement readers, the income statement became the more meaningful report. Of course the shift in emphasis from balance sheet to income statement had causes other than the changed method of corporate financing. These included long-run institutional and technological changes, such as the regulation of quasi-public corporations and the growth of railroads.[17] Income taxation also shifted attention to revenues and expenses, as did the rapid development of cost accounting. Even long-term creditors found earning power more significant than tests of solvency. It began to be argued that determining net asset values at the balance sheet date was not only of secondary importance but was impossible to accomplish. Later the same would be said of income measurement.

THE FUNDS STATEMENT

The balance sheet and income statement, compiled directly from ledger balances, provide an overall financial view whose predictive power can be sharpened by analysis of working capital changes. Funds statements have been used in American practice for over 100 years.[18] By 1903 at least four types existed: reports summarizing changes in cash, in current assets, in working capital, and in all financial activities. But there was no agreement as to which type should be generally adopted or what form it should take.

In four textbooks published between 1908 and 1921,[19] William Morse Cole illustrated a statement designed to summarize changes in all balance sheet accounts. He reasoned that increases in asset accounts indicated that expenditures had been made to acquire property of some kind, just as decreases in liability accounts showed that debts had been paid. Similarly, net decreases in assets indicated something taken from the asset account during the year and spent elsewhere, while liability increases suggested that the firm had borrowed assets. Cole labeled such individual increases in liabilities and decreases in assets "Where-got (or Receipts or Credits)," and listed asset increases and liability decreases as "Where-gone (or Expenditures or Debits)." By comparing beginning and ending balance sheet items in this way he hoped to show the effects of internal transactions and especially to portray shifts in liquidity. But in cumulating net changes in *all* balance sheet accounts, he failed to isolate liquidity changes and thereby to reveal the sources of receipts or the ultimate effect of expenditures. He also tacitly assumed that each such change increased or decreased the total amount of a firm's resources.

The present funds statement format is largely the work of H. A. Finney, who led the drive for a report which focused on liquidity by showing the causes of working capital changes. His solution to a 1921 CPA Examination problem on resource application featured a "Statement of Application of Funds" divided into two parts, "Funds Provided" and "Funds Applied."[20] He was among the first to favor grouping current account balances into a "pool" of values. In a 1923 article,[21] Finney pointed out that some balance sheet changes, for example land revaluations and goodwill writeoffs, are the result of arbitrary book entries and neither provide nor dispense funds. To isolate the real changes he demonstrated a worksheet approach which aggregated most (though not all) of the fluctuations which affect working capital, and offered a routine, systematic method for deriving them. By 1925 textbook presentations could be found which approximated both the format and contents of today's funds statements.

During the interwar period where was a tendency to eliminate from funds statements all transactions not affecting current asset and liability balances. The substitution of a single working capital account for the detailed listing of changes in current accounts left room for more consideration of underlying transactions. After World War II attempts were made to measure the actual flow of funds, not just the sum of working capital changes between balance sheet dates.[22] The funds statement appeared much more frequently in published reports. Beginning in September 1971, the AICPA required its inclusion in annual reports to stockholders.[23]

THE TRADITIONAL STATEMENTS TODAY

The balance sheet and income statement have emerged in their present form only during the last 100 years. Yet they seem appropriate to a much simpler socio-economic environment. They came to maturity at a time when inflation was almost never the problem it has since become. Their makers faced no comparable regulatory pressure to increase disclosure or broaden the scope of published reports. In each era they could cater to a single dominant user group. They were not required to conform to a set of "generally accepted" but vaguely defined accounting principles. Nor were accountants normally expected to provide really precise asset valuations or profit measurements. In the case of the balance sheet one result is that today, as in Tudor England, the descriptions of asset and equity items are often more revealing than the valuations attached to them.

FOOTNOTES

1. A.C. Littleton, *Accounting Evolution to 1900* (New York: American Institute Publishing Co., 1933), 117.
2. *Ibid.*
3. *Ibid.*, 90.
4. Edward Peragallo, *Origin and Evolution of Double Entry Bookkeeping, A study of Italian Practice from the Fourteenth Century* (New York: American Institute Publishing Co., 1938), 8.
5. Edward Peragallo, "Origin of the Trial Balance," in A.C. Littleton and B.S. Yamey, eds., *Studies in the History of Accounting* (Homewood, Ill. Richard D. Irwin, 1956), 216.
6. *Ibid.*, 218.
7. Littleton, *op. cit.*, 132.

8. Jacques Savary, *Le Parfait Negociant*, 6th ed. (Paris: 1712); quoted in Littleton, *op. cit.*, 136.
9. Littleton, *op. cit.*, 137-38.
10. A.C. Littleton and V.K. Zimmerman, *Accounting Theory: Continuity and Change* (Englewood Cliffs, N.J.: Prentice-Hall, 1962), 76. See also Littleton, *op. cit.*, 133-34.
11. *Ibid.*, 76.
12. *Ibid.*, 85.
13. *Ibid.*, 88.
14. *Ibid.*, 82-83.
15. *Ibid.*, 92-93.
16. *Ibid.*, 95-96.
17. Eldon S. Hendriksen, *Accounting Theory*, rev. ed. (Homewood, Ill. Richard D. Irwin, 1970), 47-48, 55.
18. L.S. Rosen and D.T. DeCoster, "Funds' Statements: A Historical Perspective," *Accounting Review* 44 (January, 1969), 126.
19. William Morse Cole, *Accounts: Their Construction and Interpretation* (Boston: Houghton Mifflin Co., 1908 and 1915); *Accounting and Auditing* (Cree Publishing Co., 1910); *The Fundamentals of Accounting* (Boston: Houghton Mifflin Co., 1921).
20. H.A. Finney, ed. "Students' Department," *Journal of Accountancy* 32 (July, 1921), 64-67.
21. H.A. Finney, "Statement of Application of Funds," *Journal of Accountancy* 36 (December, 1923), 460-72.
22. See Colin Park and John W. Gladson, *Working Capital* (New York: Macmillan Company, (1963).
23. Accounting Principles Board, "Reporting Changes in Financial Position," *Opinion No. 19* (New York: AICPA, 1971).

SELECTED BIBLIOGRAPHY

Anton, Hector R. *Accounting for the Flow of Funds*. Boston: Houghton Mifflin Co., 1962, 45-64.

Brown, Sister Isidore. *The Historical Development of the use of Ratios in Financial Statement Analysis to 1933*. Unpublished Ph.D. dissertation, Catholic University of America, 1955. University Microfilms, Ann Arbor, Michigan.

Daniels, Mortimer B. *Corporation Financial Statements*. Ann Arbor: University of Michigan, 1934, chap. one.

Dev, Susan. "Ratio Analysis and the Prediction of Company Failure." In Harold Edey and B.S. Yamey, eds. *Debits, Credits, Finance, and Profits*. London: Sweet and Maxwell, 1974, 61-74.

Edey, H.C., and Panitpakdi, Prot. "British Company Accounting and the Law 1844-1900." In A.C. Littleton and B.S. Yamey, eds. *Studies in the History of Accounting*. Homewood, Ill. Richard D. Irwin, 1956, 356-79.

Foulke, Roy A. *Practical Financial Statement Analysis*. 6th ed. New York: McGraw-Hill, 1968, chap. one.

Gregory, R.H., and Wallace, E.L. "Solution of Funds Statement Problems—History and Proposed New Method." *Accounting Research* 3 (1952), 99-132.

Hay, L.E. "Executorship Reporting—Some Historical Notes." *Accounting Review* 36 (January, 1961), 100-4.

Hendrikson, Eldon S. *Accounting Theory*, rev. ed. Homewood, Ill. Richard D. Irwin, 1970, 60-62, 237-50.

Horrigan, J.O., "A short History of Financial Ratio Analysis." *Accounting Review* 43 (April, 1968), 284-94.

Howard, S.E. "Public Rules for Private Accounting in France, 1673 and 1807." *Accounting Review* 7 (June, 1932), 91-102.

Käfer, K. and Zimmerman, V.K. "Notes on the Evolution of the Statement of Sources and Application of Funds." *International Journal of Accounting* 2 (1967), 89-121.

Littleton, A.C. *Accounting Evolution to 1900*. New York: American Institute Publishing Company, 1933. Reprinted by Russell and Russell, New York, 1966, chaps. seven through ten.

Littleton, A.C., and Zimmerman, V.K. *Accounting Theory: Continuity and Change*. Englewood Cliffs, N.J.: Prentice-Hall, 1962, chaps. three and four.

Moyer, C.A. "Trends in Presentation of Financial Statements and Reports." Chapter fifteen of Morton Backer, ed. *Handbook of Modern Accounting Theory*. Englewood Cliffs, N.J.: Prentice-Hall, 1955.

Myer, J.N. "Statements Accounting for Balance Sheet Changes." *Accounting Review* 19 (January, 1944), 31-38.

Park, Colin, and Gladson, John W. *Working Capital*. New York: Macmillan Company, 1963, especially chaps. one and two.

Penndorf, B. "The Relation of Taxation to the History of the Balance Sheet." *Accounting Review* 5 (December, 1930), 243-51.

Peragallo, Edward. *Origin and Evolution of Double Entry Bookkeeping, A Study of Italian Practice from the Fourteenth Century*. New York: American Institute Publishing Company, 1938. Reprinted by Nihon Shoseki, Osaka, 1974.

_____. "Origin of the Trial Balance." In A.C. Littleton and B.S. Yamey, eds. *Studies in the History of Accounting*. Homewood, Ill. Richard D. Irwin, 1956, 215-22.

Rosen, L.S., and DeCoster, D.T. "Funds' Statements: A Historical Perspective." *Accounting Review* 44 (January, 1969), 124-36.

Schmalenbach, Eugene. *Dynamic Accounting*. London: Gee, 1959, chap. one.

Takatera, Sadao. "Early Experiences of the British Balance Sheet." *Kyoto University Economic Review* 37 (October, 1967), 34-47. Reprinted in O. Kojima, ed. *Historical Studies of Double-Entry Bookkeeping*. Kyoto: Diagakudo Shoten, 1975, 299-305.

Ten, Have, O. "Simon Stevin of Bruges." in A.C. Littleton and B.S. Yamey, eds. *Studies in the History of Accounting*. Homewood, Ill. Richard D. Irwin, 1956, 236-46.

Walker, R.G. "Asset Classification and Asset Valuation." *Accounting and Business Research* 4 (1974), 286-296.

Winjum, James. "Accounting in its Age of Stagnation." *Accounting Review* 45 (October, 1970), 743-61.

_____. *The Role of Accounting in the Economic Development of England: 1500-1750*. Urbana: Center for International Education and Research in Accounting, 1972.

Yamey, B.S. "Some Topics in the History of Financial Accounting in England, 1500-1900." In W.T. Baxter and S. Davidson, eds. *Studies in Accounting Theory*. Homewood, Ill. Richard D. Irwin, 1962, 14-43.

_____. "Closing the Ledger." *Accounting and Business Research* 1 (1970), 71-77.

_____. "Pious Inscriptions; Confused Accounts; Classification of Accounts: Three Historical Notes." In Harold Edey and B.S. Yamey, eds. *Debits, Credits, Finance, and Profits*. London: Sweet and Maxwell, 1974, 143-160.

Yamey, B.S., Edey, H.C., and Thomson, H.W. *Accounting in England and Scotland: 1543-1800*. London: Sweet and Maxwell, 1963.

Chapter 7

ADVENT OF THE CORPORATION

The legal doctines underlying modern corporations derived from three much older ideas: (1) that each such firm is an independent, property-owning entity in its own right, (2) that therefore, the individuals comprising it have limited liability for corporate activities, and (3) that it has continuity of existence apart from the lives of its owners. Three leading institutions of the medieval world, the church, the town, and the craft guild all were treated as separate entities with perpetual existence.[1] Monastery property was never considered as belonging to individual monks or abbots, nor were they personally responsible for church obligations. Medieval municipalities were also viewed as entities apart from their inhabitants, and they often obtained articles of incorporation which legally recognized their separate status. Craft guilds offered mutual association for the protection of an occupational group. Like the church and town, they held property in their own names and had permanent offices through which many individuals passed.

In each case the entity's independent existence provided the rationale underlying limited liability for its members. If a business exists apart from its owners, its property cannot logically be made available to their personal creditors, because the owners themselves have only an indirect claim on corporate assets. Similarly, if the corporation is a separate entity with the power to contract and hold property, its creditors cannot expect to reach stockholders' personal assets to satisfy corporate debts.

Italian *Commenda* partnerships were direct ancestors of the limited liability corporation. During the Renaissance, investors evaded the church usury laws, which held that money was barren, by entrusting their cash to overseas traders for a share in the profits of joint ventures. Besides nicely combining venture capital and trading ability, the partnership contract *en commendite* established the precedent that while trading partners were fully liable for partnership debts, a nonparticipating investor might get a share of profits while risking only the amount of his investment.

Influenced by Italian practice, many European commercial codes made a distinction between the liability of active and silent partners, holding the latter responsible only to the extent of their contribution. The French Code Savary of 1673 provided specifically for limited partnerships in the Italian manner. But in England the concept of partnership rested on the agency relationship, in which each partner could bind the others and all were jointly and severally liable for debts. This made corporations especially hard to establish in the nation which first required them on a large scale. Early in the seventeenth century certain English companies extended a type of limited liability to their investors as an inducement to buy stock. The "par value" doctrine did not protect investors' personal assets from company creditors, but merely assured subscribers to fully paid shares that the company would not call on them for further capital.[2] But even before this, the British government had begun promoting limited liability companies for reasons of its own.

THE STATE IN BUSINESS

Mercantilism was a set of economic theories and also a political policy based on developing business strength and increasing national wealth by trading. It affected accounting development because of its dominance between the sixteenth and eighteenth centuries when the corporation and other modern business forms were maturing. Like Adam Smith, the mercantilists saw business profits as a source of both personal and public good. But the mercantilist trader aspired to monopoly in theory as well as in practice. The American Revolution has been described as a struggle between British and Colonial mercantilists for control of the land west of the Allegheny mountains.[3] Mercantilist doctrine held that the state should encourage trade and industry by granting monopoly patents to inventors and by chartering companies with exclusive franchises to perform certain services or to exploit particular overseas areas. In emphasizing foreign trade, the nation should also be sure exports exceeded imports, creating a favorable trade balance which would enlarge the national treasury through an influx of gold and silver. Since the imports tended to be raw materials and the exports manufactured products, this policy led naturally to the more sophisticated one of exporting surpluses and acquiring needed foreign goods in exchange.

Commerce in Elizabethan England, as in Pacioli's Venice, typically took the form of desultory venture-speculations. In this environment incorporation promoted business continuity—it was at first a privilege conferred only by royal charter and always for monopoly purposes. Trade guilds interested in dominating areas of commercial life had begun incorporating as early as 1394. Soon there were municipal corporations for activities such as firefighting and banking, and for almost 200 years such livery companies monopolized various public services.

CHANGING FORMS OF BUSINESS ORGANIZATION

The discovery of America and the opening of sea routes to China and India turned investors' attention to overseas trading. The earliest British "Companies of Adventurers" formed to carry on this trade were partnerships but, as with the Italian *Commendas,* certain partners wished to trade actively while others merely wanted to invest. In a field where risks as well as rewards were great, some form of limited liability was needed if investor and adventurer were to collaborate effectively.

The first joint stock companies were partnerships with a few corporate features. They generally had limited life and imposed unlimited liability for company debts, but they also in many cases issued transferable shares. Their purposes ranged from trade to colonization and included military expeditions and voyages of discovery. Parliament preferred them to competitive businesses because they were easier to regulate and tax. They were granted monopoly rights partly as compensation for the large initial investments such ventures required. The Russia Company (lumber), the Virginia Company (tobacco), the East India Company (spices), and the Hudson's Bay Company (furs) were four of the best known. In chartering companies such as the Bank of England, whose activities touched vital national interests, the government allowed shareholders individual immunity from the bankruptcy laws if the firm failed. The effect was to make them liable for company debts only up to the amount unpaid on their shares.

The East India Company, chartered by Elizabeth I in 1600, evolved in just sixty years from a system of speculative voyages with terminable stocks to a continuing corporation with permanently invested capital. Between 1600 and 1617 the company sponsored 113 voyages, each supplied with newly subscribed capital and treated as a separate venture.[4] This made liquidation necessary after each voyage so that those who wished to drop out might do so and new "adventurers" might be admitted. It also meant the stock was not readily negotiable, since there was no way to enter a venture in progress other than by buying unissued stock or a fraction of a share held by a present member. At the end of each voyage assets as well as earnings were subject to "divisions" among the shareholders. Profit was easily measured by the individual investor: he gained to the extent that he got back more than he had paid in.

But ships, trading posts and other long-lived resources had a bothersome way of carrying over from one venture to the next, until finally the company's accounts became a jumble of successive voyages. As unliquidated balances or "remains" of earlier voyages were merged with later ones, it became necessary to juggle assets and profits of many distinct ventures in various stages of completion. Also, during the seventeenth century trading abroad had developed into a fairly continuous process requiring permanent capital. It now became more useful to view the business as a going concern.

In 1613 the East India Company stopped issuing stocks for each venture and began selling four-year subscriptions, with a fourth of the stock price to be paid each year and used to finance that year's voyages. A new charter in 1657 established the principle of permanently invested capital and extended the right to transfer individual shares before liquidation. Stock was to be priced by the company, first at the end of seven years, then every three years thereafter. Any shareholder could at any time sell his stock at these prices. This not only simplified the problem of transferring shares but, from the company's view, made it easier to attract new capital. In 1661, following out the logic of permanently invested capital, the company's Governor announced that future distributions would consist of "dividends" paid from profits rather than the familiar "divisions" of profits and assets.[5]

THE SOUTH SEA BUBBLE

There remained the problem of regulating these new companies. A corporation created by Crown charter had virtually an unlimited scope of activities, whatever its original purpose. Also, in the late seventeenth century many unincorporated firms began to behave like corporations, issuing transferable shares without having the legal right to do so. Subject to almost no control, they were used to promote fraudulent and sometimes fantastic schemes. Companies were formed to raise Spanish galleons, to make perpetual motion machines,

> To make deal boards out of saw-dust; to grow mulberry trees in Chelsea
> Park so that silk-worms might be cultivated; to furnish funerals to any part
> of Great Britain; for extracting silver from lead; for encouraging the breed
> of horses in England, and improving of glebe and church lands, and
> repairing parsonage and vicarage houses.[6]

Another promoter, offering a subscription to anyone paying two guineas, advertised a scheme whose purpose he kept secret, but promised to reveal later. "In one forenoon this adventurer received a thousand of these subscriptions; and in the evening set out for another kingdom."[7]

The South Sea Company was the most spectacular of these ventures, and the one with major accounting implications. It was chartered in 1710, mainly to fund about ten million pounds of floating national debt. For ten years it tried without much success to develop an overseas trade. Then, during England's first great era of stock speculation, the company decided to take over the entire national debt and to pay for it by issuing large amounts of new stock. The directors inflated share prices by selling on 10 percent margin, spreading rumors of dividends, and offering loans equal to half the stock's market value.[8] In 1720, after wild speculation, stock prices fell to 15 percent of their highest level. Finally there was not enough money in the country to meet subscription installments as they came due or to buy the shares that were being thrown on the market. Though the company continued in business for another 130 years, millions of pounds of investor funds had been lost and the nation's commercial development was slowed for half a century. A secret parliamentary committee, appointed to investigate, found that the accounts had been altered. A director was imprisoned in the Tower and the estates of others were confiscated.

Like the 1929 crash, the South Sea Bubble's collapse led to demands for better accounting verification. Charles Snell, a writing master and accountant, was retained by the defense to examine the records of Sawbridge and Company, a subsidiary of the South Sea Company. Snell was the first English accountant employed to audit the records of a public company, and the first to conduct what we would call a corporate fraud investigation. His published report was inconclusive. He had discovered fictitious entries, but offered no opinion as to why they were made.

The final result of this speculative frenzy was popularly known as the Bubble Act of 1720. It aimed to correct four evils: (1) excessive stock speculation, (2) formation of fraudulent joint stock companies, (3) the use of corporate prerogatives by unincorporated firms, and (4) the use of corporate charters to conduct inappropriate types of businesses.[9] This Act not only denied limited liability status to all firms not incorporated by Crown or Parliament, but was used as a policy instrument to restrain the formation of new corporations. Its effect was to inhibit the natural growth of limited liability companies for 100 years.

This prohibition came at the worst possible time, retarding at the start of the Industrial Revolution the type of enterprise most suitable for rapid industrial expansion. Manufacturers were forced to establish partnerships in which every member, no matter how small his investment, was by law personally responsible for all the company's debts. Being unable to protect investors, such partnerships had very limited ability to raise capital. Often they consisted of a large, fluctuating body of individuals, and a person dealing with them might not be sure with whom he was contracting. A number of canals, railroads, and other public utilities were given limited liability status between 1720 and 1844, but most commercial and industrial firms were not. They could incorporate only by charter or by special act of Parliament, both cumbersome and very expensive processes.

Early in the nineteenth century a series of court decisions undermined the Bubble Act.[10] A statute of 1825 repealed it entirely and enabled the Crown to specify in company charters exactly what degree of liability or nonliability stockholders had for corporate debts. Beginning in 1837 the Crown was empowered to grant unincorporated firms letters of patent which in effect chartered them as joint stock companies. The 1844 Companies Act allowed nearly all businesses to incorporate by registration, but still with unlimited liability. An 1855 statute permitted firms registered under the 1844 Act to get certificates of limited liability for their shareholders. The 1862 Companies Act codified earlier rules for incorporating and regulating joint stock companies, removing the last barriers to corporate dominance of England's basic industries. Ironically, the state became an arbiter in these industries long after its mercantilist premise had given way to a belief in *laissez-faire.*

ACCOUNTING IMPLICATIONS OF THE GOING CONCERN

It was continuity of operations, not limited liability or the corporation's separate entity status, which radically changed accounting technique. Whereas bookkeeping for a completed venture was entirely historical, for a going concern it became a problem of viewing segments in a stream of continuous activity. Not only were results much more tentative, but the whole emphasis of record keeping shifted toward the future. Asset valuation now depended mainly on the firm's long-run earning power; this made liquidation prices less appropriate than historical costs. Continuity also brought with it the idea that assets should not be revalued unless such changes reflected the value of the going concern.

With business continuity came a need for capital maintenance. A corporation cannot rationally claim to have indefinite life while dissipating its invested capital. Both limited liability and the economic need for permanent investments require that paid-in capital be kept in the business.[11] The presence of large permanent assets makes capital maintenance an *economic* necessity. The corporation must keep its capital intact to insure real continuity of existence and to preserve its economic power so that investors, consumers, employees, and all others who depend on it will not lose because of its diminished wealth and earning ability. The statutory recognition of limited liability creates a *legal* obligation to preserve capital intact. The law denies corporate creditors recourse to a stockholder's personal assets, but compensates them by protecting their claims against corporate assets.

To make certain that invested capital was maintained intact, a series of landmark court decisions, reinforced by statutes both in England and the United States, required that dividends could be declared only from current and accumulated income.[12] As a result, in Yamey's strong phrase, "What had often been incidental, became central."[13] Calculating the amount of profit available for dividends became the corporate accountant's most important task. It required that a sharp distinction be made between assets and expenses, and that revenues be associated with the costs of producing a particular period's income.

But at first there was very little precision or consistency in profit measurement. There was no body of doctrine which every corporation had to follow.

Legal decisions which hinged on fine distinctions between capital and revenue expenditures helped clarify and standardize income finding. It was held proper to capitalize interest paid during construction, but improper to pay "interest" on corporate capital.[14] The courts also ruled that provision for future operations must be made before stockholders were entitled to cash dividends, and specifically that profit finding indicated a need for bad debt writeoffs, depreciation allowances, and for equity reserves in general. Littleton believes such decisions reflected quite well the views of mid-nineteenth century accountants.[15] They were in a sense substitutes for codified accounting principles, a way of identifying and giving public approval to the better accounting methods in use at the time.

But Yamey considers that such legal principles of accounting were generally more lenient than professional accounting rules, and that accounting restraints, not legal requirements, imposed the main discipline on profit calculation.[16] There were almost no effective disclosure requirements. If statements were prepared in good faith and approved by auditors, courts preferred not to intervene. Yamey also stresses management's ability to create secret reserves, manipulate book profits, and control dividend policy within the law. There was the same abuse of accrual accounting which is so evident today. Indeed much of the ambiguity in modern financial reporting results from the continuation of late nineteenth century practices. Just as significant as the new emphasis on profit finding was "The victory of the needs of company management over the developing accent on meticulous accounting calculations."[17]

Since dividend payments affected corporate liquidity, there was a tendency to equate the profit figure with realized asset increases. It was inferred from this that unrealized gains should not be recorded in the accounts because, unlike sales, they added nothing to liquid assets or to the ability to pay dividends. This tendency was counteracted by the increasing use of accrual accounting. When revenues and expenses were related to a firm's performance during a particular accounting interval, net worth and periodic income began to be calculated quite apart from cash receipts and disbursements. For instance, bookkeepers began to realize that interest ran day by day and that a certain amount would be earned by a given date even if the money was not received by then. In this sense recognition of periodicity brought accounting practice nearer reality by making entries hinge on the receiving and giving of goods, not on the collecting and paying of money.

We have seen that corporate continuity tended to shorten and regularize accounting periods. The life of a business now eclipsed not only specific ventures but even the lifespans of its owners. Periodic accounting reports were helpful in pricing company shares. They were sometimes required by legal and tax authorities. The calculation of profits for a particular time interval became a major determinant of dividend payments. Often shareholders were absentee owners who had little direct contact with company affairs. The periodic profit figure became an index of managerial effectiveness in the minds of many who lacked the time to study operations in detail.

The calendar year proved to be a convenient corporate reporting period. It was usually long enough to encompass one or more complete cycles of business activity, yet short enough to give investors fairly current information. Useful comparisons could be made when statements covered the same time span and appeared on the same date each year. As record keeping became more standardized, there was a tendency for corporations to prepare statements at progressively shorter intervals until they arrived at an annual reporting basis. A fiscal year ending at the low point in annual operations—a natural business year— was used as early as the 1770s, and reappeared at various times and places during the nineteenth century.[18] But by 1800, in England at least, the usual practice was to close the books either at year end or on the anniversary of the firm's inception.

CORPORATE INFLUENCES ON ACCOUNTING

Public acceptance of the idea that certain institutions had existence apart from their owners led to the doctrine that such owners should have limited liability for corporate debts. This in turn created an obligation to preserve invested capital by limiting dividend payments to the amount of accumulated profits, both to protect creditors and to preserve enterprise continuity. Restricting dividends in this way required systematic profit measurement, including a more precise distinction between assets and expenses.

Eldon Hendriksen concludes that "Few basic ideas in accounting theory can be traced solely to the corporate form."[19] However, the same influences which produced the corporation also produced major changes in accounting thought. Joint stock companies "were the catalyst in whose presence the permanent investment of capital assets was united with the mechanism for measuring income."[20] The corporation gave legal validity to the notion of continuity. By fostering an impersonal view of transactions it helped put an end to the personification of accounts. The creation of surplus reserves to cover future contingencies became common only after conservatism became a key principle of corporate finance. More than any other factor, the advent of the corporation established the year as the basis for segmenting reporting periods and as the dividing line between current and long term assets and debts.

Corporate accounting extracted new potential from the Renaissance integration of real and nominal accounts. The larger scale of corporate operations encouraged routinization, consistency, and bookkeeping economy. Subsidiary journals and ledgers came into general use. The need to inform absentee investors made periodic reporting more important than the reference use of the ledger. The need for audited statements encouraged the professionalization of accountancy both in England and America. The need to stabilize the money market and protect investors' savings involved the government in corporate reporting. And with its ability to quickly concentrate large amounts of capital, the corporation also set the stage for factory production and industrial accounting.

FOOTNOTES

1. A.C. Littleton, *Accounting Evolution to 1900* (New York: American Institute Publishing Company 1933), 242-244.
2. *Ibid.*, 249.
3. Amaury de Riencourt, *The American Empire* (New York: Dial Press, 1968), 8-9.
4. Littleton, *op. cit.*, 210.
5. *Ibid.*, 211.
6. C.J. Hasson, "The South Sea Bubble and Mr. Snell," *Journal of Accountancy* 54 (August, 1932), 131.
7. *Ibid.*, 132.
8. *Ibid.*, 131.
9. Littleton, *op. cit.*, 248 fn.
10. *Ibid.*, 251-52.
11. *Ibid.*, 245-46.
12. *Ibid.*, 215.
13. B.S. Yamey, "Some Topics in the History of Financial Accounting in England 1500-1900." in W.T. Baxter and Sidney Davidson, ed., *Studies in Accounting Theory* (Homewood, Ill.: Richard D. Irwin, 1962), 38.
14. Littleton, *op. cit.*, 218-19.
15. *Ibid.*, 221.
16. Yamey, *op. cit.*, 41.
17. *Ibid.*, 42.
18. Nicholas Stacey, *English Accountancy, 1800-1954* (London: Gee and Company, 1954), 16-21.
19. Eldon S. Hendriksen, *Accounting Theory*, rev. ed. (Homewood, Ill.: Richard D. Irwin, 1970), 47.
20. Littleton, *op. cit,*, 213.

SELECTED BIBLIOGRAPHY

Beard, Miriam. *A History of Business*, 2 vols. Ann Arbor: University of Michigan Press, 1962 and 1963, vol. 1, 325-453.

Edey, H.C., and Panitpakdi, Prot. "British Company Accounting and the Law 1844-1900." In A.C. Littleton and B.S. Yamey, eds. *Studies in the History of Accounting.* Homewood, Ill.: Richard D. Irwin, 1956, 356-79.

Hasson, C.J., "The South Sea Bubble and Mr. Snell." in M. Chatfield, ed., *Contemporary Studies in the Evolution of Accounting Thought.* Belmont, Cal.: Dickenson Publishing Company, 1968, 86-94.

Hendriksen, Eldon S. *Accounting Theory*, rev. ed. Homewood, Ill.: Richard D. Irwin, 1970, 47-52.

Irish, R.A. "The Evolution of Corporate Accounting." In M. Chatfield, ed. *Contemporary Studies in the Evolution of Accounting Thought.* Belmont, Cal.: Dickenson Publishing Company, 1968, 57-85.

Littleton, A.C. *Accounting Evolution to 1900.* New York: American Institute Publishing Company, 1933. Reprinted by Russell and Russell, 1966, chaps. thirteen and fifteen.

Pollard, Sidney. *The Genesis of Modern Management: A Study of the Industrial Revolution in Great Britain.* London: Edward Arnold, 1965, chap. two.

Pollins, H. "Aspects of Railway Accounting Before 1868." In A.C. Littleton and B.S. Yamey, eds. *Studies in the History of Accounting.* Homewood, Ill.: Richard D. Irwin, 1956, 332-55.

Sainsbury, Ethel Bruce. *A Calendar of the Court Minutes etc. of the East India Company, 1660-1663*. Oxford, England: Oxford University Press, 1922.

_____. *A Calendar of the Court Minutes etc. of the East India Company, 1664-1667*. Oxford, England: Oxford University Press, 1925.

_____. *A Calendar of the Court Minutes etc. of the East India Company, 1671-1673*. Oxford, England: Oxford University Press, 1932.

Scott, William. *The Constitution and Finance of English and Irish Joint-Stock Companies to 1720*. Cambridge, England: Cambridge University Press, 1910.

Stacey, N.A.H. *English Accountancy: A Study in Social and Economic History, 1800-1954*. London: Gee and Company, 1954.

Sterling, Robert R. "The Going Concern: An Examination," *Accounting Review* 43 (July, 1968), 481-502.

Ten, Have, O. *The History of Accountancy*. Palo Alto: Bay Books, 1976, 52-55.

Watzlaff, R.H. "The Bubble Act of 1920," *Abacus* 7 (June, 1971), 8-28.

Wren, Daniel A. *The Evolution of Management Thought*. New York: Ronald Press Company, 1972, chap. two.

Yamey, B.S. "The Case Law Relating to Company Dividends." In W.T. Baxter and S. Davidson, eds. *Studies in Accounting Theory*. Homewood, Ill.: Richard D. Irwin, 1962, 428-42.

_____. "The Development of Company Accounting Conventions." *Accountants' Magazine* 65 (October, 1961), 753-63.

_____. "Some Topics in the History of Financial Accounting in England 1500-1900." In W.T. Baxter and S. Davidson, ed. *Studies in Accounting Theory*. Homewood, Ill.: Richard D. Irwin, 1962, 14-43.

_____. "Scientific Bookkeeping and the Rise of Capitalism." In W.T. Baxter, ed. *Studies in Accounting*. London: Sweet and Maxwell, 1950, 13-30.

Part 2

ACCOUNTING ANALYSIS IN THE INDUSTRIAL ERA

Chapter 8

ACCOUNTING PROBLEMS OF THE INDUSTRIAL CORPORATION

THE INDUSTRIAL REVOLUTION IN ENGLAND

The Industrial Revolution was of course a movement, not an historical period. Its impact on eighteenth century England and on the United States and Germany after 1870 is paralleled in many ways by the experiences of developing nations today. At the end of the seventeenth century, improvements in medical care and sanitation, better dietary habits, and a trend toward town living combined to cause a fall in death rates and rapid population increases throughout Western Europe. In England, where the population doubled in seventy years, an agricultural economy could no longer support such numbers. A new form of productive power was needed.

Many factors favored industrial development.[1] Savings rates were high in Britain and capital was cheap. Rising prices and high profit expectations encouraged investment in new industrial ventures. The Enclosure Acts had made labor available. The division of tasks inherent in factory production helped foster a series of innovations and inventions which quickly spread from the textile industry to pottery making, mining, ironmaking, and transportation.

An essential physical change was the concentration of production in factories using powered equipment. Large firms employing factory production methods existed throughout Western Europe, but most of them, like the English mercantilists, were privilege manufacturers who attempted to profit by creating monopolies. Their problems were different from those of the British industrialist, who typically sold widely used consumer goods in competition with other firms and tried to broaden his product's distribution by reducing its cost. This strong price sensitivity of English manufacturers and their ability to develop and exploit a mass market set England apart and helped put it first into the Industrial Revolution.

A new socioeconomic doctrine emerged. In *The Wealth of Nations,* Adam Smith advanced *laissez-faire* as a practical ideal: the state's withdrawal from business, to be replaced by the acts and choices of individual producers and consumers. Under his influence the concept of a fixed volume of employment and trade gave way to the notion of unlimited progress in an unregulated and expanding economy.

The eighteenth century industrialist faced an array of problems new in history. Sidney Pollard writes that:

> The large-scale entrepreneur of the day began with very limited manage-
> rial, clerical or administrative staff: he wrote his own letters, visited his
> own customers, and belabored his men with his own walking-stick. Yet his
> range of responsibilities was much wider than that of today's entrepreneur,
> who is concerned almost exclusively with the activities inside the factory,
> with buying, producing and selling. In the early years of industrialization
> many outside services now taken for granted or dealt with by the single
> action of paying taxes, had to be provided by the large manufacturer
> himself.[2]

These included creating towns and transportation systems where none existed, recruiting and training the first generation of factory workers, and with very limited powers of compulsion regulating the lives of thousands of men. Besides problems of manufacturing technique, the sheer volume of operations was new. No longer could one man personally supervise the activities of a major company.

The two main responses of large firms to the problems of industrialization were the appointment and training of managerial staffs, and the development of industrial accounting.[3] In an unstable environment accounting represented a familiar and rational element. And industrial managers badly needed specific accounting data:

1. To find the profit available for dividends they needed sophisticated capital-income accounting, including asset valuation and depreciation procedures.
2. They had to prevent fraud and theft, meet payrolls, and preserve liquidity.
3. They needed production control data. For example, raw materials stocks had to be large enough to prevent delays due to shortages, yet not so large as to waste capital.
4. To test operating efficiency they had to check the output and expenditures of different processes, in absolute terms and comparatively.
5. They needed cost accounting (a) to calculate the value of ending inventories and

goods sold, (b) to determine how far prices could be cut during recession periods and still cover variable costs, and (c) to make rational decisions based on estimates of future and alternative costs.

NEW DEMANDS ON ACCOUNTING PRACTICE

During the Industrial Revolution accountants first came to grips with the major problems which still concern them. This chapter therefore describes the earliest contemporary accounting practice, which occurred moreover at a time when each firm had great freedom to develop whatever accounting methods and principles suited its particular needs.[4] The accounting profession lacked influence. Unless fraud was involved, courts generally—and philosophically—chose not to interfere in questions of accounting doctrine. Nor were companies encouraged to narrow areas of reporting difference by the implied threat of government regulation.

Far more than today, accounting behavior was a response to the objectives of individual managers. They could in each business very largely make the rules by which assets were valued and income was determined. The early industrial firm may be seen as a laboratory in which accounting experiments were conducted without the noneconomic constraints we take for granted. This being so, it is instructive to see how accountants responded to management's needs, or failed to do so, in an environment where problem-solving methods evolved almost solely in response to managerial requirements.

MANORIAL ACCOUNTS

Existing accounting systems available to the eighteenth century industrialist had been developed by merchants and by the proprietors of landed estates. Manorial accounting as described in Chapter Two centered around the need of stewards for evidence that they had performed their duties honestly and well. It was widely used in industries developed from the estates themselves, such as mines, canals, and even ironworks.[5] The textile industry and others employed agricultural labor and hiring practices and often located in the countryside, near rivers which could be used to turn a water wheel for power. Where factories were managed by estate owners, the manorial steward was usually the industrial manager's superior, and often kept accounts in the estate form.

Manorial accounting was unsuitable for any business which had to innovate and operate in a competitive society. The success of large landowners depended less on the market mechanism than on social and political privileges which allowed them, for example, to force passage of the Private Enclosure Acts. Agricultural techniques tended to change slowly and improvements were not usually made for direct competitive advantage. Nor had the landlord a profit motive in the capitalistic sense. Industrial firms using the charge and discharge method typically had no capital account, made no distinction between capital and revenue expenditures, and failed to determine total income or return on investment. Such accounts revealed neither the efficiency with which capital had been used, nor the benefits of innovation, nor the firm's position relative to its competitors. Manorial accounts soon went out of use in industry.

MERCHANT'S ACCOUNTS

The more important source of industrial accounting was double entry bookkeeping as developed by merchants since the Middle Ages. "Accountancy in Britain was dominated by the requirements of the merchant, all the formal training, all the prestige derived from him."[6] This "training," by rote and personification, was unrealistic in terms of industrial processes. Still, mercantile bookkeeping had much to offer. In eighteenth century England most large industrial firms were partnerships and required a bookkeeping system which would permit a precise division of profits. The industrialist, like the merchant, wished to prevent errors, control theft, and to be able to estimate his net worth at any time. He had to be sure there was money available to pay current bills. He needed a systematic record of transactions for dealing with outsiders, and for his own use, a ready reference in the form of ledger balances.

Industrial accounting immediately added two new factors to mercantile bookkeeping: (1) the use of large quantities of fixed assets, and (2) an increased need for periodic reporting. Most industrial accounting problems centered around the handling of fixed capital, which had rarely been important to the merchant. He invested mainly in inventory, not equipment, and in calculating profit could ignore depreciation, maintenance, and overhead expense. Nor had he any reason to relate profit to fixed assets or total capital. His calculations showed the income from individual transactions, commoditites, and voyages, and were designed to allow a division of profits among a changing group of venture partners.

Pacioli, writing in 1494, made no provision for financial statements and no serious attempt to determine the profits earned during any given period of time. Since business in his day was typically a series of disconnected ventures, there was little interest in unfinished operations and few of the modern reasons for assigning costs and revenues to specific years. Owners were usually in personal contact with their affairs, operations could easily be observed, and profits were not hard to estimate. Most financial information was taken directly from the ledger accounts. Statements were normally prepared only at the end of a major project, such as a trading voyage, or after all the pages in a ledger had been filled. Accounting periods were usually uncessary. The pace of operations guided the accounting process.

But when a firm's life lasted through many ventures it was no longer practical to wait till liquidation before preparing financial statements. Account regularity was only one aspect of a new sense of timeliness which emerged from the Industrial Revolution. The adoption of periodic routines enabled managers to handle masses of detail and to regulate operations too extensive to be supervised directly.[7] Periodic reports also helped solve the problem of management from a distance, when a company's plants were in different places, or when an entrepreneur was travelling as a salesman or buyer. Reporting convenience dictated the use of calendar intervals: many expense items, such as wages, were paid weekly or monthly, and others, such as interest, had an annual connotation. Ironically, the regularizing of accounts forced the natural rhythm of work into uniform reporting segments just when machine techniques made operational time more important than ever before.

CHANGING CONCEPTS OF CAPITAL AND INCOME

We have said that the corporation, with its indefinite existence and permanent investment in fixed assets, assumed a legal and economic obligation to maintain its productive power intact. During the nineteenth century it became generally accepted that dividends should not exceed accumulated profits, and the calculation of annual income available to stockholders became a primary accounting task. But the key to income measurement was usually asset valuation, not the matching of costs and revenues. "The expressed purpose of accounting at that time was to show a true balance sheet with capital maintained intact and profit, if any, clearly indicated."[8]

While there was much diversity—and inconsistency—in asset valuation practices, two viewpoints predominated. Manufacturing companies commonly accounted for depreciable assets as if they were unsold merchandise, that is, they revalued assets at the end of each accounting period, charging increases or decreases directly to profit and loss. In contrast, most railroads, utilities, and other public service corporations used some type of replacement accounting. Original investments were capitalized but asset replacements and maintenance charges were expensed. Depreciation was considered unnecessary so long as property was kept in good working order.

THE INVENTORY METHOD

The "inventory" technique was a traditional method of valuing fixed assets. John Mellis described it in his *Briefe Instruction* (1588), as did Stephen Monteage in *Debtor and Creditor Made Easie* (1683) and John Mair in the Fifth Edition of *Bookkeeping Methodiz'd* (1757). While it had many variations in practice, assets had to be appraised or at least revalued at the end of each accounting period. Typically the new value was debited and the old one credited to the asset account; in this way the "inventory" portion was carried forward and any shrinkage in value reduced profit. Depreciation in these terms was wholly a valuation concept, and for the majority of firms using this method, profit was the change in value of net assets between two successive accounting periods.[9]

Valuation methods of depreciation have always been difficult to standardize. The inventory technique had innumerable variations. There was no agreed-on set of best practices, nor was there a definitive answer to the question: what is value? Fixed asset "values" included cost, lower of cost or market, and other valuations used in inventory accounting.[10] Asset appreciation between balance sheet dates tended to be ignored, while decreases were generally written down. Nonrecurring changes were usually not included. Moreover, revaluing fixed assets at the end of each accounting period was awkward and expensive compared to the use of a depreciation rate. Some firms compromised by using average rates to write assets down each year, then making partial revaluations at longer intervals.

The larger fault of a method which adjusted for every kind of value change —even those caused by inflation and business cycle fluctuations—was that many of these changed market values were independent of the asset's use and were determined by factors which the company could not control and which therefore did not reflect management's efficiency in using the assets. Systematic depreciation implies that fixed assets contribute directly to a product's value and thus, like materials and labor expense, should be allocated to its cost. The growth of corporations with large fixed asset investments made it essential for accountants to deal directly with the problem of capital consumption, because in a setting of increasing manufacturing competition costs needed to be known as exactly as possible. The inventory method neatly sidestepped the real issues of asset and enterprise valuation, particularly the need to distinguish between capital and revenue expenditures.

REPLACEMENT ACCOUNTING

Railroads were the first industrial enterprises to reflect the whole range of asset valuation problems. Requiring much larger capital investments and more long-lived equipment than most nineteenth century businesses, they were compelled to isolate asset expenditures and account for them methodically. Corollary to this was concern for capital maintenance through depreciation. During the boom of the 1840s, many railroads had paid large dividends out of capital, creating a windfall for short-term speculators at the expense of long-term investors and creditors. In response to the resulting scandals, some lines adopted cost-based depreciation, but in most cases abandoned it when such depreciation provisions were found inadequate to replace fixed assets. The commonest valuation method came to be some form of replacement accounting.

The usual approach was to relate depreciation to asset maintenance, on the assumption that original invested capital was permanently maintained in good working order by expenditures for repairs and renewals. Thus, fixed assets purchased from the proceeds of bond and stock issues were capitalized at original cost and never depreciated. Instead, asset replacements as well as repairs were charged directly to expense; only expenditures for additions and betterments were normally capitalized. Railroad operations encouraged replacement accounting because most of the assets involved—stations, trains, rails, and so on—had long lives, and because maintenance was the railways' prime operating problem. Again, there were many variations in practice.[11] Some railroads charged *all* capital costs to expense if repair charges were thought to cover depreciation. Some formed a "depreciation fund" by setting aside for repairs an annual percentage above ordinary charges. Others ignored depreciation only if repairs were sufficient to make good wear and tear.

Replacement accounting, like the inventory valuation method, was simple and flexible in practice, and gave managers a wide range of accounting options. It avoided the complex problem of forecasting the useful lives of long-term assets. Most important, since original capital investments created no charges to expense until they were replaced, this method made railroads seem an attractive investment by maximizing reported profits during the first years of their life cycle when they most needed capital. George O. May believed that the rapid development of American railroads would probably have been impossible if periodic cost-based depreciation had been required. He added however that "It is no doubt true that as a result of accounting methods followed, large amounts of capital have been lost by investors."[12]

Replacement accounting created serious liquidity problems. Railroad asset valuation policies had two conflicting purposes: to attract investors with the prospect of high earnings and dividends, while at the same time accumulating funds to replace equipment. Lines which paid large dividends from inflated profits in their early years had to trust to future income to provide cash for asset replacements. Also, it was assumed that repairs and maintenance would keep rolling stock in working order, but this was not always true: obsolescence as well as use decreased asset values. An ulterior aim of interweaving repairs, replacements, and depreciation was to facilitate internal financing by enabling managers to create secret reserves. Since depreciation expense was not recognized until assets were replaced, there was often an incentive to expense betterments or to keep income high by not replacing worn out equipment.

The replacement method has been called an inherently unstable offshoot of cash basis accounting.[13] In an era of chronic business depressions the amounts spent on maintenance and charged to expense were apt to fluctuate widely. Reporting inconsistency was the rule, within and between quasi-public corporations, and the variety of valuation methods used made comparison of published results very difficult. Until the 1868 Regulation of Railways Act, English law did not try to specify which expenditures belonged to capital and which to revenue. Stockholders were misled as to actual income, future earnings potential, and managerial efficiency. Nor were they the only ones deceived by the tendency of replacement accounting to understate capital consumption charges. Half the track mileage constructed in the U.S. before 1900 was ultimately placed in receivership.[14] In their defense it must be said that nineteenth century businessmen were in doubt as to the essential function of depreciation. Should it be used to refine income calculations, reflect true asset values, finance asset replacements, maintain capital intact, or stabilize dividend payments? Definitive answers to this question waited on the development of a theory of depreciation.

THE ORIGINS OF COST-BASED DEPRECIATION

Louis Goldberg describes four senses in which depreciation is used in accounting: (1) as a fall in asset price, (2) as a fall in value, (3) as physical deterioration, and (4) as an allocation of cost.[15] Though some of these concepts originated long before the Industrial Revolution, all were applied in practice by nineteenth century industrial firms.

Perhaps the oldest theory of depreciation is that of falling price—the idea that taking possession of an asset reduces it to secondhand, lowering its value, though not always its usefulness. This concept of falling price depreciation was expressed by Vitruvius, the Roman writer on architecture. Describing annual depreciation as "the price of the passing of each year," Vitruvius set the rule that in valuing a masonry wall, one-eightieth of its cost should be deducted for each year it had stood.[16] Depreciation in these terms was a reduction in the price to be paid for a limited life asset. Vetruvius' purpose was merely to arrive at a valuation for a legal settlement. He was concerned with the durability of materials and with the legal and customary method of valuing a particular kind of wall, not with asset use in the modern sense.

To the merchant depreciation usually meant a fall in asset value, not much different from a casualty loss. His practice was to inventory fixed assets and reduce their book value to allow for all factors which had caused it to decline.[17] The practical limitations of this method have been described. Conceptually it was weak because the practice of annual asset revaluations ignored the going concern concept which the use of those very assets had helped make important.

Systematic depreciation was at first simply an attempt to measure physical deterioration in money terms. Everyone could see, as Hatfield put it, that "All assets are on an irresistible march to the junkheap." The use of equipment in production meant it was being used up. Less obvious was the idea that physical depreciation is related to the economic services which such assets render.

It is hardly surprising that the essential problem of depreciation was not recognized until quite late. Before the Industrial Revolution most firms were small, fixed assets were relatively unimportant, and precise income finding was not generally necessary. Courts did not require that companies take depreciation, nor did English tax authorities allow it until 1878. As a rule, not only depreciation but all accruals were crudely handled. Furthermore, each party at interest wanted something different from the depreciation figure. Creditors wished to be sure capital was maintained intact. Management needed a cash reserve to finance asset replacements. Stockholders wanted an accurate, consistent statement of income available for dividends. There was increasing agreement that an asset's cost should be apportioned over the periods until its retirement. But should this allocation be based on historical or replacement cost? A debate ensued between those accountants who wished above all to refine income measurement, and those who saw depreciation chiefly as a means of maintaining company liquidity.

Replacement accounting was based on the idea that management should retain in the business cash equal to the value of fixed assets used up. Since most corporate officials viewed depreciation expense as a means of financing asset replacements, it was logical to make the charge for depreciation a managerial option. If managers did not plan to replace assets, or if profits were not available for dividends, they saw no reason to provide for depreciation. And since no cash outlays were involved, charging depreciation only in profitable years allowed a firm to smooth income and equalize dividends without endangering its liquidity position. If obsolescence was a factor, accelerated depreciation might be taken. The only imperative was that capital replacements should be assured before distributable profits were recognized. The result of this essentially funds statement view of asset conversions was that the allowance for depreciation came to be regarded as a kind of surplus reserve, a segregation of profits for asset purchases.[18] As an alternative to taking depreciation, some companies actually created funds or retained earnings reserves to finance asset replacements.

Near the end of the nineteenth century, a few accountants began to see depreciation as part of the general problem of allocating joint costs—that is, as a system of cost allocation rather than of asset valuation. O. G. Ladelle viewed the cost of an asset as joint to the periods of its use, and suggested that the allocation of depreciation to each period should be based on the expected net benefit to be derived during that period, after adjusting for an agreed rate of interest on the unallocated portion of asset cost.[19] However, several conceptual problems remained. Depreciation was not seen by most accountants as a cost of production if only because no clear cost concept existed. Nor was there a generally understood notion of matching costs and related revenues, or even of converting asset values to expense.[20] The transition from crude measurement to matching was a qualitative jump in sophistication as great as the present movement from matching to a precise measurement of asset values.

The consensus on asset valuation which emerged from the nineteenth century was that historical cost should normally be the maximum asset value and that depreciation expense was a factor in income calculation which should be reported even though it turned a profit into a net loss. Cost-based depreciation was aided by the growing importance of the income statement. Still it was slow to take effect in practice, even after industrial developments had made it a logical solution. Until the twentieth century most American firms made no specific provision for depreciation. Those which did typically wrote it off directly, without using an allowance account. In 1900 the inventory method of asset valuation was still the most widely used. The bookkeeping treatment of depreciation continued to vary widely, and much experimentation was evident. But there began to be less diversity in published reports. Historical cost valuations and the percentage writedown of assets were easier to standardize than were the older methods which required periodic asset revaluations.

They were also more compatible with an accounting framework in which allowable procedures are determined by reference to general principles.

EMERGING PRINCIPLES

Accounting theory became important for the first time during the Industrial Revolution. According to Hendriksen, the indirect effects of industrial technology were (1) a greater adherence to cost as a valuation basis, (2) greater significance of the distinction between capital and income, and (3) development of the going concern concept.[21] Most theoretical improvements centered around attempts to refine profit finding. While income still was usually calculated in the capital section of the balance sheet, asset valuation gradually became subservient to it. Also, with investors and creditors so dependent on accounting data, rules were needed for the organization of financial statements. Account classifications were introduced. It would be misleading to speak of codified body of accounting principles. Rather, a series of conventions became widely accepted in practice. Some of them—continuity, periodicity, historical cost, and conservatism—only emerged in their modern form after being adopted by nineteenth century manufacturers.

Continuous industrial production, like regular mercantile trading, produced a demand for accounting reports at intermediate points in operations. Periodicity in turn created or affected other accounting concepts. To make the continuity principle technically feasible, events of different accounting periods had to be sharply distinguished. The idea of estimating periodic income by matching costs and related revenues followed naturally. Profit estimates were refined by a system of accruals and deferrals which allowed the effects of transactions to be split between periods.

But the transition from venture to going concern made record keeping more subjective and left a wide area of accounting discretion to management. In apportioning costs between periods, accountants had to make estimates whose accuracy largely depended on the course of future events. Honest differences of opinion about inventory pricing and asset lifespans could lead to large variations in reported profits. Or industrial managers could deliberately blur periodic results by shifting income from one period to another, overdepreciating assets and charging capital goods to expense. There was also a considerable time lag between adoption of the period notion and acceptance of comparability, consistency, and other doctrines needed to answer questions it had raised.

And from the beginning there was a contradiction between the continuity assumption and the periodicity assumption which it made necessary. The one tells us to look at operations as a continuous flow; the other says we must break this flow into comparable time segments. The root of the period problem is that in assigning revenues and expenses to time intervals, the accountant is doing something that is absolutely necessary but is at the same time quite arbitrary and artificial.

Most corporate officials took the view that so long as they acted in good faith, it was up to them what disclosure to provide in financial statements. The stockholder's main defense against management's wide choice of accounting options was the doctrine of conservatism, which held that it was better to err on the side of understatement by anticipating possible losses while deferring gains until they were realized. Acceptance of this concept depended partly on investor attitudes. Early accounting practices which favored short-term speculators often continued until investors became willing to forgo current dividends to assure larger future ones. For example, after 1850 a tendency to understate profits began to replace the deliberate overstatement which had characterized the speculative inception of the railroads. Besides safeguarding legal capital against excess dividend payments, this convention of understatement reinforced the use of lower of cost or market inventory valuations, and of historical cost in fixed asset accounting.

The accounting literature of the time and other evidence suggests that conservatism was widely ineffective in the face of management's desire to equalize income over the phases of the business cycle.[22] The creation of secret reserves was a characteristic abuse of this doctrine. A systematic understatement of income and assets allowed managers to convey an appearance of stability which was attractive to potential investors, while distorting analyses of managerial effectiveness and of future earning potential. It is probable that the resulting large, unstable accounting error influenced resource allocation, prices and output, the business cycle, and economic growth in general.[23]

MANAGEMENT ACCOUNTING

THE ORIGINS OF COST ACCOUNTING

Though certain cost finding techniques are as old as double entry bookkeeping, systematic costing hardly existed at the start of the Industrial Revolution. Yet to find operating income, factory accountants had to calculate the value not only of finished products but of goods in various stages of completion. So at the same time that financial accountants were rationalizing the assignment of costs to particular time intervals, industrial accountants were given the task of somehow synchronizing the flows of cost and production. So urgent was this need for internal data that during the nineteenth century "Corporate costs attached to the product, only secondarily to the period."[24]

Between the Renaissance and the late eighteenth century cost accounting techniques had developed scarcely at all. Bookkeeping texts were written for the merchant's use and generally ignored internal transactions. However, a few examples of preindustrial cost finding stand as exceptions to a generally low level of practice. Among other ventures, the Fugger family operated silver and copper mines and smelters in the Tyrol and Carinthia districts of Austria. As early as 1577, material and labor costs were accumulated in a "Mine and

Foundry Account," and transportation and other expenses were summarized. Smelter accounts were charged with operating costs and credited with shipments. Total costs of production were calculated, and profits on the sales of various types of ore were determined.

Christopher Plantin, a sixteenth century Antwerp printer and publisher, maintained what amounted to a job order cost system, with a separate ledger account for each book he published. In each such account he accumulated costs of paper used, wages paid, and other printing expenses identifiable with a particular book. The cost and financial accounts were coordinated: after a book had been printed, an entry was made transferring the account balance to a finished goods account called "Books in Stock." Here quantities of books on hand were recorded together with costs, creating a perpetual inventory record.

James Dodson, in *The Accountant, or The Method of Bookkeeping* (1750), demonstrated batch costing in shoemaker's accounts, showing the flow of costs from one production stage to the next, the increasing value of work in process and the division of costs according to the different types of shoes.

None of these forerunner systems had any traceable influence on modern cost accounting. When industrial accountants faced similar problems and devised many similar solutions, they did so independently and without reference to what A. C. Littleton has called "pre-cost accounting." The interest for us of such accounts is less that modern cost techniques had earlier origins than that manufacturing processes themselves have a logic which suggests solutions to the recurring problems which they create. Most cost records which survive from the pre-industrial period have two features in common: (1) the segregation and accumulation of costs in control accounts, and (2) the comparison of a product's total cost with its sales price to determine its profitability.

THE PUTTING-OUT SYSTEM

The direct ancestors of industrial cost accounts were venture accounting and the domestic or putting-out systems of early manufacturers. Venture bookkeeping had the advantage of allowing merchants to reckon profits in separate ledger accounts for each business activity, type of goods, temporary partnership, or trading voyage. Factory accountants adapted this method when they allocated costs to particular departments, processes, or product lines of an industrial firm.

Domestic manufacturing first became important in fourteenth century Italy, where increasing commerce and improved production techniques led bankers and merchants to establish industrial affiliates.[25] The Medici textile manufacturers purchased raw wool and sold finished cloth which had been produced by individual craftsmen in their own homes. Because every phase of production was performed by a different guild, separate cost records were needed for each process. In the Medici industrial partnership, each step in the conversion process was represented by a memorandum book which showed the quantities of wool delivered to various households, the amounts of processed goods returned, and wages due or paid. A clearing account, "Cloth Manufactured and Sold," matched costs and revenues on batches of material, showing on balance the profit on all the cloth sold during an operating period. Since outworker production required little machinery, overhead could be ignored and selling prices calculated in terms of direct costs. The Italian putting-out manufacturers may not have been the first to use cost accounting to rationalize production, but in their time they had no peers. They could for example import raw wool from England, manufacture it, and ship back the finished textiles to sell in England below English prices.

Many eighteenth century industries went through a putting-out phase before concentrating production in central factories. Like the Medici, the English domestic manufacturer needed a bookkeeping check on materials given to outworkers, on equipment rent, wages paid, and on the quantity and quality of finished work returned. And like any merchant he wished to know the cost of his wares and his profit on different lines. Among the first generation of factory owners were many men who had began as putting-out manufacturers. They were most familiar with accounting systems which emphasized internal control rather than cost finding. The typical putting-out firm was small and its owner could personally supervise operations. He was thus not overly concerned about systematic asset valuation or periodic profit finding. Since he used almost no heavy machinery, his unit costs might not vary greatly with changes in output. He did not have to measure the benefits of technical innovations. Nor had he the factory owner's need to closely coordinate production.

ACCOUNTING AND FACTORY MANAGEMENT PROBLEMS

"The germ of cost accounting . . . lay in the factory system of production."[26] With the benefit of hindsight we can see that the main new fact confronting both financial and cost accountants was the presence of large amounts of capital sunk in plant and equipment. But to early industrial managers the central importance of invested capital was less apparent. Investing in fixed assets did not seem very different from buying inventories. The differences which became troublesome were dealt with in isolation. Three of the most insistent were the problems of setting prices, of allocating overhead, and of integrating cost and financial accounts.

During the Industrial Revolution cost accounting was valued more as an aid to rational price setting than as a control tool. Equipment manufacturers and engineering firms customarily made cost estimates and tendered bids to prospective clients. Having accepted a contract on these terms, it was natural for them to keep a job cost sheet not only to find profit but to acquire knowledge useful in making future bids. The competitive manufacturer also needed to know how much prices could be cut during seasonal or cyclical slumps and still cover variable costs. Sometimes additional uses were found for cost data generated to test pricing policies. Sidney Pollard writes of one eighteenth century firm in which "Costing figures were used not only to determine prices but also wages, and they became the starting-point for changes in the methods of work and of payments, and of technical changes."[27]

Such calculations raised the problem of overhead allocation. The modern view is that overhead forms part of a product's cost. The eighteenth century attitude was that overhead resulted from unproductive labor, not engaged in transforming raw materials, and thus did not add to the value of finished products. This position became less tenable as the adoption of powered machinery increased the ratio of overhead to wages. But alternatives were slow to develop. It should be remembered that subdividing a product's cost was in itself a revolutionary idea. Also, most factory accountants were not chiefly concerned with purely internal processes. Trained in the use of mercantile bookkeeping systems which emphasized accounting for persons and events, they found it hard to describe the processing of inanimate objects.

More apparent but equally puzzling was the need to integrate cost and financial accounting records, or rather to fit cost accounts into the framework of double entry bookkeeping. Industrialists had inherited an accounting system designed for the merchant, in which inventories were assumed to be purchased complete. Some managers saw in cost accounting a way to refine the matching process and improve income measurement—by standardizing expense classifications, attaching costs to particular products, and sharpening the distinction between capital and revenue expenditures. Underlying this attempt to force industrial accounts into the mercantile accounting format was the assumption that factory costs could be transferred from account to account within the double entry system, using inventory as a control account. But there was no general understanding as to how this should be done. Until the twentieth century most cost records were developed independently and not tied in directly to the double entry accounts.

Several pioneering authors attacked the problem of coordinating financial accounts and manufacturing records. Robert Hamilton devoted a few pages of his book, *Introduction to Merchandise* (Edinburgh, 1788), to the accounts of "artificers and manufacturers." He described a system comprising work in process and finished goods accounts, and subsidiary books for manufacturing. These included a book of materials in which quantities bought and sold were recorded, a book of wages, and a book of "work" where the quantities of material delivered to workers, the quantities of goods received in return, and the value of material, wages, and finished goods were entered in separate columns. A manufacturing account was debited each year-end for balances of material and expense, and credited for the value of goods manufactured. The resulting balance, after allowing for the value of work in process, was meant to show profit and loss.[28]

The first comprehensive descriptions of factory accounting systems were given by Anselme Payen (1817) and F. W. Cronhelm (1818).[29] Using the example of a woolen mill, Cronhelm set up memorandum books for raw materials, work in process and finished goods, with labor costs subdivided by spinning, weaving, and finishing processes. While showing only quantities, not money values, these memorandum accounts were probably the earliest textbook example of perpetual inventories. A raw materials account was debited for purchases and credited for wool put into process. A manufacturing account debited pounds of wool put in process and credited finished pieces of cloth. The finished goods account was debited for materials completed and credited for goods sold. An inventory control sheet drew quantities from these three materials books and extended them into money values, work in process being averaged at the "middle stage." Cronhelm's system permitted the calculation of inventory and cost of goods sold, but not the analysis of costs by processes or lots of goods. The absence of money values in the memorandum books also meant that internal transactions were poorly coordinated with the records of purchases and sales.

Payen described accounting systems suitable for a carriage maker and a glue manufacturer. In his carriage making example he set up a job cost system, using a journal and ledger in money for transactions with outsiders and another in quantities for internal transactions. These journals accumulated material and labor costs for each of three carriages and compared total costs to the selling price of each, leaving profit or loss as a final balance. The glue factory was used to illustrate process costing. Again, quantities and money values were accounted for in different books, but total costs, including interest and depreciation, were collected in something very like a manufacturing account. In both examples Payen's attempts to compare total cost summaries with selling prices or cost of goods sold brought him nearer than Cronhelm to a final integration of cost and financial accounts. Garner suggests that the only missing link was a journal entry tying the ledger-in-kind inventory to the manufacturing account in the ledger-in-money. He concludes that "both of these writers were far superior to any who wrote for the next fifty years."[30]

He goes on to emphasize the slow development of cost accounting between 1820 and 1880, the lag of theory behind practice, and the slow spread of new techniques. Payen and Cronhelm had showed how to transfer costs between accounts, how to accumulate total costs in control accounts, how to isolate ending inventory balances and link manufacturing balances to general ledger totals. But by the mid-nineteenth century almost no firms were able to show the movement of manufacturing costs from one account to another in the general ledger. Few distinguished between factory overhead and commercial expenses. The techniques for allocating and absorbing overhead were not generally understood. This absence of cost innovation—and of management demands for cost data—is in striking contrast to the rapid development of industrial production techniques during this period.

One possible explanation is that only in the later stages of the Industrial Revolution did competitive pressures provide an important motive for systematic cost accounting. Many early capitalists, competing largely with nonfactory producers, had what amounted to a temporary monopoly position. Selling prices were far above costs and successful innovation produced large profits with or without the help of accounting data.

Moreover, it was difficult to disseminate knowledge about factory accounting. Cost accounting techniques were considered industrial secrets. Bookkeeping was still dominated by mercantile trading, few texts discussed manufacturing accounting, and few accountants took a generalized view of the subject. Most "works accountants" did not write down their ideas or methods, and often these were transmitted only when an employee changed jobs.

A prime incentive for scientific costing resulted from the increasing use of heavy machinery, which required recognition of overhead expense. But early industrialists used relatively primitive equipment and overhead was a small enough part of their total cost to be ignored in inventory calculations. Also, not until the nineteenth century was it common for one firm to make a great variety of products. Before then, managers could mentally adjust prime costs to include overhead.

Manufacturers seeking an overview of operations were also hampered by accountants' inability to tie cost figures to overall income calculations. One result was that cost systems which produced useful analyses of individual products or departments tended to break down when applied to the whole firm. The first generation of industrial accountants never found a reliable basis for making overall cost studies, and "There were owners of large coal-mines who did not know the cost of bringing a ton of coal to market."[31]

Accountants knew how to allocate costs on the basis of past operations, but not how to use these costs to predict the future. This was especially harmful to management decision making in that such unintegrated cost forecasts are the most sophisticated accounting records which have survived from eighteenth century industrial firms. The best of them took account of variations between expected costs and volume, included detailed calculations of depreciation and interest (sometimes compound interest), as well as the probable opportunity costs of different methods, locations, and different uses of a particular machine.[32] Of course many cost estimates from this era seem much less precise and modern, especially when overhead was an important factor. And many of the ancillary techniques needed to predict costs accurately had not been invented. Inaccuracies in cost forecasts which began with crude estimates of inventory turnover, the size of markets, or the extent of coal or mineral reserves cannot be blamed entirely on the accountant.

Another impediment to a fruitful use of accounting data resulted from the prevailing attitudes toward administration. The art of management was in its infancy and was based on assumptions which the Industrial Revolution itself largely invalidated. A tradition of personal supervision persisted long after companies became too large to make it feasible. Better management was seen as one remedy for the technical inefficiency and lack of planning and control which had caused so many business failures. But no clear relationship was perceived between the quality of management and its use of accounting figures. In a period of rapid, basic innovation it was hard to isolate managerial from technical functions, and administrative ability tended to be equated with technical competence. With the major emphasis on production, accounting and managerial staffs were chronically undermanned and had to spend most of their time on routine tasks.

SUMMARY: COSTS AND DECISION MAKING

Until the twentieth century accounting data was not widely used as a direct aid to industrial decision making. When available it was often unreliable and entrepreneurs became adept, not so much at analyzing accounting reports as at finding substitutes for them. Partly this was caused by the accountant's failure to develop full cost procedures oriented toward the industrial manager. Only a few techniques, such as departmental cost allocations, were originally intended to facilitate decision making. But at least equally this failure was caused by the lack of administrative ability to use accounting data. Before the Industrial Revolution, the size of firms was limited by their owners' inability to cope with the management problems involved in large-scale operations.[33] After 1750, developments in technology and marketing made it essential that progressive companies should grow beyond the size where a small group of partners could directly oversee operations. The main contribution of industrialization to accountancy was an indirect one: it created the managerial skills which required and could make use of accounting information.

ACCOUNTANCY AND CAPITALIST DEVELOPMENT

What effect had accounting on the Industrial Revolution? Among others the sociologist Max Weber, the historian Werner Sombart, and the economist Joseph Schumpeter have given double entry bookkeeping a central place in their theories of capitalist development.[34] In *Der Moderne Kapitalismus,* Sombart advanced three arguments for the importance of "scientific" bookkeeping. First, *rationalization.* The balancing features and mathematical logic inherent in double entry bookkeeping, together with manufacturing capitalism, helped quantify, systematize, and control business affairs, and gave a new rationality to resource allocation. Second, *abstraction.* By reducing assets and equities to numerical abstractions and by expressing the total results of operations as profit and loss, double entry bookkeeping clarified the aim of business as the "rationalistic pursuit of unlimited profits." Third, *depersonalization.* By substituting an abstract concept of capital for the notion of personal ownership, double entry bookkeeping facilitated the separation of business firms from their owners and thereby aided the growth of large corporations. So for Sombart accounting had far-reaching economic implications. It defined the entrepreneur's goals, rationalized his activities, and summarized for judgment the results of his operations.

These arguments are vulnerable in being based almost entirely on accounting *effects* while largely ignoring accounting *practices.* Studies of double entry methodology by three accounting historians have produced the counter-thesis that industrial accounting techniques grafted onto double entry bookkeeping were not especially efficient and were dictated less by a desire for rationality than by expediency and self-interest.

Basil Yamey[35] points out that Sombart's claims for the double entry system cannot be reconciled with its use in actual business situations. He suggests that knowing total capital or total income is rarely useful to those faced with the problem of allocating *particular* resources. Double entry records did not help the early industrialist in choosing among markets, production techniques, or product lines because there was no stable history on which to base predictions about the future. In fact, as a problem-solving tool, double entry bookkeeping was hardly better than the manorial system which preceded it. It did not help the capitalist maximize return on investment, nor did the lack of a total profit figure inhibit the merchant's pursuit of gain. Double entry bookkeeping provided a framework for recording and classifying a company's routine financial affairs. When nonroutine decisions had to be made, businessmen used other criteria.

Sombart emphasized the quantification and abstraction of data as virtues of the double entry method, but Yamey believes they were less important to decision makers than was access to the numerical detail underlying ledger balances. Sombart's third point, that double entry bookkeeping was needed to separate the firm from its proprietors, is also invalid. Well into the Industrial Revolution, business and personal assets were mixed in double entry accounts. Little can be inferred from the fact that a particular firm used double entry bookkeeping. Many large companies operated without it and apparently did no worse than their competitors. Yamey concludes that its introduction had few major economic consequences.

Sidney Pollard[36] finds two "heresies" in eighteenth century industrial accounting practice which refute Sombart's thesis. One was the tendency to confuse capital and revenue. The other was the assumption that profits were not directly related to the amount of capital invested, and thus were not a return on investment. The presence of large amounts of fixed assets posed novel problems which early industrial accountants could not solve. Their inability to distinguish between capital and revenue expenditures meant that capital changes affecting the relationship among classes of equityholders were obscured, and without "purposeful capital accounting, there could be no rational use of accounts for managerial guidance."[37]

Unlike the classical economists, eighteenth century businessmen had no clear concept of capital as "wealth for profit" seeking a maximum return. Their accountants did not calculate return on investment in the modern sense. Worse, they failed to see that capital produced income. Even large industrial firms were usually partnerships, whose profit was commonly understood to be the surplus after interest was paid to partners on their invested capital. Income was considered the businessman's reward for risk taking, ingenuity, or sheer luck, not for investing *per se.* Thus capital was peripheral, not central to accounting measurements. It was simply a factor of production paid for by interest at the market price.

Examining nineteenth century industrial accounting in England and America, Richard Brief[38] concludes that it failed to distinguish systematically between capital and revenue expenditures, or to periodically allocate the cost of fixed assets to expense. Often the resulting "error" was deliberately fostered by management. The replacement accounting used by railroads enormously understated capital consumption charges. Industrial accountants did not solve the overhead problem, nor could they agree on preferred depreciation methods or asset valuation techniques. Nor was accounting theory logically consistent or very influential. Accounting as it developed continued to be mainly a matter of conventions.

SUMMARY AND CONCLUSIONS

The accounting results of industrialization can be seen as a series of additions to the older framework of double entry bookkeeping. Asset valuation, income finding and reporting to absentee owners became important and were to some extent systematized. The concepts of continuity, periodicity, and accrual became practical necessities for large manufacturers. New developments and rediscoveries included systematic cost accounting, the nonverbal audit, and a statistical concept of capital with enhanced theoretical potential.

Technology advanced much faster than the accounting response to industrial problems. Accountants confronting these problems achieved few solutions we would call definitive. They did not rationalize bookkeeping methodology. Because Sombart generalized from results, without considering the evolution of bookkeeping technique, he tended to describe the form rather than the substance of industrial accounting practice. His theory ignores the paradox of "rational" industrial corporations continuing to use essentially Renaissance bookkeeping methods. But wherever capitalism appeared, more accurate accounting practices soon followed. And double entry bookkeeping undoubtedly enhanced managerial planning and decision-making capabilities.[39] The real strength of scientific bookkeeping was shown less by its immediate benefit to entrepreneurs than by its ability to adapt to a business environment completely different from any foreseen by its inventors.

FOOTNOTES

1. T.S. Ashton, *The Industrial Revolution, 1760-1830* (London: Oxford University Press, 1962), 7-22.

2. Sidney Pollard, *The Genesis of Modern Management: A Study of the Industrial Revolution in Great Britain* (London: Edward Arnold, 1965), 198.
3. *Ibid.*, 209.
4. Richard P. Brief, "The Origin and Evolution of Nineteenth Century Asset Accounting," *Business History Review* 40 (1966), 1-2.
5. Pollard, *op. cit.*, 211.
6. *Ibid.*, 213.
7. *Ibid.*, 215-17.
8. D.A. Litherland, "Fixed Asset Replacement a Half Century Ago," *Accounting Review* 26 (October, 1951), 475.
9. Brief, *op. cit.*, 6-7.
10. *Ibid.*, 7-9, 22.
11. A.C. Littleton, *Accounting Evolution to 1900* (New York: American Institute Publishing Company, 1933), 227-236.
12. George O. May, *Twenty-Five Years of Accounting Responsibility, 1911-1936* (New York: American Institute Publishing Company, 1936), Vol. 2, 341.
13. Richard P. Brief, "Nineteenth Century Accounting Error," *Journal of Accounting Research* 3 (Spring, 1965), 21.
14. *Ibid.*, 20.
15. Louis Goldberg, "Concepts of Depreciation," in W.T. Baxter and S. Davidson, eds., *Studies in Accounting Theory* (Homewood, Ill.: Richard D. Irwin, 1962), 239.
16. *Ibid.*, 240-41. See Vetruvius, *On Architecture*, translated by F. Granger (London: William Heinemann, 1931), vol. 2, chap. 8, 8-9.
17. Goldberg, *op. cit.*, 246-53.
18. Brief, "Nineteenth Century Accounting Error," *op. cit.*, 25.
19. Richard P. Brief, "A Late Nineteenth Century Contribution to the Theory of Depreciation," *Journal of Accounting Research* 5 (Spring, 1967), 27-38.
20. In the literature the words "expense" and "loss" were commonly used interchangeably.
21. Eldon S. Hendriksen, *Accounting Theory*, rev. ed. (Homewood, Ill.: Richard D. Irwin, 1970), 33.
22. Brief, "Nineteenth Century Accounting Error," *op. cit.*, 29-31.
23. *Ibid.*
24. Littleton, *op. cit.*, 321.
25. S. Paul Garner, *Evolution of Cost Accounting to 1925* (Alabama: University of Alabama Press, 1954), 7-21.
26. Littleton, *op. cit.*, 368.
27. Pollard, *op. cit.*, 247.
28. Robert Hamilton, *Introduction to Merchandise, 2d ed. (Edinburgh: Creech, 1820).*
29. Anselme Payen, *Essai sur la tenue des Livres d'un Manufacturies* (Paris: 1817). F.W. Cronhelm, *Double Entry by Single* (London: Longmans, Green, 1818).
30. Garner, *op. cit.*, 64.
31. Pollard, *op. cit.*, 225.
32. *Ibid.*, 219-21.
33. *Ibid.*, 23-24.
34. Max Weber, *General Economic History* (New York: Collier Books, 1961). Joseph Schumpeter, *Capitalism, Socialism and Democracy, 3d ed.*, The University Library (New York: Harper and Row, 1962). W. Sombart, *Der Moderne Kapitalismus*, 6th ed. (Munich and Leipzig, 1924).
35. Basil S. Yamey, "Scientific Bookkeeping and the Rise of Capitalism," *Economic History Review*, Second Series, vol. 1 (1949), 99-113. "Accounting and the Rise of Capitalism: Further Notes on a Theme by Sombart," *Journal of Accounting Research* 2 (Autumn, 1964), 117-36.
36. Sidney Pollard, "Capital Accounting in the Industrial Revolution," *Yorkshire Bulletin of Economic and Social Research* 15 (November, 1963), 75-91.
37. Pollard, *The Genesis of Modern Management, op. cit.*, 245.
38. Brief, "Nineteenth Century Accounting Error," *op. cit.*, 14.
39. Kenneth S. Most, "Sombart's Propositions Revisited," *Accounting Review* 67 (October, 1972), 722-734.

SELECTED BIBLIOGRAPHY

Ashton, T.S. *The Industrial Revolution, 1760-1830.* London: Oxford University Press, 1962.
Boer, G. "Replacement Cost: A Historical Look." *Accounting Review* 41 (January, 1966), 92-97.

Brief, Richard. "A Late Nineteenth Century Contribution to the Theory of Depreciation." *Journal of Accounting Research* 5 (Spring, 1967), 27-38.
_____. "Depreciation Theory in Historical Perspective." *Accountant* 163 (November 26, 1970), 737-39.
_____. "Nineteenth Century Accounting Error." *Journal of Accounting Research* 3 (1965), 12-31.
_____. *Nineteenth Century Capital Accounting and Business Investment*. Ph.D. Dissertation, Columbia University, 1964. Reprinted by Arno Press, New York, 1976.
_____. "The Origin and Evolution of Nineteenth Century Asset Accounting." *Business History Review* 40 (1966), 1-22.
Crossman, P. "The Genesis of Cost Control." *Accounting Review* 28 (October, 1953), 522-27.
De Roover, Florence Edler. "Cost Accounting in the Sixteenth Century." *Accounting Review* 12 (September, 1937), 226-37.
Edey, H.C., and Panitpakdi, Prot. "British Company Accounting and the Law 1844-1900." In A.C. Littleton and B.S. Yamey, eds. *Studies in the History of Accounting*. Homewood, Ill.: Richard D. Irwin, 1956, 356-79.
Edwards, R.S. "Some Notes on the Early Literature and Development of Cost Accounting in Great Britain." *Accountant* 97 (1937), 193-95, 225-31, 253-55, 283-87, 313-16, and 343-44.
Freear, J. "Robert Loder, Jacobean Management Accountant." *Abacus* 6 (September, 1970), 25-38.
Frishkoff, Paul. "Capitalism and the Development of Bookkeeping: a Reconsideration." *International Journal of Accounting* 5 (Spring, 1970), 29-37.
Gambino, A.J., and Palmer, J.R. *Management Accounting in Colonial America*. National Association of Accountants Research Study. New York: National Association of Accountants, 1976.
Garner, S. Paul. *Evolution of Cost Accounting to 1925*. Alabama: University of Alabama Press, 1954, chaps. one and two.
_____. "Highlights in the Development of Cost Accounting." In M. Chatfield, ed. *Contemporary Studies in the Evolution of Accounting Thought*. Belmont, Cal.: Dickenson Publishing Company, 1968, 210-21.
Goldberg, Louis. "Concepts of Depreciation." In W.T. Baxter and S. Davidson, eds. *Studies in Accounting Theory*. Homewood, Ill.: Richard D. Irwin, 1962, 236-58.
Hartwell, Ronald M. *The Causes of the Industrial Revolution in England*. London: Methuen, 1967.
Hendriksen, Eldon S. *Accounting Theory*, rev. ed. Homewood, Ill.: Richard D. Irwin, 1970, 28-41.
Hume, L.J. "The Development of Industrial Accounting: the Benthams' Contribution." *Journal of Accounting Research* 8 (Spring, 1970), 21-33.
Irish, R.A. "The Evolution of Corporate Accounting." In M. Chatfield, ed. *Contemporary Studies in the Evolution of Accounting Thought*. Belmont, Cal.: Dickenson Publishing Company, 1968, 57-85.
Johnson, H. Thomas. "Early Cost Accounting for Internal Management Control: Lyman Mills in the 1850s." *Business History Review* 46 (Winter, 1972), 466-474.
Lee, Geoffrey A. "The Concept of Profit in British Accounting, 1760-1900." *Business History Review* 49 (Spring, 1975), 6-36.
Litherland, D.A., "Fixed Asset Replacement a Half Century Ago." In M. Chatfield, ed. *Contemporary Studies in the Evolution of Accounting Thought*. Belmont, Cal.: Dickenson Publishing Company, 1968, 167-75.
Littleton, A.C. *Accounting Evolution to 1900*. New York: American Institute Publishing Company, 1933. Reprinted by Russell and Russell, New York, 1966, chaps. fourteen and twenty.
McKendrick, Neil. "Josiah Wedgewood and Cost Accounting in the Industrial Revolution." *Economic History Review*, 2nd Series, 23 (April, 1970), 45-67.
Mantoux, Paul. *The Industrial Revolution in the Eighteenth Century*, rev. ed. New York: Macmillan Company, 1961.
Mason, Perry. "Illustrations of the Early Treatment of Depreciation." *Accounting Review* 8 (September, 1933), 209-18.
Mee, G. *Aristocratic Enterprise. The Fitzwilliam Industrial Undertakings 1795-1857*. Glascow: Blackie, 1975.
Most, Kenneth S. "Sombart's Propositions Revisited." *Accounting Review* 67 (October, 1972), 722-34.
Parker, R.H. *Management Accounting: An Historical Perspective*. New York: Augustus M. Kelly, 1969, chap. two.

Peragallo, Edward. *Origin and Evolution of Double Entry Bookkeeping, A Study of Italian Practice from the Fourteenth Century*. New York: American Institute Publishing Company, 1938. Reprinted by Nihon Shoseki, Osaka, 1974, 38-49.

Pollard, Sidney. "Capital Accounting in the Industrial Revolution." In M. Chatfield, ed. *Contemporary Studies in the Evolution of Accounting Thought*. Belmont, Cal.: Dickenson Publishing Company, 1968, 113-34.

_____. "Fixed Capital in the Industrial Revolution in Britain." *Journal of Economic History* 24 (September, 1964), 299-314.

_____. *The Genesis of Modern Management: A Study of the Industrial Revolution in Great Britain*. London: Edward Arnold, 1965, especially chap. six.

Pollins, H. "Aspects of Railway Accounting Before 1868." In A.C. Littleton and B.S. Yamey, eds. *Studies in the History of Accounting*. Homewood, Ill.: Richard D. Irwin, 1956, 332-55.

Shenkir, W.G., Welsch, G.A., and Bear, J.A., Jr. "Thomas Jefferson: Management Accountant." *Journal of Accountancy* 133 (April, 1972), 33-47.

Solomons, David. "The Historical Development of Costing." In D. Solomons, ed., *Studies in Costing*. London: Sweet and Maxwell, 1952, 1-52.

Stacey, N.A.H. *English Accountancy: A Study in Social and Economic History, 1800-1954*. London: Gee and Company, 1954.

Stone, Williard E. "An Early English Cotton Mill Cost Accounting System: Charlton Mills, 1810-1889." *Accounting and Business Research* 4 (1973), 71-78.

Ten Have, O. *The History of Accountancy*. Palo Alto: Bay Books, 1976, 79-93.

Winjum, James O. "Accounting and the Rise of Capitalism: An Accountant's View." *Journal of Accounting Research* 9 (Autumn, 1971), 333-350.

_____. *The Role of Accounting in the Economic Development of England: 1500-1750*. Urbana: Center for International Education and Research in Accounting, 1972, especially 5-24.

Wren, Daniel A. *The Evolution of Management Thought*. New York: Ronald Press Company, 1972, chaps. three and four.

Yamey, B.S. "The Case Law Relating to Company Dividends." In W.T. Baxter and S. Davidson, eds. *Studies in Accounting Theory*. Homewood, Ill.: Richard D. Irwin, 1962, 428-42.

_____. "The Development of Company Accounting Conventions." *Accountant's Magazine* 65 (October, 1961), 753-63.

_____. "Some Topics in the History of Financial Accounting in England 1500-1900." In W.T. Baxter and S. Davidson, eds. *Studies in Accounting Theory*. Homewood, Ill.: Richard D. Irwin, 1962, 14-43.

_____. "Scientific Bookkeeping and the Rise of Capitalism." In W.T. Baxter, ed. *Studies in Accounting*. London: Sweet and Maxwell, 1950, 13-30.

_____. "Accounting and the Rise of Capitalism: Further Notes on a Theme by Sombart." *Journal of Accounting Research* 2 (Autumn, 1964), 117-36.

Chapter 9

BRITISH ACCOUNTING REGULATION AND AUDIT

Every society which has developed systematic record keeping has also produced some kind of account verification. It is natural for a prudent man who is unable to directly supervise his property to arrange for an independent check on the stewardship of those entrusted with his wealth. The ancient Egyptians achieved this kind of control by having tax receipts recorded independently by two officials.[1] In Greece the accounts of officeholders were audited at the expiration of their terms. The Romans developed an elaborate system of crosschecking between the records of officials who authorized expenditures and those who actually received and paid money. Renaissance Italy's emergence as a trading center led to the first extensive use of auditing in commercial ventures. The Genoa Commune ledger was duplicated by another ledger kept by city auditors. The overseas traders of Venice and Genoa employed auditors to verify the accounts of ship captains who were responsible for carrying on the actual trading.[2]

THE ENGLISH AUDIT BEFORE 1844

The feudal English audit followed a similar pattern of development.[3] The royal revenue was audited beginning in the reign of Henry I (1100–1135). Written records of manorial audits survive from the thirteenth century. About this time the practice of investigating servants and tax collectors was extended to the financial reports of other officials who handled public money. Such examinations had strictly limited aims. "Auditing as it existed to the sixteenth century was designed to verify the honesty of persons charged with fiscal responsibilities."[4] In other words, the early audit tested the personal integrity of stewards, not the quality of their accounts. Proof of bookkeeping accuraey and fairness were sought only insofar as they might indicate the existence of fraud.

The medieval audit included a painstaking review of every transaction. Entries were examined and traced back to underlying documents; balances were refooted and compared with amounts on hand and other physical evidence. Financial statements were scrutinized, and sometimes the verification process ended with a public reading of tax receipts or a bailiff's charge and discharge statement. Bookkeeping skill was required, but rarely professional judgment in the modern sense. Nor was a manorial auditor independent of the parties at interest. He acted on behalf of the nobleman who had appointed him.

Yet underlying feudal audit procedures was a system of beliefs which has changed very little.[5] Basic was the idea that men in positions of trust should be subject to public scrutiny. Corollary was the notion that expectation of audit made such stewards more honest. Also that examination of a subordinate's records benefitted him as well as the interests he served. And it was seen that this examination was most effective when made by outsiders, and that publicizing the audit increased public confidence in the organization. In the nineteenth century these beliefs became the foundation for the British statutory audit, which in turn set standards for verification all over the world.

Beginning with the first Bankruptcy Act in 1542, the English government intervened directly to protect creditors against fraud. Recurring business crises during the nineteenth century resulted in a series of new statutes and a continuing demand for men trained in bookkeeping and asset appraisal. The Victorians chose to regard insolvency as a moral shortcoming. There was often a presumption of asset concealment, and the examination of debtors' accounts introduced an element of extreme skepticism not usually found in the master-servant audit. And in both trustee and bankruptcy audits, court-appointed accountants were involved as third parties interested not only in creditor protection but in the administration of the auditee's affairs. The resulting tradition of examination and reporting by impartial experts added a new dimension to the verification process. Even more significant, investors in prosperous companies began to demand audits.

Up to this time audit objectives had hardly changed in 2000 years. The advent of double entry bookkeeping had introduced technical refinements, but fraud detection remained the goal. An entirely new audit environment was created by the combination of large-scale factory production and limited liability corporations organized to attract funds from the general public. Many more people became involved in business affairs than ever before, and as operating control passed from individual proprietors to hired professionals, reporting to absentee owners became a major accounting task. We have seen that corporate accounting conventions were often influenced by changing business conditions and changes in management policy, and that bookkeeping "error" which misstated profits was not always accidental. It was realized that the credibility of financial statements which represented management's communication with stockholders would be enhanced by outside verification. The employment of independent experts to stand between company directors and investor-owners was another instance of the English gift for adapting traditional methods to new situations.

Before 1850 auditing comprised a small part of the average accountant's practice, which was sometimes extremely varied. The self-styled "expert in accounts" might be a bookkeeper, appraiser, attorney, actuary, bankruptcy auditor, executor of estates, or winder-up of dissolved companies.[6] Collectively these men possessed all the skills auditing required, but they generally had no incentive to coordinate their talents. Business audits were usually made only in exceptional circumstances, such as liquidation, or when assets had to be revalued prior to a company's sale. In the absence of an organized accounting profession there was little agreement as to what an audit investigation should consist of or who should make it. Financial statements might be examined by company officials and signed by the firm's chairman. In other cases auditors acted merely as clerks, checking the final ledger balances and the correctness of vouchers. Since they often lacked formal certifying power, auditors who pointed out faults in the accounts might safely be ignored. Yet even before the Companies Act of 1844, the medieval audit with its tradition of giving discharge to individual accountants had been replaced by the scrutiny of an entire entity's records and an analysis of reports in terms of their meaning to outsiders.

THE COMPANIES ACTS, 1844–1862

The companies acts were intended to regulate the formation of corporations and to permit continuing supervision of their directors' handling of company affairs.[7] To achieve these goals a reporting obligation was imposed in exchange for the right to incorporate. Between 1844 and 1900 the Acts tried principally to establish minimum auditing and reporting standards. Since 1900 they have concentrated on improving financial statement quality by raising standards of disclosure.

Incorporation by registration, but with unlimited liability, was first permitted by the Joint Stock Companies Act of 1844. This act was soon amended and reissued as the Companies Clauses Consolidation Act of 1845. It required that account books be kept and periodically balanced and that directors prepare and sign a "full and fair" annual balance sheet, which would then be examined by one or more of the stockholders. It was hoped that these shareholders would be able, through their knowledge of conditions obtained by audit, to learn what directors were doing, to make them justify their actions, and to influence their subsequent behavior. Such investor-auditors were entitled to inspect the company's books and to question officers and employees. Their main task was to evaluate the balance sheet and report to the assembled stockholders whether it displayed a "true and correct View of the State of the Company's Affairs." Directors were to send printed copies of the balance sheet together with the auditor's report to stockholders ten days before their general meeting, and were to file an identical balance sheet with the Registrar of Joint Stock Companies.

Though ambitious in intent, this first effort at audit legislation was weak procedurally and far ahead of its time in the sense that means to implement it did not yet exist. Moreover, audit attention was fixed on the traditional issues of company solvency and managerial integrity, ignoring questions of profit measurement and dividend policy which the shareholders of most companies would have found more relevant. The acts provided for appointment of auditors but were silent as to their qualifications, tenure, renumeration, and specific duties. No attempt was made to specify the form or contents of the statutory balance sheet or the asset valuation methods to be used. This lack of precision would have been less damaging had there been a coherent body of doctrine to give substance to the phrase "true and correct." But the 1844–45 Acts were needed precisely because there was no professional control over practice. The very factors which made accounting regulation necessary made it inadequate.

The acts assumed that stockholders themselves would form a committee, check the books, and report back to their colleagues. And at midcentury one might actually find teams of investors making periodic visits to corporations in which they held shares, ticking off ledger balances against their printed balance sheets and seeing that each cash payment was covered by a voucher. This was nothing but the traditional stewardship audit in modern dress, with shareholders taking the part of manorial lords and company directors cast in the role of medieval bailiffs. One writer calls audits under the 1845 Act a "complete farce," and certainly directors found it easy to file misleading or simply uninformative statements.[8] Parliament had neglected to provide enforcement machinery, and the Companies Registrar had no authority to reject balance sheets submitted to him. The law did not require the date of the statutory balance sheet to be related to the date of the stockholder's meeting, and some firms filed identical statements year after year. In other cases meetings were called with minimum notice, or shareholders friendly to management were appointed as auditors. It soon became evident that only an examination by professionals could provide the meaningful check on directors intended by the law. The 1844–45 statutes provided for the employment of skilled accountants as "assistants" to the stockholder-auditors. Finally these assistants took over the whole audit examination.

The Companies Acts of 1855–56 introduced corporate registration with limited liability. It would have been logical to remedy the defects of the 1845 Act and protect against abuses of the new law by strengthening the mandatory audit requirements. Instead, Parliament struck out the compulsory bookkeeping, reporting, and audit clauses of the earlier act, leaving most commercial corporations completely unregulated in accounting matters. This abandonment of statutory requirements may actually have increased the auditor's importance, but it weakened the idea of incorporation as a privilege which implied an obligation of financial disclosure. Only after 1900 was there a gradual return to the kind of regulation Parliament had approved in 1844, but worked out with greater precision and attention to detail, as development of the audit art caught up with the intention of the original law.

In place of statutory requirements, the 1855–56 Acts included a model balance sheet and model corporate articles of association (bylaws). These were permissive. Any registered company which chose to adopt its own articles could ignore the model set, which was compulsory only for firms which did not bother to register articles of their own. The model balance sheet was extremely progressive. Assets and liabilities were classified by type, bad debts were provided for, depreciation was shown for both plant and inventories, and retained earnings was divided into portions reserved for contingencies and available for dividends.[9] The model articles included nearly all the audit and accounting provisions of the 1845 Act plus others even more advanced.[10] Books were to be kept in double entry form. No dividend was to be paid which reduced capital. An income statement was not required but different sources of revenue were to be distinguished. By specifying that auditors no longer had to be shareholders in the company, the model articles simplified the employment of outside professionals. As additional protection the new law provided that, even if no auditor was appointed, a petition by 20 percent of the stockholders required the Board of Trade to name an inspector who would investigate the company's affairs.

The 1862 Companies Act reproduced the model balance sheet and articles of association with only a few important changes. The auditor's examination was described in greater detail, and a standard form audit certificate was presented for the first time. It was stated explicitly that dividends could only be paid from accumulated income. This Act completed the *conceptual* framework of English company law. Though there have since been many procedural additions and refinements, its basic provisions have changed very little during the last hundred years.

FAILURES AND FRAUD CASES

Between 1862 and 1900 several unsuccessful attempts were made to reinstate compulsory accounting clauses in the companies acts.[11] But the turnabout from detailed regulation to a policy of *laissez-faire* had resulted not only from the weaknesses of the 1845 Act but from the prevailing philosophy that accounting disclosure was a personal matter best settled by agreement between shareholders and company directors. Underlying this feeling was the perennial question as to how far accounting uniformity could usefully be carried, considering the real diversity among the businesses involved and the known tendency of laws to inhibit innovation. Managers were often afraid disclosure would weaken their competitive position, while many stockholders feared that specifying audit procedures might limit the auditor's work to a mere mechanical check of balance sheet figures. It was even suggested that, while compulsory audit measures could easily be evaded by unscrupulous directors, they had the effect of causing investors to relax their vigilance.[12] It must be remembered that in the 1860s relatively few firms were incorporated and not many people realized how great a role the "limited" company was to play in English commercial life. As the importance of the corporate form rapidly increased, so did demands for more reliable accounting information, even if the price was compulsory disclosure and enforced uniformity of reporting methods.

Contributing to this change in public opinion was the spectacular failure in 1878 of the incorporated City of Glasgow Bank. By overvaluing assets, undervaluing debts, and misdescribing balance sheet items, the bank's directors had for years hidden its insolvency while continuing to pay dividends. The immediate response to this fraud was a clause in the 1879 Companies Act requiring annual audits for all banks registered thereafter with limited liability. And despite its policy of noninterference with commercial corporations, Parliament had always been willing to regulate companies whose failure was apt to dislocate the whole economy. The 1855–56 Acts had excluded banks and insurance companies from the privilege of limited liability, and when this right was granted them a few years later, it was on condition that they publish semiannual balance sheets and file copies with the Board of Trade. Compulsory accounting and audit requirements had never been abandoned for corporations chartered directly by Parliament, among them the railroads. The Regulation of Railways Act (1868) was a forerunner of similar laws prescribing accounting methods and audit for building societies, waterworks, gasworks, and electric light companies.[13] By the 1880s statutory regulation was an accepted fact of life for nearly all public service corporations.

The scope of audit engagements and the responsibilities of auditors were clarified by a series of landmark court decisions, the first of which was *Leeds Estate Building and Investment Co. v. Shepard* (1887). Leeds' articles of association provided that the manager and directors were entitled to bonuses based on the amount of income available for dividends. To increase these bonuses they inflated profits by overstating asset valuations. Without making a detailed examination, the auditor certified to the correctness of financial statements given him by the directors, and dividends were illegally paid out of capital. When the company went into liquidation the auditor and directors were sued, and the auditor, though he had been elected by the stockholders, maintained that he was simply a servant of management. The judge disagreed, saying that it was the auditor's duty to inquire into the "substantial accuracy" of the balance sheet provided by management, not merely its arithmetic correctness.[14] It followed that an auditor had to examine the records from which statements were taken and satisfy himself as to the existence and approximate value of company resources.

In the Kingston Cotton Mill Company case (1896), the court ruled that an auditor, having no reason to suspect dishonesty, had no duty to verify inventory figures given him by a company official who himself certified to the amount of inventory on hand. A stricter interpretation of audit responsibility resulted from the London and General Bank case (1895). The bank had been organized to make loans to a group of building companies, and for several years most of its funds had been loaned to four such companies, the loans being secured by inadequate collateral. The bank's auditor called the directors' attention to the bank's weak financial position, and in his 1891 report concluded that no dividend should be paid. But the directors persuaded him to delete this from his report to the stockholders, after which they paid a dividend which was in fact a return of capital. The stockholders sued the auditor, who was found guilty of misfeasance. The court held that while an auditor is not "an insurer" of the balance sheet, he must be honest and prudent, must never certify what he knows to be untrue, and must exercise "reasonable care and skill" before expressing his opinion. Previously it had been usual for either an affirmative audit opinion to be given, or none at all. The precedent established by this case required auditors to express an opinion even if it was negative.[15]

The rule that dividend payments could not reduce capital below the amount paid in by stockholders was modified by *Lee v. The Neuchatel Asphalte Co.* (1889). The Court of Appeals held that in calculating profits from which dividends were to be paid, the company could ignore declines in the value of wasting assets.[16] This and similar decisions led accountants to distinguish sharply between the valuation of fixed and current assets and to emphasize the latter as being more important.[17] Also, to avoid the legal risks which resulted from paying dividends out of capital, accountants tended to go to the other extreme by deliberately understating asset values and income. The lower of cost or market rule became more respectable. Judicial rulings on capital maintenance gave the doctrine of conservatism legal support at one of the most formative stages in the development of asset valuation and profit measurement concepts.

A more balanced view of financial understatement emerged from *Rex v. Kylsant* (1931).[18] The auditor of the Royal Mail Steam Packet Company was accused of aiding and abetting in the publication of false annual reports. The company had placed two million pounds earned during World War I into a funded taxation reserve, and during the 1920s it turned operating losses into apparent profits by crediting portions of this reserve to the profit and loss account. The auditor's defense was that management had a right to smooth income; that in fact such conservative practice was needed to stabilize dividends and promote investor confidence. The only explanation given in the company's report was the phrase "including adjustment of taxation reserves," and the case turned on whether these words gave statement readers sufficient warning. The auditor was acquitted of intent to deceive, but the court made it clear that conservatism was no longer a substitute for accounting disclosure.

Very often the courts seemed afraid of their own power. Yamey's comment on the philosophy underlying the *Lee v. Neuchatel* decision applies to many others: "Business men were to be the judges on business matters."[19] But case law, like the companies acts, was a factor making for accounting uniformity. If this pattern of judicial legislation had been allowed to continue, British audit requirements would today be more like those which finally developed in the United States. But beginning in 1900 Parliament reasserted its right to direct the profession by statute, passing a series of new acts aimed at detailed audit regulation.

THE COMPANIES ACTS, 1900–1967

In 1895 the Davey Committee recommended that annual audits be made compulsory for all registered companies, and this proposal was incorporated into the 1900 Companies Act. This in effect restored the main statutory requirements of the 1844 Act, since by requiring an audit the law inferred an obligation to prepare annual balance sheets. The act also specified that at the first stockholder's meeting of a new corporation there be submitted a summary of receipts and payments incurred since the date of incorporation, including details of organizational expenses, contracts entered into, and stock issued, all of which was to be certified as correct by the auditor. But there was still no prescribed form of balance sheet and no provision that *professional* auditors be appointed.

The 1907 Companies Act required that publicly held corporations file annual audited balance sheets. These were to disclose the amount of capital on which interest had been paid, the rate of such interest, commissions paid on stock or debentures, and discounts on debentures. The auditor's certificate and report were combined in one document, which had to be attached to the balance sheet or referred to thereon. The report was reworded to indicate explicitly that the law required an examination which went beyond mere comparisons of ledger balances with balance sheet figures. To strengthen auditor tenure and independence, two weeks' notice of intention to change auditors had to be given the management, the stockholders, and the retiring auditor.

The Companies Act of 1928–29 contained major changes in accounting and audit regulations: (1) For the first time an annual income statement had to be submitted to stockholders, though it did not have to be filed with the Registrar of Companies and was not specifically covered by the auditor's report. (2) On the balance sheet, current and fixed assets had to be segregated, and corporations were required to state how they had valued fixed assets. Authorized and issued capital stock were to be distinguished, and organizational expenses, goodwill, patents, and trademarks were to be stated as separate items. Disclosure had to be made of loans to directors and officers, of loans made for the purchase of the firm's own shares for the benefit of employees, and of discounts on shares issued. Corporations could no longer file out of date balance sheets with the Registrar. (3) While not requiring a consolidated balance sheet, the new law defined holding companies and required disclosure of the treatment of subsidiary income. The holding company's balance sheet was to describe investments in and loans to and from subsidiaries. (4) Prospectuses of new stock issues were to be accompanied by auditors' reports on past profits of the company whose securities were to be issued, as well as past profits of any business that was to be acquired from the proceeds of the sale.

The Cohen Committee on Company Law Amendment recommended in its 1945 report that only members of a recognized professional body be allowed to serve as corporate auditors, and a clause to this effect was included in the Companies Act 1947, then consolidated into the Act of 1948. The Committee further recommended, and the 1947–48 Acts provided, that the auditor's report should state whether in his opinion the company had kept proper account books, whether he had obtained all data necessary for the audit, and whether the balance sheet and income statement were in agreement with the books and gave a "full and fair" view of the company's financial status and operating results. Consolidated financial statements were required for the first time. The principle of independence was reinforced by giving the auditor tenure from one stockholder's meeting to the next and the right to attend such meetings and defend himself before the stockholders if he received notice that he would not be reappointed.

The 1967 Companies Act, following the report of the Jenkins Committee, set additional disclosure requirements. Like the AICPA's *Accounting Principles Board Opinion No. 9*, it required the all-inclusive income statement. Balance sheets now had to show: (1) the basis of inventory valuation; (2) totals of fixed assets acquired, disposed of, or destroyed during the year; (3) capital expenditures authorized by directors but not contracted for; (4) total amounts of quoted and unquoted investments; (5) a subdivision of land into freehold, long leasehold, and short leasehold categories; (6) the total of loans other than bank loans and overdrafts, which are not repayable within five years, and including terms of repayment and interest rates; (7) the name of each subsidiary of a holding company, with details of the nature of the stock investment; (8) or, in the case of a subsidiary, the name and country of incorporation of its ultimate holding company.

AUDIT TECHNIQUE

Though English feudal experience and other factors[20] affected the development of nineteenth century audit technique, the companies acts were undoubtedly a dominant influence. The audit was seen as an instrument of stockholder control over the performance of duties which they had delegated to management. Accordingly its primary goals were the verification of managerial stewardship and the detection of fraud.

The investigation which followed from this approach had two aspects. Most important was a careful and complete check of the bookkeeper's work. It was thought useful to examine every transaction which had occurred. Vouchers and other documents were compared with journal entries, postings were traced from journal to ledger, which was refooted and checked against the trial balance and balance sheet. Since the balance sheet summarized bookkeeping detail, proof that this detail was correct seemed a logical basis for an auditor's opinion of the resulting financial statement.

Even though all transactions were properly journalized and the balance sheet conformed to the ledger, there was always the chance of judgmental error —accruals or deferrals omitted or miscalculated, account categories confused, incorrect asset valuations, and so on. The account analysis portion of a British audit program of the 1880s has a modern sound.[21] The auditor examined securities, assayed notes for genuineness and collectability, aged accounts receivable, wrote off bad debts and provided for possible uncollectibles, and confirmed by mail *all* outstanding receivables. He saw to it that inventory count and price sheets had been signed by department heads, with totals correctly entered in the ledger, and that obsolete and damaged goods had been written down. He verified that fixed assets were recorded at cost, that capital items had not been charged to expense or *vice versa,* and that some form of depreciation had been taken. He checked to see that dividend payments had not reduced capital, that directors had not exceeded their authority to borrow, that leaseholds and patents had been properly amortized, and that all direct and contingent liabilities were listed on the balance sheet. Finally he compared the record of shares purchased, sold, and outstanding with the company's authorization and with stockholder membership lists.

It was this part of the audit examination which involved real expertise rather than simply the ability to backtrack a company bookkeeper, and the history of auditing from the 1890s is one of upgrading analysis and deemphasizing routine verification. This required a radical shift in priorities. Perhaps the chief obstacle to change was the mental attitude of stockholders, who had hired the auditor as a detective. But the immediate problem was to investigate steward-ship with much less detailed checking, thereby saving time which could be used to extend the scope of audit analysis. Before 1890 little interest was shown in internal control systems for assets other than cash,[22] and little was said about sampling as an alternative to a complete check of bookkeeping detail. Where testing was used, it seems to have been viewed not as an application of probability to shorten the work, but as a way to make a partial examination in cases where stockholders refused to pay for a complete audit. But after 1900 sampling became a common practice in English auditing, and a 1910 text stated that the first step in any examination should be to "ascertain the system of internal check."[23] While verification remained important, the acceptance of internal control and sampling procedures allowed audit emphasis to shift from the detection of fraud and clerical errors toward a more refined scrutiny of reporting fairness.

The emergence of professional societies capable of imposing their own standards was another factor in improving audit quality. Although the English accounting profession received much of its impetus from the companies acts, auditing became an important specialized function only after 1875.[24] In 1880 five regional organizations were incorporated by royal charter into the Institute of Chartered Accountants in England and Wales. Beginning in 1882 the Institute admitted new members by examination only, and these examinations included questions on auditing, which soon became one of the major subject areas for professional preparation.

Nationwide organization and testing encouraged the development of a specialized audit literature. *The Accountant* was established in 1874, but only in the 1880s, under the Institute's influence, did articles begin to appear regularly on audit procedure, auditor's duties, and related topics. The earliest important textbook on the subject was F. W. Pixley's *Auditors, Their Duties and Responsibilities* (1881). Its first edition described accounting and audit provisions of the companies acts, bookkeeping and the forms of accounts, financial statement categories, the nature of an audit, and of course the duties and responsibilities of auditors. Later editions added chapters on profits available for dividends and on certification. But the most influential and durable text to emerge from this period was Lawrence R. Dicksee's *Auditing* (1892). It was very different from modern American books on the subject, being composed mainly of extracts from company law, citations from court decisions, and, in its later editions, the British Institute's recommendations on accounting procedure. In its eighteenth edition (1969) it remains one of the best known auditing textbooks in the world.

THE AUDITOR AS THEORIST

Yet to certain questions raised by the audit investigation no answers were forthcoming. And it soon became clear that even balance sheets certified "true and correct" were often misleading because of the ease with which validated facts could be distorted or hidden. In coming to grips with problems of capital, income, and asset use created by the industrial corporation and absentee ownership, the auditor was forced to reason beyond existing rules of thumb and finally to elaborate his ideas of proper treatment into accounting principles. His scrutiny of financial statements ultimately rationalized bookkeeping itself, not only through the use of internal control procedures but more directly by refining transaction analysis, account classifications, and the rules of financial statement disclosure. English social conditions had created a need for audit services and had produced accountants more highly skilled than any before them. By subjecting customary methods to analysis, these auditors gave accounting theory some of its earliest practical applications. And in attempting to standardize British practice, Parliament through the companies acts codified parts of this theory. The next step was to seek agreement on a set of broad standards by which accounting actions might be judged. But this was to be largely an American contribution.

TOWARD ACCOUNTING UNIFORMITY

The companies acts were designed to meet an industrial society's need for uniform reporting standards. Such standards were essential if Britain was to maintain a rational pattern of resource allocation and a stable capital market. The statutory English audit provides a striking contrast with American attempts to achieve accounting uniformity through the use of general principles, and with the reliance of several Western European countries on uniform charts of accounts.

Statutory regulation may fail because its requirements are too minimal, or because it tries to achieve too much uniformity of detail, or because of legislative ignorance as to the state of the accounting art. Or the system may stagnate if existing laws prove difficult to amend. Or "preoccupation with the importance of not misleading investors obscures the desirability of enlightening them." Critics have claimed that the companies acts nullified themselves by following rather than anticipating improvements in practice; that, for example, most well-managed corporations had annual audits long before they became compulsory in 1900. The acts set lower limits beneath which practice could not legally fall, but also perhaps a ceiling above which accountants had no incentive to rise. It has sometimes seemed that the prime motive of American advocates of the principles approach has been the avoidance of statutory regulation. Yet, except for the fact that English auditors are hired by stockholders rather than management, the British and American systems have produced roughly similar results, often promoting the same reforms at about the same time. In later chapters we shall trace the influence of British company law on the SEC Act and on the American Institute's endorsement of accounting principles beginning in the 1930s.

FOOTNOTES

1. Richard Brown, ed., *A History of Accounting and Accountants* (London: Jack, 1905), 21-30, 74.
2. J.C. Ray, ed., *Independent Auditing Standards* (New York: Holt, Rinehart and Winston, 1964), 3.
3. See Chapter Two.
4. L. Fitzpatrick, "The Story of Bookkeeping, Accounting, and Auditing," *Accountants Digest* 4 (March, 1939), 217.
5. A.C. Littleton and V.K. Zimmerman, *Accounting Theory: Continuity and Change* (Englewood Cliffs, N.J.: Prentice-Hall, 1962), 104-5.
6. Brown, *op. cit.*, 201; A.C. Littleton, *Accounting Evolution to 1900* (New York: American Institute Publishing Company, 1933), 305-6.
7. Littleton, *op. cit.*, 293 ff.
8. *Ibid.*, 290; H.C. Edey and Prot Panitpakdi, "British Company Accounting and the Law, 1844-1900," in A.C. Littleton and B.S. Yamey eds., *Studies in the History of Accounting* (Homewood, Ill.: Richard D. Irwin, 1956), 360-61.
9. See Chapter Six.

10. Summarized in Edey and Panitpakdi, *op. cit.*, 362-68.
11. *Ibid.*, 368-69.
12. *Ibid.*, 367.
13. Littleton, *op. cit.*, 302-3.
14. Wiley D. Rich, *Legal Responsibilities and Rights of Public Accountants* (New York: American Institute Publishing Co., 1935), 327.
15. *Ibid.*, 26.
16. B.S. Yamey, "The Case Law Relating to Company Dividends," in W.T. Baxter and S. Davidson, eds., *Studies in Accounting Theory* (Homewood, Ill.: Richard D. Irwin, 1962), 429-32.
17. Edey and Panitpakdi, *op. cit.*, 378-79.
18. Sir Patrick Hastings, "The Case of the Royal Mail," in W.T. Baxter and S. Davidson, eds., *op. cit.*, 452-61.
19. Yamey, *op. cit.*, 432.
20. See "the relativity of auditing" diagram, Littleton, *op. cit.*, 364.
21. *Ibid.*, 312-13.
22. E.D. McMillan, "Evaluation of Internal Control." *The Internal Auditor* 13 (December, 1965), 39; R. Gene Brown, "Changing Audit Objectives and Techniques," *Accounting Review* 37 (October, 1962), 698.
23. E.V. Spicer and E.C. Pegler, *Audit Programmes* (London: H. Foulkes Lynch and Co., 1910), 4.
24. Littleton, *op. cit.*, 290, 306-7.

SELECTED BIBLIOGRAPHY

Brown, R. Gene. "Changing Audit Objectives and Techniques." *Accounting Review* 37 (October, 1962), 696-703.
Brown, Richard, ed. *A History of Accounting and Accountants*. London: Jack, 1905. Reprinted by B. Franklin, New York, 1966, chap. four.
Davies, P.M., and Bourn, A.M. "Lord Kylsant and the Royal Mail." *Business History* 14 (July, 1972), 102-123.
Dicksee, Lawrence R. *Auditing: A Practical Manual for Auditors*. London: Gee, 1892. Reprinted by Arno Press, New York, 1976.
Edey, H.C. "Company Accounting in the Nineteenth and Twentieth Centuries." in M. Chatfield, ed. *Contemporary Studies in the Evolution of Accounting Thought*. Belmont, Cal.: Dickenson Publishing Company, 1968, 135-43.
Edey, H.C., and Panitpakdi, Prot. "British Company Accounting and the Law 1844-1900." In A.C. Littleton and B.S. Yamey, eds. *Studies in the History of Accounting*. Homewood, Ill.: Richard D. Irwin, 1956, 356-79.
Hastings, Sir Patrick. "The Case of the Royal Mail." In W.T. Baxter and S. Davidson, eds., *Studies in Accounting Theory*. Homewood, Ill.: Richard D. Irwin, 1962, 452-461.
Hein, L.W. "The Auditor and the British Companies Acts." *Accounting Review* 38 (July, 1963), 508-20.
Lee, T.A. "The Historical Development of Internal Control from the Earliest Times to the End of the Seventeenth Century." *Journal of Accounting Research* 9 (Spring, 1971), 150-157.
_____ "A Brief History of Company Audits: 1840-1940." *Accountant's Magazine* 74 (August, 1970), 363-368.
Littleton, A.C. *Accounting Evolution to 1900*. New York: American Institute Publishing Company, 1933. Reprinted by Russell and Russell, New York, 1966, chaps. sixteen, eighteen, and nineteen.
Littleton, A.C., and Zimmerman, V.K. *Accounting Theory: Continuity and Change*. Englewood Cliffs, N.J.: Prentice-Hall, 1962, chap. five.
McMillan, E.D. "Evaluation of Internal Control." *The Internal Auditor* 13 (December, 1965), 36-41.
Manly, P.S. "Clarence Hatry." *Abacus* 12 (June, 1976), 49-60.
_____. "Gerard Lee Beran and the City Equitable Companies." *Abacus* 9 (December, 1973), 107-115.

Murray, Alasdair, "A History of Internal Audit." *Accountant* 173 (November, 20, 1975) 585-586.

Pixley, F.W. *Auditors: Their Duties and Responsibilities.* London: Good, 1881. Reprinted by Arno Press, New York, 1976.

Rich, Wiley D. *Legal Responsibilities and Rights of Public Accountants.* New York: American Institute Publishing Company, 1935.

Tyson, R.E. "The Failure of the City of Glascow Bank and the Rise of Independent Auditing." *Accountant's Magazine* 78 (April, 1974), 126-131.

Vamplew, Wray. "A Careful and Most Ingenious Fabrication of Imaginary Accounts: Scottish Railway Company Accounts before 1868." *Accountant's Magazine* 78 (August, 1974), 307-312.

Woolf, A.H. *A Short History of Accountants and Accountancy.* London: Gee, 1912. Reprinted by Nihon Shoseki, Osaka, 1974. Chapter Thirteen.

Yamey, B.S. "The Case Law Relating to Company Dividends." In W.T. Baxter and S. Davidson, eds. *Studies in Accounting Theory.* Homewood, Ill.: Richard D. Irwin, 1962, 428-42.

_____ "The Development of Company Accounting Conventions." *Accountants' Magazine* 65 (October, 1961), 753-63.

Chapter 10

THE AMERICAN AUDIT PROGRAM

The American audit, like the British, was subject to three institutional influences: government regulation, court decisions, and rules made by accounting societies. English auditing got much of its impetus from the companies acts. In the absence of such statutory requirements, American audit authority in its formative period depended largely on the profession's own efforts and on their acceptance by the consumers of certified financial statements—managers, creditors, and to a lesser extent, stockholders. This meant that improvements in audit technique usually reflected the business community's estimate of what was commercially desirable; there was less emphasis on public protection than in England. Legislative regulation and judicial interpretation became important factors only after the groundwork of American auditing had been laid.

THE BRITISH ACCOUNTING TRADITION IN AMERICA

After the Civil War a rapidly industrializing American economy attracted large amounts of European and particularly British capital. In the 1880s it became common for Scots and English chartered accountants to visit the United States to make fraud, value, and status audits of American properties and firms in which their clients had investments.[1] Finding local accounting practitioners but no organized auditing profession in a nation which was already one of the world's leading manufacturers, some of them stayed on, to found the American branch of Price Waterhouse and several others among the largest present CPA firms. Besides auditing expertise, they brought with them the solidarity and sense of responsibility appropriate to recognized professional men. Establishing connections with influential industrialists, bankers, and lawyers, they formed the first truly nationwide accounting partnerships.

These English auditors transplanted the British stewardship examination to the United States without much consideration for differences in American law, industrial history, or financial practices. The attest function as they saw it depended mainly on verification of bookkeeping detail. Even in large companies this might include examining all cash payment vouchers and checking every footing and posting. Distaste for such "bookkeeper audits" figures largely in the memoirs of early American accountants. Walter Staub recalled that the usual audit made by his firm focused on the integrity of employees who handled cash, to the exclusion of almost everything else.[2] Robert Montgomery estimated that three-fourths of audit time was spent examining footings and postings, whereas experience showed that three-fourths of defalcations were hidden by failure to account for cash receipts or income.[3] His colleagues considered it sufficient to check the bookkeeper's work and write "audited and found correct," without any analysis of balance sheet quality.[4] Montgomery concludes that the auditor of the 1890s "was little recognized because the matters which were referred to him were relatively unimportant and this unimportance tended to reduce him to the level of a clerk."[5]

There were valid reasons for the detailed audit approach. Bookkeeping error was very common; detailed checking was often needed to correct ledgers which had been out of balance for months or even years. Staff embezzlement was also common, and the high failure rate among early industrial ventures was partly due to fraud by promoters and managers. But the British statutory audit was the end product of a long history of speculative collapses and restricted incorporation which had no parallel in the United States. In America the federal government neither incorporated companies nor regulated their accounting. These powers were left to the states, almost none of which required audits of corporate accounts. Nor could American auditors easily be elected by stockholders. Variations in state commercial codes resulted in a wide variety of corporate bylaws, making it hard to standardize the relationship between investors and auditors. It was difficult, in such a large country, even to get shareholders to annual meetings. So from the first the American audit had to justify its expense to proprietors and corporate directors, not to stockholders or the government. Extensive checking of managerial stewardship was costly in comparison with perceived benefits, and a substitute for the detailed audit was sought.

THE BALANCE SHEET AUDIT

The American capital market during the late nineteenth century was mainly local and regional rather than national, and companies financed themselves by bank borrowing far oftener than by issuing stock. In that period of alternating inflation and depression, wholesalers reacted to uncertainty by shortening their credit terms and offering cash discounts for quick payment of accounts receivable.[6] Local bankers proved willing to make short-term loans on the basis of promissory notes to wholesalers whom they knew personally. The retailer purchased goods on credit, believing that rapid turnover would allow him to pay for most of them out of the cash receipts from their sale. The wholesaler, offering discounts as an incentive for prompt payment, expected to use collections from receivables to pay his note at the bank. The second phase of American audit development was built on bankers' need for reliable financial data about loan applicants.

As short-term lending outgrew its local origins based on personal acquaintance with borrowers and the details of their business, bankers began to ask credit applicants to submit signed balance sheets. A signed statement of assets not only gave clues about the merchant's liquidity, but in case of default could be introduced as evidence in court. Applicants found credit forthcoming even more readily if they could present a balance sheet certified by an expert and disinterested third party. Between 1900 and 1914 the certification of balance sheets for use by bankers became a major part of the CPA's work.[7]

Bankers wanted assurance that a merchant could repay his loan at maturity. They judged that the best indications of future liquidity were to be found in the relationship between current assets and current liabilities. A safe margin of working capital and a two-to-one current ratio became the standards for credit granting. Because this analysis of working capital rarely involved questions of company solvency, fraud, or managerial stewardship, a "general audit" of the English type was unnecessary. Nominal accounts, long-term assets and equities, and bookkeeping accuracy might be reviewed briefly, but the balance sheet was the focus of audit analysis, and verification of current assets and liabilities got far more attention than the mechanical details of bookkeeping. The result was an examination which looked to the future, but with a strong conservative bias. It was only natural for bankers to anticipate potential losses but not gains, to favor the writedown of inventories to the lower of cost or market price, and to encourage the use of depreciation reserves and bad debt allowances. Hendriksen considers that the balance sheet audit influenced accounting theory by temporarily counteracting those forces which otherwise would have shifted accounting emphasis to the income statement much sooner.[8]

Several of the earliest American audit texts recognized the potential advantages of a selective examination. The balance sheet audit was made on the assumption that certain accounts were more important than others, and that because of this a company's records could be evaluated without looking at each transaction which produced the final results. In other words, an intensive, in-depth scrutiny of a few key accounts might be an effective substitute for the detailed checking of a whole year's transactions. But to make this possible it was necessary to decide how much the less important parts of the examination could safely be curtailed. While most English authors concentrated on the detailed audit program, Montgomery, Staub, and other American writers explicitly linked the extent of required audit sampling to an appraisal of the client's internal control system.[9] The stronger the system of internal control, the less time need be spent on detailed checking for errors and fraud, and the more time an auditor would have for a qualitative analysis of the accounts that really mattered.

But the literature was a generation ahead of practice. The American auditor, unlike his English counterpart, could only sell those services his clients considered worth buying. Sampling became popular, not because a better theory was forthcoming, but because a detailed audit of large firms was considered too expensive.[10] To cut costs, many auditors simply reduced the scope of their examinations, but without necessarily changing their attitudes or objectives. R. Gene Brown describes the period 1905–1933 as one which combined "detailed verification and testing" with only "slight recognition" given to the importance of internal controls.[11] At the start of this period there was little understanding that scrutiny of a few systematically chosen transactions could reliably indicate the quality of a firm's record keeping. And not until the 1920s would auditors as a group base their examinations on preliminary appraisals of internal control, in effect making their clients partners in the audit process.

UNIFORM ACCOUNTING (1917)

The advent of progressive income taxation during World War I not only multiplied the number of firms employing outside auditors,[12] but inspired government interest in the fairness of reported income. The Federal Reserve Board began requiring audited financial statements to support applications for the discount of commercial paper by member banks. Regulatory agencies and the New York Stock Exchange indicated that guidelines for financial statement preparation were needed. A group of investment bankers urged that statements distributed to the public be audited under government standards. The absence of uniform and "generally accepted" standards was particularly felt within the accounting profession. The individual auditor had nothing but precedent to guide him; his duties varied according to his judgment of the circumstances in each audit situation.

The first authoritative guide to what an American audit should cover was prepared in 1917 by the American Institute of Accountants at the request of the Federal Trade Commission. After being approved by the Commission and by the Institute's Council, and following the Federal Reserve Board's tentative endorsement, it was published under the title *Uniform Accounting* in the April 1917 issue of the *Federal Reserve Bulletin.* In 1918 it was reissued under the same joint sponsorship, with minor changes and a new title, *Approved Methods for the Preparation of Balance-Sheet Statements.* Copies were sent to all

Institute members. The text began by outlining a balance sheet audit program for a merchandising or manufacturing firm. It followed with specific instructions for examining particular accounts. Suggested formats for a balance sheet and a comparative income statement appeared at the end. While its contents had only the force of recommendations, the 1917 statement was the beginning of audit self-regulation in the United States, and the first step toward a merger with the British experience of statutory audit. It directly affected the methods used by the Institute and the SEC in developing audit standards during the 1930s.

The short form audit report needed standardizing as much as the examination, and the 1917 bulletin suggested this format:

> I have audited the accounts of the ABC Company for the period from January 1, 1917 to December 31, 1917 and I certify that the above balance sheet and statement of profit and loss have been made in accordance with the plan suggested and advised by the Federal Reserve Board and in my opinion set forth the financial condition of the firm at December 31, 1917, and the results of its operations for the period.

This and most other audit certificates used in the United States before 1932 reflected a strong British influence.[13] Though there were many variations,[14] the auditor usually "certified" that in his opinion the balance sheet exhibited a "true and correct view" of the company's affairs as shown by the account books. But underlying the British certificate were statutes and accepted procedures which gave these phrases a precise technical meaning which did not yet exist in the United States. Also, the American audit had different purposes. The basis for English certification was largely bookkeeping accuracy, but it was useless for an American accountant making a credit examination merely to show that the financial statements agreed with a properly posted ledger. In the American context "true and correct" was inappropriate and even dangerous, conveying a false sense of exactness but leaving the CPA's audit responsibility in doubt and his legal liability undefined. Should the certificate be simply a report on the balance sheet and income statement, or should it express the auditor's judgment of his client's entire business situation? A verbal formula was needed which would tell the reader unmistakably what the auditor had done and what reliance could be placed on the financial statements as a result of his work.

STOCKHOLDERS AND CORPORATE DISCLOSURE

During the 1920s, when the general public first began buying corporate securities, auditors faced the problem of certifying financial data for distribution to investors who had little or no accounting knowledge. J. M. B. Hoxsey of the New York Stock Exchange believed that overconservatism and other accounting practices which might have been excusable in an era of smaller firms and short-term bank borrowing were misleading in reports to this much less sophisticated class of readers.[15] Arguing for improved corporate publicity, he pointed out that many corporations kept sales figures secret, others did not take depreciation, still others failed to treat nonoperating income consistently, to separate retained earnings from paid-in capital, or to disclose arbitrary asset writeups. Harvard Economics Professor William Z. Ripley's analysis of annual reports during the 1920s produced a similar picture of withheld information and deceptive reporting methods. Criticizing the absence of uniform accounting standards, he advocated that the Federal Trade Commission enforce disclosure of corporate affairs.[16] In retrospect it seems that the rapid expansion of equity financing, the existence of so many questionable accounting options, and the profession's inability to standardize practice made some form of federal regulation inevitable.

A revised edition of the 1917 Federal Reserve-American Institute bulletin was published in 1929. *Verification of Financial Statements* still emphasized the balance sheet audit made for companies seeking bank credit. But income statement accounts were discussed in detail, as were reporting procedures. The preface to the 1929 edition also stressed reliance on internal control systems:

> The extent of the verification will be determined by the conditions in each concern. In some cases the auditor may find it necessary to verify a substantial portion or all of the transactions recorded upon the books. In others, where the system of internal check is good, tests only may suffice. The responsibility for the extent of the work required must be assumed by the auditor.[17]

Following issuance of the 1929 bulletin, changes were made in the audit certificate used by many leading CPA firms. The new report, worded to emphasize reporting fairness, omitted references to the examination of the books and to the "correctness" of financial statements:

> We have examined the accounts of the ABC Company for the period from January 1 to December 31, 1929.
> We certify that the accompanying balance sheet and statement of profit and loss, in our opinion, set forth the financial condition of the company at December 31, 1929 and the results of operations for the period.[18]

THE MODERN AUDIT EXAMINATION

The first important court decisions affecting American auditing were handed down during the 1920s. An auditor's responsibility to his clients was ruled on in *Craig v. Anyon* (1925).[19] Barrow, Wade, Guthrie & Co., CPAs, had audited the accounts of Bache and Company, brokers, from 1913 to 1917 without discovering that over a five-year period a Bache employee had stolen more than a million dollars from the firm. A trial court found the CPAs guilty of negligence and assessed damages for the amount of the plaintiff's loss. On appeal the damages were reduced to $2000, the amount of the auditor's fee, on the grounds of contributory negligence—Bache should not be allowed to recover for losses they themselves could have avoided by establishing an effective internal control system. The *Craig* decision seemed to reaffirm precedents set by earlier English cases, to the effect that an auditor's legal liability to his client was extremely limited so long as he exercised "reasonable care" in performing his duties.

THE ULTRAMARES CASE

Until the case of *Ultramares Corporation v. Touche, Niven & Company* (1931),[20] auditors admitted no liability whatsoever to third parties. The common law rule was that even a negligent professional man could normally be sued only by his clients. Having no contract with outsiders, he owed no responsibility to them unless he had committed fraud. In 1924 Touche Niven gave an unqualified audit certificate to a rubber importer, Fred Stern and Company, failing to discover that management had falsified entries in order to overstate accounts receivable. The auditors supplied Stern with thirty-two numbered copies of the certified balance sheet, knowing the company would use them in applying for credit. Ultramares Corporation, a factor, made loans to Stern Company on the basis of these certified balance sheets. When Stern declared bankruptcy in 1925 Ultramares sued the auditors for the amount of Stern's debt, on the grounds that a careful audit examination would have showed that Stern was insolvent on the balance sheet date. The auditors were acquitted on a fraud charge but were found guilty of negligence. But the trial judge set even this aside, applying the doctrine of privity which protected auditors from third party negligence suits. An intermediate appelate court affirmed dismissal of the fraud count, but reinstated the negligence verdict. The case then went to the New York Court of Appeals.

Judge Cardozo agreed that third parties could not hold an auditor liable for ordinary negligence, only for fraud. But in a brilliantly reasoned decision he argued that courts could infer fraud from grossly negligent actions, and in doing so could subject the auditor to liability from any injured party who relied on the auditor's report, whether or not the accountant knew of his intention to do so. In short, the greater the negligence, the more widespread the legal recourse. Even an honest mistake or oversight so gross as to support the inference that an auditor did not believe his own opinion might justify a fraud verdict and open the door to almost indefinite third party liability. So in *Ultramares* the substantive question became whether the audit had been so grossly negligent as to constitute constructive fraud. Deciding that it had been, Cardozo ordered a new trial. Before it could be held, the suit was settled out of court. But the precedent established has been reiterated in similar cases ever since,[21] until today the auditor's liability to the public at large is nearly as extensive as to his own clients.[22]

Ultramares led to changes in the short form audit report. The court had criticized Touche Niven for not clearly indicating the scope of their examination, and particularly for failing to distinguish their statement of the audit's scope from their statement of opinion. The profession's response was defensive. The form of audit report which now came into general use read:

> We have examined the accounts of the ABC Company for the year ended December 31, 1931. In our opinion the accompanying balance sheet and statement of profit and loss set forth the financial condition of the company at December 31, 1931, and the results of its operations for the year ended that date.[23]

The word "certify" was eliminated and the American Institute emphasized that the auditor's certificate was an opinion, not a guarantee. Moreover it was an opinion of the *client's* actions, not the auditor's. His examination of the books was not intended to "prove" anything, but simply to put his mind in contact with the company's affairs. His knowledge and his skill in applying audit techniques then allowed him to express a professional opinion of management's financial statements.[24]

INSTITUTE AND STOCK EXCHANGE

The belief that loose accounting practices had contributed to the 1929 market crash and the depression led to the first effective agitation for compulsory audit requirements. For years George O. May had argued that the powers and duties prescribed for auditors under the English companies acts could be applied in the United States to remedy American reporting defects.[25] An enforcement mechanism existed in the New York Stock Exchange, whose stock listing rules gave it regulatory power over most major American corporations. Since the early 1920s the Exchange had required companies whose stock it listed to submit financial statements, and though these could be prepared by company accountants, independent audits were encouraged. Discussions and correspondence between the Exchange and the American Institute, aimed at improving reporting standards, began in 1930 and continued for more than three years.

Instead of trying to formulate uniform procedures to be followed by every company, the Institute's special Committee on Cooperation with Stock Exchanges, headed by George O. May, proposed that corporations be free to choose their own accounting methods within the framework of "accepted accounting principles," provided they disclosed such methods and used them consistently from year to year.[26] In October 1933 these recommendations were approved by the New York Stock Exchange, which earlier in the year had announced that corporations requesting permission to list their stock on the

Exchange must produce financial statements certified by independent public accountants, and must then file similar audited statements annually.

The auditor's report was reworded to make accounting principles the criteria for measuring reporting fairness. The new report was divided into two sections, one dealing with the examination's scope, the other with the auditor's opinion. Financial statements were the representations of management; the auditor accepted responsibility only for the judgment he expressed on them. For the first time a reporting format was recommended by the Institute for use by all CPAs, so that any deviation from the approved wording would put the reader on guard that something was wrong.

> We have made an examination of the balance sheet of the ABC Company as at December 31, 1933, and of the statement of income and surplus for the year 1933. In connection therewith, we examined or tested accounting records of the company and other supporting evidence and obtained information and explanations from officers and employees of the company; we also made a general review of the accounting methods and of the operating and income accounts for the year, but we did not make a detailed audit of the transactions.
>
> In our opinion, based on such examination, the accompanying balance sheet and related statement of income and surplus fairly present, in accordance with accepted principles of accounting consistently maintained by the company during the year under review, its position at December 31, 1933, and the results of its operations for the year.[27]

THE SECURITIES AND EXCHANGE COMMISSION

The Securities Act of 1933 provided for the registration of securities issues with the Federal Trade Commission before they were offered for sale in interstate markets, and also, as part of this registration, required the filing and public disclosure of financial statements certified by independent public accountants. The Securities Exchange Act of 1934 called for the registration of stock issues prior to their listing on the national exchanges, and for the submission of annual audited statements to a federal agency created to administer both acts, the Securities and Exchange Commission. Reinforcing the *Ultramares* decision, other provisions of the 1934 Act exposed the auditor to lawsuit by any investor who suffered loss as a result of relying on audited statements, either because material facts were omitted, or because untrue or misleading statements were made, or because the audit examination was incomplete, or because an opinion was given on inadequate evidence. Like the English companies acts, these new laws were a government's response to managerial abuse of the reporting function. But the American statutes called for much more detailed disclosure of financial data, and their regulatory potential was far greater. The SEC was authorized not only to prescribe the form and contents of financial statements submitted to it, but even to dictate the book-keeping methods used by regulated corporations.

However, in carrying out its mandate to protect investors, the SEC made limited use of these powers, preferring to reinforce the independent auditor's position. The American Institute was allowed to take the lead in developing accounting principles and improving reporting procedures. Yet an authority greater than the accounting profession's had established itself, and SEC bulletins and rulings, underlined by the threat of government intervention, made it clear that CPAs must at a minimum adhere to their own professional standards. The SEC's influence on auditing was mainly progressive. It promoted the fairness examination, required disclosure, emphasized the income statement, and encouraged extension of the balance sheet audit into new areas. Audit attention was diverted from the banker to the stockholder, and from small and medium-sized firms seeking credit, to the nation's largest corporations. The Securities Acts applied only to corporations registered with the SEC, but it soon became evident that the audits and financial reports of other companies might be considered inadequate unless SEC standards had been met.

Nothing illustrates better the difference between the Institute's approach and the SEC's than their attitudes toward auditor independence. The Institute had always regarded independence as a state of mind and a matter of character. It was reflected in objective, impartial decision making. A CPA did not subordinate his judgments to those of his client. To specify formally that auditors should be independent was almost insulting.

The SEC was concerned not only with the auditor's actions but also with the public's view of them. Appearance was as important as mental attitude because stockholders, whose confidence in the securities market was all important, often lacked the sophistication to interpret financial statements for themselves. They had to trust the auditor's interpretation, which in turn required that he should *seem* trustworthy. Many of the auditor's actions, even the manner of his appointment by a corporate board of directors, made the appearance of independence hard to maintain. The SEC ruled that it would not consider an auditor independent if he had a "substantial" interest in a client company, was an officer or director, or had any other relationship with management which might subconsciously impair his objectivity. Several *Accounting Series Releases* described borderline cases in which an auditor's interest in his client had been judged substantial, or where particular relationships were considered likely to impair independence.[28] In 1941 the Institute reluctantly added a general rule on independence to its code of ethics. Twenty years later, under SEC pressure, this rule was rewritten to prohibit auditors from having *any* financial interest in businesses whose statements they certified.

THE 1936 STATEMENT

In 1936 the Institute published a second revision of its 1917 bulletin on audit procedure. *Examination of Financial Statements by Independent Public Ac-*

countants closely followed portions of the Institute's correspondence with the New York Stock Exchange, and also reflected SEC influence. Financial statements were now "prepared for credit purposes or for annual reports to stockholders." References to the balance sheet audit were eliminated; the income statement and balance sheet were given relatively equal status.[29] Recognizing that auditing *standards* as well as procedures were needed, the 1936 statement made the first attempt to link auditing to recent developments in accounting theory. What Littleton called "a mild approach" to auditing theory appeared in references to the going concern concept, consistency, cost basis valuation, and the belief that cost transfers to the income statement were more important than the residuals which remained on the balance sheet.

But the 1936 statement compromised on two procedural questions which would shortly become crucial. For years there had been disagreement about the auditor's responsibility for verifying inventories and receivables. Some CPAs preferred to obtain direct confirmation of accounts receivable balances from debtors; others considered this unnecessary if internal controls were adequate. Similarly, many auditors insisted on witnessing and test checking inventory counts, but traditional practice in England and America had been to rely on inventory sheets signed by management, the theory being that accountants were not skilled appraisers and that any statement that they had physically inspected inventories might convey the impression that they accepted responsibility for inventory valuations. As a result of these differences of opinion, the 1936 bulletin suggested but did not require physical checking of inventories and direct mail confirmations of accounts receivable.

THE McKESSON & ROBBINS CASE

Early in 1938 Julian Thompson, a creditor of McKesson & Robbins drug company, noticed that while the firm's crude drug division was its most profitable operation, these profits were immediately reinvested and no cash ever accumulated. It was also curious that crude drug inventories shown on the books were very much underinsured. Previously the company's directors had voted to reduce inventory balances, and now asked President Philip Coster to do so. Instead, by the end of 1938 inventories had increased by a million dollars. Becoming suspicious, Thompson refused to sign three million dollars in debentures until management furnished proof that the crude drug inventories really existed. An SEC investigation followed.

The SEC examiners found that Philip Coster was an ex-convict living under a false name, assisted by his three brothers, also using false names and holding strategic executive positions in the company.[30] McKesson & Robbins' domestic drug business was legitimate; its foreign crude drug operation existed only on paper. Using company funds, Coster pretended to buy crude drugs from five Canadian vendors, who held the nonexistent "merchandise" at warehouses for the account of McKesson & Robbins. Coster then made imaginary sales to foreign dealers and collected "payments" of fictitious accounts receivable from imaginary debtors. The fraud was concealed by an elaborate facade of false documents: invoices, purchase orders, receiving tickets, shipping notices, bills of lading, debit and credit memos, inventory tally sheets and signed summaries, statements from bankers, confirmations from outside suppliers, forged contracts and guarantees, even forged credit ratings. Over a period of twelve years Coster and his brothers had stolen about $2.9 million from McKesson & Robbins.

In January 1939 the SEC opened public hearings on the case in New York City. A parade of expert witnesses testified that in auditing McKesson & Robbins, Price Waterhouse and Company had adhered to generally accepted procedures as described in the Institute's 1936 statement. During examinations made before 1935 the auditors had been given inventory sheets signed or initialed by company employees. After 1934 they had obtained written confirmations of inventory quantities held by the Canadian "suppliers," and had test-checked them to purchase orders. Each year two or more company officials formally certified as to the condition and quantity of inventories shown on the balance sheet. Though receivables were not confirmed by mail, credits to customers' accounts were compared with entries in the cash receipts book, and records of crude drug sales were test-checked to the perpetual inventory records and to copies of customers' invoices and shipping advices (all were forgeries). Price Waterhouse's defense was that they had conformed to prevailing professional standards.[31] Frauds involving managerial collusion were notoriously elusive and a balance sheet audit could not be expected to uncover them. In any case more extensive testing would simply have encountered additional expertly forged documents.

The SEC Committee agreed, but with reservations. Every standard procedure had been followed in annual examinations by the largest accounting firm in the United States. It seemed reasonable that even an audit program not geared to fraud detection should have found *something* wrong with a consolidated balance sheet which included nine million dollars in fictitious receivables and ten million in fictitious inventories. Not only were existing audit standards inadequate, the Committee concluded, but the type of audit being performed by American CPAs was not serving even its ostensible purposes. Auditors should extend verification outside the books to establish the actual existence of the assets and liabilities shown on the balance sheet. If the auditors had inspected McKesson & Robbins' inventories the fraud would have been discovered. Direct mail confirmation of receivables and observation of inventory counts, including physical tests if necessary, should become mandatory audit procedures. When inventories were located in other countries correspondent firms could make such observations. The Committee also recommended changes in the form of the auditor's report, proposed that the opinion be addressed directly to stockholders, and even suggested that auditors be elected by the stockholders.

The McKesson & Robbins fraud forced a long overdue appraisal of audit priorities. In fifty years American accountants had gone from one extreme to the other. The detailed stewardship audit had been tried and rejected as being unsuited to local conditions and too expensive. Then for a generation most American audits had been dangerously superficial credit investigations. The voluntary refund of over $500,000 in fees by Price Waterhouse to McKesson & Robbins indicated the scale of potential liability faced by auditors who failed to make the type of examination which would disclose major fraud. The result was a final break with the balance sheet audit and the older British tradition of auditing the accounts instead of the business. The new tendency to seek physical contact with company affairs was part of a general expansion of audit responsibility to embrace fixed as well as current assets, the income statement equally with the balance sheet. Between the detailed examination on the one hand and the balance sheet audit on the other, a new point of equilibrium was sought, an investigation comprehensive enough to inform the public and protect the accountant, yet economical enough to justify its cost to the client.

On January 30, 1939, only three weeks after the first SEC hearings in the McKesson & Robbins case, the American Institute formed a Special Committee on Auditing Procedure. Its report, "Extension of Auditing Procedure," recommended that physical observation of inventory counts and the direct confirmation of receivables should be normal audit techniques, and that if either of these tests was omitted, an exception must be noted in the auditor's opinion. The Committee also recommended changes in the standard auditor's report, to emphasize reporting consistency and the fact that audit tests had been based on a review of the internal control system:

> We have examined the balance sheet of the ABC Company as of December 31, 1939, and the statements of income and surplus for the fiscal year then ended, have reviewed the system of internal control and the accounting procedures of the company and, without making a detailed audit of the transactions, have examined and tested accounting records of the company and other supporting evidence, by methods and to the extent we deemed appropriate.
>
> In our opinion, the accompanying balance sheet and related statements of income and surplus present fairly the position of the ABC Company at December 31, 1939, and the results of its operations for the fiscal year, in conformity with generally accepted accounting principles applied on a basis consistent with that of the preceding year.[32]

Following acceptance of these proposals by the Institute's Council, the Committee on Auditing Procedure was continued as a standing committee, parallel to the Committee on Accounting Procedure. "Extension" was republished as the first of more than forty interpretive *Statements on Auditing Procedure* similar in form to the *Accounting Research Bulletins.*

AUDITING STANDARDS

In 1941, as a final result of its McKesson & Robbins investigation, the SEC issued *Accounting Series Release No. 21,* amending Regulation S-X to include the following: "The accountants' certificate . . . shall state whether the audit was made in accordance with generally accepted auditing standards applicable in the circumstances."[33] The American Institute then added this sentence to the scope paragraph of its short form audit report:

> Our examination was made in accordance with generally accepted auditing standards and included all procedures which we considered necessary in the circumstances.

Like the phrase "accepted principles of accounting" which appeared in the 1933 auditor's report, this reference to "auditing standards" was essentially a bluff. There were no agreed on auditing standards in 1941, and no serious attempt was made to define any until after World War II. But there was an evident need to standardize the auditor's examination and to specify the minimum level of work necessary for financial statement certification. In 1947 the Institute's Committee on Auditing Procedure issued a special report, *Tentative Statement of Auditing Standards—Their Generally Accepted Significance and Scope.* Its introduction described audit procedures as "acts to be performed," whereas standards "deal with measures of the quality of the performance of those acts, and the objectives to be attained in the employment of the procedures undertaken."[34] The text offered guidance in planning field work, appraising internal control systems, and critically evaluating audit evidence prior to expressing an opinion.

In 1949 the audit report was again revised to reflect the profession's adoption of specific auditing standards:

> We have examined the balance sheet of ABC Company as of December 31, 1949, and the related statements of income and surplus for the year then ended. Our examination was made in accordance with generally accepted auditing standards, and accordingly included such tests of the accounting records and such other auditing procedures as we considered necessary in the circumstances.
>
> In our opinion, the accompanying balance sheet and statements of income and surplus present fairly the financial position of ABC Company at December 31, 1949, and the results of its operations for the year then ended, in conformity with generally accepted accounting principles applied on a basis consistent with that of the preceding year.[35]

The only subsequent change in this format was the substitution of the phrase "retained earnings" for the word "surplus."

Since the McKesson & Robbins case several trends have become evident in the American audit program. A review of internal controls is now the normal starting point for an audit, and the results of that review largely determine the extent of testing required. Where sampling indicates a reliable control system, detailed verification may almost be eliminated. At the same time, the auditor's concept of internal control has expanded to include the totality of the firm and its operations, and even questions of managerial policy. In choosing to evaluate internal control beyond its direct effects on the accounting system, the auditor found himself in an excellent position to diagnose and suggest solutions for a client's operating problems. The modern concept of management services emerged from this environment. R. Gene Brown believes that the appraisal of internal control in this larger sense will become the predominant means of judging financial statement fairness.[36] The future auditor will concentrate on systems control techniques and spend even less time reviewing the historical accounting records.

The last thirty years in auditing, as in financial accounting, have been characterized by a search for principles which could be used to rationalize procedures.[37] Not surprisingly, the same criticisms made of accounting theory apply to auditing standards. Certified financial statements still are not comparable within or between companies. Too many unnecessary and even conflicting options are tolerated. Critics charge that much of auditing theory seems designed for the convenience of auditors who, like corporate managers, have developed a vested interest in the traditional examination. The sparseness of auditing theory has made it difficult for practitioners to assimilate new techniques, with the result that potentially revolutionary developments such as electronic data processing and statistical sampling were for years used mainly to implement the conventional audit program. In the aftermath of the McKesson & Robbins fraud, audit standards were promoted partly to educate report readers about the role of the auditor and the extent of his attest function. But studies made of the recent "litigation explosion" indicate that while the public's idea of audit duties and responsibilities has rapidly expanded, auditors themselves continue to define their functions much as they did a generation ago.[38]

A CRISIS IN LEGAL LIABILITY

Because of the time constraints involved and the incompatibility of fraud and fairness examinations, auditors have taken the position that they have a duty to test for fraud, but no legal liability if they fail to uncover it.[39] In the past, courts generally agreed. But the public's position as seen in prosecutor's arguments and recent jury decisions is that fraud detection is the main reason for hiring an auditor and thus his principal duty.[40]

For many years following the *Ultramares* decision, auditors assumed that they could be held liable to clients for negligence but to third parties only for gross negligence or fraud. Recently the accountant's privity defense has deteriorated. The *Bar Chris, Westec* and *Yale Express* cases included as plaintiffs third parties who were not in a contractual relationship with the auditors. Negligence actions by third parties have been successful in SEC hearings and in the courts.

Under common law a professional man is held to the standard of performance which may reasonably be expected of his peers. Before the 1960s any auditor who could prove that he had adhered to American Institute standards had what seemed an infallible legal defense.[41] Recent cases have established that an accountant following all of the profession's "generally accepted" auditing standards and procedures can be successfully sued by stockholders and others who rely on financial statements which turn out to be misleading.

This traditional defense was effective largely because the accounting profession's standards were superior to those found in common law. Rule making was nearly always left to the profession. In recent decisions courts have indicated that the auditor has a social responsibility over and above his expressed standards, and must look beyond a client's financial data to other circumstances of interest to the investing and lending public. Judges and juries composed of laymen have not only found deficiencies in the way auditors examine accounts, but have assumed leadership in setting auditing standards, and have even interpreted accounting principles and ruled on their validity.

In most earlier cases, accountants were sued for failing to *discover* misfeasance or fraud. In recent cases, they have more often been sued for failing to *disclose* all that they had discovered.

THE CONTINENTAL VENDING CASE

The most publicized of these decisions involved the auditors of Continental Vending Machine Corporation,[42] and resulted in the first criminal conviction of a major accounting firm in seventy years. Harold Roth, the president of Continental Vending, owned about 25 percent of its stock. Between 1958 and 1962 he financed his personal stock market dealings by having Continental Vending loan money to an affiliate, Valley Commercial Corporation, whose funds he then borrowed. During the 1962 audit of Continental Vending, President Roth informed the auditors that Valley was unable to repay Continental Vending because he was unable to repay Valley. He agreed to post collateral for Valley's $3.5 million debt to Continental Vending, and the auditors decided that if this was done there was no need for them to examine Valley's books, which were regularly audited by another accounting firm. The loan to Valley was footnoted on Continental Vending's balance sheet, but the footnote failed to disclose that 80 percent of the collateral used to secure Valley's debt consisted of Continental's own securities, which were worth only $2.9 million on the date of the auditor's opinion. The footnote stated in effect that the receivable from Valley was backed by securities with a greater market value than the *net amount* owed by Valley to Continental Vending (Continental also owed Valley about a million dollars). Shortly after the statements were certified, Continental Vending Machine Corporation filed a bankruptcy petition.

The auditors were sued by the federal government for conspiring to file false statements and use the mails to defraud. Their main defense was that they had followed generally accepted accounting principles and auditing standards, which included no specific obligation to disclose the nature of loan collateral or examine the accounts of affiliates which had other auditors. The prosecution argued that they should have inquired into the affairs of Valley Commercial Corporation; that failure to do so gave them a reason to falsify Continental's 1962 balance sheet. It did not dispute that they had followed professional standards, but continually urged that this was not sufficient. "Generally accepted auditing standards express only the minimum requirements and do not attempt to spell out what an accountant must do as a matter of practice under [individual] circumstances."[43] Judge Mansfield agreed that compliance with auditing standards, even if proved, "is not conclusive on the issue of the defendant's good faith and intention, and the fact that a defendant's conduct was in accord with such standards and principles does not necessarily or automatically constitute a complete defense.[44] At the end of the trial he added ominously "The accounting profession would do well to revise its accounting principles and standards."[45] In June 1968, after an earlier trial had ended in a hung jury, an audit manager and two partners were found guilty and were fined. The conviction was upheld on appeal, and the Supreme Court declined to review the case.

One can feel sympathy for men who suddenly find themselves held to standards of performance they knew nothing about, while being blamed for adhering to standards which no one told them were inadequate. The Continental Vending decision created immediate pressure to expand the scope of the audit examination, and this may have been the government's motive in pressing fraud charges. In effect it indicted the accounting profession for not modifying its rules to meet changing public needs. The American Institute saw this judicial standard-setting as a challenge to its own authority, and filed "on behalf of the entire profession" a memorandum *amicus curiae.*[46] Its thesis was that audit standards are the result of public exposure, debate, and general acceptance by auditors of ideas which prove useful in practice. Standards exist because the profession sanctions them. They are not logical imperatives or natural laws, nor can they be manufactured in a jury room. Until they are codified by an accounting body they cannot even be enforced in an orderly way.

CONCLUSIONS

One possible response to the liability crisis is for auditors to seek protection within the traditional framework of historical cost, objectivity, consistency, and conservatism. The actions of the courts and the SEC can be seen as attempts to make this solution unfeasible. Another alternative is to broaden the attest function to meet the demands being made on it. An inference to be drawn from recent court decisions is that the public accountant is underemployed in his role as certifier of historical financial statements. Without fully realizing it, the profession may have come full circle, from the nineteenth century accounting generalists, through a phase of intensive audit specialization, into a new era dominated by operational auditing and management services in which the accountant is returning to a vocational concept of multiple tasks. Auditing may yet prove less important than the functions it has helped create.

FOOTNOTES

1. James Don Edwards, *History of Public Accounting in the United States* (East Lansing: Michigan State University, 1961), 48-51.
2. Walter A. Staub, *Auditing Developments During the Present Century* (Cambridge, Mass: Harvard University Press, 1942), 9-10.
3. Robert H. Montgomery, *Auditing Theory and Practice*, 1st ed. (New York: Ronald Press Company, 1912), 258.
4. Robert H. Montgomery, *Fifty Years of Accountancy* (Privately Printed by the Ronald Press Company, 1939), 17.
5. *Ibid.*, 316.
6. A.C. Littleton and V.K. Zimmerman, *Accounting Theory: Continuity and Change*, (Englewood Cliffs, N.J.: Prentice-Hall, 1962), 110-11.
7. *Ibid.*, 115.
8. Eldon S. Hendriksen, *Accounting Theory*, rev. ed. (Homewood, Ill.: Richard D. Irwin, 1970), 62.
9. C.A. Moyer, "Early Developments in American Auditing," *Accounting Review* 26 (January, 1951), 3-8.
10. R. Gene Brown, "Changing Audit Objectives and Techniques," *Accounting Review* 37 (October, 1962), 699-700.
11. *Ibid.*, 696.
12. M.E. Peloubet, "The Historical Development of Accounting," in Morton Backer, ed., *The Handbook of Modern Accounting Theory*, (Englewood Cliffs, N.J.: Prentice-Hall, 1955), 19.
13. G. Cochrane, "The Auditor's Reprot. Its Evolution in the U.S.A.," *Accountant* 123 (November 4, 1950), 449-50.
14. For example, see Edwards, *op. cit.*, 90-92; John L. Carey, *The Rise of the Accounting Profession*, vol. 1 (New York: AICPA, 1969), 28-29.
15. J.M.B. Hoxsey, "Accounting for Investors," *Journal of Accountancy* 50 (October, 1930), 251-84.
16. William Z. Ripley, "Stop, Look, Listen!" *Atlantic Monthly* 180 (September, 1926), 380.
17. *Verification of Financial Statements* (Washington, D.C.: U.S. Government Printing Office, 1929). Reprinted in *The Journal of Accountancy* 47 (May, 1929), 323-24.
18. Cochrane, *op. cit.*, 450.
19. *Craig v. Anyon*, 212 App. Div. 55, 208 N.Y. Supp. 259 aff'd 242 N.Y. 569, 152 N.E. 431 (1926).
20. *Ultramares Corporation v. Touche, Niven & Company*, 255 N.Y. 170; 174 N.E. 441 (1931).
21. *State Street Trust Co. v. Ernst*, 15 N.E. 2d 418 (1938); *National Surety Co. v. Lybrand*, 256 App. Div. 226; 9 NYS 2d 554 (1939); *Duro Sportswear v. Cohen*, 131 NYS 2d 20 (1954).
22. Wayne A. Label, "The Accountant's Legal Liability: Its Impact Upon the Profession," (Unpublished Ph.D. Dissertation, University of California, Los Angeles, 1971), 123.

23. Cochrane, *op. cit.*, 451.
24. Littleton and Zimmerman, *op. cit.*, 119.
25. George O. May, "Corporate Publicity and the Auditor," *Journal of Accountancy* 42 (November, 1926), 321-26.
26. See George O. May, *Twenty-Five Years of Accounting Responsibility, 1911-1936* (New York: American Institute of Accountants, 1936), 119-20.
27. Cochrane, *op. cit.*, 453.
28. SEC *Accounting Series Release No. 2* (1937); SEC *Accounting Series Release No. 47* (1944).
29. *Examination of Financial Statements by Independent Public Accountants* (New York: American Institute of Accountants, 1936), 4.
30. Philip Coster (Philip N. Musica), who had previously been convicted of commercial fraud carried out in collusion with his brothers, committed suicide during the investigation.
31. C.W. DeMond, *Price, Waterhouse and Company in America* (New York: Comet Press, 1951), 273; quoted in Edwards, *op. cit.*, 166-67.
32. Cochrane, *op. cit.*, 455-56.
33. SEC *Accounting Series Release No. 21* (1941), 39.
34. *Tentative Statement of Auditing Standards–Their Generally Accepted Significance and Scope* (New York: American Institute of Accountants, 1947), 9.
35. Cochrane, *op. cit.*, 456.
36. Brown, *op. cit.*, 703.
37. See R.K. Mautz and Hussein A. Sharaf, *The Philosophy of Auditing*, American Accounting Association Monograph No. 6 (Menasha, Wisconsin: American Accounting Association, 1961).
38. Label, *op. cit.*, 39.
39. American Institute of CPAs, *Codification of Statements on Auditing Procedure* (New York, AICPA, 1951), 11-12.
40. Label, *op. cit.*, 39.
41. *Ibid.*, 69.
42. *The United States of America v. Carl Simon, et. al.*, U.S. Dist. Ct. S.D.N.Y. Docket No. 66, Crim. 831 (1968).
43. Charge of the Court, *United States of America v. Carl Simon, et. al.*, New York, June 20, 1968, 39.
44. *Ibid.*, 15.
45. *The Wall Street Journal*, Friday, September 27, 1968, 5.
46. Memorandum of American Institute of Certified Public Accountants, *Amicus Curiae*, in *USA V. Simon, et. al.*, August 23, 1968. Reprinted in *The Journal of Accountancy* 126 (November, 1968), 54-64.

SELECTED BIBLIOGRAPHY

Boutell, W.S. *Auditing with the Computer*. Berkeley and Los Angeles: University of California Press, 1965, 46-59.
Brown, R. Gene. "Changing Audit Objectives and Techniques." *Accounting Review* 37 (October, 1962), 696-703.
Carey, John L. *The Rise of the Accounting Profession* (2 vols.). New York: AICPA, 1969-1970.
Cochrane, George. "The Auditor's Report. Its Evolution in the U.S.A." *Accountant* 123 (November 4, 1950), 448-60.
DeMond, C.W. *Price, Waterhouse and Company in America*. New York: Comet Press, 1951.
Dicksee, Lawrence R. *Auditing*. R.H. Montgomery, ed. Authorized American edition. New York: 1905. Reprinted by Arno Press, New York, 1976.
Earl, Victor M. "The Litigation Explosion." *Journal of Accountancy* 129 (March, 1970), 65-67.
Edwards, James Don. *History of Public Accounting in the United States*. East Lansing: Michigan State University, 1961.

Gassmann, Rosa-Elizabeth. "Survey of the Development of Auditing in Germany." *Academy of Accounting Historians Working Paper No. 4*. University, Alabama: Academy of Accounting Historians, 1974.

Johnson, J.T., and Brasseaux, J.H., eds. *Readings in Auditing*, 2nd ed. Cincinnati: Southwestern Publishing Company, 1965.

Levy, Saul. *Accountants' Legal Responsibility*. New York: American Institute of Accountants, 1954.

Littleton, A.C., and Zimmerman, V.K. *Accounting Theory: Continuity and Change*. Englewood Cliffs, N.J.: Prentice-Hall, 1962, chap. five.

Mautz, R.K., and Sharaf, Hussein A. *The Philosophy of Auditing*. American Accounting Association Monograph Number 6. Menasha, Wisc.: American Accounting Association, 1961.

May, George O. *Financial Accounting—A Distillation of Experience*. New York: Macmillan, 1946. Reprinted by Scholars Book Company, Houston.

_____. *George Oliver May: Twenty-Five Years of Accounting Responsibility, 1911-1936*. Bishop Carlton Hunt, ed. New York: Price, Waterhouse, 1936. Reprinted by Scholars Book Company, Lawrence, Kansas, 1971.

Montgomery, Robert H. *Auditing Theory and Practice*. New York: Ronald Press Company, 1912. Reprinted by Arno Press, New York, 1976.

_____. *Fifty Years of Accountancy*. Privately printed by the Ronald Press Company, 1939. Chapters one and two.

Moyer, C.A. "Early Developments in American Auditing." *Accounting Review* 26 (January, 1951), 3-8.

Rappaport, Louis H. *SEC Accounting Practice and Procedure*, 2d ed. New York: Ronald Press Company, 1963.

Rich, Wiley D. *Legal Responsibilities and Rights of Public Accountants*. New York: American Institute Publishing Company, 1935.

Staub, Walter A. *Auditing Developments During the Present Century*. Cambridge, Mass.: Harvard University Press, 1942.

Chapter 11

PROFESSIONAL DEVELOPMENT

Italy, where modern bookkeeping originated, also produced the first societies of professional accountants. The oldest of these was the *Collegio dei Rexonati* (college of accountants) of Venice, founded in 1581. The applicant for membership had first to obtain a certificate of fitness from a magistrate. He was then required to serve a six year apprenticeship in the office of a public accountant, usually between the ages of eighteen and twenty-four, the latter being the minimum age for admission to the society. Before being eligible for the entrance examination, the candidate had to get another declaration by a magistrate that he met the legal requirements, plus a certificate from the accountant with whom he had served his apprenticeship. He then appeared before a commission of forty-five examiners, including thirty accountants. Two thirds of the commissioners having decided that he should be admitted to examination, he answered orally two questions drawn by lot. To pass he needed the approval of two thirds of the commissioners. Thereafter he had to submit to a similar examination given by the controllers of accounts and five learned merchants. If he got three fourths of their votes he was granted a certificate of admission to the college, in effect a license to practice. By 1669 the college had become so powerful that no Venetian could do accounting work, either in connection with public administration or the law, unless he was a member.[1]

A similar organization was established in 1739 by the practicing accountants of Milan. Its admission requirements included a familiarity with commerce, economics, and public affairs, a knowledge of Latin and arithmetic, a five-year apprenticeship, the attainment of age twenty-five, and passing a formal examination in accounting. Unlike the state-supported association in Venice, the college in Milan was entirely a private society, and never succeeded in monopolizing the practice of accounting for its members. But in 1742 the city government established a uniform scale of charges for accounting work and disbarred from practice any accountant charging more or less than this legal tariff. The colleges at Venice and Milan had imitators throughout Italy, and by the nineteenth century a majority of the Italian States had passed laws providing that no one could practice as an accountant without being a member of a recognized association.[2]

These early accounting societies had no traceable influence on British and American developments, and are chiefly interesting as prototypes. Then as later, what might be called the pattern of professionalization began with a recognized public need for accounting data, which led to government regulation of certain accounting functions and to legal encouragement of attempts to organize groups of practitioners. The profession's acceptance of social responsibility took the form of licensing, of admission standards to separate the qualified from the less qualified, of training programs to raise levels of competence, and of ethical codes to maintain cohesion among the initiated. Other professions developed in a similar way at about the same time,[3] yet accountancy never has attained the status of medicine or law. American and British accounting societies have been unable to impose uniform standards on all practitioners, or control the education of their members, or eliminate competition by the unlicensed. Their continuing insecure position among professional groups has limited accountants' effectiveness in every effort where public understanding and confidence were important factors.

ENGLAND AND SCOTLAND

The eighteenth century accountant had as many functions as the Babylonian scribe. Indeed the variety of his tasks and the different degrees of skill involved were major impediments to professional identity. Anyone who kept accounts might be considered and could consider himself an accountant. "Merchant and accountant" and "accountant and agent" were commonly used titles. Much accounting work was subsidiary to the practice of law and was performed in solicitors' offices. Others calling themselves accountants held government posts or court appointments in which their bookkeeping skill was less important than impartiality and personal integrity. Accountants in public practice tended to be concerned with unusual events in the life of a business. They were appraisers, executors of estates, actuaries, trustees in bankruptcy, liquidators of dissolved companies. In 1773 the city directory of Edinburgh contained the names of seven accountants, and in the following year seventeen. The earliest mention of a public accountant in London occurred in 1776. By 1800 there were about 600 accountants in England and Wales, most of them practicing accountancy as a sideline to more profitable businesses, such as auctioneering, rent collecting, or stockbrokerage.[4] Littleton concludes that at that time there was still no accounting profession in Great Britain.[5]

The rapid increase in commerce and industry during the nineteenth century was a necessary but not sufficient reason for the rise of professional accountancy. Professional coherence also required specialization in a few skilled tasks and identification with them. And it was important that such duties should include recognizable public service functions as well as the traditional record keeping services performed for individual businessmen. Fortunately or unfortunately, the economic turbulence of the time caused these requirements to be amply fulfilled. The British accounting profession "was born through bankruptcies, fed on failures and frauds, grew on liquidations and graduated through audits."[6]

AUDITS AND LIQUIDATIONS

Accounting investigations became an almost traditional response to financial disaster. The collapse of the South Sea Bubble in 1720 had produced Charles Snell's audit of Sawbridge and Company. When the American Revolution precipitated a wave of bankruptcies among Glascow merchants in 1777, accountants were appointed as trustees for the creditors.[7] Then came the crisis of 1793, during which more than twenty banking companies failed. Accountants were commissioned to settle their affairs. The need for safeguards against fraud on the part of corporate promoters and directors led to the inclusion of audit provisions in the companies acts. During the "railroad mania" of the 1840s, the Companies' Clauses Consolidation Act provided for the appointment of shareholder-auditors by railways and specified that they might hire professional accountants to assist them. As representatives of the stockholders, such accountants assumed a quasi-judicial position independent of management.

The Companies Act of 1862 soon became known as "the accountant's friend."[8] By requiring that dividends could be paid only from income, it made the services of skilled accountants absolutely necessary. Auditors no longer had to be stockholders, and their precise duties for examination and reporting were set forth. The 1862 Act also created the position of official liquidator for the purpose of winding up insolvent companies, and this job was usually given to a professional accountant. The first important liquidations under the act followed the collapse of Overend, Gurney and Company, Ltd., together with four large banks, during the crisis of 1866. The failure of the City of Glasgow Bank in 1878 directed attention to public accountants when leading Glasgow practitioners took charge of the liquidation while others testified for the prosecution or the defense. A law passed in the following year required annual audits of financial institutions in return for the privilege of incorporation with limited liability.

THE BANKRUPTCY ACTS

H. A. Shannon estimates that just over 30 percent of all English corporations formed between 1856 and 1883 ended in insolvency, and that a majority of these were liquidated within six years of their inception.[9] Business depressions followed one another with machinelike regularity. The British government responded to these crises, with their attendant upsurge of business failures, by passing a series of bankruptcy acts.[10] It is likely that no other laws enacted during the nineteenth century, not even the companies acts, provided so much work for accountants. The stewardship provisions of these statutes varied, but all required the appointment of administrators to take control of the bankrupt's property, both in his interests and to protect his creditors from asset concealment and conversion.

The 1825 Bankruptcy Act authorized the appointment of commissioners in bankruptcy to manage the properties of insolvent debtors. The 1831 Act created a court of bankruptcy and gave the lord chancellor authority to select not more than thirty official assignees, "being merchants, bankers, accountants, or traders." This was the first governmental recognition of English accountants, who were particularly fitted for these jobs because the reasons for insolvency were sought by a process of tracing back through the debtor's accounts to the time when he was solvent. The Bankruptcy Act of 1849 created a specific role for accountants by requiring every bankrupt to deliver his account books to an official assignee and help him prepare a summary of his financial condition. The bankrupt also had to file such balance sheets and accounts as the court directed, and swear to their truth. Passing the final hearing in bankruptcy court depended on a favorable report by the official assignee regarding the accuracy of the accounts. It became usual for the debtor awaiting discharge to employ a public accountant to make sure that his statement of affairs and deficiency statement would pass inspection. This was also prudent because creditors opposed to a bankruptcy settlement sometimes hired accountants of their own to investigate the statements filed by a debtor with the court.[11]

The 1861 Bankruptcy Act abolished the position of official assignee and placed the debtor's property in the hands of assignees chosen by the creditors. The latter usually preferred outright liquidation to bankruptcy proceedings, and they now had the power to make compositions and distribute the bankrupt's assets as they pleased without court intervention. Under the Act of 1869, accountants were engaged not only to appraise and manage the property of bankrupts, but actually to liquidate insolvent businesses on behalf of the creditors. So many unqualified men began calling themselves accountants to obtain this employment that "within a few years after the act accountants doubled in numbers."[12] A nationwide professional organization sanctioned by the government was needed to help the public distinguish competent practitioners from these opportunists.

PROFESSIONAL SOCIETIES

The profession developed earlier in Scotland than in England, due partly to the Scots tradition of allowing accountants to handle certain fiduciary duties which in England were given to court-appointed officials. The first accountant's organization in Great Britain was the Society of Accountants in Edinburgh, founded in 1853 and in 1854 granted a royal charter which permitted its members to designate themselves "chartered accountants." The Institute of Accountants and Actuaries in Glasgow received a similar charter in 1855, as did the Society of Accountants in Aberdeen in 1867. Local accountants' societies were formed in London (1870), Liverpool (1870), Manchester (1871), and Sheffield (1877). Within a few years membership in the London society was made available to practitioners in all parts of the United Kingdom, and the name was changed from the Institute of Accountants in London to the Institute of Accountants. In March 1880 the five existing English societies were incorporated into the Institute of Chartered Accountants in England and Wales. The new organization began with 527 members; before February 1881, its membership had increased to 1025.[13]

The dilemma of professional association is that unless every practitioner is allowed to enter, some will form rival groups; but if all are accepted, the major purposes of association will be frustrated. The Institute's tenure as the only English accounting society was brief. During the 1880s alone four new accounting groups were organized in England. Since the founding members of each society were admitted without examination, it was tempting and only natural for those excluded or overlooked by the Institute to protect their competitive position by forming organizations of their own. In this way the tendency to combine was offset by a tendency for successful organizations to spawn imitators with less strict admission standards, creating a hierarchy of similar groups each a step lower down on the professional scale. Moreover, the growing demand for accounting services furnished a living for many who remained completely unorganized, and produced thousands of additional "accountants" whose skills were essentially secretarial.

The Institute's charter provided that public accountants who had been in continuous practice for five years from January 1, 1879 were to be admitted as Fellow Chartered Accountants (FCA), while those who prior to charter had been for three years in public practice or employed for five years as public account-clerks were to be admitted as Associate Chartered Accountants (ACA). After this initial registration, aspirants for Institute membership had to pass a series of examinations and serve a five-year, full-time apprenticeship in the office of a chartered accountant. The "articled clerk" received no salary; in fact chartered accountants were offered premiums of from $250 to $2500 by prospective apprentices for the privilege of working in their office.[14]

Beginning in July 1882, candidates for Institute membership were required to pass three examinations, whose subject matter was as follows:

Preliminary examination—
Writing from dictation, writing a short English composition, arithmetic, algebra, Euclid, geography, history of England, elementary Latin, *options:* two of the following—Latin, Greek, French, German, physics, chemistry, animal physiology, electricity, magnetism, light geology, higher mathematics.

Intermediate examination—
Bookkeeping, accounting, auditing, adjustment of partnership and executorship accounts, rights and duties of trustees, liquidations and receiverships.

Final examination—
In addition to further questions on the topics in the intermediate examination: principles of the law of bankruptcy, joint-stock companies, mercantile practices, arbitration and award.[15]

The tests given by the Scots societies covered a similar but even wider range of subjects.[16]

Preparation for such examinations clearly required more than office training. Yet most English accounting societies were located in commercial centers which had no universities, and so the technical education of apprentices depended mainly on the profession's own efforts.[17] These were reflected first in an upgrading of the periodical literature, particularly in the increased attention given auditing.[18] *The Accountant,* founded in 1874, became the recognized voice of English chartered accountants, while the three Scots societies in 1897 established *The Accountants' Magazine.* Textbooks by Pixley and Dicksee gave auditing methods an academic and conceptual basis. In 1883 *The Accountant Student's Journal* appeared. Student societies formed in Edinburgh (1886) and London (1890) sponsored lectures and discussions for apprentices. In 1893 the Institute established its own library in London.

The number of British accountants nearly quadrupled between 1840 and 1870.[19] The variety of their tasks also grew, and by 1900 public accountants increasingly specialized in a particular type of work, or even in auditing certain types of companies. Throughout Western Europe professional accounting development during this period followed a generally similar course.[20] Government regulation of corporate relations with investors and creditors required professional identification among accountants because it required that accounting's public-service functions be performed in a socially responsible way. As the last of the major techniques to attain professional status in Britain, accountancy was recognized as important but not yet as prestigious. Few who had the choice of practicing the older professions seem to have been attracted to it.[21]

THE UNITED STATES

Late in the nineteenth century British accountants became frequent visitors to the United States, where they investigated the accounts of railroads, breweries, and other properties in which their clients had investments. Their arrival coincided with major developments in American finance. Industrial firms were beginning to incorporate and offer their securities to the public. A growing merger movement created a demand for auditors. The federal government was becoming involved in economic regulation, and an income tax seemed inevitable. Four of the present "big eight" CPA firms were founded by immigrant chartered accountants. Members of Price, Waterhouse and Company were active in the United States as early as 1873, and the company's first American office was opened in 1890. The Scots accountants James Marwick, John B. Niven, and Arthur Young helped establish other major firms. The fact that America was repeating so many aspects of their own country's experience gave these men a great competitive advantage over the typical American practitioner, who was still occupied with bookkeeping and low-level management services.[22] British accountants formed the first national firms in the United States. They actively promoted the idea of professional organization. At a time when there was almost no native accounting literature, they trained American staff members in English comprehensive audit techniques. The profession in America was built largely on British foundations.

PROFESSIONAL SOCIETIES

The first practitioners' group which aspired to national influence was the American Association of Public Accountants, founded in 1886. Though it adopted bylaws similar to those of the English Institute, and in 1894 proposed rules for presenting balance sheet items "in order of quickest realization," the Association remained a poor imitation of the British societies. This was due partly to the absence of federal audit and bankruptcy statutes which in Britain had stimulated public-service accounting and given it a focus. Whereas the English Institute had begun with over 500 members, the Association started with just thirty-one, and after ten years had increased this to only forty-five, most of them residents of the New York City area.[23] Under such conditions the benefits of restrictive admission standards always had to be balanced against the need to compete with rival groups for a basic cadre of members. Accordingly the Association required no examination for membership. It never produced workable programs of apprenticeship or education, and its members did not even have the sole use of an identifying title. The profession in America simply was not strong enough to be exclusive.

In 1896 New York State passed the first law providing for issuance of CPA certificates to qualified practitioners. During the next twenty-five years this type of state licensing was extended throughout the country. It amounted to statutory recognition of the right to use a title, but the CPA certificate was not a degree which followed a course of study, nor did it confer the right to monopolize any area of accounting practice. It was soon evident that professional accreditation under state laws made uniform federal legislation impossible and standardization of practice more difficult than in England, where the societies themselves licensed their members. There was the problem of dealing with forty-eight state legislatures, each of which had its own rules for certification and reciprocity. The founders of the American Association had hoped to create a national organization which would govern the profession. But following passage of the CPA laws, the Association became virtually a federation of autonomous state societies, and as such proved incapable of enforcing ethical or technical standards.

In 1916 the American Association of Public Accountants became the American Institute of Accountants in the United States of America. The new organization could not hope to supplant the state CPA societies or offer a form of accreditation superior to the CPA certificate. But by setting respectable admission standards, enforcing its own code of conduct, and remaining free of legislative influence, it could promote a common professional identity for accountants throughout the country. Full membership required five consecutive years of practice as a partner or sole practitioner, plus the passing of a written or oral examination. Associate members, who had no vote, only had to present "satisfactory" evidence of education, training, and experience in public accounting, and pass an examination. At the end of its first year the American Institute of Accountants as it was now called had 1100 members and 120 associates. There were at that time only about 3300 CPAs in the United States,[24] and enrollment was not limited to them. Indeed, one purpose of the new group was to organize public accountants who could not meet the requirements of state CPA societies. Dissatisfaction with this and other Institute policies led to the formation of the rival American Society of CPAs in 1921, and it was not until sixteen years later, when the Institute restricted its membership to CPAs, that the two groups of practitioners were finally united.

The Institute's Board of Examiners began preparing "uniform" CPA examinations in 1917, and within a few years these were being used in nearly every state. As tests both of a candidate's fitness to practice and for admission to the Institute, standard examinations furthered the cause of professional cohesion. Efforts to restrict the practice of public accounting proved less successful. A provision of the 1917 Oklahoma Accountancy Act which limited public accounting practice to CPAs was declared unconstitutional in 1924. Most states had enacted "permissive" laws which allowed anyone to perform the functions of a public accountant, merely reserving use of the title "CPA" to those licensed as such. A series of court tests did establish the right of states to limit public practice to CPAs and registered noncertified accountants, and a number of such "regulatory" laws were passed during the 1920s. They may or may not have raised levels of competence, but their visible effect was to create different and mutually antagonistic classes of practitioners: CPAs who were licensed by examination, and Public Accountants, Licensed Public Accountants, and so forth who were not. In general, the legal regulation of accountancy during this period lagged behind the profession's own efforts to improve the qualifications of new accountants and the public image of its members.[25]

The United States was the first nation to recognize accounting as a discipline deserving a place in the university curriculum.[26] In 1883 the Wharton School of the University of Pennsylvania offered the first course in the subject. By 1900 twelve American universities included accounting courses in their curricula, and this number increased to fifty-two in 1910 and 116 in 1916. By 1920 most large universities were offering degrees in business administration with a major in accounting.[27] When college education became a normal means of preparation, accountancy became accessible to many who would not have considered a long apprenticeship. Even more significant was the fact that practitioners established strong academic ties at a formative stage in the profession's development. The universities produced a coterie of accounting theorists who, as in no other country, established a conceptual basis for practice. In 1916 academic accountants organized the American Association of University Instructors in Accounting, later renamed the American Accounting Association. In 1926 *The Accounting Review* began publication.

STANDARDS OF CONDUCT

Self-regulation is an identifying feature of every professional group, and the progress of American accountancy can be traced through the evolution of its rules of conduct. Attempts to narrow differences in practice by establishing technical standards based on accounting principles would almost certainly have failed without prior agreement on standards of behavior. The division of authority within the profession meant that there were several sources of accounting ethics: the Institute, each state CPA society, the state boards of accountancy, and later the SEC. An accountant might be bound by one of these, by several, or by none, and a frequent complaint was that the licensed and organized put themselves at a competitive disadvantage. But all these codes were similar enough so that the Institute's can be taken as representative.

The earliest rules of conduct stressed professional identification and the creation of a group image typical of the established professions. The bylaws of the American Association of Public Accountants (1889) prohibited members from splitting fees and from allowing nonmembers to practice in their names. Following establishment of *The Journal of Accountancy* in 1905, much concern was expressed about practices which led the public to confuse accountants with laymen. By 1907 the Association had passed three additional rules: (1) a member could not take part in any business incompatible with public accounting; (2) he could not certify work done by nonaccountants; and (3) he could not use the initials "CPA" unless he was licensed by the state.[28]

But to a foreign observer[29] it seemed that there were no restrictions at all on the practice of American accounting. Accountants advertised in the newspapers, bid against one another for jobs, and gave advance estimates of fees. One reason for the founding of the Institute in 1916 was that the American Association, having enrolled the members of state societies *en masse,* failed in its attempts to impose discipline by proxy. In 1917 the Institute's Council approved the following eight rules:

1. A CPA firm cannot describe itself as "members of the American Institute of Accountants" unless every partner in the firm is an Institute member.
2. A member shall not knowingly certify to financial statements which contain an essential misstatement of fact or omissions which amount to an essential misstatement.
3. He shall not allow anyone to practice in his name who is not his partner, employee, or a member of the Institute.
4. He shall not share fees with the laity or accept "kickbacks" for referrals.
5. He shall not engage in any activity which is incompatible or inconsistent with his accounting practice.
6. He shall not express an opinion on financial statements unless they have been examined under his supervision, or that of his partner, his employee, a member of the Institute, or a member of a similar association abroad.
7. He shall not participate in any effort to enact or alter legislation affecting accounting practice, without informing the Institute.
8. He shall not solicit the clients or encroach upon the business of another member of the Institute.[30]

These rules and those which followed showed concern for professional identity, but also for technical performance and the practitioner's responsibility to his clients and the public. Before 1917 the most debated ethical issue was whether or not accountants should advertise; afterwards, and especially since 1933, it has been auditor independence.[31] The original "state of mind" doctrine of independence meant simply that the relations between client and accountant should be such that the latter's findings would be influenced only by facts. The later "appearance to others" concept showed the profession's growing maturity by placing less emphasis on *actions* and more on *relationships.* The value of the CPA's opinion to those who relied on audited statements was seen to depend not only on his examination of the records but specifically on his independence and integrity. In other words, the accountant now sought the public's confidence not so much to enhance his professional status as to increase the importance of his work.

The more significant later rules, in order of their adoption, were:

9. A member shall not solicit a fellow member's employees without first informing the member (1919).
10. He shall not engage in the corporate practice of public accounting (1919).
11. He shall not make the amount of his fees contingent on the results obtained (1919).
12. He shall not advertise (1922).
13. He shall not vouch for the accuracy of forecasts of future earnings (1932).
14. He shall not make competitive bids for engagements (1934).

15. He shall have no substantial financial interest in companies he audits (1941).
16. He shall not violate his confidential relationship with his clients (1941).
17. In rendering services of a type performed by public accountants, he must observe the Institute's ethical code (1948).
18. Before accepting engagements obtained by referral he must consult with his prospective client's former accountant (1958).
19. He shall not allow an employee to perform a service he himself is not allowed to perform (1958).
20. He shall not commit an act discreditable to the profession (1962).
21. He shall have no financial interest in companies he audits (1964).

Ethics violations have never been a major problem. As Institute membership multiplied, the number who were admonished, suspended, or expelled remained about the same each year.[32] Overt forms of competition among practitioners gradually became more subdued.[33] The beliefs that accountants should be independent, that they should not advertise or solicit business, and that they should adhere to certain technical standards were as old as the profession. The members' willingness to make these unwritten rules explicit was itself evidence of professional self-confidence and growth.

THE SUMMING UP

Speaking at the annual meeting of the American Institute in 1924, Henry Rand Hatfield offered a partly satirical but largely objective assessment of the profession's status:

> But accounting is, alas, only a pseudoscience ... its products are displayed neither in the salon nor in the national academy; one finds it discussed by neither realist, idealist, nor phenomenalist. The humanists look down upon us as beings who dabble in the sordid figures of dollars and cents instead of toying with infinities and searching for the elusive soul of things; the scientists and technologists despise us as able only to record rather than to perform deeds.
>
> The contempt for accounting is not limited to university circles, but is well-nigh universal. It is evidenced by ignorance of the subject, by condescension toward its devotees, by their exclusion from polite literature.[34]

Clearly the profession's status did not accord with its accomplishments. In 1917, the year in which the Institute brought out the first comprehensive American ethical code for accountants, it also offered the first uniform CPA examination and published in the *Federal Reserve Bulletin* the first set of technical standards for auditing and financial reporting. American cost accounting was probably the best in the world. Montgomery, Cole, Sprague, and Hatfield himself had produced the only body of accounting textbook literature which had a theoretical content. The transition from serving individual businessmen to accounting for large corporations and reporting to their investors was already under way, but its success depended on public understanding, and the social importance of accountancy was only gradually being recognized. Events of the 1930s, in particular the publicizing of accounting shortcomings by the SEC, would show practitioners that to be ignored was not the worst that could happen.

FOOTNOTES

1. Richard Brown, ed., *A History of Accounting and Accountants* (Edinburgh: Jack, 1905), 177.
2. *Ibid.*, 178-80.
3. K.L. Milne, *The Accountant in Public Practice* (London: Butterworth, 1959), 251-58.
4. N.A.H. Stacey, *English Accountancy: A study in Social and Economic History, 1800-1954* (London: Gee, 1954), 17.
5. A.C. Littleton, *Accounting Evolution to 1900* (New York: American Institute Publishing Company, 1933), 268.
6. H.W. Robinson, *A History of Accountants in Ireland* (Dublin: Institute of Chartered Accountants in Ireland, 1964), 30.
7. James Don Edwards, *History of Public Accounting in the United States* (East Lansing: Michigan State University, 1961), 6-12.
8. Brown, *op. cit.*, 318.
9. H.A. Shannon, "The First Five Thousand Limited Companies and their Duration," *Economic History* 2 (1932).
10. See Littleton, *op. cit.*, 277.
11. A.H. Woolf, *A Short History of Accountants and Accountancy* (London: Gee, 1912), 174.
12. Quoted in Littleton, *op. cit.*, 282.
13. *Ibid.*, 316.
14. Edwards, *op. cit.*, 24.
15. Littleton, *op. cit.*, 316-17.
16. *Ibid.*, 317.
17. R.H. Parker, "Lower of Cost or Market in Britain and the United States: An Historical Survey," *Abacus* 1 (December, 1965), 163.
18. Littleton, *op. cit.*, 317-18.
19. A.C. Littleton, "Public Accounting in the United States," in *Essays in Accountancy* (Urbana: University of Illinois Press, 1961), 98.
20. See Brown, *op. cit.*, 281-301; E. van Dien, "The Development of Professional Accounting in Continental Europe," *Accountant* 81 (1929), 409-17, 439-48.
21. Stacey, *op. cit.*, 50.
22. M.E. Peloubet, "The Historical Development of Accounting," in Morton Backer, ed., *Modern Accounting Theory* (Englewood Cliffs, N.J.: Prentice-Hall, 1966), 5.
23. Edwards, *op. cit.*, 84.
24. John L. Carey, *The Rise of the Accounting Profession*, 2 vols. (New York: AICPA, 1969-1970), vol. 1, 317.
25. Edwards, *op. cit.*, 101-47.
26. *Ibid.*, 60-61.
27. C.E. Allen, "The Growth of Accounting Instruction Since 1900," *Accounting Review* 2 (June, 1927), 160.
28. Carey, *op. cit.*, 85-86.
29. Brown, *op. cit.*, 279.
30. Quoted in Edwards, *op. cit.*, 255-56.
31. Carey, *op. cit.*, 88-90.
32. Darwin, J. Casler, *The Evolution of C.P.A. Ethics: A Profile of Professionalization* (East Lansing: Bureau of Business and Economic Research, Michigan State University, 1964), 117.
33. *Ibid.*, 116.
34. Henry Rand Hatfield, "An Historical Defense of Bookkeeping," *Journal of Accountancy* 37 (April, 1924), 241.

SELECTED BIBLIOGRAPHY

Allen, C.E. "The Growth of Accounting Instruction Since 1900." *Accounting Review* 2 (June, 1927), 150-66.
Anyon, James T. *Recollections of The Early Days of American Accountancy, 1883-1893.* New York: 1925. Reprinted by Nihon Shoseki, Osaka, 1974.
Brief, Richard P. "The Accountant's Responsibility in Historical Perspective." *Accounting Review* 50 (April, 1975), 285-297.
Brown, Richard, ed. *A History of Accounting and Accountants.* Edinburgh: Jack, 1905. Reprinted by B. Franklin, New York, 1966, 173-452.
Carey, John L. *The Rise of the Accounting Profession,* 2 vols. New York: AICPA, 1969-1970.
_____. "The C.P.A.'s Professional Heritage." *Academy of Accounting Historians Working Papers 1 and 5.* University, Alabama: Academy of Accounting Historians, 1974.
Carey, John L., and Doherty, William O. *Ethical Standards of the Accounting Profession.* New York: AICPA, 1966, chap. one.
Casler, Darwin J. *The Evolution of C.P.A. Ethics: A Profile of Professionalization.* East Lansing: Bureau of Business and Economic Research, Michigan State University, 1964.
Dickenson, Arthur Lowes. *Accounting Practice and Procedure.* London: 1914. Reprinted by Scholars Book Company, Houston, 1975. Chapter ten.
Dien, E. van. "The Development of Professional Accounting in Continental Europe." *Accountant* 81 (1929), 409-17, 439-48.
Edwards, James Don. *History of Public Accounting in the United States.* East Lansing: Michigan State University, 1961.
_____. "The Antecedents of American Public Accounting." In M. Chatfield, ed. *Contemporary Studies in the Evolution of Accounting Thought.* Belmont, Cal.: Dickenson Publishing Company, 1968, 144-66.
Grady, Paul, ed. *Memoirs and Accounting Thought of George O. May.* New York: Ronald Press Company, 1962.
Green, Wilmer. *History and Survey of Accountancy.* Brooklyn: Standard Text Press, 1930. Reprinted by Nihon Shoseki, Osaka, 1974, 95-122.
Hunthausen, John M. "The Evolution of Accountancy Education and Certification Standards." *Colorado CPA Report* (Spring, 1975), 15-24.
Johnson, T.J., and Caygill, M. "The Development of Accountancy Links in the Commonwealth." *Accounting and Business Research* 1 (1971), 155-173.
Knight, C.L., Previts, G.J., and Ratcliffe, T.A. *A Reference Chronology of Events Significant to the Development of Accountancy in the United States.* University, Alabama: Academy of Accounting Historians, 1976.
Littleton, A.C. *Accounting Evolution to 1900.* New York: American Institute Publishing Company, 1933. Reprinted by Russell and Russell, New York, 1966, 265-87.
_____. *Essays on Accountancy.* Urbana: University of Illinois Press, 1961, 93-99, 115-41, 445-70.
Lockwood, J. "Early University Education in Accountancy." *Accounting Review* 13 (June, 1938), 131-44.
Mendes, H.E., "The Development of Uniform Examinations." *Accounting Review* 19 (April, 1944), 139-42.
Merino, Barbara D. *The Professionalization of Public Accounting in America: A Comparative Analysis of the Contributions of Selected Practitioners 1900-1925.* Unpublished Ph.D. dissertation, University of Alabama, 1975. University Microfilms, Ann Arbor, Michigan.
Murphy, Mary E. *Advanced Public Accounting Practice.* Homewood, Ill.: Richard D. Irwin, 1966, chaps. one and two.
_____. "The British Accounting Tradition in America." *Journal of Accountancy* 111 (April, 1961), 54-63.
_____. "The Rise of the Profession in England." *Accounting Review* 15 (March, 1940), 62-71.
Murray, David. *Chapters in the History of Bookkeeping, Accountancy, and Commerical Arithmetic.* Glascow: Jackson, Wylie, 1930, 52-122.
Parker, R.H. *Management Accounting: an Historical Perspective.* New York: Augustus M. Kelley, 1969, chap. six.
Peloubet, M.E., "The Historical Development of Accounting." In Morton Backer, ed. *Modern Accounting Theory.* Englewood Cliffs, N.J.: Prentice-Hall, 1966, 5-27.

Simpson, R.J. "American Accounting Education, Textbooks, and Public Practice Prior to 1900." *Business History Review* 34 (1960), 459-66.

Stacey, N.A.H. *English Accountancy: A Study in Social and Economic History, 1800-1954.* London: Gee, 1954, chap. one.

"Steps in the Evolution of the Profession in the United Kingdom." *Accountant* 137, (November 9, 1957), 544-45.

Stewart, J.C. "Qualification for Membership a Hundred Years Ago." *Accountant's Magazine* 78 (July, 1974), 263-265.

———. "The Emergent Professionals." *Accountant's Magazine* 79 (March, 1975), 113-116.

Sullivan, John P. "The Accountant as Consultant: a Historical Review." *Journal of Accountancy* 138 (November, 1974), 92-95.

Woolf, A.H. *A Short History of Accountants and Accountancy.* London: Gee, 1912. Reprinted by Nihon Shoseki, Osaka, 1974. Chapters fourteen, fifteen, and sixteen.

Chapter 12

THE GENESIS OF MODERN COST ACCOUNTING

We have seen that early industrial corporations largely reinvented the type of prime cost system first developed in Renaissance Italy. Before 1885 neither accountants nor industrialists showed great interest in rationalizing factory accounts. Manufacturers guarded their cost methods as industrial secrets. Bookkeeping texts generally ignored the subject, and the few which considered it had almost no effect on later practice. English and American cost finding in the 1870s was only marginally better than that of the Medicis 400 years earlier.[1]

This slow development of factory accounting was due partly to the very limited use made of cost data. The usual motive was simply to cumulate the ending inventory figure needed to complete financial accounting records and reports.[2] This could be done by opening a manufacturing account in the general ledger, which was debited for the costs of material and labor put into process and credited with sales proceeds, the remainder being profit and inventory. It was also recognized that careful records of past costs were needed to improve price estimating in firms which customarily got jobs through competitive bidding. Solomons considers that the most important factor leading to a growth of interest in costing was the increasing difficulty of price setting in the engineering industry.[3] As engineering firms grew and became more competitive, precise cost estimates were needed for bidding on the type of job which was specially contracted for and for which there was no scale of market prices.

159

Yet even here accounting figures were at first rarely used as direct aids to managerial control or decision making.

Cost control was stimulated by falling prices during the last quarter of the nineteenth century, and even more by the increasing complexity and scale of industrial operations. Intricate production processes had to be organized; the work of thousands of men had to be coordinated. The tendency of industrial corporations to acquire subsidiaries created a need for centralized control of widely scattered operations. The introduction of heavy powered machinery in the iron, coal, and textile industries made indirect costs important just at the time when the broadening of product lines complicated overhead calculation and allocations. In the 1870s American industry still served a largely agrarian economy. Businesses tended to be small and usually bought and sold locally. But by 1900 most major industries had become dominated by a few vertically integrated corporations producing for national markets. In many cases production costs now became more important than interfirm competition in determining the selling prices of consumer goods.

Under these new conditions the usual prime cost system left many questions unanswered. There was some theoretical understanding of overhead before 1885, but great difficulty in assigning it to products because the cost records and the double entry books were not coordinated. Only past costs were calculated, and the process was normally one of simple accumulation, with no attempt made to record the conversions of value which occurred during the manufacturing process. There was little uniformity of technique or sense of best practice. No clear distinction was made between factory and administrative costs, or even between expenses and losses. The effect of volume changes on costs was not generally understood, and almost no one thought of segregating fixed and variable cost elements. Cost authorities had little to say about making systematic choices among alternative methods of operation or production. Nor was there any sense of holding individuals responsible for their performance by comparisons between actual and standard costs.

Between 1885 and 1920 cost accounting evolved from a level where the methods used seem almost as remote as medieval bookkeeping, to a point where most of the descriptions in today's texts were approximated by the best practice. The economic progress of large corporations urgently required this transformation and perhaps made it inevitable, but it does not seem that the corporations themselves directly added much to the discipline's growth. Though hundreds of accountants and engineers made contributions to this "cost accounting renaissance," its main lines of development can be traced in the writings of ten men. Metcalfe, Garcke and Fells, Norton, Lewis and Church were pioneers who introduced radically new cost concepts. Arnold and Nicholson consolidated these ideas and helped promote them in practice. Whitmore and Emerson added another dimension in the form of standard cost procedures.

BASIC INNOVATIONS
HENRY METCALFE
The first modern book on cost accounting was Captain Henry Metcalfe's *The Cost of Manufactures* (1885).[4] Metcalfe was an American Army ordinance officer, and his experience with arsenal production and discussions with commercial foremen convinced him that a better method was needed for assigning material and labor costs to jobs. Since the usual production records were informal memoranda books carried by shop foremen, only the most cursory data was kept on orders, which were often verbally authorized and were sometimes lost track of entirely. Neither the foreman's jottings nor the formal shop ledger seemed a proper mechanism for on-the-spot recording of shop floor events.

Metcalfe proposed that each material requisition or transfer be recorded on a separate "shop order card," which included spaces for pricing the article and for the job number to which it was charged. Similarly each workman was given a book of cards, and as he moved from job to job, he noted the time spent on each to the nearest quarter day. In this way a written record of costs literally followed the work through every factory department. Each day the cards were to be collected and a cost sheet compiled showing the materials and labor applied to particular jobs. Until an order was completed, the cards were filed by job numbers; afterwards, the cards for that job were summarized and entered in the shop order book. Metcalfe's system offered a novel and effective solution to the prime cost gathering problem, and there is evidence that it was widely used.

In 1885 overhead was not the problem it later became, and Metcalfe gave it relatively less attention. He demonstrated four overhead allocation methods: an arbitrary charge, a percentage of gross cost, a percentage of labor cost, and a charge varying with the time spent on production. He preferred the last, a forerunner of the direct labor hours method, on the grounds that indirect expenses were incurred mainly to increase labor's effectiveness. Pointing out that overhead costs were never precisely known till the year was over, he suggested dividing the total overhead charge for the preceding year (or the average of the past several years) by the total hours of shop work done during that period, to get a predetermined burden rate which could be applied to present jobs through his card system. But he never explained exactly how this was to be done or how absorbed overhead was to be reconciled with actual expenditures.

At least Metcalfe's instincts about overhead were sound. His attempt to tie cost accounts into the financial accounting system was an unredeemed and admitted failure. He was able partially to reconcile prime costs with the general ledger balances, but integrating overhead costs seemed impossible, or at least so difficult as not to be worth the trouble. "Substantial truth" he felt, would be "neglected for the sake of striking a balance."[5]

Though his book was intended for general use, Metcalfe's direct experience seems to have been limited to military production in an Army arsenal. His environment was in effect a large machine shop which required expensive capital equipment, specialized labor, and complicated production techniques involving a high probability of waste. His writing implies a continuous need to evaluate different complex situations. But he never had to worry about selling finished products or earning a profit on invested capital. Most private businesses of the time operated in a simpler cost environment, but with a wider range of problems. If he had shared their circumstances his book might have been different in scope and emphasis.

GARCKE AND FELLS

Two years after Metcalfe's book appeared, Emile Garcke, an English electrical engineer, and John Manger Fells, a chartered accountant, published *Factory Accounts*.[6] This was certainly the nineteenth century's best known and most influential work on costing[7] (it ran through seven editions by 1922). Garcke and Fells' description of the routine by which prime costs are passed through a series of ledger accounts from raw materials to finished goods sounds familiar and in fact has hardly been improved on. Material and labor expenses were transferred from stores and wages accounts to a summary "manufacturing" (work in process) account in the general ledger, which also received debits from the cashbook for expenditures directly applicable to the production process. Periodically the prime costs of goods completed were transferred from "manufacturing" to "stock" (finished goods), leaving the work in process in "manufacturing" and accumulating the cost of goods manufactured in "stock." Two entries were required when a sale was made. One credited "stock" and debited "trading" for the cost of goods sold; the other debited the customer for the selling price and credited "trading." The balances of the stores, manufacturing, and stock accounts showed ending inventories. The trading account showed total sales revenues in opposition to total cost of goods sold, and its balance was gross profit.[8]

Garcke and Fells were among the first to insist that all cost accounts be kept in double entry form and completely integrated with the financial accounting records.[9] This integration was not to be sacrificed simply because a plant had many departments or subsidiary ledgers; these only made coordination more imperative. Tying the two systems together obviously facilitated accounting control over materials and labor in the factory. In theory at least the stores account could at any time be reconciled with the stores ledger, the manufacturing account with the prime cost ledger, and the stock account with the stock ledger balances. The advantages of a coherent perpetual inventory were added to those of a job order cost system.

Only after cost and financial records were effectively combined in this way did cost finding become mainly an accounting task. According to Garner "It may be safely stated that the profession of cost accounting developed out of the attention which was shown in the subject by early industrial engineers."[10] Many engineers had argued that double entry bookkeeping, invented to record the exchange of finished goods with outsiders, was quite unsuitable for planning and controlling plant activities, where physical units were often more useful than monetary standards, and timely estimates better than later, more accurate measurements.

The merging of cost and financial accounting records which enhanced double entry bookkeeping as an administrative tool also influenced accounting theory.[11] The fact that balance sheet figures were supported not only by the general ledger but by subsidiary records added credibility to the historical cost principle at a time when valuation methods were very much in flux. The ability to measure internal and external value conversions on the same scale made the accrual concept more important and supported the emerging doctrines of realization and matching. Investments in future services, which often previously had been treated as expenses, began to be classed as deferred charges.

Garcke and Fells showed a conceptual understanding of overhead. They distinguished between factory costs and administrative expenses, and realized that the former should be allocated to jobs while the latter should go directly to profit and loss. They were far ahead of their time in reasoning that fixed costs, since they did not vary with changes in production volume, were a hindrance to managerial analysis and should be excluded from overhead allocations. But they confused the distinction between fixed and variable costs by inferring that all "shop expenses" were variable while nonfactory costs were not. Assuming that overhead was incurred to assist labor, they proposed to develop an allocation rate by dividing indirect costs by total direct labor hours. But this was to be done only after the whole year's expenses had been determined, and the actual procedure for passing overhead costs through the inventory accounts eluded them as it had Metcalfe.

GEORGE NORTON

The next important work on costing was *Textile Manufacturers' Bookkeeping* (1889)[12] by G. P. Norton, an English chartered accountant. As the title suggests, Norton drew his illustrations from the textile industry, where he was concerned with the departmental analysis of costs rather than their allocation to particular jobs. His explanation of process costing centered around a "manufacturing account," which was not a ledger account but a detailed summary of departmental operations.[13] Its first section included as debits the actual cost of materials used and the processing costs which *would have been incurred* if all the work done in the factory had instead been "put out" to subcontractors. The total of material costs and hypothetical processing costs was then deducted from sales and the cost of unsold goods to arrive at the gross profit which *would have been earned* by the traditional putting-out textile manufacturer. In Section II of Norton's manufacturing account, the actual gross profit of each department was contrasted with the hypothetical figures from Section I, any differences being the income or loss resulting from the owner's decision to have all work done in his own factory. The sum of these departmental profits and losses, plus the gross profit from Section I, less administrative expenses, equaled net operating income for the whole business.

Norton's comparisons of actual and imputed expenses seems to have been the nineteenth century's nearest approach to standard costing. It was modern in the sense that emphasis was less on *finding* costs than on *using* them to test operating efficiency. Norton's system helped managers judge whether a mill was producing economically, which departments did and did not pay, and whether selling prices were realistic. It was true that his "putting-out" prices could not readily be combined with the amounts in the double entry ledger. Norton kept his cost records separate from the commercial accounts, and thought it impractical and undesirable to consolidate the two. Also, he treated each department as a separate costing entity. There was as yet no method for cumulating process costs and passing them on from one operation to the next. Nonetheless his manufacturing account was adopted by textile mills in England and America, and was not improved on for a decade.[14]

J. SLATER LEWIS

Beginning about 1900, accountants began to pay serious attention to the overhead element of cost. It had become not only a problem in its own right, but one which blocked solutions to other problems. Earlier writers had been unable to agree on what expenses should be included in the overhead charge to jobs, or what basis of allocation should be used. Garcke and Fells had shown how prime costs could be brought into the double entry system, but no one had yet demonstrated a practical method for distributing overhead to work in process through the ledger accounts.

The English factory accountant Slater Lewis[15] was an early advocate of integrating cost and financial accounts, but his preferred treatment of overhead was to bring it in contact with prime costs only at the end of an accounting period. In 1896 he proposed that accounts containing overhead items be closed to profit and loss like ordinary expenses. At the same time work in process and finished goods would be debited with their respective shares of assignable overhead cost and a suspense account in the general ledger would be credited. At the start of the next period a reversing entry was to be made debiting suspense and crediting profit and loss. Then suspense was again debited and finished goods and work in process were credited, bringing the inventory accounts back to a prime cost basis and leaving the overhead cost as a balance in suspense. During the period this balance was to be absorbed gradually into the cost of goods sold, though Lewis failed to specify exactly how this would be done. Although his system was complicated, its effect was orthodox. It allowed overhead to be handled as a unit, avoided the problem of running it through the inventory accounts, and made sure that the amount applied to jobs exactly coincided with actual expenditures.

As if realizing that this solution skirted the essential difficulties, Lewis suggested an alternative. Certain overhead charges might be reduced to rates and absorbed directly into work in process. Overhead accounts would be debited to record actual expenditures, then credited for allocations to jobs according to the types of direct labor used on different projects. This of course is essentially the modern method, but one senses that Lewis did not feel safe with it. He thought that in most cases ratable burden allocations were not worth the trouble. And there was always the danger of a wrong absorption rate which would overallocate actual overhead and "create a fictitious asset." Compared to his suspense account allocation method, he was vague about procedure.

ALEXANDER HAMILTON CHURCH

Born in England, Hamilton Church was employed there as an expert in factory organization, and was at one time assistant to Slater Lewis. In 1898 he emigrated to America where, "shy and retiring, he lived for many years of his life almost as a recluse."[16] Church was the first important writer to place cost finding in the context of the manufacturing enterprise as a whole. His central theme was not simply better cost accounting but the rational organization of factory operations, which he found were frequently subject to the fallacy of "confounding bookkeeping with organization." (Though trained in accounting, he did not think much of accountants, and said so.) His particular interest was overhead expense, which he saw not as waste or unproductive cost but as a legitimate expenditure worth controlling, and indeed as a barometer of managerial skill. His six articles on "The Proper Distribution of Establishment Charges" in *Engineering Magazine* (1901) "at once took rank as a standard reference work on one of the most difficult questions of cost-finding."[17]

Church believed that while the usual overhead allocation methods might be satisfactory for historical reporting purposes, they failed as aids to management decision making. The manufacturer needed to know his product's cost before the goods were sold, not months later when all the indirect expenses for the period had been accumulated and distributed. Furthermore, the overhead charge to jobs was often distorted by outside events. Church had noticed that during business depressions, as idle capacity increased, the fixed cost element in overhead allocations caused unit costs to vary inversely with production volume, resulting in the highest costs per unit just when the need to lower prices was greatest. He felt that part of the problem was due to the allocation procedures commonly used. The labor rate, labor hours, and percentage of prime cost methods had been developed mainly for inventory valuation purposes and were not sensitive enough to variations in wage rates and machine performance. They were in effect averaging techniques, which might give adequate results under stable conditions, but not otherwise.

The widely used machine hours rate was also crude, but it did take into account differences in the cost of work done on different types of equipment. Church reasoned that if overhead could be assigned to each individual machine or group of similar machines, then the machine hours method might become a precise allocation formula. He envisioned a factory divided into many "little shops" or production centers, with the overhead cost of each attached to the work passing through at a predetermined hourly rate. Most costs which had formerly been averaged over all the jobs in the plant could then be assigned to these production centers on some logical basis, such as floor space or the value of equipment, leaving just a residue to be allocated arbitrarily. Management need only single out a few key factors, such as power, depreciation, rent, and insurance. Overhead could then be allotted to departments based on the usage rates for these factors, from there to production centers, and finally to work in process using "scientific machine rates" based on the assumption of full capacity operations.

There remained the problem of idle capacity. Church saw the fallacy of recording an increase in product costs between periods simply because the volume of output fell more rapidly than expenditures for overhead. Continuing his analogy of little shops, he said that if every production center worked at full capacity and if actual overhead was allocated using his scientific machine rate, the balance left in the overhead account should consist entirely of residual items which had no logical allocation basis, such as supervisory salaries. But if a shop worked only half the time, the unabsorbed overhead would also include expenses which could and should be charged to particular production centers. Church proposed to distribute such expenses by means of a "supplementary rate," for which he claimed two advantages. First, the ratio between the scientific machine rate and the supplementary rate would serve as an index of plant capacity during the period. Second, the fact that overhead absorption no longer depended on the extent of plant utilization would allow management to make far more valid comparisons between the costs of jobs or products produced in different accounting periods.

When applied in an English factory, Church's system proved overelaborate and difficult to keep current.[18] His theory was also deficient in several ways. His supplementary rate was not a pure index of shop efficiency, since an increase in overhead expense due to inflation or changes in demand would increase the rate even if all machines were in full use. It also tended to equate capacity production with optimal efficiency. Church's supplementary rate soon went out of use, and in his later writings he himself largely abandoned it. But he remained adamantly opposed to predetermined or standard rates based on expected production volume, though his scientific machine rate required a pre-estimate of costs. In attempting to distinguish between normal and abnormal costs and to assign responsibility for unabsorbed overhead, Church was trying to achieve the results of a standard cost system while rejecting the use of standard costs.

Though parts of his theory were criticized for the next twenty years, Church's basic assumptions about the content of overhead expense and its allocation became points of departure for later American writers. Whitmore (1908), Nicholson (1909), Webner (1911), Moxey (1913), Scovell (1916), and Jordan and Harris (1920) showed the direct influence of his work. As a former president of the Institute of Cost and Works Accountants put it, Church, "probably did more than anyone, both directly and indirectly, to promote costing as it is now known, chiefly because he promoted thought."[19]

THE CONSOLIDATION PERIOD

It should be remembered that these pioneering authors had as their audience a small minority of firms. Cost textbooks played a vital role in standardizing practice and facilitating the interaction of ideas, but their impact on industrial practice was not at first great. Even as late as 1900 formal cost accounting systems were a rarity in England and America.[20] Most manufacturers had some informal procedure which enabled them to estimate the costs of labor and material embodied in particular jobs. Overhead was generally ignored. Those few who allocated it usually did so on a labor time or rate basis, preferring simplicity to precision. The need at this point was less for new ideas than for a wider dissemination of work which had already been done.

H. L. ARNOLD

Around the turn of the century H. L. Arnold wrote a series of books which in effect summarized the American cost accounting methods then in vogue. These were the kind of studies now made by academics, perhaps under the auspices of the National Association of Accountants, but which then came from a relatively uneducated man. Arnold was a journeyman machinist before becoming superintendent and then designer for Pratt and Whitney. His work is of interest today for what it reveals about the evolution of ideas during a period of rapid change, and the interplay of textbook theories with actual practice. In *The Complete Cost-Keeper* (1899)[21] he described the cost systems of fifteen industrial firms which he considered representative of the best accounting of the day. Overhead allocation was always on the basis of historical experience, and in most cases both factory and administrative expenses were distributed to jobs. It was common practice to keep cost accounts completely separate from the financial accounting records. Knowing of a few firms which had partially integrated the two, Arnold still felt that nothing could be done in a consolidated system that could not be done separately.

In *The Factory Manager and Accountant* (1903)[22] he offered new examples of the latest American practice, and his own views on the objectives of cost

accounting. In essence these were as follows: since the factory past is unaltera-
ble, there is no reason to record it except as a guide to the best management
of future costs. The factory accountant hopes by finding the cost of past
production to be able to predict and control the cost of similar future production. Arnold now opted for the integration of cost and financial accounts,
which had become a popular viewpoint among American authors, though it
was about 1910 before the English took it up.[23]

J. LEE NICHOLSON

Lee Nicholson, industrial consultant and university lecturer, organized the
National Association of Cost Accountants and was its first president. His
Factory Organization and Costs (1909)[24] summarized and refined many of the
then-known theories and practices of cost finding. For example, he not only
described the methodology of job order and process costing but also the
circumstances in which each was appropriate. He was one of the first to explain
how departmental costs might be cumulated and passed on from one factory
operation to the next. He also proposed a summary of requisitions as an aid
in posting to stores ledgers and cost records, originated several methods of
accounting for scrap, and suggested an improved perpetual inventory system.

Noting that he knew of hundreds of firms whose overhead accounting was
inadequate, Nicholson devoted many pages to a discussion of seven common
allocation methods. He argued that selling and administrative expenses added
nothing to the value of goods produced in the factory and should be excluded
from overhead distributions to product. His "new machine rate" elaborated
on Church's scientific machine rate. All labor and overhead costs were collected by departments and then divided among units produced on the basis of
time incurred in various machine processes. The "new pay rate" combined
labor and overhead expense to create a joint rate for applying costs to product.

Nicholson's second book,[25] in 1913, showed the effects of his teaching
experience at New York and Columbia Universities. Its most important contribution was a system of reciprocal accounts which permitted coordination
between cost and financial ledgers that were separately kept and balanced. He
distinguished clearly between operating and service departments with respect
to burden allocation, and introduced a technique for collecting overhead expense in control accounts before charging it to production. He also recommended a method for estimating cost of goods sold at current prices which
foreshadowed LIFO.

In his later writings Nicholson anticipated post-1920 developments in the
use of cost data by management and in the psychology of cost control.[26] As
a staff man dealing with line personnel, the factory accountant must be diplomatic, yet forceful enough to take full advantage of the discipline which costing
made possible. Nicholson stressed the importance of supplying information
appropriate to each executive level, and the need to educate foremen and

department heads about overhead costs as a first step toward controlling such costs. Top management should be given comparative figures; accounting summaries prepared for the sales and production departments should show the effect of volume changes on costs.

THE ORIGINS OF STANDARD COSTING

Traditional cost systems relied on stores records of material requisitions and on foremen's accounts of the time spent by workers on each job. If overhead was added, it was usually applied as a flat percentage of the current or previous year's labor or prime costs. The total of material, labor, and overhead gave a figure which was accepted as the actual cost of a job or product. Only gradually did it become evident that this "true" cost was not very useful in fixing prices or controlling efficiency. There was no agreement as to how materials bought at different prices should be charged to jobs, how overtime pay should be assigned, what expenses should be included in overhead or how it should be allocated. Actual costs also required a great deal of repetitive, detailed work to establish and maintain, and they were affected by so many random factors that the final results seemed almost accidental. The absence of cost standards led to a widespread ignorance of the expense of doing business.

The possibility of comparing actual and "ideal" costs was implied in the writings of Garcke and Fells, Church, and others. Refinements in overhead allocation methods were an attempt to escape from the limitations of crudely determined actual costs. So were systems designed to isolate and quantify the effects of volume changes and other distorting influences on unit costs. But it truly required a conceptual leap of faith for accountants trained in the preparation of historical summaries to begin estimating the cost of a product *before* it was produced. The tendency among early authors was to follow out lines of reasoning which led them to the notion of predetermined costs, which notion they then repudiated.

Engineers and efficiency experts had no such inhibitions. In their efforts to increase output and reduce expense they found information before the event far more valuable than historical data. Standard costs were a natural outgrowth of the production standards and work routines developed by Frederick Taylor and his followers. The advent of scientific management accelerated a shift in emphasis from the inventorying of costs to cost control through comparisons between actual operating results and preset standards.

The earliest known writings on standard costing were by Percy Longmuir, an American engineer, and J. Stanley Garry, an English accountant. In 1902 Longmuir, in an article on foundry costs,[27] proposed that the labor cost of each type of work should be related to production quantities to give standard factors for each type of labor, which then could be used to provide timely cost data for managerial decision making. In a paper on "Factory Costs"[28] read to the Society of Chemical Industry in 1903, Garry postulated the use of a "normal standard price" for materials, and introduced the concepts of volume and price variances. Neither his proposal nor Longmuir's was worked out in technical detail, and neither had any noticeable effect on contemporary practice.

JOHN WHITMORE

The first detailed description of a standard cost system was given by an American accountant, John Whitmore. A disciple of Church, Whitmore in 1906 wrote a series of articles[29] which provided the ledgers, accounts, and entries needed to make Church's system operative in a factory situation. While largely accepting Church's scientific machine rate for overhead allocation, Whitmore disapproved of his treatment of idle capacity costs. He saw idle time essentially as waste, not as a "proper cost" of production, and criticized Church's supplementary rate which charged it to work in process. Whitmore was ambivalent as to whether idle capacity costs should be written off as period expenses. But he strongly urged that they be segregated from normal production costs in a ledger account called "factory capacity idle."

Two years later[30] Whitmore elaborated on his idea that true cost does not necessarily include every expense incurred in producing an article. If idle capacity expense is not really part of a product's cost, might there not be other costs resulting from waste or accident which should also be excluded? He thought it practical, on the basis of labor efficiency and material quantity standards, to calculate in advance what "proper costs" should be and then to show the variances between them and actual expenditures. He knew of industries in which the manufacturing orders were so numerous that it was impossible to set up a separate cost account for each order, but quite possible to calculate a standard cost for every article. Using as his example a shoe factory, Whitmore showed how each grade of leather could be valued at a "proper" price, and how variances would result if either prices or quality of material was different from the standards. He also explained how direct labor could be charged to work in process at standard rates. Though admitting that he had not made an application of overhead by the same methods, he believed it could be done. He did not, however, show standard costs developed from scientific efficiency studies. While not ruling out the use of engineered standard costs for internal purposes, he preferred to show only "probable costs" in the financial records.

HARRINGTON EMERSON

The American efficiency engineer Harrington Emerson made a more clinical study of standard costs in a series of articles titled "Efficiency as a Basis for Operations and Wages" (1909).[31] In distinguishing between standard and actual cost systems, he spoke of the latter almost with contempt:

> There are two radically different methods of ascertaining costs, the first method to ascertain them after the work is done, the second method to

ascertain them before the work is undertaken. The first method is the old one, still used in most manufacturing and maintenance undertakings, the second method is the new one, beginning to be used in some very large plants, where its feasibility and practical value have already been demonstrated.[32]

Emerson showed that the figures provided by actual cost systems were not only hopelessly delayed, but were wrong, mixing legitimate costs with avoidable losses which had nothing to do with the final product and only impeded attempts to eliminate waste and poor methods. Knowledge of what costs should be under normal conditions made any excess immediately visible and directed managerial attention to substandard performance. Really the question was one of allocating the supervisor's time in the most useful way. "Standard costs are the mariner's compass of a business enterprise, showing as they do from month to month the proper course of the business ship."[33]

Though he was not an accountant and gave no directions for the ledger treatment of standard costs, Emerson stressed the need to tie such costs into the regular accounting records, not only to allow systematic comparisons with actual expenditures but to offer proof to line executives that the methods used were producing the promised results. He gave more attention to standard setting than Whitmore had. Though vacillating between ideal and attainable standards, he advocated the use of the hour as the "real standard unit of cost." A man's rate of pay for a given hour and his speed of work could be scientifically measured, and these smaller time units made possible precise cost standards. He failed to locate the exact sources of inefficiencies because he attempted nothing more detailed than an overall variance between actual and standard results. Like Whitmore, he may have been describing and interpreting a system he had seen in operation.

LATER DEVELOPMENTS

The notion that predetermined costs were more useful than a cumulation of actual amounts became well established in the literature between 1910 and 1920. During this period standard cost analyses began to be used in practice not only to control expenditures and eliminate waste, but also in budgeting, and to anticipate the costs of new products. In 1911 G. Charter Harrison, an associate of Emerson, designed the earliest known complete standard cost system.[34] He elaborated on this in a series of articles in 1918,[35] and in 1920 brought out the first set of formulae for the analysis of cost variances.[36] His descriptions of accounts, ledgers, and cost analysis sheets were detailed enough to be used in cookbook fashion, and seem to mark the completion of basic cost accounting development.

But once again the attainment of a certain level of sophistication intimated the need for further refinements. The usual item-by-item comparison of actual and standard costs was distorted by the different behavior of fixed and variable cost elements when production volume fluctuated. As early as 1913, C. H.

Scovell[37] suggested that fixed costs be segregated, like the expenses of waste and idle time, in order to make variance analysis more meaningful. The introduction of full or absorption costing, which resulted in the inclusion of fixed factory costs in overhead allocation rates, would eventually lead to cost-volume-profit analysis, flexible budgeting, and direct costing.

SUMMARY AND CONCLUSIONS

Perhaps because it lagged behind accounting progress in other areas, and even behind industrial growth, cost accounting developed remarkably quickly once it got started. Between 1885 and 1920 the essentials of present methodology were not only formulated but were to some extent standardized in practice. A manageable overhead allocation procedure was devised, the mechanics for integrating the cost and financial records were worked out, and standard cost procedures were developed. Little had been done before and not much has been done since, except for refinements and new applications of existing techniques. In fact the great majority of factory accounting problems were either solved fairly easily during this period, or still concern us.

Paul Garner ends his *Evolution of Cost Accounting to 1925* with the following nine conclusions:

1. Although there was some interest in cost theories and practices before 1885, few authorities prior to that time had considered the subject worthy of their undivided attention.

2. English cost accountants contributed a large proportion of the original ideas and procedures before 1900. After that date the American theorists and practitioners forged ahead of their British contemporaries, the latter never regaining their relative standing.

3. Prime cost systems came into use much sooner than the more complete factory costing arrangements.

4. The third element of cost (factory overhead) was comparatively neglected in the period before 1900, but after that date more attention was devoted to it than to the two other elements of cost combined.

5. Subject to considerable qualification and opinion, it seems from the evidence available that the so-called "depression years" in industrial activity have been especially fruitful periods for introducing and developing new cost techniques and procedures.

6. Industrial engineers, rather than cost or general accountants, took a more active interest in costing problems in the early development of the subject in this country.

7. Theories and methods for valuing factory inventories did not attract as much attention in the early American cost discussions as in the English.

8. The integration of factory and financial records proceeded at a very slow pace until well after the turn of the century, all of the details not being worked out until around 1920.

9. Cost theories and techniques have evolved as a product of their

industrial environment, and their rapid development has been necessitated by the continually increasing complexity of manufacturing processes.[38]

FOOTNOTES

1. S. Paul Garner, *Evolution of Cost Accounting to 1925* (Alabama: University of Alabama Press, 1954), 9, 27.
2. A.C. Littleton, *Accounting Evolution to 1900* (New York: American Institute Publishing Company, 1933), 355-357.
3. David Solomons, "The Historical Development of Costing," in David Solomons, ed., *Studies in Costing* (London: Sweet and Maxwell, 1952), 19.
4. Henry Metcalfe, *The Cost of Manufactures* (New York: John Wiley and Sons, 1885).
5. *Ibid.*, 289.
6. Emile Garcke and John Manger Fells, *Factory Accounts, Their Principles and Practice*, (London: Crosby, Lockwood and Son, 1887).
7. S. Paul Garner, "Highlights in the Development of Cost Accounting," *The National Public Accountant* (March, 1950), 10.
8. For a diagrammatic description, see Littleton, *op. cit.*, 349.
9. Garner, *Evolution of Cost Accounting to 1925, op. cit.*, 257.
10. *Ibid.*, 346.
11. Eldon S. Hendriksen, *Accounting Theory*, rev. ed. (Homewood, Ill.: Richard D. Irwin, 1970), 36.
12. George P. Norton, *Textile Manufacturers' Bookkeeping* (London: Simpkin, 1889).
13. Norton's manufacturing account is illustrated in Littleton, *op. cit.*, 346-47, and in Garner, *Evolution of Cost Accounting to 1925, op. cit.*, 278-79.
14. Garner, *Evolution of Cost Accounting to 1925, op. cit.*, 246.
15. J. Slater Lewis, *The Commerical Organisation of Factories* (London: E. and F.N. Spon, 1896).
16. Joseph A. Litterer, "Alexander Hamilton Church and the Development of Modern Management," *Business History Review* 33 (Summer, 1961), 225.
17. Quoted in Solomons, *op. cit.*, 26.
18. *Ibid.*, 29.
19. Roland Dunkerley, in a paper titled "A Historical Review of the Institute and the Profession" read to the eighteenth National Cost Conference of the I.C.W.A. on May 10, 1946.
20. Solomons, *op. cit.*, 17-18.
21. H.L. Arnold, *The Complete Cost-Keeper* (New York: The Engineering Magazine Press, 1899).
22. H.L. Arnold, *The Factory Manager and Accountant* (New York: The Engineering Magazine Press, 1903).
23. Garner, *Evolution of Cost Accounting to 1925, op. cit.*, 258.
24. J. Lee Nicholson, *Factory Organization and Costs* (New York: Kohl Technical Publishing Company, 1909).
25. J. Lee Nicholson, *Cost Accounting—Theory and Practices* (New York: Ronald Press Company, 1913).
26. L.W. Hein, "J. Lee Nicholson: Pioneer Cost Accountant," *Accounting Review* 34 (January, 1959), 110.
27. Percy Longmuir, "Recording and Interpreting Foundry Costs," *The Engineering Magazine* (September, 1902).
28. H. Stanley Garry, "Factory Costs," *The Accountant* (July 25 and September 12, 1903).
29. John Whitmore, "Factory Accounting As Applied to Machine Shops," *Journal of Accountancy* (August, 1906–January, 1907).
30. John Whitmore, "Shoe Factory Cost Accounts," *Journal of Accountancy* 6 (May, 1908), 12-25.
31. Harrington Emerson, "Efficiency as a Basis for Operation and Wages," *The Engineering Magazine* (July, 1908–March, 1909).
32. *Ibid.*, vol. 36, 336.
33. *Loc. cit.*

34. Solomons, *op. cit.*, 50.
35. G. Charter Harrison, "Cost Accounting to Aid Production," *Industrial Management* (October, 1918–June, 1919).
36. G. Charter Harrison, "Scientific Basis for Cost Accounting," *Industrial Management* (December, 1918), 459.
37. C.H. Scovell, "Cost Accounting Practice, With Special Reference to Machine Hour Rate," *Journal of Accountancy* 17 (1914).
38. Garner, *Evolution of Cost Accounting to 1925, op. cit.*, 341-42.

SELECTED BIBLIOGRAPHY

Brummet, R. Lee, "Brief History of Overhead Costing since 1875." 1-13 of his *Overhead Costing*, Ann Arbor: Michigan Business Studies, 1957.

Chatfield, Michael. "The Origins of Cost Accounting." *Management Accounting* 52 (June, 1971), 11-14.

Church, Alexander Hamilton. *Production Factors in Cost Accounting and Works Management.* New York: Engineering Magazine Press, 1910. Reprinted by Arno Press, New York, 1976.

Crossman, P. "The Genesis of Cost Control." *Accounting Review* 28 (October, 1953), 522-27.

Edwards, R.S. "Some Notes on the Early Literature and Development of Cost Accounting in Great Britain." *Accountant* 97 (1937), 193-95, 225-31, 253-55, 283-87, 313-16, 343-44.

Epstein, Marc Jay. "The Effect of Scientific Management on the Development of the Standard Cost System." Unpublished Ph.D. dissertation, University of Oregon, 1973. University Microfilms, Ann Arbor, Michigan.

Epstein, Marc J., and Epstein, Joanne B. "An Annotated Bibliography of Scientific Management and Standard Costing to 1920." *Abacus* 10 (1974), 165-174.

Feller, R.E. "Early Contributions to Cost Accounting." *Management Accounting* 55 (December, 1973), 12-16, 27.

Garcke, Emile, and Fells, John Manger. *Factory Accounts, Their Principles and Practice.* London: Crosby, Lockwood and Son, 1887. Reprinted by Arno Press, New York, 1976.

Garner, S. Paul. *Evolution of Cost Accounting to 1925.* Alabama: University of Alabama Press, 1954, chaps. three to twelve.

――――. "Highlights in the Development of Cost Accounting." In M. Chatfield, ed. *Contemporary Studies in the Evolution of Accounting Thought*. Belmont, Cal.: Dickenson Publishing Company, 1968, 210-21.

――――. "Historical Development of Cost Accounting." *Accounting Review* 12 (October, 1947), 385-89.

Hein, L.W. "J. Lee Nicholson: Pioneer Cost Accountant." *Accounting Review* 34 (January, 1959), 106-11.

Horn, C.A. "How Victorian Industrial Advances Brought Cost Accountancy to the Fore." *Management Accounting* (England) 52 (January, 1974), 7-10.

Jackson, J. Hugh. "A Half Century of Cost Accounting Progress." In M. Chatfield, ed. *Contemporary Studies in the Evolution of Accounting Thought*. Belmont, Cal.: Dickenson Publishing Company, 1968, 222-36.

Jones, D.M.C. "The Development of Accounting in Commerce and Industry." *Accountant's Review* (March, 1975), 7-23.

Littleton, A.C. *Accounting Evolution to 1900.* New York: American Institute Publishing Company, 1933. Reprinted by Russell and Russell, New York, 1966. Chapter twenty-one.

Litterer, Joseph A. "Alexander Hamilton Church and the Development of Modern Management." *Business History Review* 33 (Summer, 1961), 211-25.

Norton, George P. *Textile Manufacturers' Bookkeeping for the Counting House, Mill and Warehouse.* London: Simpkin, 1889. Reprinted by Arno Press, New York, 1976.

Schoenfeld, Hanns-Martin. *Cost Terminology and Cost Theory: A Study of its Development and Present State in Central Europe.* Urbana: Center for International Education and Research in Accounting, 1974.

_____. "Development and Present State of Cost Theory in Germany." *International Journal of Accounting* 8 (Fall, 1972), 43-65.

Solomons, David. "The Historical Development of Costing." In David Solomons, ed., *Studies in Costing*. London: Sweet and Maxwell, 1952, 1-52.

Sowell, Ellis Mast. *The Evolution of the Theories and Techniques of Standard Costs*. University, Alabama: University of Alabama Press, 1973.

Weber, Charles. *The Evolution of Direct Costing*. Urbana: Center for International Education and Research in Accounting, 1966.

Weber, Karl. *Amerikanische Standardkostenrechung: Ein Uberlick*. Winterthur: Verlag P.G. Keller, 1960.

Chapter 13

COST ANALYSIS FOR DECISION MAKING

By 1920 answers had been found to the major technical problems of industrial accounting. Factory managers were provided with schedules of past production costs, and standard cost systems were increasingly used. In the following decade refinements were made in burden distribution, in cost control and variance analysis, in the extension of cost methods to distribution expenses, and in the design of cost summaries and reports. But the striking change after 1920 was managerial recognition of cost accounting's value, not only in reducing factory expense, but for policy and decision making. Given this broader mission, the question became not so much one of deriving cost figures as of deciding which figures were important and what use should be made of them.

The development of costs to rationalize decision making was mainly an application of economic theory and engineering technique.[1] It included methods of cost-volume-profit analysis (the break-even chart, flexible budgeting, and direct costing), capital budgeting, and attempts to implement uniform cost accounting standards.

THE CONCEPT OF RELEVANT COST

The relevant costs for decision making are those which will be different depending on whether or not a particular action is taken. It is natural for businessmen to think in these terms, and early authors calculated the effect on profits of sowing different types of grain and of using different kinds of factory lighting.[2] The first formal analyses of differential costs were made by neoclassical economists late in the nineteenth century. Pointing out that "In commerce, bygones are for ever bygones,"[3] W. S. Jevons in 1871 maintained that asset values depend on future utility rather than historical cost. The Austrian economist Friedrich von Wieser in 1876 first expressed the idea that the cost of any article is the value of productive forces which could have been employed elsewhere but instead were bound up in it.[4] The American economist D. I. Green reasoned that because the number of good opportunities is usually limited, and since taking one usually means forgoing others, the cost of these forgoings in effect becomes the cost of the opportunity chosen.[5] P. H. Wicksteed argued that what a person will give for something can be determined by comparing the difference which he believes having it will make to him, with the difference caused by the loss of whatever he must give for it, or could have instead of it. He added that the entrepeneur's talent consists of increasing or decreasing his expenditures for materials, labor, and overhead to exactly that level where their differential importance to him coincides with their market prices.[6]

But economic theorists were not writing for and were rarely read by practicing accountants and businessmen.[7] And neither training nor experience fitted most accountants to think in terms of future alternative costs. There was also a practical problem: relevant variable costs were mixed in the overhead accounts with much less controllable fixed cost elements, and no one seemed sure how to identify or separate the two. Since the eighteenth century it had been understood that costs do not always vary proportionally with changes in production volume, and that the cost of making an article changes with the number of units produced. Turgot and Malthus had applied this idea to the question of diminishing returns in agriculture. In the 1830s Charles Babbage showed its relevance to machine costs.[8] After 1850 it became common for economists, engineers, and even accountants to distinguish between the behavior of fixed and variable expenses. A few, like Garcke and Fells, emphasized the importance of this distinction. But even after it was generally understood how and why factory costs were affected by volume changes, the technique of isolating controllable costs for analysis eluded accounting practitioners.

COST-VOLUME-PROFIT ANALYSIS

Several of the earliest applications of cost-volume-profit analysis were made in the field of railway economics. In 1850 the Irish mathematician Dionysius Lardner suggested that it was necessary to anticipate the effect of railway rate changes on the volume of traffic. Too large a fare increase would decrease the amount of business to a point where total receipts actually declined. Setting rates to maximize income required a segregation of variable and fixed costs, since the latter by definition were not affected by rate changes and could be ignored.[9] The American civil engineer A. M. Wellington, discussing the profitability of railroad investment in 1887, tried to show systematically the influ-

ence of cost and volume changes on profit levels. After explaining that the large
fixed costs incurred in railroad construction meant that even a small decline
in volume could have major effects on receipts and income, he illustrated the
results of alternative cost patterns and even set up a crude break-even analysis.
But he failed to sufficiently distinguish between fixed and variable operating
expenses, nor did he reduce his examples to mathematical formulas which
would show the break-even point and the marginal income at each level of
activity.[10]

THE BREAK-EVEN CHART

The first published descriptions of the break-even chart were by the American
engineer Henry Hess (1903)[11] and the Scots accountant Sir John Mann
(1904).[12] Letting the vertical axis of his chart represent dollars and the horizontal axis represent both output and time, Hess plotted a series of straight
lines which showed the effect of volume changes on total net receipts, total
costs, total variable costs, direct and indirect expenses, and fixed costs. The
intersection of the total receipts and total cost lines was of course the point
at which the company exactly broke even. Above this point marginal income
appeared and increased proportionally with the increase in output. Hess intended his chart to be used for control as well as profit planning. He claimed
that graphical comparisons between budgeted and actual figures dramatized
variances and facilitated quick corrective action.

According to Ned Chapin,[13] two distinct versions of the break-even chart
evolved from Hess's model. Both showed how costs and revenues varied with
volume changes, but they differed in the way costs were plotted and in the type
of analysis made from the resulting data. The less popular version, developed
by C. E. Knoeppel and Fred V. Gardner, plotted costs according to account
classifications (sales, material, labor, and so on), allowing their fixed or variable
character to be inferred from the slopes and intercepts of the lines. This type
lent itself particularly to flexible budgeting, and in his later writings Knoeppel
described his "profitgraph" as "essentially a *graphic master budget,* for a year
or shorter period."[14]

The American engineer Walter Rautenstrauch coined the phrase "break-
even chart" and pioneered the type of diagram in general use today. Describing
his chart as the "graphic basis of a budget," he built it around the relationship
between expenses and sales (not expenses and receipts, as Hess had), and
plotted costs according to their degree of variability.[15] In 1922 John H. Williams showed that the break-even point could be calculated arithmetically by
dividing fixed costs by the contribution to fixed costs and profits.[16] Formulas
for break-even analysis were published by Rautenstrauch (1930) and by Arthur J. Minor (1932), and descriptions of profit-volume charts began to appear
in the accounting literature.

THE FLEXIBLE BUDGET

Even its inventors had warned that the break-even chart oversimplified cost-volume-profit analysis by assuming a linear relationship between output and expense. That is, the usual classification of costs as either entirely fixed or entirely variable ignored the fact that most costs included both elements. The first accounting treatment of semivariable costs was made in 1922 by John H. Williams.[17] He believed that by interpolating between the amounts of semivariable expense appropriate to a firm's minimum and maximum outputs, it was possible to accurately predict how much individual costs should be at every likely production volume. It would then be feasible to develop detailed budgets for a range of different output levels.

Variable budgeting was first used to adjust overhead allocation rates for volume changes. Unexpected fluctuations in output obscured comparisons between budgeted indirect expenses and actual results, making it difficult to evaluate executive performance and preventing responsibility for waste and overspending from being definitely placed. In 1928 a group of Westinghouse engineers and accountants attacked this problem by devising what they called a "flexible budget." Spending allowances were tied into the company's standard cost system by means of volume variance accounts which neutralized the effect of output changes. The Westinghouse method was widely imitated. As other manufacturers combined standard costs systems with flexible budgets, CPAs began to accept the resulting figures for external reporting purposes, provided the standard costs were reasonably close to actual historical averages.

During the next decade the flexible budget was popularized as a money-saver. In many businesses hit by the depression, even though spending was kept within budgeted limits, it was higher than necessary given the rapid decline in production and sales volume. Short-run cost control was perhaps a lesser motive for flexible budgeting than the evaluation of managerial efficiency, but the effect in both cases was to make the budgetary process less arbitrary and the analysis of variances more meaningful. Its success was so dramatic that in 1946 Raymond P. Marple claimed that the greatest single advance in industrial accounting during the 1930s was the general adoption of flexible budgeting.[18]

DIRECT COSTING

The first technical paper on direct costing was written by Jonathan N. Harris and appeared in the *NAA Bulletin* for January 15, 1936.[19] In it he described the conditions which led to his installation of a "direct standard cost manufacturing plan" at Dewey and Almy Chemical Company in 1934. Rarely has an accounting innovation been described in such detail at its first exposition, and this article is worth reviewing at length.

Writing in a pseudo-dramatic style, Harris begins with a paradox. Sales are up, but income is down, because in the current month his firm produced only half as much as it sold, resulting in writeoffs to expense of underabsorbed overhead which more than ate up the increase in gross profit from sales. The root of this problem is absorption costing, which assigns fixed as well as variable overhead expenses to products. Each month's standard cost allocation is based on the average planned level of production for the year. But in a seasonal business which must build up stocks from which it can sell during peak demand periods, neither monthly production nor sales will conform to the standard volume. There will nearly always be large over-or underabsorbed overhead balances. When production is at capacity and sales are low, income will be inflated to a point where it may even exceed sales (a hard result to explain, Harris adds). The reverse situation creates fictitious monthly losses. The practice of writing off underabsorbed overhead to profit and loss while dividing overabsorbed balances between inventories and cost of goods sold is not only inconsistent, but leads to an improper valuation of inventories and a mismatching of costs and revenues, and defeats the purpose of the normal capacity concept. The rate of production is allowed to influence profit, and current sales are charged with the cost of goods to be sold in the future.

Harris then asks: if we can isolate fixed costs, is it permissible to exclude them when calculating factory inventory prices? He reasons that all costs which would have been incurred even if the product had not been made are a function of time rather than of production, and should be charged to expense. Allocating only variable costs to products simplifies standard costing by eliminating the need to estimate "normal" capacity. It ends all the problems and distortions caused by volume variances. Fixed overhead expenses tend to be the result of top management decisions. Assigning them to production often means that department heads are unfairly held responsible for expenditures they cannot control. Pricing, control, and decision making are facilitated by direct cost income statements which segregate variable cost elements and show marginal income as a separate figure.

Harris admits that working capital balances would be decreased by the introduction of direct costing, that lower inventory valuations might tempt sales managers to cut selling prices, and that the new method would be unacceptable for tax reporting and for use in audited financial statements. He suggests that the problem of annual statement presentations might be solved by adding to direct cost inventories an amount equivalent to indirect factory overhead. And in general, the advantages of direct costing outweigh the disadvantages. Using disguised figures from Dewey and Almy, Harris concludes by comparing the statement formats and operating results obtained under the old and new methods.

Direct costing was a natural extension of break-even analysis and flexible budgeting, and the publicity from Harris's article brought to light a number of earlier experiments. G. Charter Harrison had used a variant of direct costing to show the managers of an agricultural equipment company that their variable cost gross margin justified the additional marketing expenses needed to secure profitable sales volume.[20] Clem Kohl, Controller of Gates Rubber Company, pointed out that his firm began using direct costing in 1919, when elimination of fixed overhead allocations to product enabled management to avoid the error of closing a plant whose revenues were covering its variable costs and making a substantial contribution to its fixed costs.[21]

The pioneer writings of 1936–37 were followed by a long dormant period. Direct costing had made an inconvenient appearance. It offered a substitute for the notion of matching revenues with full costs just at the time when the accounting profession was doing everything possible to standardize this principle and make it "generally acceptable." In 1947 C. Robert Fay, a member of the Westinghouse team that developed the flexible budget, installed a direct standard cost system in the Glass Division of Pittsburgh Plate Glass Company, the first large corporation to adopt this method. Direct costing gained adherents from the success of this system. Still the pressure for conversion came mainly from operating management. CPAs, the Internal Revenue Service, and the SEC were agreeable to direct costing for managerial use so long as published figures were adjusted to include fixed overhead. During the ten-year period 1951–1960 the National Association of Accountants' Topical Index listed forty-four major articles on direct costing, plus many shorter items, as against only two articles published during the 1940s.[22]

CAPITAL BUDGETING

A refined evaluation of investment decisions requires not only a forecast of cash inflows and outflows, but knowledge of compound interest and a calculation of the discounted value of money. Compound interest was understood in Babylonian times, and the use of rate of return concepts has a long history.[23] Compound interest tables were first published by Jan Trenchant (Lyons, 1558) and by Simon Stevin (Antwerp, 1582). Stevin was also the first to apply the net present value approach to financial investments. He explained that the difference between the present values of two or more proposed loans, calculated at a given interest rate, showed how much more profitable one loan was than another. Knowledge of compound interest was a prerequisite for the development of scientific life insurance during the seventeenth and eighteenth centuries. Later its use was extended to the computation of bond yields and rates on leased facilities. It was more difficult to set out the cash implications of capital budgeting decisions, where expected receipts and expenditures were less definitely known, and only toward the end of the nineteenth century did writers on economics and engineering take up this subject.

In the 1887 edition of his book on the location of railroads, A. M. Wellington anticipated the capital budgeting problem in its modern form and offered some tentative solutions.[24] Railroad construction required massive cash outlays before any returns were received, and prior to committing itself to such projects, management had to judge whether there was sufficient need for a new line to assure a fair return on construction expenses. This primary question— whether to build a new line at all—should be decided systematically on the basis of estimated cost, probable receipts, the capital available for construction, and the expected return on investment. Wellington pointed out that the cost of capital increases with the amount invested, and that rate of return is a better measure than gross receipts. He suggested analysis of the present value of cash inflows and outlays, and reproduced the appropriate compound interest tables in his book. Stressing that forecasts into the distant future become progressively less precise, he concluded that while the tendency is for railway traffic to increase, it is generally inexpedient and even dangerous to anticipate such increases more than five years ahead in order to justify immediate capital outlays.

Alfred Marshall's *Principles of Economics* (1890) established a conceptual basis for capital budgeting. Marshall stated that return on investment must exceed outlay by an amount which increases, at compound interest, in proportion to the time of waiting. The longer an investor has to wait, and the greater his risk of loss, the richer his ultimate compensation should be. Changes in the general purchasing power of money are a complicating factor. An alert businessman will continue a particular type of speculation until he feels that the marginal gains resulting from further investments will no longer compensate him for his outlays.[25]

Irving Fisher[26] described four methods of choosing among investment alternatives, and claimed that each gave the same result. Out of all suitable opportunities, one should select: (1) that which has the highest present value, calculated at the market rate of interest; (2) the one whose returns in present value outweigh by the greatest margin its present value costs when both returns and costs are discounted at the market rate of interest; (3) the one whose rate of return over cost exceeds the interest rate by the greatest amount; and (4) where options differ by continuous gradations, select the one whose difference from its nearest rivals gives a rate of return over cost equal to the interest rate.

As might be expected, early attempts to apply capital budgeting in practice were less sophisticated than this. Though he did not use discounted cash flow procedures, the engineer John T. Van Deventer in a 1915 article[27] offered a systematic method for evaluating investment choices in a machine shop: (1) estimate the probable saving that a new appliance will make; (2) assign it a probable life span; (3) estimate what it will cost, and (4) decide on the minimum acceptable rate of return.

During the 1930s John Maynard Keynes, Kenneth Boulding, Paul Samuelson, and other economists considered the question of return on capital.[28] Refinements such as salvage value and sinking fund depreciation were added to capital budgeting calculations during this period. But the periodical accounting literature contained few references to investment decisions, nor was the subject well covered in American cost or financial accounting textbooks. Before World War II the time value of money seems rarely to have been an important consideration in managerial decisions to expand or contract operations.[29]

During the war capital expenditures tended to be justified on grounds other than expected monetary return, and in the immediate postwar period demand pressed on capacity and profits were attainable without careful selection among investment alternatives. Not until the yearly 1950s did business interest in capital budgeting become widespread. At that time managerial economist Joel Dean studied the handling of investment proposals by fifty "well-managed" companies. He found that "decisions are made on the basis of ill-defined standards and intuitive judgement."[30] Managers did not rank proposals systematically, they could not defend their choices logically, and they did not understand the economic concepts involved. The most commonly used decision criteria seemed to be degree of necessity or postponability. Admitting the importance of interpretation and judgment in dealing with critical forecasting factors, Dean nonetheless saw the need for an analytical framework which would help executives decide which proposals meant most to the firm's long-run prosperity. He favored rate of return analysis based on discounted cash flows. His aim was to sum up all relevant data in one figure, which would be applicable to all types of capital budgeting alternatives and would permit appraisal in terms of a single set of standards.

Studies made during the 1950s indicated that more businesses were adopting discounted cash flow procedures.[31] But the "payback period" and "rate of return" methods based on financial accounting techniques remained by far the most popular, though neither the accrual nor realization methods used in accounting practice were refined enough for capital budgeting. And it was typically accountants, as financial experts in residence, who were consulted on capital budgeting decisions, despite the fact that nearly all the writing on this subject before the 1960s had been done by nonaccountants. These seeming contradictions are explained only partly by the accountant's preoccupation with historical and external reporting. They were also a result of his highly specialized education which seldom included much economic theory. Accounting interest in discounted cash flow methods can be dated from the point at which the profession began to pay serious attention to economic and statistical concepts. If nothing else, the history of capital budgeting provides a compelling argument for interdisciplinary studies.

UNIFORM COST SYSTEMS

The search for financial accounting principles had its counterpart in attempts to set up industry-wide cost standards. As early as 1889 the National Association of Stove Manufacturers introduced a standard "formula" for costing the industry's products. The printing industry and many others followed suit.[32]

According to the NAA Research Department, sixty-nine such uniform systems existed in 1920. Though these may have helped to rationalize production, their usual purpose was to reduce competition by fostering price-fixing agreements based on cost estimates. Enforcement of the antitrust laws discouraged this type of uniform costing. In later years a number of industrial trade associations persuaded their members to report operating results according to uniform charts of accounts. Averages compiled from the resulting figures gave individual manufacturers a standard of comparison by which to judge their relative efficiency. Very recently the federal government has attempted to standardize the cost methods used by civilian contractors and subcontractors with whom it deals.

Admiral Hyman Rickover, testifying before the Senate Housing and Banking Committee in 1963, called the lack of uniform cost standards the most serious deficiency in government procurement. Each year the federal government placed orders for billions of dollars worth of military hardware, usually at contracted prices set in relation to estimated production costs, sometimes on a cost-plus-fixed-fee basis. But accounting systems used by civilian contractors and subcontractors varied so widely that it was almost impossible to compare contracts, set fair prices, determine defense equipment costs, or assess true defense industry profits. Rickover added that industry had no interest in changing this situation and that the accounting profession had had ample time and opportunity to do so nething about it, but "pays only lip service to the concept." He felt that if uniform cost standards were ever to be implemented, government must take the initiative. In 1970 Congress established the Cost Accounting Standards Board to develop uniform cost procedures to be used in accounting for defense procurement contracts exceeding $100,000. Standards have since been set for depreciation, overhead distribution, and for the traceability, allocability, and auditability of costs.[33] The General Services Administration, NASA, and the Atomic Energy Commission have incorporated similar standards into their contracts.

COST ACCOUNTING PRINCIPLES

There seems to be a consensus that while cost standards *should* be compatible with generally accepted accounting principles, the latter are too narrowly defined to serve as a basis for contract costing or for managerial decision making generally.[34] The 1962 report of the American Accounting Association's Management Accounting Committee,[35] after enumerating the areas of conflict between financial and managerial accounting concepts, also concluded that differences between the reporting objectives of the two areas justify the formulation of a separate body of principles for internal reporting.

However, the American Institute of CPAs proposes that Accounting Principles Board recommendations be the starting point for developing cost standards used in government contract negotiations.[36] It argues that both managerial and financial accounting are largely concerned with cost allocations and matching. A unified statement of accounting principles would allow similar problems in each area to be attacked on an integrated basis. During the "costing renaissance" internal accounting procedures were superimposed on double entry bookkeeping, and cost accounting has lived on borrowed theory ever since. Many cost problems have been created or aggravated by the constraints imposed by financial accounting concepts. For example, if revenues were realized on an accretion basis, there would be less need for a precise allocation of costs to inventories. Conversely, the tenability of financial accounting principles governing asset valuation, matching, and realization depends on the cost bases underlying the accumulation of asset values. Direct costing, the assumptions about inventory flow, and the lower of cost or market rule are all responses to the same questions. If cost procedures are viewed in this larger context, the question of managerial intent in incurring factory expenses becomes more important, and there is less justification for omitting idle capacity costs and similar "losses" from allocations to product. A synthesis of cost and financial accounting theory might reverse the trend toward direct costing and cause the assignment to production of many expenditures now charged against current revenues.

SUMMARY AND CONCLUSIONS

Modern financial accounting grew out of an earlier tradition of cash basis exchanges. In time this disbursements concept of cost gave way to accrual accounting, periodicity and realization, but financial accountants have never followed out the implications of these doctrines; they continue to reject the use of imputed costs, discounted cash flow procedures, and even current market valuations. Cost accounting as we know it developed much later and never had a personalistic or money bias. On the contrary, it urges advanced concepts of accrual and realization on a financial accounting system still preoccupied with cash outlays. Homburger and Dent believe that "Users of published financial statements are interested in substantially the same type of information which management has developed to meet its own needs."[37] They suggest that the relevant costs for managerial decision making could be more useful to investors than the figures produced under generally accepted accounting principles. The comparison of actual and budgeted results, direct costing, the breakdown of profits to disclose the marginal contribution of product lines, divisions, and subsidiaries, the use of capital budgeting methods to derive replacement costs, and the market valuation of current assets, are techniques which might enhance the credibility of published statements. It would seem that in many ways management accounting concepts represent a level of aspiration for financial accountants.

FOOTNOTES

1. R.H. Parker, *Management Accounting: an Historical Perspective* (New York: Augustus M. Kelley, 1969), 12.
2. *Ibid.*, 15-16.
3. W.S. Jevons, *The Theory of Political Economy* (London: Macmillan, 1871), 159.
4. Friedrich von Wieser, *Natural Value*, C.A. Malloch, trans. (London: Macmillan, 1893), 175.
5. D.I. Green, "Pain-Cost and Opportunity-Cost," *Quarterly Journal of Economics* 8 (1893-1894), 228.
6. P.H. Wicksteed, *The Common Sense of Political Economy and Selected Papers and Reviews of Economic Theory*, Lionel Robbins, ed. (London: Routledge, 1934), vol. 2, 772-800.
7. J.M. Clark's *Studies in the Economics of Overhead Costs* (Chicago: University of Chicago Press, 1923), included the first critical discussion by an economist of cost accounting in terms of relevant costs.
8. Charles Babbage, *On the Economy of Machinery and Manufactures* (London: Charles Knight, 1832).
9. Dionysius Lardner, *Railway Economy* (London: Taylor, Walton and Maberly, 1850).
10. A.M. Wellington, *The Economic Theory of the Location of Railways*, 2d ed. (New York: Wiley, 1887). For a summary, see R.J. Stephens, "A Note on Early Reference to Cost-Volume-Profit Relationships," *Abacus* 2 (September, 1966), 78-83.
11. Henry Hess, "Manufacturing: Capital, Costs, Profits and Dividends," *Engineering Magazine* 26 (1903), 367-79.
12. Sir John Mann, "Oncost or Expenses," in *Encyclopaedia of Accounting*, G. Lisle ed. (Edinburgh: William Green & Sons, 1903-1907), vol. 5, 199-225.
13. Ned Chapin, "The Development of the Break-Even Chart: A Bibliographical Note," *Journal of Business* 28 (1955), 148-49.
14. C.E. Knoeppel, *Profit Engineering* (New York: McGraw-Hill, 1933), 91.
15. The break-even charts of Hess, Mann, Knoeppel, and Rautenstrauch are illustrated in Parker, *op. cit.*, 63-69.
16. John H. Williams, "A Technique for the Chief Executive," *Bulletin of the Taylor Society* 7 (1922), 51.
17. *Ibid.*, 47-68.
18. Raymond P. Marple, "Combining the Forecast and Flexible Budgets," *Accounting Review* 21 (April, 1946), 140.
19. Jonathan N. Harris, "What Did We Earn Last Month?" *N.A.A. Bulletin* 18 (January 15, 1936), 501-27.
20. G. Charter Harrison, *New Wine in Old Bottles* (New York: privately printed, 1937).
21. Clem Kohl, "What is Wrong with Most Profit and Loss Statements?" *N.A.A. Bulletin* 19 (July 1, 1937), 1207-19.
22. Raymond P. Marple, "Historical Background," 3-14 of his *National Association of Accountants on Direct Costing: Selected Papers* (New York: Ronald Press, 1965), 12.
23. Parker, *op. cit.*, 34.
24. Wellington, *op. cit.*, 13-80.
25. Alfred Marshall, *Principles of Economics*, 8th ed. (London: Macmillan Company, 1920), 352-56.
26. Irving Fisher, *The Rate of Interest* (New York: Macmillan Company, 1907), chap. eight.
27. John Van Deventer, "Jigs and Fixtures in a Small Shop," *American Machinist* 42 (1915), 807-9. Summarized by George A. Wing, "Capital Budgeting, Circa 1915," *Journal of Finance* 20 (1965), 472-9.
28. Parker, *op. cit.*, 45-48.
29. *Ibid.*, 49.
30. Joel Dean, *Capital Budgeting* (New York: Columbia University Press, 1951), preface.
31. Parker, *op. cit.*, 55-56.
32. David Solomons, "The Historical Development of Costing," in David Solomons, ed. *Studies in Costing* (London: Sweet and Maxwell, 1952), 50-51.
33. Cost Accounting Standards Board. *Standards, Rules, and Regulations as of June 30, 1975.*

34. "Uniform Cost Accounting Standards," four commentaries in *The Federal Accountant* (September, 1969), 63-94; William J. Vatter, "Excerpts from 'Standards for Cost Analysis,' " *The Federal Accountant* (September, 1970), 65-87.
35. American Accounting Association, "Report of the Management Accounting Committee," *Accounting Review* 37 (July, 1962), 523-37.
36. "Institute Offers Assistance in Setting Cost Standards," *Journal of Accountancy* 129 (May, 1970), 9, 10, 12, 14, 16.
37. Richard H. Homburger and William C. Dent, "Management Accounting Concepts and the Principles Dilemma," *Management Accounting* 50 (April, 1969), 14-15.

SELECTED BIBLIOGRAPHY

American Accounting Association. "Report of the Management Accounting Committee." *Accounting Review* 37 (July, 1962), 523-37.

Amey, Lloyd. "On Opportunity Costs and Decision Making." *Accountancy* 72 (July, 1961), 442-451.

Barton, A.D. "The Break-Even Chart." *Australian Accountant* 26 (September, 1956), 375-88.

Benninger, L.J. "Accounting Theory and Cost Accounting." *Accounting Review* 40 (July, 1965), 547-57.

Chandra, Gyan, and Paperman, Jacob B. "Direct Costing vs. Absorption Costing: a Historical Review." *Accounting Historian* 3 (Winter, 1975), 1, 9, 10.

Channon, Geoffrey. "A Nineteenth Century Investment Decision: the Midland Railway's London Extension." *Economic History Review* 25 (August, 1972), 448-470.

Chapin, Ned. "The Development of the Break-Even Chart: A Bibliographical Note." *Journal of Business* (1955), 148-49.

Clark, J. Maurice. *Studies in the Economics of Overhead Costs*. Chicago: University of Chicago Press, 1923.

Elnicki, R.A. "The Genesis of Management Accounting." *Management Accounting* 52 (April, 1971), 15-17.

Garner, S. Paul. *Evolution of Cost Accounting to 1925*. Alabama: University of Alabama Press, 1954.

Gould, J.R. "Opportunity Cost: The London Tradition." In Harold Edey and B.S. Yamey, eds. *Debits, Credits, Finance, and Profits*. London: Sweet and Maxwell, 1974, 91-107.

Homburger, Richard H., and Dent, William C. "Management Accounting Concepts and the Principles Dilemma." *Management Accounting* 50 (April, 1969), 14-15.

Jackson, J. Hugh. "A Half Century of Cost Accounting Progress." In M. Chatfield, ed. *Contemporary Studies in the Evolution of Accounting Thought*. Belmont, Cal.: Dickenson Publishing Company, 1968, 222-36.

Johnson, H.T. "The Role of Accounting History in the Study of Modern Business Enterprise." *Accounting Review* 50 (July, 1975), 444-450.

————. "Management Accounting in an Early Integrated Industrial Firm: E.I. du Pont de Nemours Powder Company, 1903-1913." *Business History Review* 49 (Summer, 1975), 184-204.

Julius, M.J. "Historical Development of Uniform Accounting." *Journal of Business* 16 (1943), 219-29.

Marple, Raymond P. "Historical Background," 3-14 of his *National Association of Accountants on Direct Costing: Selected Papers*. New York: Ronald Press, 1965. This book also includes the pioneering articles on direct costing by Harris, Kohl, Kramer, and Clark.

Most, Kenneth S. "The History of Uniform Cost Accounting." 40-48 of his *Uniform Cost Accounting*. London: Gee, 1961.

National Association of Accountants. "Current Applications of Direct Costing." *NAA Research Report 33* (New York). National Association of Accountants, 1961.

Nielson, Oswald. "A Predecessor of Direct Costing." *Journal of Accounting Research* 4 (Spring, 1966), 119-20.

Parker, R.H. *Management Accounting: an Historical Perspective*. New York: Augustus M. Kelley, 1969.

———. "Early History of Cost Concepts for Decision-Making." *Accountancy* 79 (September, 1968), 621-624.

———. "Discounted Cash Flow in Historical Perspective." *Journal of Accounting Research* 6 (1968), 58-71.

Raymond, Robert H. "History of the Flexible Budget." *Management Accounting* 47 (August, 1966), 9-15.

Schoenfeld, Hanns-Martin. *Cost Terminology and Cost Theory: A Study of its Development and Present State in Central Europe.* Urbana: Center for International Education and Research in Accounting, 1974.

———. "Development and Present State of Cost Theory in Germany." *International Journal of Accounting* 8 (Fall, 1972), 43-65.

Scorgie, M.B. "Rate of Return." *Abacus* 1 (September, 1965), 85-91.

Sizer, J. "The Development of Marginal Costing." *Accountants' Magazine* 72 (January, 1968), 23-30.

Solomons, David. "The Historical Development of Costing." In David Solomons, ed. *Studies in Costing.* London: Sweet and Maxwell, 1952, 1-52.

Stephens, R.J. "A Note on an Early Reference to Cost-Volume-Profit Relationships." *Abacus* 2 (September, 1966), 78-83.

Villers, Raymond. "The Origin of the Break-Even Chart." *Journal of Business* 28 (1955), 296-7.

Weber, Charles. *The Evolution of Direct Costing.* Urbana: Center for International Education and Research in Accounting, 1966.

Wing, G.A. "Capital Budgeting, Circa 1915." *Journal of Finance* 20 (1965), 472-79.

Chapter 14

GOVERNMENT AND BUSINESS BUDGETING

Many early civilizations attempted state planning, but at a time when human activities depended so largely on natural events, their efforts were usually unsystematic. Planting and harvesting, construction projects, hunting, and even war were seasonal enterprises. Unable to dominate his environment, man budgeted at the sufferance of nature.

Industrial development greatly extended human influence over the economic future. Modern budgeting implies a two-sided view of future events—what is to be done and what it will cost—and one author has even called it the "application of double entry bookkeeping to planning."[1] Certainly the control function of accounting presupposes a prior planning function, and the comparison of performance with expectations which the budget formalizes is implicit in every accounting system. Moreover, during this century accounting has acted as a catalyst facilitating the exchange of methods and ideas between government and business budgeting.

GOVERNMENT BUDGETING IN ENGLAND AND FRANCE

The origins of English budgeting are most easily understood as part of a long struggle to democratize taxation. The Twelfth Article of *Magna Carta* restricted King John's right to levy taxes on the nobility. In 1689 the Bill of Rights provided that no one could be taxed without the consent of Parliament. To further strengthen the people's "control of the purse," legislative authority to authorize Crown expenditures was gradually extended to include control over the details and purposes of spending programs. The accession of William and Mary was followed by establishment of the Civil List, which segregated the funds appropriated for public use from those of the king, and limited the latter to a specific amount.

During the eighteenth century Parliament further curbed the king's powers by requiring him to prepare annual estimates of his expenditures for the following year together with similar spending estimates for all other government departments. It became customary for the Chancellor of the Exchequer, speaking for the king, to deliver in Parliament at the beginning of each fiscal year a three-part report on the national finances.[2] This included a formal accounting for the past year's government expenditures, an estimate of the coming year's expenditures, and a recommendation for a tax levy to supply the needed funds. Parliament debated and sometimes altered the Chancellor's budget proposals. Taxes were then levied and the approved appropriations became spending limitations for the following year.

Having taken over the king's taxing and spending powers, Parliament faced the problem of holding officials at all levels accountable for their use of public funds. This required a formal system of responsibility accounting, and much of the budgetary procedure which was now adopted was intended simply to improve accounting control. In 1785 an "Act for the Better Examining and Auditing of the Public Accounts of this Kingdom" was passed to replace the Joint Auditors of the Imprest with five Commissioners "with the largest and most stringent powers of auditing the public accounts of every department."[3] Passage of the Consolidated Fund Act in 1787 provided an overall basis for accountability by establishing a general fund through which all state revenues and expenditures passed. A comprehensive annual statement of finances was published by the government starting in 1802. After 1822 these statements included details of revenues and expenditures and indicated the prospective surplus or deficit.

The English budgetary process nicely combined the advantages of popular sovereignty with the advantages of centralized administration. The royal prerogatives had been eroded but the concept of unified executive authority was retained. While Parliament could reject or modify proposed expenditures, the budget remained an executive document. The Crown was ultimately responsible for specifying the purposes of budget requests, for coordinating revenue and expenditure proposals, and for collecting and spending public money. The system was further centralized in 1800 when responsibility for financial planning was given to the Cabinet, which acted in several capacities. It was a central executive authority, formulating a statement of the government's needs for the coming fiscal year and providing an account of its stewardship over public funds. As a committee of the House of Commons, the Cabinet then asked for approval of its program and defended and explained it in the House. After approval was granted it undertook, again in its executive role, to administer the budget and to control spending by the Crown's ministers.

This concentration of legislative and executive powers made it inevitable that the budget would reflect the priorities of the majority party. Beginning with the Peel-Gladstone era in the 1840s, the maxim became "expenditure depends on policy." In enacting his program of social and economic reforms, Gladstone theorized that:

> Budgets are not merely matters of arithmetic, but in a thousand ways go to the root of prosperity of individuals, and relation of classes, and the strength of kingdoms.[4]

The English budget has since become the major instrument for defining national objectives, and Parliamentary debate on government policy often centers on questions of expenditure.

FRANCE

The development of budgeting in Continental Europe also depended on the emergence of democratic institutions. In France before 1789 there were only occasional efforts to assert a popularly controlled "budget right" or establish responsibility accounting. Theoretically ministers of departments were held accountable for their spending of public funds, but the old General Assemblies rarely inquired into the use of subsidies, and in practice:

> The expenditure of the various departments shall be determined and decided by His Majesty, the nation trusting itself with confidence to His Majesty's promises with regard to economies.[5]

Normanton cities this eighteenth century crisis of accountability as an important cause of the French Revolution.[6]

Beginning with a decree of June 17, 1789, it became a basic principle of French constitutional practice that "No tax whatever can be levied without the consent of the nation."[7] This injunction was repeated in the Constitution of 1814. Following British precedent, the French government began presenting to the National Assembly an annual budget bill, which on passage became the finance act of that year. A general fund was established, and in 1817 the Assembly ruled that each minister's expenditures could not exceed the total funds appropriated for his use. Beginning in 1831 the Assembly examined the details of expenditure requests. But the centralized executive responsibility represented by the Chancellor of the Exchequer was never fully duplicated in the French system. The National Assembly as a body retained and exercised the authority to increase, reduce, or eliminate individual items of expenditure and taxation.

AMERICAN GOVERNMENT BUDGETING, 1780-1929

The United States was founded in the midst of grievances over arbitrary taxation. The right to "control the purse" was established in America by the

English Parliamentary Bill of March 11, 1778, which repealed the duty on tea and declared that no similar tax would be levied. Article 1, Section 9 of the American Constitution required that:

> No money shall be drawn from the treasury, but in consequence of appropriations made by law; and a regular statement and account of the receipts and expenditures of all public money shall be published from time to time.

An Act of September 2, 1789 established the Treasury Department and directed the Secretary of the Treasury "to prepare and report estimates of the public revenue and public expenditures." On his own initiative Alexander Hamilton not only prepared budget estimates but established direct, personal relations with Congress in the style of a Chancellor of the Exchequer. His efforts were reinforced in 1800 by a law directing the Secretary of the Treasury to "digest, prepare and lay before Congress" at the start of each session "a report on the subject of finance, containing estimates of the public revenue and public expenditures, and plans for improving or increasing the revenues. . . ."

There is no evidence that the Treasury Department ever complied with this request. From 1789 to 1921 the various agencies of the federal government prepared their financial estimates individually, each setting forth its own needs. These were then assembled by the Treasury staff and presented to Congress without comment or revision. Until 1865 the House Ways and Means Committee served as a planning mechanism, at least to the extent of permitting a comprehensive review of departmental requests. At that time a House Committee on Appropriations was established, and thereafter such unity as was achieved by congressional budget review began to be dissipated. By 1885 there were eight House committees with authority to recommend budget appropriations. Later this number was increased to ten, and the Senate delegated appropriating authority to eight of its standing committees. American budgeting developed almost a century later than in Western Europe not only because American executive power was less centralized, but also because of the relative unimportance of government operations before World War I. Between 1790 and 1900, the total receipts of the federal government, mostly from customs duties, amounted to only fifteen billion dollars, and expenditures were a little over sixteen billion.[8] This made average expenditure, including the cost of four wars, less than $150 million a year.

THE NEED FOR A NATIONAL BUDGET

So long as its major fiscal problem was the annual disposal of large surpluses, Congress had little incentive to impose rigorous spending controls on government departments. But following the Spanish-American War and America's emergence as a world power, federal expenditures increased more rapidly than sources of income. Congressional committees had become notorious for their tendency to favor special pleaders, and growing public hostility to government waste and corruption led muckrackers and even Congressmen to agitate for budget reform. The executive branch also favored a national budget, simply because without it the president's economic policies could not be implemented coherently.

In 1911 President Taft appointed a Commission on Economy and Efficiency which made the first detailed study of the federal government's organizational structure and pattern of expenditures. Its report, endorsed by the president, went to Congress in June 1912. *The Need for a National Budget* recommended that the president be made responsible for financial planning and fiscal management. His duties would include submitting a budget to Congress at the start of each year's regular session. This executive budget was to include a statement of policy, contain summary estimates of revenues and expenditures, an historical review of the past year's financial operations, and a summary of changes in the law. The Secretary of the Treasury was to prepare for Congress detailed reports supporting the executive conclusions and recommendations. Each department and agency of the government would in turn submit annual accounts to the Treasury and to Congress.

The 1912 election resulted in Taft's defeat, the loss of his influence as head of the Republican Party, and the return of a Congress controlled by Democrats. Nonetheless he submitted a 1913 budget to Congress, but partisan opposition and the inclination to defend congressional privileges caused its referral to the Committee on Appropriations, where it was allowed to die. Woodrow Wilson, inaugurated in March, did not push the budget issue. Business was good, the Treasury had no immediate financial problems, and with passage of the Sixteenth Amendment a new source of federal income became available.

STATE AND MUNICIPAL BUDGETS

Despite the federal government's failure to act, budgeting was an idea whose time had come. Cities and states, businesses, social organizations, and public institutions of all kinds were rapidly placed on a budgetary basis. The need was particulary felt for a clarification of administrative responsibility, and the appeal for "economy and efficiency" united social elements which had little else in common. Civic reformers saw in the budget a way to control expenditures and hold politicians accountable to the people. The business community favored budgeting as a means of easing tax burdens and making their dealings with government units more systematic, since competitive bidding on contracts and other reforms tended to accompany the introduction of budgetary procedures.

Very often the overriding motive for budgeting was economic necessity, as government units were asked to expand their activities without receiving a proportional increase in revenues. During the 1890s a number of big city administrations felt the need to establish budgetary systems, and over the next thirty years nearly all American municipalities followed their example. The states also faced increasing financial pressures, and between 1910 and 1920 forty-four of them enacted budget laws.[9] Considering that budgeting was promoted as a way to protect the citizen against arbitrary government, the results of these efforts must have surprised many of their sponsors. In the process of centralizing fiscal responsibility, the government and especially the executive branch enormously increased its power. Budgeting was of course only one aspect of a general movement away from *laissez-faire,* small government, and the rigid separation of legislative and executive authority. And the same thing was happening in other industrial countries. But America was the one major nation which established its budgetary system first at the lower levels and only afterwards on a national scale.

ADOPTION OF A NATIONAL BUDGET

Public interest in a national budget continued after the defeat of Taft's proposal, and increased with the expansion of federal activities following America's entry into World War I. All three major political parties included budget planks in their 1916 election platforms. In 1919 both Houses of Congress appointed committees to study the problem. The congressional debate centered on what type of budget was most suitable and particularly what the president's powers were to be. Agreement was reached, and Warren G. Harding signed the National Budgeting and Accounting Act on June 10, 1921.

This act made the president responsible for submitting to Congress at the start of each fiscal year a complete budget of federal revenues and expenditures. While the legislature could reject or revise these executive proposals, the budget, as in England, was meant to be the financial expression of the government's policies and programs for the coming year. A centralized Bureau of the Budget was created not only to prepare budget estimates, but also to make reorganization proposals which would reduce duplication, waste, and inefficiency within and between government agencies.

Though the Bureau was also authorized to make policy recommendations, its practical emphasis during the 1920s was on the development of expenditure controls. As its first Director said:

> The Bureau of the Budget is concerned only with the humbler and routine business of Government. Unlike cabinet officers, it is concerned with no question of policy, save that of economy and efficiency.[10]

A federal deficit in 1919 was followed by eleven years of surpluses, and during this period of business prosperity and frugal administration, a balanced budget and a reduced national debt were the only visible policy aims. This total emphasis on the negative aspects of budgeting suggests that a modern fiscal instrument had been placed in the hands of men who were unwilling to make full use of it.

GOVERNMENT AND INDUSTRIAL INTERACTIONS

In theory at least, a government unit should be able to decide on the actions it wishes to take, estimate their cost, and assess taxes adequate to finance them. But a business must first forecast its revenues and only then consider its operating alternatives within the limitations this forecast imposes. The motive underlying government budgeting is most often efficiency; in a business the motive is usually to increase profits.

The first business budgets were adopted for the purpose of limiting expenditures.[11] Many companies began by budgeting expenses they considered discretionary, such as advertising, research, and capital additions. There was no attempt to measure the effectiveness of such expenditures. The aim at first was merely to control them by keeping them within fixed limits.

SCIENTIFIC MANAGEMENT

The two main sources of systematic business budgeting were industrial engineering and cost accounting. Until the twentieth century, industrial planning was largely intuitive and precise computation of production costs was rarely considered necessary. But the expansion of heavy industry and the divison of labor tasks which accompanied assembly line production complicated the problems of factory planning and created conditions favorable to the introduction of budgetary procedures. Recognizing that production scheduling and control depended on meticulous preparation, Frederick Taylor tried to standardize industrial operations by applying scientific method to questions of "task management." Henri Fayol identified planning and forecasting as the first steps in the process of managerial control, and wrote of the need for "unity of direction" in plans and leadership. H. L. Gantt developed visual aids to planning and controlling, stressing the importance of time as a vital ingredient in the planning process.[12]

For these men, budgeting offered a means of placing responsibility and measuring performance rather than simply a way of limiting expenditures. Not until Taylor and others had made time and motion studies and test runs of each plant operation could production costs be accurately computed and a "science of work" be developed. The resulting production standards not only facilitated scheduling and worker incentive schemes but permitted far more precise budget estimates of plant capabilities and future operations. Performance standards and work measurement techniques developed in business were later introduced into such government agencies as the Forest Service, the Census Bureau, and the Bureau of Reclamation.[13]

THE ACCOUNTING CONTRIBUTION

Cost accountants helped systematize budgeting by establishing a system of records within which standard costs could be developed and routinely compared with actual results. Their early efforts to apply overhead to production on the basis of activity estimates led naturally to the idea of estimating expected costs in the form of a budget. Later they took the lead in setting standards for selling and financing expenses. We have seen how the distinction between fixed and variable overhead costs made by pioneers such as Garcke and Fells eventually led to flexible budgeting and the possibility of meaningful variance analysis even when volume fluctuated unexpectedly. Direct costing and refined methods of capital budgeting were other industrial accounting techniques which found applications in government budgeting.

But the extension of financial accounting techniques to serve government needs had hardly begun before World War II. At that time both commercial and nonprofit accounting were needlessly specialized. Government accountants concerned themselves largely with cash receipts and disbursements and the legal status of appropriations. To many orthodox financial accountants, budgeting seemed an entirely new medium involving prediction and comparison, subjective estimates of future conditions, and inferences which had to be derived partly from events outside the company. Littleton and Zimmerman conclude that the art of *policymaking* was better supported by government accounting systems, but the techniques for *decisionmaking* on the basis of accounting data were much better developed in commerical businesses.[14]

AMERICAN GOVERNMENT BUDGETING, 1929-1949

Fiscal 1931 brought a drop in receipts, a rise in expenditures, and the first of sixteen successive federal deficits. Keynes and other advocates of planned capitalism would argue that budgeting over the business cycle was necessary to maintain economic stability, and that such a policy on the government's part could have checked the overexpansion of the 1920s and prevented the subsequent depression. The way in which the private sector's collapse had affected government operations made it clear that effective budgeting must include projections for the whole economy. There was renewed interest in national income accounting.[15]

The New Deal plans for economic recovery required a greatly expanded Bureau of the Budget. In 1936 the Bureau was asked to assist the president in preparing executive orders and proclamations. The following year it was given authority to examine nonfiscal legislation for conformity with the government's general program. Nevertheless a report by the president's Committee on Administrative Management in 1937 criticized the Bureau's routinized, control-minded approach. The Reorganization Act of 1939 transferred the Bureau from the Treasury Department to the president's Executive Office, made it directly responsible to him, and authorized it to suggest improved management policies and procedures within the executive branch as well as reorganization plans for government agencies and departments.

Preplanning for the American war effort was sadly deficient. Military leaders were unable to:

> ... envision even remotely the extent of prospective supply needs of a total war waged all over the world. ... The plans and designs made in the War and Navy Departments were not too valuable. The administrative plans ... were quite inappropriate. War was not what the planners thought and did not come as they had imagined.[16]

There was no comprehensive system of priorities, and as military and civilian demands for crucial production elements exceeded available supplies, the impossibility of controlling each commodity separately became apparent. In 1941 the Production Requirements Plan was introduced to identify overall military needs in relation to existing inventories and industrial capacity. From 1943 to 1945 production and the distribution of output were budgeted through the Controlled Materials Plan. Novick considers this the first federal performance budget because it included: (1) identification of major goals, program objectives, and program elements; (2) the systematic analysis of supplies and needs, with Army, Navy and nonmilitary requests judged on the same basis; and (3) an extended time horizon encompassing long-range projects.[17]

POSTWAR INNOVATIONS

In the early postwar period, as William Vatter proposed a fund theory of accounting for business corporations,[18] the federal government began to adopt commercial accounting practices on a large scale. The Government Corporations Control Act of 1945 required that government-owned corporations use accrual accounting and separate their capital and revenue expenditures. Corporate budgets were to be supported by accounts that provided cost information, and the Comptroller General's audits were to appraise the corporation's performance rather than merely the legality and propriety of its expenditures.

The Cold War created a fiscal situation unique in American history. Defense spending continued for years at a high level, but without the excuse of a specific emergency to justify waste or extravagance. The high social costs of such a budget structure made it imperative that military expenditures somehow be related to results achieved. This required *economic* analysis of matters which had formerly been considered strictly political or military. Since 1921 federal budgeting had been conducted in terms of executive departments and their subdivisions. So long as each department performed an identified function, changes in its total expenditures could be roughly equated with changes in the scale of its efforts. But in the more sophisticated postwar environment, a government unit often performed several tasks, and numbers of personnel or dollars spent became less reliable guides to the quality of performance or even to the government's policy intentions.[19] Also, the traditional one-year budget failed to show the significance of capital expenditures, whose effects were often spread over much longer periods.

PERFORMANCE BUDGETING

In place of budgets which simply listed the objects of expenditure (personnel, travel, and so on), the Commission on Organization of the Executive Branch, chaired by Herbert Hoover, recommended that:

> the whole budgetary concept of the federal government should be re-fashioned by the adoption of a budget based on functions, activities and projects: this we designate a "performance budget."

In 1949 the National Security Act was amended to require performance budgeting in the Department of Defense. Other amendments to the same Act authorized the establishment of working capital funds and comptroller positions in the Defense Department, and gave the Comptroller General authority to set accounting requirements in terms of principles and standards. The Budgeting and Accounting Procedures Act of 1950 made no specific reference to performance budgeting, but required that budgets set forth "Functions and activities of the government." Narrative descriptions of programs and activities were added to the 1951 federal budget to give readers a general picture of the work to be done by the organizational units requesting funds. But neither these descriptions nor the revised defense budgets permitted objective assessment of the effectiveness of government expenditures.

The Bureau of the Budget was comfortable in its role of fiscal management and understandably reluctant to venture into areas requiring new expertise. Even the AICPA had described performance budgeting as "something that is, and isn't accounting."[20] Consistent with tradition:

> The professional backgrounds and philosophical orientations of several Directors of the Bureau during the 1950's led to emphasis on accounting aspects, negative controls, and routine approaches—without much effort to encourage long-range planning.[21]

The Bureau encouraged government agencies to adopt commercial methods of fixed asset and inventory accounting. The second Hoover Commission in 1955 recommended continued use of "program budgeting" and proposed that annual budget appropriations be based on accrued expenditure estimates. A 1956 law provided for subsidiary fixed asset records as part of each agency's accounting system. Financial statements were developed to show financial status, operating results, and the cost of performing assigned functions. The General Accounting Office undertook a program of management audits, designed to evaluate the effectiveness of an agency's discharge of its responsibilities.

THE PROGRAMMING-PLANNING-BUDGETING SYSTEM

Performance budgeting was especially hard to apply in agencies whose spending patterns were unstable. Before 1961 defense budgeting, and the planning of strategy and forces were:

> ... almost completely separate activities, done by different people, at different times, with different terms of reference and without any method of integrating their activities. Forces and strategy were developed by the military planners; budgeting was done by the civilian secretaries and the comptroller organization.[22]

Whether this divorce of planning and budgeting was a cause or an effect, information was not available about the costs of alternative military strategies or about the effects on them of different budgetary levels. Programs were still formulated within the particular department responsible for them, without considering their impact on other areas. The defense budget ceiling, based on administrative estimates of available revenue, did not refer to military requirements; the recommendations of the military services and the Joint Chiefs of Staff did not refer to costs. Differences were settled through a bargaining process whose results were hard to defend empirically. The ongoing effectiveness of military construction programs and new weapons systems was especially difficult to evaluate because the budgetary time horizon was only a year.

When Robert McNamara became Secretary of Defense in 1961, he added a programming capability to the Defense Department's existing performance budget, creating what is called the Programming-Planning-Budgeting System (PPBS). Department planners produced a range of alternative courses of action; programmers more specifically determined the priorities in accomplishing each of nine military "missions." No fixed budget ceiling was set. Instead, each spending proposal was judged on its merits in terms of need, contribution to increased military effectiveness, and cost in national resources. A series of completely costed "packages," which often required contributions by all three services, was projected five years into the future, and each annual budget was integrated with these long-range plans. Recognizing the need for a continuous rather than an annual review of ongoing programs, the Department in 1964 adopted the Program Change Proposal System to allow immediate modification in the approved Five Year Force Structure and Financial Program.

So successful was PPBS in the Defense Department that President Johnson called for its adoption throughout the federal government. His 1968 budget message summarized the advantages of a system which would enable the government to:

1. Identify our national goals with precision and on a continuing basis
2. Choose among those goals the ones that are most urgent

3. Search for alternative means of reaching those goals most effectively at the least cost
4. Inform ourselves not merely on next year's costs, but on the second, and third, and subsequent year's costs of our programs
5. Measure the performance of our programs to insure a dollar's worth of service for each dollar spent.

The installation of PPBS in twenty-one other government agencies produced mixed results. The Defense Department had ten years of experience with performance budgeting before adopting PPBS. In departments lacking such experience the new system was sometimes misunderstood and misused. Organizations with shorter-term or less complex planning needs did not always require such elaborate budgetary procedures. The success of PPBS was also found to depend on prolonged encouragement, and not every government agency had a McNamara to implement the "McNamara Method" in practice.

To the military planner, cost effectiveness may mean enhanced retaliatory capability, while to the entrepeneur it may imply increased market share or return on investment. The managerial task in both cases involves balancing needs and resources to reach specified objectives with minimum expenditure. Experience in defense planning and the recent history of business budgeting suggest that this is done best when annual and long-run plans are coordinated and when goal-setting, planning, and program analysis are based on an ordered sequence of analytical steps.

FOOTNOTES

1. Frederick C. Mosher, *Program Budgeting: Theory and Practice* (New York: Stratford Press, 1954), 48.
2. The word budget (from the Latin "bulga," meaning leather bag for carrying food supplies) originally referred to the money bag used as a receptacle for state revenues. Later the word was applied to the leather portfolio in which the Chancellor's budget speech was carried to Parliament. Finally it was extended to include the documents in the bag and the budget speech itself.
3. Edwin L. Theiss, "The Beginnings of Business Budgeting." *Accounting Review* 12 (January, 1937), 44.
4. Quoted in Jesse Burkhead. *Government Budgeting* (New York: John Wiley and Sons, 1959), 6.
5. Quoted in the Rene Stourm, *The Budget* (New York: D. Appleton and Company, 1917), 41-42.
6. E.L. Normanton, *The Accountability and Audit of Governments* (New York: Praeger, 1966), 17.
7. Stourm, *op. cit.*, 39.
8. Percival Flack Brundage, *The Bureau of the Budget* (New York: Praeger, 1970), 6.
9. Frederick A. Cleveland and Arthur E. Buck, *The Budget and Responsible Government* (New York: Macmillan, 1920), 124.
10. Quoted in Charles G. Dawes, *The First Year of the Budget of the United States* (New York: Harper and Brothers, 1923), xi.

11. Theiss, *op. cit.*, 49.
12. See Daniel A. Wren, *The Evolution of Management Thought* (New York: Ronald Press, 1972), 495.
13. Fremont Lyden and Ernest G. Miller, eds., *Planning Programming Budgeting: A Systems Approach to Management* (Chicago: Markham Publishing Company, 1968), 37.
14. A.C. Littleton and V.K. Zimmerman, *Accounting Theory: Continuity and Change* (Englewood Cliffs, N.J.: Prentice-Hall, 1962), 244.
15. For a detailed history from the seventeenth century, see P. Studenski, *The Income of Nations* (New York: University Press, 1958).
16. Mosher, *op. cit.*, 54.
17. David Novick, *Origin and History of Program Budgeting* (Santa Monica, Cal.: RAND Corporation, 1966), 5.
18. See William J. Vatter, *The Fund Theory of Accounting and its Implications for Financial Reports* (Chicago: University of Chicago Press, 1947).
19. David Novick, ed. *Program Budgeting* (Cambridge, Mass.: Harvard University Press, 1965), 29.
20. "Budgeting *a la* McNamara," *Journal of Accountancy* 121 (February, 1966), 16.
21. "Budgeting for National Objectives—Three Cheers and One Criticism," *Journal of Accountancy* 121 (May, 1966), 34.
22. *Planning-Programming-Budgeting*, Hearings, Subcommittee on National Security and International Operations, Committee on Government Operations, United States Senate, 90th Congress, 1st Session (Washington, D.C.: U.S. Government Printing Office, 1967), part 2, 67.

SELECTED BIBLIOGRAPHY

Brundage, Percival Flack. *The Bureau of the Budget*. New York: Praeger, 1970, chaps. one and two.
Burkhead, Jesse. *Government Budgeting*. New York: John Wiley and Sons, 1959, chap. one.
Cleveland, Frederick A., and Buck, Arthur E. *The Budget and Responsible Government*. New York: Macmillan, 1920.
Harrill, E. Reese. "Performance Budgeting and Accounting." *The Federal Accountant*, 14 (Spring, 1965), 35-58.
Harris, R.D. "Necker's *Compte Rendu* of 1781: A Reconsideration." *Journal of Modern History* 42 (June, 1970), 161-183.
Herbert, L. "A Perspective of Accounting." *Accounting Review* 46 (July, 1971), 433-440.
Jennings, R.M., and Trout, A.P. "Internal Control—Public Finance in 17th Century France." *Journal of European Economic History* (1972), 647-660.
Kendrick, J.W. *Economic Accounts and their Uses*. New York: McGraw-Hill, 1972, 10-20.
_____. "The Historical Development of National-Income Accounts." *History of Political Economy* 2 (Fall, 1970), 284-315.
Lyden, Fremont, and Miller, Ernest G., eds. *Planning Programming Budgeting: A Systems Approach to Management*. Chicago: Markham Publishing Company, 1968.
Mattessich, Richard. "On the Evolution of Budgeting and Budget Simulation." Chap. 2, pp. 5-10 of his *Simulation of the Firm Through a Budget Computer Program*. Homewood, Ill.: Richard D. Irwin, 1964.
Morse, Ellsworth, H., Jr. "The Accounting and Auditing Act of 1950—Its Current Significance to GAO." *GAO Review* (Summer, 1975), 23-31.
Mosher, Frederick C. *Program Budgeting: Theory and Practice*. New York: Stratford Press, 1954.
Normanton, E.L. *The Accountability and Audit of Governments*. New York: Praeger, 1966, chaps. one and two.
Novick, David. *Origin and History of Program Budgeting*. Santa Monica, Cal.: RAND Corporation, 1966.

_____. ed. *Program Budgeting*. Cambridge, Mass.: Harvard University Press, 1965, especially chap. one.

Raymond, Robert H. "History of the Flexible Budget." *Management Accounting* 47 (August, 1966), 9-15.

Rogers, D.M. "Development of the Modern Business Budget." *Journal of Accountancy* 53 (1932), 186-205.

Staats, Elmer B. "Government Auditing–Yesterday, Today, and Tomorrow." *GAO Review* (Spring, 1976), 1-9.

Stourm, Rene, *The Budget*. New York: D. Appleton and Company, 1917.

Studenski, P. *The Income of Nations*. New York: University Press, 1958.

Theiss, Edwin L. "The Beginnings of Business Budgeting." *Accounting Review* 12 (January, 1937), 43-55.

Chapter 15

THE ACCOUNTING ROLE IN INCOME TAXATION

FORERUNNER LEGISLATION

Income taxation is as old as civilization. The Old Testament and histories of ancient India mention taxes based on personal income. The regular, direct income taxation of Roman citizens began shortly after establishment of the Empire. Many medieval principalities taxed personal earnings. The Florentine Republic levied an income tax in the fifteenth century, as did the French monarchy beginning in the reign of Louis XIV.

Yet no preindustrial society relied mainly on the income tax for its revenues. Such a tax requires a concept of income separate from capital, and this was largely absent during the Middle Ages. It is also harder to assess and needs more elaborate administrative machinery than either sales or property taxes. To some extent its success depends on the growth of commerce and industry, as well as on widespread literacy, an abundance of savings and capital, a tendency to urban living, and a society mature enough to accept taxation as a self-imposed discipline. Another prerequisite for a successful income tax is accurate record keeping. The use of a self-calculated tax is in itself evidence of considerable accounting sophistication.

Though several European countries had been moving toward income taxation since the seventeenth century,[1] the modern income tax dates from the Napoleonic Wars. In 1793 France adopted a general income tax as a war finance measure. England did the same in 1799. The British assessment procedure was noteworthy partly because of its influence on later American tax laws. While not formally progressive, it allowed exemptions for families with children. Deductions were granted for payment of life insurance premiums and for the cost of income-producing buildings. This tax was repealed in 1816 and no similar law was enacted until 1842, when the permanent British income tax came into force. Peacetime income taxes were first adopted by Austria in 1849, by Germany in 1850, and by Italy in 1864.

AMERICAN INCOME TAX LAWS, 1646–1913

During the seventeenth century, several of the American colonies[2] supplemented property taxes by exacting levies on "estates or faculties," that is, on the skilled aptitudes possessed by "laborers, artificers and handicraftsmen." The faculty tax was therefore levied on assumed, not actual income. Such laws were hard to enforce and were usually short-lived. But prior to the Revolutionary War a number of colonies revived the faculty tax, and during the war more than a third of them taxed profits. When the colonies had won their independence these statutes were allowed to lapse. During the early nineteenth century six states tried to impose income taxes, but with little more effect than to create systems of licensing.[3]

A federal income tax was proposed during the War of 1812, but between 1780 and 1860 tariffs remained the main source of government revenue. The first federal income tax was a war measure passed in 1861. It was so badly drafted that it never became operative, and in the following year Congress replaced it with a more workable law. The 1862 act provided for progressive rates of 3 percent on incomes above $800, and was scaled up to 10 percent on incomes above $5000. The rates were increased until in 1865 earnings between $600 and $5000 were taxed at 5 percent and those above $5000 at 10 percent. Taxpayers were required to submit lists of annual income and taxable property from which an assessor calculated the amount owed. Though affecting only 1 percent of the population, this Civil War legislation established a number of taxing principles and precedents which became part of Revenue Acts passed after the Sixteenth Amendment. A concept of "taxable net income" developed. Rent, dividends, and interest were taxable, but legacies and life insurance proceeds did not constitute income. Losses sustained on stock or other property were allowed only when the asset was disposed of. Casualty losses were deductible. Asset repairs were distinguished from permanent improvements. Tax was withheld from the wages of government employees and from interest paid on certain corporate securities. Most important, the notion became established that a tax on earnings is the fairest measure of a man's ability to pay.

Despite lack of adequate enforcement machinery (and in contrast to the Confederate income tax), the tax was a fiscal success, yielding $347 million in eleven years, a fifth of all federal internal revenue during the Civil War. However, most of this money was raised in the Eastern states and spent elsewhere. Eastern financial interests opposed the tax and their thinking controlled the then dominant Republican Party. Congress allowed it to lapse in 1873.

The tariff was still the main source of revenue during the last third of the nineteenth century, but its yield fluctuated widely according to business conditions and had little relation to government needs for income. Moreover, the economy was unstable, with depressions in 1873, 1884, and 1893. The income tax was seen by its advocates as a way to make the federal government big enough to control the business cycle and regulate large corporations. Inequalities in wealth furnished a second argument for the income tax. While farmers and small businessmen paid both state and local taxes, the rich often escaped taxation almost entirely. Farm and labor organizations made the income tax part of their program. In Congress a political battle was joined between southern and western Democrats, who viewed the tariff as a burden, and eastern legislators who favored protective tariffs to reduce European competition. Grover Cleveland's election in 1892 on a platform of tariff for revenue only meant that another source of federal income was needed, and in 1894 Congress passed an income tax law modeled on the Civil War legislation. The tax applied to both personal and corporate income. Capital gains, gifts, and inheritances were taxable, and a flat 2 percent rate was applied with a $4000 exemption for personal taxpayers. Seligman says the act was so carelessly written that it was in some ways fortunate when the Supreme Court declared it unconstitutional.[4]

The Constitution gave Congress power to levy taxes, but to prevent shifting an unfair burden to sparsely settled farm states, required that direct taxes be allotted according to state population. No one knew exactly what a direct tax was, but all the legal precedents favored the new income tax.[5] However, in a landmark case, *Pollack v. Farmer's Loan and Trust,* the Supreme Court in 1895 declared it unconstitutional on the grounds that (1) the federal government lacked the power to tax income from state bonds, and (2) a tax on income was in effect a tax on the source of that income; thus a tax on rents was a direct tax on the land from which rents were received, and was invalid because it was not apportioned equally as the Constitution specified. At the rehearing asked for by both sides, the Court concluded that the parts of the act invalidated were so important as to void the whole law. This meant that no federal personal income tax could be levied until the Constitution was amended or the Supreme Court reversed its decision.

The Spanish-American War was financed largely by excise taxes, but as the twentieth century began, the federal government again felt the need for new sources of revenue. There were also renewed demands for a tax based on ability to pay. In 1908 Theodore Roosevelt recommended an income tax, and Democrats committed to it under Bryan joined forces with insurgent Republicans. In 1909 conservative Republicans, forced to compromise, joined with President Taft to propose a constitutional amendment authorizing an income tax unhampered by apportionment:

> The Congress shall have power to lay and collect taxes on incomes, from whatever source derived, without apportionment among the several States, and without regard to any census or enumeration.

While awaiting ratification of the Sixteenth Amendment, Congress in 1909 passed a corporate income tax bill disguised as a "special excise tax" of 1 percent on net incomes over $5000, to be paid "on the privilege of using the corporate form to do business." This law was hastily constructed and badly worded, but its constitutionality was upheld in *Flint v. Stone Tracy Co.* However, it ignored the commercial accounting methods then in use, provoking an immediate reaction from the accounting profession which gave a foretaste of things to come.

There had been little comment by accountants on the 1862 and 1894 statutes. Accountancy in America had been in its infancy. But by 1909 a number of sizable public accounting firms were established, and the large corporations most affected by the new tax had already developed modern methods of determining income. Accrual accounting was widely used; most corporations depreciated plant assets; bad debts and contingent liabilities were typically provided for, and many firms had adopted the natural business year. The Corporate Excise Act provoked a rash of indignant letters and articles from practicing accountants. An open letter appeared in July 1909, signed by twelve prominent accounting firms, pointing out the "errors" in the proposed act, stating that it "was absolutely impossible of application," and that it "violates all the principles of sound accounting."[6] Other articles asked why the accounting society had not been consulted by Congress and why the act made no provision for loss carryovers or for a continuing credit for the $5000 exemption.[7] Another CPA pointed out that by requiring the use of cash basis accounting and the calendar year, the act worked a hardship on taxpayers since "taxable net earnings received will sometimes be greatly in excess of net profits."[8] And why was depreciation allowed only if the corporate records showed a direct writedown of an asset's cost, rather than through the commoner use of an allowance account?[9]

Not for the last time, tax authorities had been trapped into making theoretical decisions without a knowledge of accounting theory. The Treasury was sensitive to these criticisms, especially since it had been given the task of administering an unworkable law. In December 1909, the Secretary of the Treasury issued an official interpretation permitting accrual income finding. Fiscal year corporations were also allowed to estimate beginning inventories. Accountants had succeeded in swinging the law at least partially back toward the recognition of orthodox accounting methods. But this was only the beginning of a continuing conflict between the language of the tax code and accounting interpretations governing its application, with a resulting confusion of ideas which still persists.

AMERICAN REVENUE ACTS SINCE 1913

Following passage of the Sixteenth Amendment, the Revenue Act of 1913, including a fifteen-page income tax section, became law on October 3, 1913. The rates were modest: a normal tax of 1 percent was placed on personal incomes above $3000 for single individuals and $4000 for married couples. A surtax ranging from 1 to 6 percent was also imposed on taxable income above $20,000. Corporations were taxed 1 percent on all income, without exemptions. Most of the essential ideas underlying this 1913 law remain in effect today. Dividends, capital gains, and undistributed profits were taxable, but not gifts, inheritances, or interest on government securities. Business expenses, taxes, interest, casualty losses, bad debts, and depreciation were deductible. As in 1909, the law passed the burden of determining taxable income onto the taxpayer but ignored the taxpayer's regular accounting system and his established accounting period. This act also was impossible to administer as written, and interpretive court decisions, often rendered by judges with no accounting knowledge, tended to further separate tax and financial accounting practice. Cases were decided in a way which ignored the idea that income accrued. Yet the 1913 law did not attract the abundance of criticism which the 1909 act had. When opponents of income taxation again appealed to the courts, citing the due process clause of the Fifth Amendment (because of exemptions and graduated rates), the tax was upheld in *Brushaber v. Union Pacific Railroad Co.* (1916).

By requiring written records to support the determination of taxable income, the tax law made accountancy mandatory and vastly increased the work of public accountants. CPAs had the immediate problem of helping thousands of businessmen who had never felt the need to make financial statements, and who now got their first statistical view of their total operations. An engagement to prepare tax returns gave the accountant opportunities to show that he could be useful in other ways. And for the first time, accounting options and accounting theory became important to many outside the profession.

The Revenue Act of 1916 improved income measurement by allowing taxpayers who kept their books on the accrual basis to prepare returns in the same way. Following America's entry into World War I, tax rates were drastically increased, exemptions were lowered, and an excess profits tax was imposed. The income tax *per se* was no longer debatable; it had become a necessity.

As a result of collaboration between accountants, lawyers, and economists, the 1918 Revenue Act for the first time set out tax rules based on commercial accounting practice, and these have remained essentially the same since. Every Act since 1918 has contained a statement similar to the declaration that "approved standard methods of accounting will ordinarily be regarded as clearly reflecting income," which should be calculated "in accordance with the method of accounting regularly employed in keeping the books. ...." The regulations included an outline of approved accounting methods. Accrual accounting and the fiscal year were specifically permitted. Inventories had to be taken where needed. Court decisions tended to support the accounting determination of taxable income. For example, in *Doyle v. Mitchell Bros. Co.* (1918) it was held that deductions from revenues to arrive at gross profit are inherent and do not depend on specific provisions of the tax law.

Though during the 1920s income taxation still affected only the well-to-do, tax courses were added to the curricula of most universities, accountants were licensed to practice before the tax courts, and tax questions appeared for the first time on the CPA examination. The tax code continued to assimilate accounting methods and concepts. The 1921 Revenue Act permitted the use of bad debt allowances, net loss carryovers, and consolidated returns. It also gave the first preferential treatment to capital gains, sharpening the separation of income and capital by recognizing that inflation cancels out part of the value of holding gains. But most important was the influence of taxation in popularizing the realization principle. From the transactions approach used in determining taxable income, and from court decisions,[10] the idea emerged that realization must occur before income is earned. And since realization is most objectively measured at the time of sale, income should be recognized then. This method replaced the older approach to income determination in which assets were inventoried at the beginning and end of each year. This change, essentially completed by the early thirties,[11] also reflected a gradual shift in accounting emphasis from the balance sheet to the income statement.

In 1939 the income tax still reached only five million people and yielded less than 20 percent of national revenues.[12] The Second World War put fifty million people on the rolls, creating the first mass tax and causing an unprecedented increase in the volume of accounting work. Though other factors were involved, a close correspondence exists between the rise in tax collections and the phenomenal growth of American Institute of Accountants' membership during the 1940s.[13] Higher rates and progressive taxation also accentuated the differences between tax and financial accounting treatments, leading to material distortions in financial statements and to the tax allocation debate of the postwar period. During the 1920s tax laws had largely caught up with commercial accounting practice; beginning in the 1930s they went beyond it in such areas as depreciation and inventory valuation, providing substitutes for theoretical changes the accounting profession was unable or unwilling to make.

In 1938 LIFO inventory valuation was allowed for a few classes of taxpayers, and in the following year its use was generalized. Thus the shift to LIFO coincided with the beginning of a thirty year rise in prices. Its ultimate justification was perhaps the accounting profession's failure to permit price level adjustments. Without LIFO, there would have been a critical cash squeeze on businesses which had to finance rapid inventory buildups. But in 1939 it was considered suitable only for firms with large investments in uniform raw materials whose cost comprised a major part of finished product value. In an attempt to limit its use, the provisions which authorized LIFO stated that it could be used for tax purposes only when also employed for financial reporting. Its predecessor, the base stock method, had never been widely adopted, and without its ability to defer tax payments in periods of rising prices LIFO would probably not have become important in financial accounting. But so great was the tax incentive that it was widely used for accounting purposes regardless of its theoretical propriety. It became the classic case of a tax treatment creating its own theoretical justifications and going on to modify existing accounting concepts.

Though accelerated depreciation had for years been described in accounting texts, until 1954 the straight line method was almost universally used both for tax and financial reporting.[14] Straight line depreciation was no more theoretically defensible: it ignored asset obsolescence and the likelihood of greater use in the early years of life, and seems to have been popular largely because of its simplicity. But as was the case in almost every country which has modified tax depreciation rules since World War II, the 1954 liberalization was promoted not to improve income measurement but to stimulate the economy by encouraging capital investment. Fast depreciation was also a response to the rising cost of equipment and to demands for depreciation on replacement cost. Since 1954 tax savings from accelerated depreciation have become a major source of industrial financing, creating interest-free government loans which in growth firms tend to become outright grants.[15] As with LIFO, first the method was permitted, then a supporting theory was developed. By tending to understate reported income, accelerated depreciation intensified the problem of reconciling tax and financial results. Ironically, the 1954 Revenue Act had been intended to narrow differences between tax and financial accounting. Instead it increased them and made the allocation problem urgent.

TAX AND ACCOUNTING INTERACTIONS

We have seen that the state of the accounting art in 1913 was far superior to the early tax laws, and that the dependency of tax rules on accounting concepts was quickly recognized. The first Revenue Acts were made workable by the addition of borrowed accounting techniques, and later tax laws gained sophistication by adopting other accounting methods. Contemporary accounting literature on taxation is heavily conditioned by this historical experience, reflecting attitudes toward income taxation which might be simplified as follows: (1) since periodic profit finding is essentially an accounting problem, it is natural for tax procedures to imitate accounting methods, and (2) conflicts between tax rules and commercial accounting practice can be minimized by making the two areas more alike. These notions retain as much impetus and inertia as the tax laws themselves, and have furnished the motivation for repeated attempts to reconcile tax and financial accounting.

The tax influence on accounting theory is hard to evaluate, if only because of its pervasiveness. Hendriksen calls it mainly indirect.[16] Tax rulings have provoked urgent discussion of neglected accounting topics. Taxation has been a prime mover in the shift in accounting emphasis from inventorying assets to measuring earnings. Tax acceptance is a means of very quickly securing mass adoption of any preferred accounting method. It undoubtedly has helped to "average up" and improve the consistency of ordinary accounting practice.

But a primary reason for codifying accounting principles was to reduce the number of acceptable alternatives in practice. The tax laws have increased accounting options without regard to accounting theory. One authority estimates that tax rulings delayed wide use of the natural business year for a generation.[17] Tax rules on gains and losses, and the administrative reasons for not allowing price level adjustments, continue to inhibit accounting efforts to depart from historical cost. The tendency of tax authorities to attack individual problems without considering accounting side effects may have encouraged the piecemeal approach to theory taken by the accounting societies. To some extent tax rules have become an American equivalent of the legal codes which regulate accountancy in France, Germany and Sweden, and like them, have tended to substitute law for professional judgment.

No real theory of income underlies the tax system. It lives on borrowed accounting theory, and has found it convenient to adopt most accounting principles. The tax laws adhere to historical cost, ignore fluctuations in the value of money, and generally respect the separateness of entities. The accounting emphasis on consistency and disclosure is in part an outgrowth of tax policy. Even more than financial accounting, tax laws emphasize determinable events, stressing uniformity, objectivity, and conservatism.

Most differences between tax rules and accounting principles center around the timing of revenue realization and expense deductibility. The tax system is a hybrid of cash and accrual methods because taxable income is computed to determine a taxpayer's ability to make an immediate cash payment. Administrative convenience and the need for current revenue collections also conflict with the accounting presumption of continuous economic life, giving each tax year a tendency to stand by itself. Periodicity rather than matching is at the heart of the tax concept of income. Profit tends to be divorced from the related expense of earning it. And in general the accounting concept of realization seems to be moving away from the tax premises which helped establish it.

If as Justice Holmes said, "Taxes are the price we pay for civilization," their benefits should be social as well as economic. The main procedural differences between tax and financial accounting result from inclusion in the tax law of social welfare, public policy, and equity provisions modifying the general concept of income. Besides the need to deal fairly with those whose ability to pay is unequal, tax administration requires detailed regulations which allow officials to make decisions with a minimum of judgment. The tendency is to rely on legal precedents rather than asking what data mean in terms of business events. Tax disputes between lawyers and accountants are not simply jurisdictional but involve a basic conflict between legal and economic approaches to income measurement.

Another obstacle to reconciling tax and financial accounting is the inability of accountants to define their own principles or to reduce the variety of methods used in handling identical transactions. The tax system includes procedures for putting disputes before the courts for definitive decisions. American accountancy lacks any such judicial body to resolve differences in practice, and the absence of a single source of accounting authority inhibits unity with tax rules, which for administrative purposes must be as precise and uniform as possible. In taxation, each allowable method is equally acceptable; in financial accounting, some are preferable to others. All these differences have become highly abrasive because of persistent efforts by accountants and the government to make the two areas as similar as possible. Both the investment credit fiasco and the continuing debate over tax allocation illustrate the dangers involved in this compulsion to reconcile tax and accounting income measurement.

The facts regarding the investment credit are well known. The 1962 Revenue Act required that the full amount of the credit be treated for tax purposes as a reduction of the basis of acquired property, and APB *Opinion No. 2* also advocated this "cost reduction" method. The 1964 Revenue Act then made the full credit available to reduce tax expense. Conceding no flaw in its original reasoning, the American Institute in 1964 reversed itself to also allow the "flow through" method. For some this about-face only illustrated the subservience of financial accounting to tax rulings. For others the moral was that unresponsiveness to taxpayer opinion can force the AICPA into untenable positions. Others, including Maurice Moonitz, cited the investment credit difficulties as evidence of the failure of accounting theory to handle situations for which no precedents exist.[18] But the problem may also be seen as part of a tendency to overapply historical experience. Perhaps the struggle to gain tax acceptance of financial accounting principles has succeeded too well, achieving more compatibility than is appropriate or desirable, and it would be wiser to accept as inherent more of the differences between tax and commercial accounting.

The AICPA view is that there should be greater conformity between tax and financial income. Its main technique for achieving this is interperiod tax allocations to eliminate the effects of timing differences. *Accounting Research Bulletin No. 23* (1944) simply stated that income taxes are an expense which like other expenses should be allocated to income. In 1945 SEC *Accounting Series Release 53* opposed allocation, as did the AAA Committee on Accounting Concepts and Standards in its 1957 statement. In 1954 *Accounting Research Bulletin No. 44* concluded that accelerated depreciation required no allocation of deferred income tax, but in the 1958 revision of the bulletin the Institute reversed itself, declaring that a future tax liability exists when accelerated depreciation is used for tax purposes but not for financial reporting. *Accounting Research Study No. 9,* "Interperiod Allocation of Corporate Income Taxes" (1966) assumed that tax allocation is "generally adopted" and "widely accepted" and that only its extent and the method of presentation remained debatable. *Accounting Principles Board Opinion No. 11,* "Accounting For Income Taxes" (1967) required comprehensive interperiod tax allocation.

Supporters of tax allocation justify it on the grounds that it helps synchronize taxation and financial accounting. They argue that commercial accounting is the better base for determining income and that allocation therefore helps achieve proper matching and a better tax measurement of actual income. To the extent that book and taxable income differ, the latter tends to include a subsidy or penalty. Thus, accepting the differences between tax and financial accounting may be saying in effect that the government has the right to tax unearned income. Or the failure to allocate may mislead statement readers about future dividend prospects by reporting income as tax free when it is not. Without allocation, businessmen would in effect have to keep two sets of books, a far more cumbersome way to eliminate the effects of tax expediencies.

Opponents of comprehensive tax allocation are also concerned with the interaction of tax rules and accounting theory. But for them the allocation problem is one of interpreting the future. Acceptance of allocation depends on the assumption that differences between tax and book income will wash out over the firm's life and that deferred income will eventually be taxed. But in a business with even a moderate growth rate the offsetting entry to this year's tax reduction may never be required. Allocation thus creates an essentially contingent liability or an asset which may never be realized. The allocation process also assumes that timing differences can be isolated and tax effects specifically attributed to them. But if timing differences turn out to be permanent instead of temporary the matching principle ceases to be an argument for tax allocation—it is illogical to provide for future taxes that will probably never be paid. Even more than the investment credit, the allocation question brings into focus all the difficulties of reconciling tax and financial accounting. Allocation is logical only if we assume that tax and book income are basically alike; it can hardly be justified if we assume they are basically different.

CONCLUSIONS

For fifty years accountants have tried to make income tax rules compatible with commercial accounting practice. In the early days of taxation this was necessary and helpful, lending the tax code workable methods and a philosophic core, hastening adoption of better accounting techniques, and stimulating critical analysis of existing theory. But there are inherent differences between tax rules and accounting methods, and much evidence suggests that attempts to reconcile the two have been carried past a point of diminishing returns. Efforts to simplify the tax code and bring it into harmony with financial accounting have failed. On the other side, accounting acceptance of tax options has resulted in theoretical inconsistencies and the proliferation of meaningless alternatives in practice. From the accountant's viewpoint, the question is not how much tax and financial accounting should differ, but how much tax expedients should be allowed to influence published financial statements. If tax policies are to be based on accounting concepts, it is in the interest of all concerned that such concepts should reflect the realities of business events and not simply be tailored to fit tax consequences. Obviously each area should stop imitating the other's methods where they do not apply. And it does seem that the profession should oppose tax regulations which try to prescribe accounting methodology. Rather than being historically conditioned as at present, its position on such questions as tax allocation should aim at a reduction of tax influence on accounting theory.

FOOTNOTES

1. Carl Sumner Shoup, *Ricardo on Taxation* (New York: Columbia University Press, 1960), 220.
2. New Plymouth, 1643; Massachusetts Bay, 1646; New Haven, 1649; Connecticut, 1650.
3. M.K. McKay, "The Background of the Income Tax." *Taxes—The Tax Magazine* 27 (June, 1949), 568-74.
4. Edwin R.A. Seligman, *The Income Tax* (New York: Macmillan, 1914), 522.
5. The Supreme Court in *Collector v. Hubbard* and *Springer v. United States* had upheld the Civil War income tax. Later in *Hylton v. United States* it had ruled that a tax on pleasure carriages was not a direct tax but an excise or "use tax" which did not have to be apportioned.
6. Open letter reprinted in *The Journal of Accountancy* 9 (July, 1909), 212-13.
7. W.S. Pangborn, "The Injustice of the Law," *Journal of Accountancy* 9 (September, 1909), 351-55.
8. R.P. Marsh, "The Corporation Tax Act and Interest," *Journal of Accountancy* 9 (December, 1909), 141-42.
9. "The Corporation Tax Act and Depreciation," editorial, *Journal of Accountancy* 14 (March, 1912), 218-22.
10. The Supreme Court in *Eisner v. Macomber* supported the realization at sale doctrine by holding that stock dividends were not realized income to the recipient.
11. See *Audits of Corporate Accounts: Correspondence with New York Stock Exchange* (New York: American Institute of Accountants, 1934), 5-7, 14, 25-26.
12. *Encyclopedia Americana*, vol. 14 (New York: Americana Corporation, 1961), 743.
13. M.E. Peloubet, "The Historical Development of Accounting," in Morton Backer, ed., *Modern Accounting Theory* (Englewood Cliffs, N.J.: Prentice-Hall, 1966), 22.
14. Dan Throop Smith, *Tax Factors in Business Decisions* (Englewood Cliffs, N.J.: Prentice-Hall, 1968), 174.
15. Sidney Davidson, "Accelerated Depreciation and the Allocation of Income Taxes." *Accounting Review* 33 (April, 1958), 173-80.
16. Eldon S. Hendriksen, *Accounting Theory*, rev. ed. (Homewood, Ill.: Richard D. Irwin, 1970), 47.
17. James M. Van Tattenhove, "The Natural Business Year and its use as a Fiscal Year by Trades and Industries in the State of Washington" (unpublished M.B.A. thesis, Graduate School of Business, University of Washington, 1956), 5-11.
18. Maurice Moonitz, "Some Reflections on the Investment Credit Experience," *Journal of Accounting Research* 4 (Spring, 1966), 47-61.

SELECTED BIBLIOGRAPHY

American Accounting Association, Committee on Concepts and Standards. "Accounting Principles and Taxable Income." *Accounting Review* 27 (October, 1952), 427-30.

American Institute of CPAs, Accounting Principles Board. "Accounting for Income Taxes." *Opinion No. 11.* New York: AICPA, 1967.

Black, Homer A. "Interperiod Allocation of Corporate Income Taxes." *Accounting Research Study No. 9.* New York, AICPA, 1966.

Cannon, Arthur M. "Tax Pressures on Accounting Principles and Accountants' Independence." *Accounting Review* 27 (October, 1952), 419-26.

Davidson, Sidney, "Accelerated Depreciation and the Allocation of Income Taxes." *Accounting Review* 33 (April, 1958), 173-80.

Drinkwater, David, and Edwards, James Don. "The Nature of Taxes and the Matching Principle." *Accounting Review* 40 (July, 1965), 579-82.

Dwight, Drake. "The Feasibility of Adjusting for Inflation in Computing Taxable Income." *Washington Law Review* (May, 1974), 874-920.

Hawkins, David F. "Controversial Accounting Changes." *Harvard Business Review* (March-April 1968), 20-41.

Hendriksen, Eldon S. *Accounting Theory*, rev. ed. Homewood, Ill.: Richard D. Irwin, 1970, 44-47, 461-77.

Keller, Thomas F. *Accounting for Corporate Income Taxes.* Ann Arbor: University of Michigan Press, 1961.

May, George O. "Accounting and the Accountant in the Administration of Income Taxation." *Columbia Law Review* 67 (April, 1947).

_____. "Historical Foreward." In Dan Throop Smith and J. Keith Butters, *Taxable and Business Income.* New York: National Bureau of Economic Research, 1949.

_____. "Taxable Income and Accounting Bases for Determining It." *Journal of Accountancy* 41 (October, 1925), 248-66.

McAnly, H.T. "How Lifo Began." *Management Accounting* 56 (May, 1975), 24-26.

McKay, M.K. "The Background of the Income Tax." *Taxes—The Tax Magazine* 27 (June, 1949), 568-74.

Moonitz, Maurice. "Some Reflections on the Investment Credit Experience." *Journal of Accounting Research* 4 (Spring, 1966), 47-61.

Norgaard, Corine T. "Financial Implications of Comprehensive Income Tax Allocation." *Financial Analysts Journal* (January-February, 1969), 81-85.

Penndorf, B. "The Relation of Taxation to the History of the Balance Sheet." *Accounting Review* 5 (December, 1930), 243-51.

Perry, Raymond E. "Comprehensive Income Tax Allocation." *Journal of Accountancy* 122 (February, 1966), 23-32.

Revsine, Lawrence. "Some Controversy Concerning 'Controversial Accounting Changes.'" *Accounting Review* 44 (April, 1969), 354-58.

Smith, Dan Throop. *Tax Factors in Business Decisions.* Englewood Cliffs, N.J.: Prentice-Hall, 1968.

Waas, R.W. "Trends in Taxation." *The Accountant* 171 (October 3, 1974), 449-453.

Winbourne, Marilynn G., and Kleepsie, Dee L. "Tax Allocation in Perspective." *Accounting Review* 41 (October, 1966), 737-44.

Part 3

A HISTORY OF ACCOUNTING THEORY

Chapter 16

ACCOUNTING THEORY: VIEWS OF THE FIRM

Despite its pragmatic origins and development, accounting has always been based on a structure of ideas. That is, there are patterns of thought underlying accounting processes which afford rational explanations for the particular methods which finally evolve. Experience may provide the initial impetus for theory and the final test of conceptual validity, but experience is itself an interpretation involving the analysis of facts in terms of standards.[1] In that sense all accounting rules have a logical foundation. This chapter describes the discovery and exposition of the theoretical framework which governs accounting practice and within which the specifics of modern theory have evolved.

ROTE LEARNING

Proprietorship was a central feature in the creation of double entry bookkeeping. The concept of capital helped bridge the gap between the reasoning involved in simple personal debt records and the Method of Venice with its integrated real and nominal accounts.[2] In Pacioli's view and that of his immediate successors, the final results of the bookkeeping cycle consisted of operating totals summarized in proprietary capital and income accounts.

But Pacioli gave no rules for teaching bookkeeping and used few specific illustrations of the type needed to make the subject part of a school curriculum. Most early writers on double entry were intent on disseminating the new system in practice. They did not theorize much, or explain how transactions should be thought out, or why a certain account should be debited and another credited.[3] A majority of later textbook authors were teachers of bookkeeping. Though their writings are our main source of information about the early development of theory, their tendency was to imitate each other, and only a few of them tried to explain the reasoning behind accounting procedures.

The essence of the first 300 years of bookkeeping instruction was first, emphasis on the journal, second, the use of rules to determine journal entries, and third, account personification. The reason for this was partly historical: the journal had been the mainstay of the Italian three book system. But whereas a fifteenth century entry expressed a complete thought, by the seventeenth century entries were prepared in a modified shorthand form which made the journal a less suitable teaching device. Teachers and authors who used it to introduce accounting failed to get a broad perspective on the subject. Each business event had to be considered as a separate problem. Nearly all texts written before the nineteenth century consisted essentially of explanations as to which journal entries were appropriate to particular transactions.[4]

Since there were thousands of possible transactions, most authors resorted to lists of rules to be memorized for use in preparing a variety of journal entries.[5] William Weston cited forty-five such rules. James Peele's method was to present forty-four sample transactions followed by the required journal entries. Dafforne gave fifteen "rules of aide" intended to cover every type of transaction. Edward Hatton illustrated twenty-nine cases for domestic trade, eighteen for foreign trade, six cases for domestic factorage, five cases for factorage in foreign trade, and sixteen cases for partnership accounts. Charles Snell's *Rules for bookkeeping* packed seventy rules into eleven pages, and his *The Merchant's Counting-House* consisted entirely of sixty-nine rules. Peele, Dafforne, Manzoni, and Dr. Kelly put their rules into verse to impress them on the student's memory. Other writers searched in vain for a general rule which would apply to all transactions and accounts.

The memorizing and copying of rules, cases and model entries became the chief means of instruction. Teaching was by example. Authors aimed to identify journal entries for every conceivable business event. There was no reasoned analysis of the latter, only a rehearsal of various transactions and of the resulting entries. First the student found in his text the case or rule which fitted a transaction, then he looked up the wastebook posting reference beside it and traced the example through the journal and ledger.[6] Though continuity of operations probably resulted in a more repetitive pattern of entries, rote teaching was obviously limited to familiar situations. Yet the use of rules was rarely questioned—it was also the common method of instruction in other areas of education. Even those seventeenth and eighteenth century authors who attacked rote learning aimed only to make the application of rules a matter of reason.

ACCOUNT PERSONIFICATION

Both the desire to rationalize bookkeeping instruction and the search for more general rules of debit and credit led to account personification. The earliest organized accounts described debtor-creditor relationships between individuals. Estate accounting also involved a bailiff who charged himself with property and receipts entrusted to him and credited himself with expenditures. The double entry system extended use of the terms "debtor" and "creditor" first to impersonal accounts such as cash and inventory and later to abstract expense accounts.[7] Pacioli used personification in describing the relation of an owner to his capital.[8] And though the words of accountability in fifteenth century Italian journals often implied a mere statistical tabulation of items, personification can be traced to very early writings on double entry, with their conscious inclusion of an imaginary proprietor (shall have, shall give) in each transaction.

Personification was strengthened in the process of translating Italian text-books into English. For lack of precisely corresponding terms, British writers rendered the Italian "debito" and "credo" as the more personal "oweth" and "trusts."[9] In Oldcastle's hands "cassa" (cash) became "chest" or storage receptacle which received and paid coins. Pacioli's "Per Cash, a Capital" became "Money Oweth to Thomas Lee." The connotation of inanimate objects possessing human qualities did help explain movements of value in nonpersonal accounts. Plant and equipment, for instance, is harder to understand as an undivided portion of total assets than as part of the owner's equity. The artificiality of this approach was not at all obvious to those employing it. From the seventeenth until the early twentieth centuries, personification remained the accepted way to set forth general rules of bookkeeping.

It took three main forms, which developed simultaneously and were sometimes found interwoven in the same text.[10] In the first, accounts were treated as living persons. In a second form, accounts merely represented the owner of a business. Edmond Degrange, Sr. based his Five Account System (1793) on the idea that cash, merchandise, receivables, payables, and profit and loss function as subsidiaries to capital and that by debiting and crediting them and their subdivisions the merchant was in effect debiting and crediting himself.[11]

The most sophisticated type of personification occurred when accounts were thought of as individuals separate from the owner but responsible to him. Augustus de Morgan in 1831 spoke of "an array of clerks" representing various accounts. He repeated this idea in an appendix to the fifth edition of his *Arithmetic* (London, 1846), which J. G. C Jackson calls "in its effect on the teaching of bookkeeping, probably the most influential piece of writing to be found during the nineteenth century."[12] Other authors quickly appropriated de Morgan's conceit of transaction analysis in terms of movements of value between clerks. Collier wrote in 1884 that:

> the whole business is *supposed* to be carried on by *clerks.* There is supposed to be a clerk called Capital or Stock who represents the owner of the business. . . . There is supposed to be a clerk called Cash who takes charge of the money. There is supposed to be a clerk called Bank who represents the firm's banker. There is supposed to be a clerk called Bills Receivable who takes charge of "Bills" payable to the Firm. . . . There is

> supposed to be a separate clerk for each and every person or firm with whom the Firm has credit transactions. . . . There is supposed to be a clerk called Profit and Loss. . . .
>
> N.B.—These clerks mind their own business and do not interfere in another's department. Thus, if perchance, "Goods" receives some money he instantly hands it over to "Cash" because he himself has no business with money.[13]

Personification resulted from contemporary attitudes toward education and from the absence of accounting theory during the seventeenth and eighteenth centuries. Both factors made it hard to explain impersonal accounts as abstractions, so they were discussed in a simpler way. Viewed as part of the general revolt against rote teaching which occurred after 1850, personification is entitled to some respect. By focusing on capital it opened the way to overall analysis of the accounting structure and helped shift instructional emphasis from the journal to the ledger. But in actual use personification was a sterile technique based on artificial reasoning. It failed to explain the true purposes of accounts or the real effects of transactions. As a result, the technical improvement of accounting was left almost entirely to practitioners, who had the advantage of describing actual business situations and were at least compelled to deal with reality. As Jackson says, the type of bookkeeping taught and the methods of instruction finally "satisfied none but the teachers."[14]

THE PROPRIETARY THEORY

Beginning in the eighteenth century a few textbook authors saw the limitations of rules and personification and tried instead to teach the logic of accounting procedures. Their reasoning about the fundamental nature of double entry marked the beginnings of accounting theory. It was a theory centered on the purpose of the firm, the nature of capital, and especially on the meaning of accounts from the owner's viewpoint. Out of this attention to owner's equity came the proprietary and entity doctrines which still serve as rationalizations for bookkeeping methodology and as an integrating framework for accounting theory.

Pacioli's transaction analysis had focused on proprietorship. Three hundred years later his interest in the motivation behind double entry was revived, under different conditions and for different reasons. The English classical economists, who were contemporary with the first accounting theorists, emphasized the distinction between a stock of wealth (capital) and its flow (income). At this same time, corporate accountants were given the tasks of calculating retained earnings available for dividends, and of making sure that invested capital was maintained intact while fixed asset balances were converted to expense. For these and other reasons "capital" became associated with ownership rather than being simply a residual balance. The accounting equation was rediscovered, and a more strategic view was taken of the book-keeping process, giving less importance to the exchange of values between accounts and more to the effect of transactions on each side of the balance sheet. The addition of theory permitted accounts to be treated as statistical categories. Words acquired special technical meanings, symbols replaced words, and finally positioning replaced symbols. The ledger was by now more important than the journal, but both were merely parts of a recording process which had become analytical rather than personal.

In 1718 Alexander Malcomb touched on the essence of proprietary theory when he distinguished between the totality of a merchant's capital and its constituent parts.[15] He also saw that profits constituted an increase to proprie-torship, and that while some transactions only shifted assets and liabilities from one account to another, others raised or lowered total equity, changing the proprietor's wealth at the same time they altered net assets. Hustcraft Stephens in 1735 made a similar distinction between the whole of a proprietor's capital and the individual assets which comprised it.[16] As he saw it, the aim of bookkeeping is to find the "Condition and Extent of a Man's Estate." This remarkable man was among the first to break away from traditional teaching methods. His design was "to offer no Rules, until he has shown them to be Consequences of Conclusions, plainly drawn from Self-evident Principles." In a long discussion at the start of his book he explained how to record assets, liabilities, and equity interests without drilling on debits and credits. Treating accounts as statistical sorting devices, he classified transactions into three categories, according to whether they affected only assets, only liabilities, or both assets and liabilities. His abstract approach to double entry was a com-plete departure from the usual explanations in terms of personification. Though his work had little direct influence on later exponents of proprietary theory, his teaching method in its freedom from rote was 100 years ahead of its time.

In 1800 James Fulton, a bookkeeper with the Board of Revenue in Bengal, India, published a more readable attempt to explain the internal equilibrium of double entry bookkeeping.[17] Noting how difficult it was to review a com-pany's financial position rapidly, he tried to develop methods which showed immediately the effects of all transactions on capital. In taking this approach he grasped one basic aspect of proprietary theory. Owner's equity is the collective expression of all other accounts, which "form merely the particulars of it: and the grand aim of double entry is, to ascertain the true state of the stock [capital] account." He also saw that the balance of capital is not only the difference between assets and liabilities but is also the original investment plus and minus operating changes since the company's inception. To illustrate this, Fulton prepared a forerunner retained earnings statement showing the effect of all transactions on capital and reconciling the capital balance with net changes in asset and liability accounts.

The exposition of proprietary theory was completed by F. W. Cronhelm in

Double Entry by Single (1818).[18] Taking Fulton's book as a point of departure, Cronhelm emphasized the equivalence of total capital with its constituent parts and argued that the purpose of bookkeeping "is to show the owner at all times the value of his whole capital, and of every part of it." In his algebraic approach to transaction analysis, the capital account became a mathematical equilibriating device, by inference a credit item opposite to assets. Transactions affected the accounting equation by increasing or decreasing assets, liabilities, or capital. He envisioned a series of conversions through the operating cycle of a business with income entering capital as a net increase in proprietorship. Expense and revenue accounts, including profit and loss, were created to avoid the inconvenience of recording every individual change in capital. Cronhelm treated them as branches of owner's equity.

The proprietary theory was refined by a New York accountant and teacher, Thomas Jones, whose *Principles and Practices of Bookkeeping* (1841)[19] has been called the first modern accounting text. He saw financial statements rather than ledger balances as the final step in the bookkeeping cycle. Accounts implied two statements of owner's affairs, the balance sheet and income statement, each of which arrived independently at the same income figure. Moreover, the interrelationship of real and nominal accounts suggested that both financial statements should have equal status. That is, expenses and revenues are not mere modifications of capital, but produce a profit figure which is valid in its own right because it includes far more detail than is revealed by asset revaluations and balance sheet changes in equities. All this was directly opposite to personification and everything it implied. Accounting as described by Jones was mainly concerned with the statistical classification of data, and hardly at all with relationships among the individuals involved.

This same thread of ideology appeared independently in continental Europe during the mid-nineteenth century. As in England it resulted from attempts to rationalize bookkeeping practice, the accounting equation, and concepts of capital. A text by Franz Hautschl (Vienna, 1840) mentioned the integration of gains and losses with original investment in the capital account and described profit and loss as a temporary resting place for additions and subtractions from owner's equity, which otherwise would be overburdened with detail. Friedrich Hugli, a Swiss government accountant, became a leading exponent of the proprietary viewpoint, summarizing and elaborating on the work of two earlier German authors, G. D. Augspurg (Bremen, 1852) and George Kurzbauer (Vienna, 1850). Kurzbauer had argued that account classifications should be derived from the two essential purposes of bookkeeping: profit finding and the inventorying of assets. These produce real and nominal accounts, in effect two independent accounting systems side by side. Double entry is the merger into one system of the "property bookkeeping" and the "results bookkeeping" of a business firm. Augspurg had also concluded that double entry bookkeeping involves the simultaneous maintenance of two sets of accounts—one presenting proprietor's net assets, the other individual asset items. Capital, representing investments as a whole, is reciprocal to the particular assets. The two totals are complementary and their agreement helps prove the arithmetic correctness of the books. Hugli and Johann Friedrich Schar (1889) approached proprietary theory from a mathematical viewpoint, showing by the use of equations and algebraic symbolizations how accounting equilibrium is maintained and how transactions affect capital. Hugli went further, arguing that a firm owns business property and does not merely owe it to a proprietor in the sense that it owes debts to third parties.

Analysis of transactions simply as increases or decreases in accounting elements was the central feature of a series of articles by Charles E. Sprague (1880). Considering accounting as a branch of mathematics, he visualized operating results in terms of an algebraic equation ("assets equal liabilities plus proprietorship") which must be constantly kept in balance. The proprietary theory was presented in complete form by Sprague in 1907,[20] and also in Hatfield's *Modern Accounting* (1909).[21] Neither of them added anything to the system described by earlier writers. But they expressed a doctrine whose time had finally come and whose underlying assumptions quickly dominated American textbook presentations. The proprietor is the center of accounting interest. Accounting records are kept and statements prepared from his viewpoint and are aimed ultimately at measurement and analysis of his net worth. Assets represent things owned by the proprietor or benefits accruing to him. Liabilities are his debts. Capital shows the firm's value to its owner. Revenues immediately increase proprietorship; expenses decrease it. Net profit accrues directly as wealth to the owner. All types of income can be treated very much alike, since all go to owner's equity and affect it similarly. For the same reason little distinction need be made between losses and expenses. Taxes and interest are expenses; dividends represent a withdrawal of capital. Realistic in the economic context in which it originated, far superior to the methodologies it replaced, the proprietary theory was already obsolete at the time of its first widespread acceptance.

THE ENTITY THEORY

The proprietary theory envisioned few parties at interest, close contact by merchants with their affairs, and data summarized only for the use of owners or creditors, who were assumed to have specialized knowledge of the business. For example, whether accounts reflected market prices or historical costs was of secondary importance because these insiders could make the needed mental and mathematical adjustments. But a corporation was legally distinct from its owners and managers, and corporate "proprietorship" typically involved a constantly changing group of shareholders. Assets could not realistically be thought of as belonging to these people because the law recognized prior claims of creditors and preferred stockholders in liquidation. Nor, because of limited liability, did investors personally owe the firm's debts. Income distributions no longer resulted from the type of informal decision involved in proprietary withdrawals. Financial statements were now communication devices between management and outsiders who had no practical access to the books and little detailed knowledge of operations.

Though the connections are only tenuous, Littleton considers medieval agency accounting a forerunner of tne entity theory, which in this sense pre-dated the corporation itself.[22] Investors in joint ventures and the parties to consignment agreements were considered to be independent of the accounting entity involved. References given by Leon Gomberg show that elements of the entity theory were described in texts published during the mid-nineteenth century.[23] In 1882 a Dutch author, I. N. Brenkman, argued that the essence of double entry lay not in the equilibrium of debits and credits but in the keeping of a statistical economic record which allowed proper accounting for business assets. Five years later a German, Manfred Berliner, independently advanced similar views. Like Brenkman, he noted the separation of the mod-ern company from its owners and concluded that bookkeeping was primarily concerned with the movement of values within business firms, not with the affairs of proprietors as such. Business assets were debts of the firm to its owners; liabilities were claims of the firm on its owners. Profit or loss measured the value of the proprietor's services, and first existed in a bookkeeping sense at the time of settlement between the firm and its ownership group.[24]

William A. Paton is the best known American advocate of the entity con-cept. His *Accounting Theory* (1922) was one of the first attempts to adapt ownership doctrine to the realities of an economy dominated by large corpora-tions. Though he took the works of Sprague and Hatfield as a starting point, Paton complained that bookkeeping texts were "saturated" with the proprie-tary viewpoint. While accounting technique had developed to meet corporate needs, theory still assumed that disclosure of proprietor's capital was the main accounting task. Paton's writings take "the conception of the business enter-prise as in all cases a distinct entity or personality."[25] If the corporation is functionally separate from its owners and creditors then it, not they, should be the center of accounting interest. This implies a wider view not only of the business but of accounting activities generally. Capital is the sum of property active in the business whether contributed by owners or creditors. So the right side of the balance sheet represents equities in assets, the left side asset market prices—not costs—since it is changes in asset values which largely determine enterprise income. Assets and debts are those of the entity, which reports to its constituents much as a trustee might account for his stewardship of resources entrusted to him. Because creditors and stockholders have similar status as equityholders, financial statements should be directed to both groups impar-tially.

Paton saw the worst effects of proprietary theory in its definition of expenses and revenues "as mere accessories of proprietorship." The notion that net profit from all sources goes directly to the owner requires no real distinction between operating and other types of income, and has "tended to shut the door to all discriminating analysis of the income sheet," making its classifications illogical.[26] Whereas proprietary theory is mainly concerned with the balance sheet and a legal concept of capital, the entity theory emphasizes corporate income and a more nearly economic idea of income measurement. Revenues and expenses are no longer simply increases or decreases in stockholder's equity. Revenues are compensation for services provided by the firm. Expenses measure the cost of services consumed in obtaining this revenue. Profit accrues to the corporation, not to its owners or creditors. Its disposition is up to the entity; income distribution is distinct from income finding. Interest payments, income taxes, and dividends are distributions of profit rather than proprietary withdrawals of capital. Retained earnings represents an undistributed allocation of income to stockholders.

Paton includes assets and expenses in one category of "services" which differ only in the timing of their matching with revenues. Assets are considered deferred costs available for future conversion rather than objects intended for liquidation to satisfy creditors. Thus, an asset's value is not directly related to the physical existence of property or to its exchange price. Rather it represents the cost applicable to services available for future conversion and delivery to the market. Asset valuation should therefore reflect the value of benefits to be received by the enterprise. These ideas were the groundwork of Paton's contribution to the 1940 monograph, *An Introduction to Corporate Accounting Standards,*[27] which may be called the high point of entity theory exposition.

THE FUND THEORY

In *The Fund Theory of Accounting (1947),* William Vatter criticized both traditional equity concepts in terms of their relevance to the modern corporation. Under proprietary theory the owner's profit is simply the difference between beginning and ending net worth as measured by changes in asset values. But because corporate equity arises from many investments made at various times, and because share prices constantly change due to factors unrelated to company asset values, it is impractical to determine the net worth or measure the profit of individual stockholder-proprietors. Since it is not feasible to continually revise asset valuations as stock market prices change, Vatter concludes that it is impossible to apply proprietary theory to the corporation.[28]

The difference between the proprietary and entity viewpoints is mainly whether books are kept for an actual or fictional owner. In the latter theory a corporate person substitutes for the proprietor. Vatter finds both concepts vulnerable in light of the realities they seek to portray. The assumed trust arrangement between a fictitious entity and real property owners is too unrealistic to govern practice. The entity with which accounting actually deals is not that which arises from the legal formula of incorporation, but is the result of relations among real equityholders. "The weakness of these personalized bases for accounting is that the content of accounting reports will tend to be affected by personal analogies; and issues will be decided not by considering the nature of the problems but upon some extension of personality."[29] For example, personalization of the entity is used to justify the cost emphasis in asset valuation. Vatter concludes that such personalization, like the account person- ification of the eighteenth century, is a simplification which may be useful for teaching but is not a satisfactory frame of reference for the integration of accounting thought.

To this general indictment Vatter adds three specific criticisms: (1) Account- ing has grown beyond the possibility of basing its operations on any single- valued theory. Large corporations are a conglomerate of personalities, resources, conditions, and relationships. The areas of use for accounting data, and the number of parties at interest are both too numerous and too varied for any single personality to maintain all the points of view involved. The single person approach must either emphasize some to the exclusion of others, or compromise all of them. (2) Neither the proprietary nor the entity theory is followed in practice. Because neither meets all the needs of modern companies, textbooks mix the two, shifting from one to the other whenever it suits their purpose. (3) Both the proprietary and entity theories break down when applied to specific situations. For example, both theories obscure the real differences between costs, expenses, and distribution of income.[30]

Vatter proposes an extension of the entity theory to embrace a less personal- istic set of ideas. The accounting area of attention should be "devoid of personal implications," yet should be sharply defined, applicable to various organizational forms and activities, and should at the same time be realistic in terms of the results accounting is expected to achieve.[31] He finds such an area of attention in the concept of a fund—an entity established to isolate and control particular activities or elements of administration. The basis for ac- counting becomes an operating area which includes a group of assets represent- ing prospective services to the fund, offset by debts and a wide range of other restrictions on asset uses. Accounting is no longer tied to any particular method of asset valuation. The income concept is depersonalized and becomes much less important as an explanation of accounting processes. As described by Vatter, the fund theory is in part a confession of weakness. Having failed to measure profits accurately, the accountant wishes to substitute budgetary measures of effort and accomplishment. The fund theory's lack of acceptance by business firms may have resulted from its inability to answer the questions report readers were conditioned to ask.

THE RESIDUAL EQUITY THEORY

The residual equity theory, developed by George Staubus,[32] makes common stockholders the center of accounting attention. In a going concern, the market value of common stock depends largely on future profit and dividend expectations. If the common shareholder's portion of assets, income, funds, and stockholder's equity can be identified, financial statements can disclose more about the prospective selling prices of common stock. Information about the residual equity may also be useful in predicting the size of common stock dividends. Accordingly, the balance sheet equity of common stockholders should be presented separately from the equities of preferred stockholders and other equityholders. The income statement should show earnings available to common stockholders after *all* prior claims are satisfied—not only interest paid to bondholders, but also dividend payments to preferred stockholders. The funds statement should segregate the funds available for payment of common stock dividends.

THE COMMANDER THEORY

Louis Goldberg[33] sees the corporate entity as a fictitious person substituting for actual decisionmakers. He agrees with Vatter that emphasis on ownership rights handicaps both the proprietary and entity theories. But he also criticizes the fund theory for failing to account for changes in the size and composition of asset groupings. Goldberg considers that stockholders, whose very numbers typically prevent them from controlling company policy, are seldom the driving force in modern corporations. He suggests that the most strategic view of corporate activities is that of the top managers or "commanders" who make the decisions and guide the organization from day to day. Rather than focusing on the special interests of one ownership group or another, accounting emphasis should be on how effectively management has used corporate resources.

The commander theory makes financial statements reports on stewardship. The balance sheet is a statement of accountability for the resources placed in management's care. The income statement expresses the results of managerial activities and shows how resources have been used to achieve these results. The funds statement describes how managers have obtained resources and what they have done with them.

This view of the firm fails to specify the recipients of accounting information. Nor does it consider the external political and social influences on decisionmaking. It is true that managers direct company operations, but the corporation must also interact with its environment. Because it focuses entirely on decisionmaking within the firm, the commander theory does not offer a comprehensive description of business activities, nor a basis for evaluating the whole spectrum of accounting concepts and methods.

THE ENTERPRISE THEORY

Eldon Hendriksen concludes that all ownership theories focus on: (1) who are the beneficiaries of net income? and (2) how should equity relationships be shown in financial statements?[34] The enterprise theory derives from the view of Peter Drucker[35] and others of the large corporation as a social institution influencing society as as whole, operating for the benefit of many interested groups, and having a reporting obligation to each of the major parties affected by its actions. It follows that financial statements should be directed not only to investors and creditors but explicitly to employees, customers, the government as a taxing body and regulatory agency, and to the general public. Income logically comprises the market value of goods and services produced by the firm, less the value of goods and services acquired from other companies. Claims against the total asset pool are treated impartially. Dividends paid to stockholders, interest to creditors, taxes to government units, and wages to employees are all considered distributions of income.[36] Because it implies a social commitment over and above any responsibility to owners, the enterprise theory dovetails nicely with regulatory policies of the past forty years which view the corporation as part of a larger system coordinating its activities with national goals.[37] It may be that accounting theory, from its egocentric beginnings, is becoming a means of fostering social consciousness in modern businesses.

TOWARD A UNIVERSAL THEORY OF ACCOUNTS

While the rules of debit and credit are so universally applied as to constitute an international language, there is still no generally accepted theory of accounts or of the business firm for which they are kept. Thus there is no definitive explanation of the double entry mechanism, of the real nature of the different accounts and their operations, or of what makes the parts of this system compatible. A valid theory of accounts "should not only answer all those questions but also should allow the deduction of those answers from one or a few general principles."[38] The ideal would be a single general rule—a categorical imperative which applied to all business events without exception. Or at least such a theory should be developed from one basic premise, such as the central importance of the business entity. And it should be fruitful as well as logically impeccable: its use should measurably improve accounting performance.

The first theories of accounts aimed only to justify the rules of double entry and to help students and practitioners understand and apply these, even in difficult or unexpected situations where rote teaching methods failed. Simple, straightforward doctrines were best suited to this educational task. Attempts were made to reduce the bookkeeping process to a set of characteristic transactions, and later to substitute stylized events or situations for real ones. Certain authors saw accounting wholly in terms of individuals and completely ignored commodity movements. Others pictured the corporation as a living entity with its own interests and motives, or converted retained earnings into a debt of the company to its owners. But business operations are too complex to be described realistically in such simplistic terms, and these theories also lacked sufficient breadth of application. On the whole they failed to adjust to changes in the business conditions which first gave them validity.

Explanations of what accounting does in the business firm remain essentially pragmatic, catering to the economic realities of the moment rather than being based on ultimate truths. The two best known theories of capital and the firm were implied by accounting practice long before they were explicitly stated in textbooks. The inventorying of assets and debts to measure net worth changes foreshadowed the proprietary doctrine, just as the subtraction of expenses from revenues to get net income anticipated the entity concept. Despite all their limitations, these theories provided a sense of direction which helped double entry bookkeeping expand to encompass industrial developments. The next four chapters examine the theoretical specifics derived from these overall views of the firm: concepts of asset valuation, income measurement, financial statement disclosure, and accounting principles.

FOOTNOTES

1. William J. Vatter, *The Fund Theory of Accounting and its Implications for Financial Reports* (Chicago: University of Chicago Press, 1947), 1.
2. A.C. Littleton, *Accounting Evolution to 1900* (New York: American Institute Publishing Company, 1933), 156-157.
3. *Ibid.*, 41.
4. J.G.C. Jackson, "The History of Methods of Exposition of Double Entry Bookkeeping in England," in A.C. Littleton and B.S. Yamey, eds., *Studies in the History of Accounting* (Homewood, Ill.: Richard D. Irwin, 1956), 288.
5. *Ibid.*, 289-92.
6. *Ibid.*, 293.
7. *Ibid.*, 295.
8. Edward Peragallo, *Origin and Evolution of Double Entry Bookkeeping, A Study of Italian Practice from the Fourteenth Century* (New York: American Institute Publishing Company, 1938), 98-99.
9. Jackson, *op. cit.*, 296.
10. *Ibid.*
11. Peragallo, *op. cit.*, 109-11.
12. Jackson, *op. cit.*, 298.
13. J. Collier, *Book-Keeping by Double-Entry* (London, 1884), preface.
14. Jackson, *op. cit.*, 304.
15. Alexander Malcomb, *A New Treatise of Arithmetick and Bookkeeping, Etc.* (Edinburgh, 1718), 132-33.
16. Hustcraft Stephens, *Italian Book-Keeping Reduced Into an Art* (London, 1735).
17. James Williamson Fulton, *British-Indian Book-keeping* (London, 1800).
18. F.W. Cronhelm, *Double Entry by Single* (London, 1818).
19. Thomas Jones, *Principles and Practices of Bookkeeping* (New York, 1841).
20. Charles E. Sprague, *The Philosophy of Accounts* (New York, 1907).
21. Henry Rand Hatfield, *Modern Accounting* (New York: D. Appleton and Company, 1909), 1-9.
22. Littleton, *op. cit.*, 193-94.
23. Leon Gomberg, *Histoire Critique de La Theorie Des Comptes* (Geneva/Berlin, 1929), 68-71.
24. Manfred Berliner, *Schwierige Fälle und Allegemeine Lehrsätze der Kaufmännischen Buchhaltung* (Leipzig, 1893).
25. William A. Paton, *Accounting Theory* (New York: Ronald Press Company, 1922), preface, iv.
26. *Ibid.*, 53.
27. W.A. Paton and A.C. Littleton, *An Introduction to Corporate Accounting Standards*, American Accounting Association Monograph No. 3 (New York: American Accounting Association, 1940), 1-8.

28. Vatter, *op. cit.*, 3-4.
29. *Ibid.*, 7.
30. *Ibid.*, 7-9.
31. *Ibid.*, 10.
32. George Staubus, *A Theory of Accounting to Investors* (Berkeley and Los Angeles: University of California Press, 1961).
33. Louis Goldberg, *An Inquiry into the Nature of Accounting*, American Accounting Association Monograph No. 7 (New York: American Accounting Association, 1965), 162-174.
34. Eldon S. Hendriksen, *Accounting Theory*, rev. ed. (Homewood, Ill.: Richard D. Irwin, 1970), 507.
35. Peter F. Drucker, *Concept of the Corporation* (New York: John Day Company, 1946).
36. Hendriksen, *op. cit.*, 503.
37. Gerhard G. Mueller, *International Accounting* (New York: Macmillan, 1967), 26.
38. Karl Käfer, *Theory of Accounts in Double-Entry Bookkeeping* (Urbana, Ill.: Center for International Education and Research in Accounting, Monograph 2, 1966), 5.

SELECTED BIBLIOGRAPHY

American Accounting Association, 1964 Concepts and Standards Research Committee –The Business Entity. "The Entity Concept." *Accounting Review* 40 (April, 1965), 358-67.
Chen, Rosita. "Social and Financial Stewardship." *Accounting Review* 50 (July, 1975), 533-543.
Drucker, Peter F. *Concept of the Corporation*. New York: John Day Company, 1946.
Goldberg, Louis. *An Inquiry into the Nature of Accounting*. American Accounting Association Monograph No. 7. American Accounting Association, 1965, 162-174.
Gynther, Reginald S. "Accounting Concepts and Behavioral Hypotheses." *Accounting Review* 42 (April, 1967), 274-290.
Hendriksen, Eldon S. *Accounting Theory*, rev. ed. Homewood, Ill.: Richard D. Irwin, 1970, 29-32, 495-507.
Jackson, J.G.C. "The History of Methods of Exposition of Double Entry Bookkeeping in England," in A.C. Littleton and B.S. Yamey, eds. *Studies in the History of Accounting* (Homewood, Ill.: Richard D. Irwin, 1956), 288-312.
Käfer, Karl. *Theory of Accounts in Double-Entry Bookkeeping*. Urbana, Ill.: Center for International Education and Research in Accounting, Monograph 2, 1966, 1-38, 69-72.
Ladd, Dwight. *Contemporary Corporate Accounting and the Public*. Homewood, Ill.: Richard D. Irwin, 1963, chaps. two and three.
Li, David H. "The Nature of Corporate Residual Equity under the Entity Concept," *Accounting Review* 35 (April, 1960), 258-63.
Linowes, David F. *The Corporate Conscience*. New York: Hawthorn Books, 1974.
Littleton, A.C. *Accounting Evolution to 1900*. New York: American Institute Publishing Company, 1933. Reprinted by Russell and Russell, New York, 1966, chaps. four, eleven, and twelve.
————. *Essays in Accountancy*. Urbana: University of Illinois Press, 1961, 22-92.
————. *The Structure of Accounting Theory*. Iowa City: American Accounting Association, 1953.
Littleton, A.C., and Zimmerman, V.K. *Accounting Theory: Continuity and Change*. Englewood Cliffs, N.J.: Prentice-Hall, 1962, chap. two.
Mattessich, Richard. *Accounting and Analytical Methods*. Homewood, Ill.: Richard D. Irwin, 1964, chap. four.
Meyer, Philip E. "The Accounting Entity." *Abacus* 9 (December, 1973), 116-126.
Paton, William A. *Accounting Theory*. New York: Ronald Press Company, 1922. Reprinted by Accounting Studies Press, Chicago, 1962, and by Scholars Book Company, Lawrence, Kansas, 1973.

Peragallo, Edward. *Origin and Evolution of Double Entry Bookkeeping, A Study of Italian Practice from the Fourteenth Century*. New York: American Institute Publishing Company, 1938. Reprinted by Nihon Shoseki, Osaka, 1974.

Schoenfeld, Hanns-Martin. Review of *Kie Kapitaltheoretische Bilanz und die Entwicklung der Bilanztheorien. Accounting Review* 46 (October, 1971), 831-835.

Sprague, Charles E. *The Philosophy of Accounts*. New York, 1907. Reprinted by Scholars Book Company, Lawrence, Kansas, 1972.

Sprouse, Robert T. *The Effect of the Concept of the Corporation on Accounting*. Ph.D. Dissertation, University of Minnesota, 1956. Reprinted by Arno Press, New York, 1976.

Staubus, George. *A Theory of Accounting to Investors*. Berkeley and Los Angeles: University of California Press, 1961. Reprinted by Scholars Book Company, Houston, 1975.

Ten Have, O. *The History of Accountancy*. Palo Alto: Bay Books, 1976, 99-106.

Vatter, William J. *The Fund Theory of Accounting and its Implications for Financial Reports*. Chicago: University of Chicago Press, 1947, esp. chap. one.

_____. "Corporate Stock Equities." In Morton Backer, ed. *Modern Accounting Theory*. New York: Prentice-Hall, 1966, 250-257.

Yamey, B.S. "Pious Inscriptions; Confused Accounts; Classification of Accounts: Three Historical Notes." In Harold Edey and B.S. Yamey, eds. *Debits, Credits, Finance and Profits*. London: Sweet and Maxwell, 1974, 143-160.

Chapter 17

CHANGING CONCEPTS OF ASSET VALUATION

Let us suppose that a modern accounting theorist could be dispatched back to the year 1900 for the purpose of compiling a catalogue of generally accepted accounting principles. If his experience had been in American practice he would not be surprised at the variety of asset valuation methods in use, or that all of them seemed equally acceptable. But he might be bewildered by the lack of coordination between sources of accounting authority. By requiring audited balance sheets the British Companies Act of 1900 had made systematic asset valuation an urgent task. But there were still few effective statutes governing accounting behavior, and the legal constraints on accounting in England and America were minor compared to those in some European countries.[1] Though several early accounting texts bristled with legal citations and the profession might have welcomed arbitration of some of its disputes, the courts, in that *laissez-faire* era, were reluctant lawgivers. Case law on asset valuation was sparse, sometimes contradictory, and it was often hard to tell how broadly a particular decision applied. Our theorist might be told that judges did not understand accounting method. Whether or not this was true, the courts, like the legislature, were of little help in standardizing asset valuation methods or in relating theory to practice.

By 1900 American and British auditors had developed asset valuation rules for their own use. But the emerging accounting profession was weak, with limited power to standardize its clients' behavior, and was generally unable to counter managerial pressures. Within wide limits each firm was left to develop accounting principles according to its own needs and goals. Naturally these were designed to protect management as well as investor interests. As a result, "Accounting varied in its general character from industry to industry, from corporation to corporation, and even from place to place."[2] English company directors were considered stewards of corporate assets and the lack of accounting uniformity was partly due to different managerial judgments about what constituted stewardship responsibility. In using their freedom to value assets some managements were ultraconservative, others were overbold. The majority of both factions showed a preference for smoothing reported income and equalizing dividend payments.

In 1900 conservatism was the dominant accounting principle, to which others were subordinated when they came in conflict. Systematic understatement of asset values was thought to offset managerial manipulation and to protect stockholders. Of course it also gave company directors wide latitude in their stewardship of invested capital. The accounting profession had grown up in a business environment of "bankruptcies, failures, frauds and disputes" which filled accountants with "a vivid sense of disaster" and had much to do with their preference for bookkeeping understatement.[3] In England conservatism corresponded to a tradition of cash basis accounting and liquidity pricing. In America it was, if possible, even more strongly entrenched. Bankers were the most influential group of statement readers, and conservatism offered them security against inflated collateral values. Conservatism's operative technique, the lower of cost or market rule, was recommended in 1900 by practically all English authorities and many American ones.[4] Price declines fostered conservatism by making asset replacement easy and compatible with low balance sheet valuations. The year 1900 marked the end of a thirty-year period of falling prices and the beginning of an inflationary trend which still continues. This meant that the premises on which asset accounting had developed during the nineteenth century were to be applied in a very different environment.

Not logically derived from conservatism, but governed and justified by reference to it, were several corollary principles. In a period of declining prices the going concern concept, which implied an obligation to maintain plant and equipment intact during the company's "indefinite" existence, did not conflict with conservatism. It required only that provision be made for asset replacements before dividends were paid. Business continuity had brought with it the idea that fixed assets should not be revalued unless such changes reflected the value of the going concern. It made historical cost valuations "both conservative and convenient." But these concepts, so similar to our own, were based on different reasoning. As Reed Storey says:

> Valuation at cost or at cost or market was defended in terms of the historical nature of accounting or the need for conservatism rather than in terms of the need for objective evidence or the process of matching. Essentially, asset valuation and income determination were based on an incomplete application of the going concern convention tempered by conservatism.[5]

Our time-travelling theorist would note without surprise a number of conventions which were widely recognized but seldom adhered to in practice. Great significance was attached to the distinction between capital and income, yet the main source of accounting error remained the inability or deliberate failure to distinguish systematically between capital and revenue expenditures.[6] Though British courts had recognized depreciation as a cost as early as 1838, few accountants in 1900 saw depreciation as an allocation problem, if only because no well-defined cost concept existed. The variety of methods in use prevented real adherence to the principles of objectivity, consistency, or comparability of data. From Adam Smith and other classicial economists had come the idea that profit could only arise from actual exchanges of goods. But realization was not yet an accounting principle, nor was there a well understood notion of matching costs with related revenues, or even of converting asset values to expense.

Anyway, practice was so different from theory that our theorist could hardly construct a set of principles which reconciled the literature with what accountants actually did. In an era when record keeping was dominated by managerial needs, the practical purpose of asset accounting was not so much correct balance sheet valuation as the provision of funds for asset replacement. In 1900 most manufacturing companies still used the single account or inventory method of asset valuation, which priced fixed assets as if they were unsold merchandise. Assets were appraised or revalued at the end of each accounting period, and for most firms using this method, profit was the change in value of all assets from all causes. No distinction was made between capital and revenue expenditures, between fixed and current assets, between depreciation and appreciation, or between inflationary increases and real income.

English railroads and certain other public service corporations were required by law to value their assets by the double account method. Historical costs of long-lived assets were recorded in a capital expenditures account and never depreciated.[7] Because it was necessary for the companies to maintain such assets permanently, their value was assumed to remain constant so long as they were kept in good working order. This made it natural to capitalize asset betterments and additions while charging replacements and repairs directly to expense. Since the timing of asset replacements was a managerial option, so logically was the depreciation charge. If taken at all, depreciation was seen not as an operating expense but as a holding back of revenue for replacement of lost asset value. There were many variations in practice. Assets might be expensed or capitalized; repairs, maintenance, and renewals might at management's discretion be charged to capital. Yet the double account method was relatively sophisticated. It was one response to the need to find going concern as opposed to liquidation values. Capital and revenue transactions were separated. Assets were divided into fixed and current portions, and increases or decreases in price levels were not allowed to affect income, which was defined as the excess of revenues over expenditures.

Most present valuation methods and much of the underlying theory were at least foreshadowed by practice in 1900. What was lacking were strong connections between the two. The theoretical improvements which followed may be seen as attempts to create an articulated set of principles which would discipline practice and make individual methods consistent with the concepts on which they supposedly were based.

1892–1929: VALUATION OF THE GOING CONCERN

Accounting practice based on conservatism had very limited theoretical potential. Its first effective critic was Lawrence R. Dicksee, senior partner in a firm of chartered accountants, Professor of Accountancy at the University of Birmingham (1902–26) and Lecturer at the London School of Economics. George O. May called his *Auditing* (1892) "perhaps the first book on modern accounting."[8] Dicksee's immediate target was the double account system, which he criticized for failing to require depreciation and for its assumption that capital consumption would not exceed the rate of asset replacement. He reasoned that the main goal of most firms is to continue in business and that asset valuation should reflect this fact. Even companies which did not take depreciation faced the certainty of asset revaluation when assets were sold or when the firm changed hands. The point of sale was a moment of truth which revealed an asset's real value. So it was not simply current sale prices—liquidation prices —which mattered, but also these *future* values. To anticipate them as nearly as possible, assets should be valued "as a going concern," meaning "at such value as they would stand in the books if proper depreciation had been provided for."[9] Dicksee also saw errors of principle arising from a failure to strictly discriminate between current and fixed assets. Fixed assets should be priced at historical cost less depreciation. The justification for ignoring value changes not caused by "time and wear" was that realization was not contemplated; such assets were bought to be used, not to be sold at a profit. The case of current assets was quite different. The logic of business continuity required that they be priced at net realizable value. Because they were bought or made to be sold, they should be sensitive to value changes and any shrinkage ought to be booked as a realized loss. By the same logic, asset appreciation should be credited to revenue, but Dicksee was not quite this bold. Since before the point of sale, "there must always be a doubt as to whether any such realization has actually occurred, it is only prudent to postpone taking credit for the assumed profit until such time as it has been actually earned."[10]

Seventy years ago these ideas were revolutionary. That they now seem orthodox is evidence of their successful application. Dicksee more than any other man established the continuity assumption as a meaningful accounting concept. In doing so he helped shift the profession's attention from the strictly historical view of valuation implied by conservatism to the view that asset values depend on future activities. He further laid the groundwork for a synthesis of theoretical concepts around the going concern principle, which remained the most important basis for asset valuation until the realization rule became dominant in the late 1920s.[11]

AMERICAN THEORISTS

Henry Rand Hatfield agreed with Dicksee that "the proper value of assets is that which they have to the holding concern, and not that which they might have to other persons. ..."[12] He stated three general valuation rules: (1) inventory prices should be those of a going concern; (2) depreciation must always be taken; and (3) conservatism requires that changes in the market prices of fixed assets be ignored. Hatfield reasoned that a firm would not buy any asset unless the value of its output was expected to equal or exceed its cost. Then, assuming the business lasted long enough to receive the asset's service benefits, liquidation prices were irrelevant. Hatfield attacked conservatism more directly than Dicksee had and particularly denounced the lower of cost or market rule. Undervaluation might at times be the lesser of two evils, but was indefensible as a policy. Writing in an era when inflation was already noticeable, he was from the first less inclined to accept historical cost as an imperative. He argued for the use of replacement costs in the balance sheet, and in his 1927 text advocated accelerated rather than straight line depreciation as corresponding better to economic realities.[13]

Dicksee and Hatfield had thought through the going concern concept to its logical conclusion: that increases as well as decreases in current asset values should be taken up as profit and loss. Both believed that if value to the going concern is the key to asset valuation, and if the selling price of fixed assets is irrelevant because they are not purchased to be sold, then conversely, the selling price of inventories should be on the balance sheet because they exist only to be sold. But as a practical matter, conservatism—both the accounting doctrine and the political instincts of accountants—prevented this, so the realization rule was substituted for the broader idea of profit implied by the continuity principle.[14]

William A. Paton was perhaps the most pragmatic theorist of this era, and among the first not only to follow out the continuity concept but to go beyond it. He saw accounting as being governed by expediency and convenient assumptions. Thus periodicity, accrual, and continuity were concepts best judged according to their usefulness, not their literal truth. He pointed out the contradictions within the historical cost doctrine, adding that ". . . even actual cost is only a tentative figure . . . accounting deals largely with judgments and estimates, not with certainty. Values are always more or less conjectural and unstable."[15] As early as 1918 he had favored recording the market values of assets rather than their costs. In 1922 he reaffirmed a belief in the consistent use of market prices. Costs of current assets should be related to realizable values, and the value of finished product is virtually selling price, regardless of the fact that no sale has occurred. When in later years inflation became a problem, Paton was "the most persistent and eloquent advocate in the U.S. of general price-level adjustments."[16]

John Canning began *The Economics of Accountancy* (1929) by considering the nature of assets, asserting that "one who seeks an answer by searching the texts on accounting for formal definitions will first be surprised that many, perhaps most, of the writers offer none at all."[17] He added that those who did define assets seldom practiced what they preached. Examining accounting practice to derive a definition from the methods accountants actually used, Canning showed that they excluded much which economists would call assets and income. He concluded that accounting practice was legally rather than economically oriented and that, while accountants practiced valuation, they had no *theory* of value.

Having given the first comprehensive definitions of balance sheet terms, Canning proposed a theory of valuation transplanted from economics. The proper valuation of any asset should be based on the expected receipts from its use. "An inventory valuation, as such, can have no significance except as an index of funds to be produced."[18] This kind of "direct valuation" applies to assets whose future cash flows can be reliably forecast. It would be best to have direct valuations of all assets, but "indirect valuation" must be applied when no estimate can be made of the funds to be provided. In either case, changes in asset values produce income, which should be recognized in the accounts as soon as reliable estimates of future conversion value can be made.

Such views were considered extreme. The adherents of historical cost valuation could point to a system which in the 1920s seemed to work fairly well. Among its most articulate spokesmen was A. C. Littleton. He considered the use of acquisition costs to be so bound up with the evolution of double entry methodology that radical departures from it, such as the substitution of current values or price level adjusted figures, could threaten an integration of real and nominal accounts which is far more important than the dollar amounts attached to individual assets and liabilities. Accounting records by their very nature cannot record values because particular prices, being transitory, quickly lose their significance during a period of inflation. Nor do price changes in themselves generate income. For example, cost increases do not always lead to higher sale prices.[19] Price level indices are less objective than historical costs and would "tend to drive a divorcing wedge between balance sheet and income statement."[20] The balance sheet might become a list of appraised values; the income statement a derivation of economic rather than realized profits. While such calculations have their uses, accounting for business events is a very different task from statistics gathering and interpretation.

SUMMARY AS OF 1929

In view of what was about to happen to asset values and to the economy generally, these debates of the 1920s may seem academic. In fact they laid the groundwork for the basic conceptual changes which have been codified since World War II. At a minimum they showed that acquisition cost was not the only feasible basis for asset valuation. As George O. May pointed out, the "tradition" of historical cost went back only seventy or eighty years.[21] Its use had been a matter of "convenience and expediency," and even during the nineteenth century other valuation bases had been more widely employed.

But if many early theorists had scant respect for conventional accounting, they had even less ability to change it quickly. Nearly all of them were university professors who could influence practice only indirectly and by a slow diffusion of ideas. During the 1920s it was the income tax laws which produced dramatic changes in valuation practice. Systematic depreciation, bad debt allowances, the wide use of historical cost valuations, the matching principle, and the realization rule owe much more to passage of the Sixteenth Amendment than to the progress of accounting theory.

Income taxation gave businessmen a vested interest in financial understatement. By 1929 the realization rule had become "the most important convention in the determination of income and the valuation of assets. . . ."[22] The continuity principle had merely ruled out liquidation prices and required asset valuation according to intended use. This implied historical cost valuation for fixed assets and net realizable value for current assets. But the realization rule provided a theoretical justification for valuing current as well as fixed assets at cost, since any higher valuation would create unrealized income. On the whole, the tax laws strengthened a conservative view of asset valuation which progressive theorists were struggling against.

THE 1930's: CODIFIED VALUATION THEORY

After the 1929 stock market crash, the accounting environment changed drastically: (1) A sudden fall in prices during the early 1930s caused concern among accountants because of misleading balance sheet values, and among businessmen because of high depreciation charges based on the higher historical costs of the past decade: (2) During the 1930s attempts were made to codify accounting theory, or better, to reconcile theory with the methods used by accountants. As a result, asset valuation practices were further standardized; (3) A third effect of the crash was the widespread realization that the market prices of a corporation's stock depend more on its earning power than on the value of its assets. Precise asset valuations soon became less important than the calculation of expense conversions from the balance sheet to the income statement.

Each of these events weakened the influence of conservatism on accounting theory. Robert Sterling calls conservatism "the most ancient and probably the most pervasive principle of accounting valuation."[23] Vance and Littleton have shown that its corollary rule, the lower of cost or market concept, is a perennial idea which originated before Pacioli's *Summa* was written.[24] But its age is deceptive; lower of cost or market has been used for different purposes at different times, being expedient in one way to the manorial steward, in another to the tax-dodging venture trader, and in still another to modern corporate managers. During the period 1900–1930 conservatism was likewise a general rule applied for special reasons. Its dominance depended largely on the balance sheet's primacy as a report to creditors.[25] The shift in emphasis toward the income statement meant that profits as well as assets had to be conservatively stated, and this was a less consistent process. Reducing inventory values when market price falls below cost reduces current income, but often inflates future profits. This style of conservatism offered more reasons to adhere to historical cost valuations than to depart from them.

In essence, though, the transition went deeper than this. It amounted to an accounting adaptation to the realities of large-scale corporate operations. Stewardship is a prime bookkeeping motive when most businesses are short-lived ventures and the main accounting responsibility is for protecting assets. In this setting conservatism is natural and rational. The steward would be foolish to raise expectations which might not be borne out by subsequent events. No one is misled so long as ownership interests are not expected to be exchanged. But in a large continuing business the profitable use of assets is more important than their physical protection. For financial statements to give relevant data about a corporation whose economic life is indefinite and whose stock is constantly changing hands requires not a conservative but the fairest and most objective possible presentation of income and asset values. Conservatism had always been arbitrary and internally inconsistent. The shift from stewardship reports to reporting economic data for investment decisions made it inappropriate as well.

This is why, despite downward price fluctuations during the 1930s, the first attempts to codify accounting theory stressed objectivity, consistency, comparability of data, the matching concept, and historical cost valuation as a stable base for income measurement. A letter dated September 1932, addressed to members of the American Institute Committee formulating principles in cooperation with the New York Stock Exchange, emphasized the need:

> to bring about a better recognition by the public of the fact that the balance sheet of a large modern corporation does not and should not be expected to represent an attempt to show present values of the assets and liabilities of the corporation. . . .[26]

George O. May, heading the Committee, derived three rather contradictory accounting "postulates": continuity, realization at the point of sale, and a monetary postulate which held that unrealized changes in asset values could be ignored.[27] But he added "the real value of the assets of any large business is dependent mainly on the earning capacity of the enterprise."[28]

The American Institute's Committee on Terminology stated in its first Bulletin that "since accounting is predominantly based on cost, the proper uses of the word *value* in accounting are largely restricted to the statement of items at cost, or at modifications of cost."[29] In *A Statement of Accounting Principles* (1938), Sanders, Hatfield, and Moore gave uncritical acceptance to the historical cost and realization doctrines.[30] The American Accounting Association endorsed historical cost asset valuation in its 1936, 1941, and 1948 statements, whose central thesis was that:

> Accounting is thus not essentially a process of valuation, but the allocation of historical costs and revenues to current and succeeding fiscal periods.[31]

Paton and Littleton's 1940 Monograph, *An Introduction to Corporate Accounting Standards,* was written as theoretical support for the 1936 AAA Statement. It was a collaboration between men who, as we have seen, began with very different premises. But they agreed that "Earning power—not cost price, not replacement price, not sale or liquidation price—is the significant basis of enterprise value."[32] The accountant's main task was income determination *via* the matching of costs and related revenues. This made asset valuation less important than the conversion of balance sheet items to expense. Assets are discussed in the chapter on "Cost" and are considered residuals, unexpired costs. "Inventories and plant are not 'values,' but cost accumulations in suspense, as it were, awaiting their destiny."[33] Acquisition prices of assets are suitable intitial balances. The question of subsequent valuation is hardly considered. Value is *assumed* to equal cost because other matters are so much more important. In this way the authors avoid the problem of *which* costs are to be associated with revenues.[34]

THE PRICE LEVEL DILEMMA

In America the first debates over historical versus replacement costing occurred not among accounting theorists, but between the railroads and the Interstate Commerce Commission.[35] The task of the I.C.C. and similar rate-making bodies was to set public utility charges just high enough so that a reasonable return could be earned on the regulated company's investment. The Commission was responsible for developing a rate base, which was then multiplied by a specific percentage to determine the total return the utility was entitled to earn. The question arose: should this rate base be developed from the original or the replacement costs of assets?

This choice presented problems because so many railroads had been built just after the Civil War, at the beginning of a long period of price declines, with the result that by 1900 the historical costs of their assets far exceeded the replacement prices. In an effort to get higher rates, the railroads argued that acquisition costs should be their rate-measure. The ICC, responsible for protecting the public from excessive railroad charges, countered that replacement costs were more appropriate. Considering this question, the Supreme Court in *Smyth v. Ames* (1898) merely noted that in each situation both types of cost should be examined if fair rates were to be set. After 1900, with price levels moving upward, the conflict between Commission and railroads continued, but the disputants exchanged arguments. Prices soon increased to a point where the railroads benefitted from the use of replacement cost accounting. The Commissioners likewise had a change of heart, becoming advocates of the now more conservative historical costs.

During the 1920s the Supreme Court set aside a number of rate decisions because of the ICC's failure to consider replacement costs. But as in earlier cases, the accounting profession got no definitive judgment from the courts concerning the use of replacement costs to offset price level changes. In 1927 the *Journal of Accountancy* criticized the ICC in an editorial for its insistence on using 1916 costs for establishing rates, noting that asset replacements would currently cost nearly double the 1916 prices.[36] The problem was still considered solely as a practical question of rate-making equity. The propriety of replacement costs *per se* was not an issue.

Following World War I most of Central Europe experienced inflation on a scale which made older acquisition costs meaningless. In Germany a method called "balance sheet stabilization" was used to adjust asset values for general price level changes. In contrast, the accounting implications of American inflation were seen mainly in terms of asset replacement rather than asset valuation. Businessmen understood that in periods of rising prices cost-based depreciation charges would not cumulate sufficient funds to replace plant and equipment. Some favored the creation of equity reserves to keep cash in the business. Others advocated accelerated depreciation. Though assets were often arbitrarily written up at management's discretion, usually without disclosure and with a credit to accounts such as "Revaluation Surplus," many businessmen expected prices to return to prewar levels, and considered that such writeups reflected temporary increases in value. At this time there was no basic conflict between managers and accountants over asset valuation because neither group anticipated continually rising price levels.

After 1929 the high original costs of the preceding decade and the higher replacement costs at which many plants had been revalued began to appear unreasonable by comparison with current price levels. As John O'Hara put it, not only were things no longer worth what people had paid for them, but the suspicion dawned that they never had been worth that much. Worse, depreciation charges based on these inflated original costs were throwing companies into a net loss position which hampered their ability to declare dividends and to support the market prices of their stocks. In retrospect the massive writeups of the 1920s were seen not just as a result of inflation but as a contributing cause of economic instability, which might be corrected by arbitrary write-downs. Accountants who had failed to protest earlier increases found them-selves in a weak position to argue against the reverse procedure. A study by Solomon Fabricant of 208 corporations randomly selected from members of the New York Stock Exchange showed that in 1931 forty companies made net fixed asset writedowns of about 96 million dollars; in 1932 sixty-four compa-nies made writedowns of $236 million; and that in each of the next two years about 60 million dollars was written off.[37] Most reported that they revalued assets because of discrepancies between historical costs and current values. When the National Association of Cost Accountants surveyed its members on the question of writing down assets, nearly 75 percent of 117 respondents favored doing so.[38] In 1938 the American Institute published an analysis of 500 corporate balance sheets which showed that 135 of 486 property items were described as "appraised or revised values" while 250 were stated at cost and 101 mentioned no valuation basis.[39]

In this atmosphere Henry Sweeney published *Stabilized Accounting* (1936), arguing for a systematic recognition of changing prices in the accounts. Draw-ing on the European experience with runaway inflation, he proposed valuation in terms of "common dollars" of uniform purchasing power. He first demon-strated how ordinary accounting went wrong: (1) it failed to provide for maintenance of capital and purchasing power; (2) it combined figures which were expressed in different measuring units; and (3) it failed to include profits and losses from changes in the value of money.[40] Since monetary assets were already stabilized at current price levels, his method concentrated on restating fixed assets and capital in terms of year end purchasing power. Sweeney considered the cost of living index the ideal deflator because men hold money for its ultimate ability to purchase goods and services. He recommended that after this index was applied to historical costs, the resulting figures be adjusted again for changes in replacement costs of land, buildings, machinery, and in-ventories on each balance sheet date, either by appraisals or by applying a suit-able replacement cost index. His method also distinguished between each period's realized income and its unrealized profits from price level changes. Retained earnings was divided into realized and unrealized portions and used as a balanc-ing figure which absorbed price level changes.

At the time Sweeney's book went largely unnoticed. In 1936 the present inflation had not begun, and accountants were already making use of the quasi-reorganization and other orthodox means of counteracting the effects of deflation on historical costs. Yet his was the rare case in which a pioneering work is also definitive. *Accounting Research Study* No. 6, "Reporting the Financial Effects of Price-Level Changes" published by the AICPA in 1963, so essentially adopts Sweeney's method that he commented, "To review the Study's main concepts, therefore, places this reviewer in the anomalous posi-tion of practically reviewing his own work."[41] Though Sweeney died before the appearance of *Accounting Principles Board Statement No. 3* "Financial Statements Restated for General Price-Level Changes" (1969), it too follows the basic method described in *Stabilized Accounting.*

Kenneth MacNeal's *Truth in Accounting* (1939) argued that "Financial statements purport to deal with present economic values, and they are apt to be useful only to the extent that they do so."[42] He blamed reporting inadequacies on the lag of accounting ideas behind business development, and backed his thesis with a plausible historical analysis which described three eras in the practice of asset valuation. In the first, accountants were concerned only with producing data for their employers. In the second, the public accounting profession originated because of creditors' need for reliable information. In the third era, from 1900 on, the owner was replaced by many stockholders and there were now three parties at interest—management, creditors, and investors. But accounting principles from all three periods remained in use regardless of changed conditions. For example, historical cost, stewardship and conservatism originated in era one and are inappropriate for reporting to stockholders, the primary party now at interest, which did not even exist when these concepts were devised. As a result the reports most useful to stockholders —the balance sheet and income statement—ignore unrealized appreciation on current assets, exclude capital gains on fixed assets, and in general treat understatement as conservative and commendable, but overstatement as dishonest. MacNeal then asks: how truthful are figures based on such principles? He concludes that accountants must become valuers rather than costers, and the market price of assets is their proper value for accounting purposes. Despite Canning's comment that "Truth may be both expensive and useless," MacNeal was only trying to do on the conceptual level what Sweeney had done with the practical problem of asset revaluation. His criticisms were simplistic, but diagnostically correct, and of a type which would become familiar after World War II.

1945–1960: THE SEARCH FOR SUBSTITUTES

A 30 percent increase in the consumer price index between 1945 and 1948 produced the first popular interest in price level adjustments, replacement costs, and other equalizing devices. Inflation on this scale impaired stockholder's equity and encouraged the creation of secret reserves and retention of the whole paraphernalia of conservatism. Price level changes also put the balance sheet and income statement in conflict, forcing the accountant constantly to choose between them. They provoked criticisms of unrealistic statement figures in audited reports. But initially the accounting profession rejected radical alternatives to historical cost in favor of solutions which it hoped would ease the pressure without upsetting orthodox valuation theory.

For management, however, the problem was entirely different and far more critical. The doctrine that value equaled cost was unhelpful to companies faced with the need to replace assets bought in the 1930s at prices which had more than doubled. Depreciation on such assets did not begin to cover replacement costs at 1947 levels. This led to sales prices too low to recover the real costs of using equipment. Depreciation based on understated asset values also inflated reported income, creating demands for higher wages, dividends, and tax payments at a time when cash was urgently needed for asset replacement. It is estimated that almost half of the seventeen billions reported as profits by American industry in 1947 was the result of inflation rather than operations.[43]

Such exceptional conditions forced major companies to go beyond existing accounting rules. In the first quarter of 1947 United States Steel Corporation deducted 30 percent ($26.3 million) more than normal depreciation charges from income, calling it "Wear and Exhaustion of Facilities" based on price indices and engineering estimates of plant replacement costs. In the same year, E. I. DuPont de Nemours and Company wrote off in advance of use that part of new plant construction costs which it deemed excessive because of prevailing high prices. Also in 1947 Chrysler Corporation began charging depreciation on historical cost at an accelerated rate, on the grounds that it had made new asset purchases at prices which were only justified by exceptional sales possibilities predicted for the next few years.[44]

U.S. Steel's auditors took exception to its supplementary depreciation charges because they ultimately would have totaled more than the historical cost of the assets. DuPont also recieved a qualified auditor's opinion because it had written off a large part of its new assets' costs before their use, violating the matching concept. The SEC issued a bulletin rejecting the use of replacement costs, and of course neither method was allowed for tax purposes. Finding no institutional support, both companies abandoned their procedures in 1948. But the "Chrysler formula," though its effect was similar, was theoretically respectable, being limited to historical cost and based on amortization over a period of economic usefulness. It led eventually to the accelerated depreciation provisions of the 1954 tax code.

In 1947 the American Institute reaffirmed its adherence to historical cost in two bulletins. Its answer to U.S. Steel was *Accounting Research Bulletin No. 33*, "Depreciation and High Costs," which advised managers to provide for asset replacements by creating surplus reserves, not by increasing depreciation charges, and which by unanimous vote recommended retention of the historical cost doctrine. *Accounting Research Bulletin No. 29*, "Inventory Pricing," described by Reed Storey as "a classic example of trying to please everyone," stated that the primary basis for inventory valuation is acquisition or production cost, but also approved virtually every orthodox departure from cost. Lower of cost or market writedowns were specifically upheld, but only "exceptionally" could inventories properly be valued above cost.[45]

In 1948 the response to a questionnaire mailed to businesses, labor organizations, accountants, and economists seemed to support the Institute's position against replacement costs. A letter sent to Institute members in October of that year reaffirmed the *Bulletin No. 33* position, while recommending that companies begin to experiment with supplementary schedules adjusted for price level changes. At the end of 1948 the Committee on Accounting Procedure again voted to support the *status quo.* In 1953, Bulletins 29 and 33 were updated and incorporated in *Accounting Research Bulletin No. 43,* which reiterated the 1947 decision that cost figures were realistic and that no basic change in historical cost accounting was justified.[46] While elaborating its definition in the lower of cost or market situation, the Committee repeated its previous statement that raising depreciation rates was not a suitable solution to the price level problem. The search continued for methods which compensated for inflationary bias without violating accounting principles.

LIFO and accelerated depreciation may be seen either as limited counter-inflationary measures or as palliatives whose effect was to delay any real solution to the price level problem during the moderate inflation of the 1950s. Both reinforced an older tradition of balance sheet conservatism, so much so that taxpayers are still not allowed to use LIFO together with lower of cost or market inventory valuations. Both gave precedence to management's need for cash retention and asset replacement, even at the expense of the accountant's desire for more precise asset valuations. Neither was designed to cope with an environment where constant price rises were a normal business expectation. Nor was either effectively used for this purpose. Both became devices for deferring income taxes in the guise of making partial price level adjustments.[47]

In 1938–39 the tax code had been revised to allow LIFO inventory valuations in certain industries which were subject to cyclical changes in raw materials prices. The intention was to avoid taxing unearned income. As Moonitz says, LIFO was compensation for the lack of an income averaging provision in the tax codes of the 1930s.[48] When instead of cyclical ups and downs, the postwar years brought continual price rises, LIFO no longer served its original purpose. Its new rationale was as a substitute for price level changes, but the real motive for its widespread use continued to be its ability to postpone tax payments in periods of rising prices.

Accelerated depreciation was more defensible theoretically and had been favored by Paton and Hatfield during the 1920s. If assets are future economic benefits, one goal of depreciation policy should be to recover enough dollars each period to equal capital consumption in original dollars. When prices rise, straight line depreciation on historical cost fails to do this; accelerated depreciation tends to more closely approximate the asset's loss of economic value. Though it may not compensate for inflationary pressures throughout the asset's useful life, fast depreciation can promote internal financing by improving company liquidity. It also offers a tax incentive for industrial replacement or expansion. Finally, it does for plant and equipment what LIFO does for inventories, transferring the bulk of asset costs to the income statement before inflation can make major inroads on their book value.

During the 1950s more than 100 articles on the price level problem were published in major accounting periodicals. By now, inflation had established itself as a permanent fact of life for which some kind of accounting allowance had to be made. American Accounting Association *Supplementary Statement No. 2* (1951) proposed that historical cost financial statements be supplemented by reports adjusted for general price level changes, and that these latter, at least in the first years of their use, need not be covered by the auditor's opinion.[49] In *Accounting and Reporting Standards for Corporate Financial Statements—1957 Revision* the Association broadened its earlier recommendations by suggesting that ending inventories and cost of goods sold should be expressed in terms of current purchasing power, and that gains and losses from price changes should be identified.[50]

The AICPA sponsored Study Group on Business Income devoted much of its attention to the effects of price level changes on income. The Study Group's report (1952) concluded that for the present, reporting emphasis should remain with historical costs, but that gradually these should be supplanted by price-level adjusted figures. In the meantime, the use of supplementary reports was recommended to show the effects of price level changes.

Accounting Research Study No. 6, "Reporting the Financial Effects of Price Level Changes" (1963) also recommended that price-level adjusted figures be added either as supplementary exhibits or as extra columns in the conventional statements.[51] Again, the justification for including such data merely as supplements was that the present and near future constituted a transition period.

The number of managements following these recommendations was very small. For most, distorted balance sheet valuations were simply not the main problem caused by inflation. Even from the accountant's viewpoint, the use of supplementary statements hardly implied a changed theoretical position. The matching of costs and revenues was still thought more important than providing for asset replacements. Balance sheet valuations were still derived as residuals from the income measuring process. Yet if the going concern has an indefinitely long life—longer than that of presently held assets—then it is *theoretically* essential to provide for depreciation sufficient to permit the physical renewal of plant assets. If reported income fails to reflect such replacement costs, capital will be depleted and business continuity undermined.

Samuel Lee describes a Korean textile mill for which the 1957 price of one yard of nylon cloth equalled the prewar cost of three acres of industrial land.[52] In such circumstances price level adjusted statements become absolutely essential and often are based on a government sponsored deflator. The American dilemma is more subtle—just enough inflation to distort published results but never quite enough to force radical changes. Even so, there are indications that the regulatory agencies and even the Internal Revenue Service would accept price level adjusted figures if the accounting profession required their use in published reports.[53] In trying to make historical costs relevant, accountants have already abstracted from them in ways which require or permit subjective judgments, especially by management. During the 1960s both major accounting societies approved systematic asset revaluations. Accounting Principles Board *Statement No. 3* (1969) recommended that companies report on the effects of general price level changes, and offered a format and procedures for doing so. In December, 1974, the Financial Accounting Standards Board issued an exposure draft, "Financial Reporting in Units of General Purchasing Power," advocating mandatory price level adjustments in audited financial statements. However, in June of 1976 the FASB announced that it had decided to defer further consideration of price level adjustments. The debate continues between supporters of the price level solution and those who favor some form of current value accounting.

REPLACEMENT COSTS OR MARKET SELLING PRICES?

If it is not premature to draw conclusions from trends in the recent literature, these would seem to include: (1) increasing advocacy for the inclusion of current replacement costs and selling prices in the balance sheet, and (2) attempts to incorporate solutions to the asset valuation problem into general restatements of accounting theory.

In *A Tentative Set of Broad Accounting Principles for Business Enterprises* (1962), Sprouse and Moonitz take the view of the 1957 AAA Committee that "Assets represent future economic benefits, rights to which have been acquired by the enterprise as a result of some current or past transaction."[54] If an asset's value equals the expected future incomes it will produce, then its balance sheet price should be determined by discounting such service potentials back to the present. To approximate this, the authors propose that normally saleable inventories should be priced at net realizable value, whether this is above or below cost. They do not discuss price level adjustments at length, and their asset valuation proposals differ little from those of Canning and other earlier writers, except that they are integrated into a general theory of accounting. Like Sweeney, Sprouse and Moonitz favor the use of price level indices together with fixed asset revaluations based on changes in replacement costs:

> In the external reports, plant and equipment should be restated in terms of current replacement costs whenever some significant event occurs, such as a reorganization of the business entity or its merger with another entity or when it becomes a subsidiary of a parent company. Even in the absence of a significant event, the accounts could be restated at periodic intervals, perhaps every five years.[55]

Depreciation in these terms is an allocation of current replacement costs, and the depreciation charge reflects the current input value of services provided by the assets. This permits profit measurement based on a matching of current input costs with current revenues. The use of replacement costs avoids the need for balance sheet conservatism, the lower of cost or market rule, and for LIFO,

FIFO and other cost flow assumptions. It places more emphasis on value changes than on cost flows, making the balance sheet as important as the income statement.

Edwards and Bell's *The Theory and Measurement of Business Income* (1961) proposes a variation of the replacement cost approach to accounting measurement. Again the center of attention is asset valuation rather than cost allocation, and current rather than historical asset prices:

> Reality, we have argued, is composed of the current events of the period being recorded. The historic costs which may be so accurately known are simply not events of the current period. Estimated current costs are certainly superior to historic costs as an approximation to true current costs.[56]

After showing the effects (in terms of lost statement comparability) of not taking up holding gains on assets, the authors demonstrate adjustment methods which account both for individual price changes and for the effects of changes in the general price level. Like Sprouse and Moonitz, they insist that the main advantage of depreciation on replacement cost is not that it improves a firm's liquidity position but that it facilitates the matching of current costs with revenues. Holding gains and losses can then be identified, and the results of management's investment decisions are more clearly revealed.

The American Accounting Association's 1963 Committee on Long Lived Assets affirmed the earlier definition of assets as service potentials. Admitting that it is hard to measure the discounted cash flows of individual assets, the Committee felt replacement cost reasonably approximates an asset's service potential, representing as it does the price a firm might pay for the asset bought in the current market. If replacement cost is higher than historical cost, the difference, in the absence of price level changes, is a holding gain which should be taken into income. Net profit can then be determined by subtracting from current revenues total expenses, including depreciation based on current replacement prices.

On March 23, 1976, the Securities and Exchange Commission issued *Accounting Series Release No. 190*, which requires certain large corporations to disclose replacement costs in the footnotes to their published financial statements. Other countries seem to be moving in the same direction. In 1973, the British Accounting Institute's Accounting Standards Steering Committee recommended general price level adjustments (ED8, later PSSAP 7). But in October, 1974, both the Institute of Chartered Accountants in England and Wales, and the Sandilands Committee, which was established by the British government, decided that replacement costs were superior to price level adjustments.

R. J. Chambers argues that "Every measurement of a financial property for the purpose of choosing a course of action—to buy, to hold, or to sell—is a measurement at a point of time, in the circumstance of the time, and in the units of currency at the time. . . ."[57] Past prices are irrelevant to such actions; future prices, in the form of discounted cash flows, are speculative and subjective. So the accountant is left with a choice between current replacement prices of assets and their current selling prices.

> But the buying price, or replacement price, does not indicate capacity, on the basis of present holdings, to go into a market with cash for the purpose of adapting oneself to contemporary conditions, whereas the selling price does. We propose, therefore, that the single financial property which is uniformly relevant at a point of time for all possible future actions in markets is the market selling price or realizable price of any or all goods held. Realizable price may be described as *current cash equivalent.*[58]

Chambers would value each asset at the price it would bring under conditions of orderly liquidation in the current market, as measured mainly by the quoted market prices for goods of a similar kind and condition. Thus the saleability of assets becomes a primary test for their inclusion in the balance sheet. Nonvendable long-term assets, including nearly all intangibles, would be written off to expense at the time of acquisition.

As a variant of the "inventory" method of asset valuation which dominated commercial bookkeeping for over 300 years, Chambers' system aims to improve the precision of accounting measurements by narrowing their scope. The firm's current market capabilities are highlighted, particularly its short-run liquidity position. The problems of predicting asset lifespans and calculating depreciation, of tracing back inventory flows to estimate historical costs, and of revaluing intangibles, disappear or are minimized. The doctrine of conservatism, with its emphasis on past prices and possible future consequences, becomes entirely irrelevant. Like other valuation methods, "continuously contemporary accounting" faces an aggregation problem, reflected in the need to find going concern prices for individual assets when the going concern by definition involves the collective use and valuation of assets. In a broader sense, the continuity principle expresses an essential difference between the present and proposed methods. Conventional accounting, in evaluating a firm's current financial position, looks both to the past and the future, creating insoluable difficulties it is true, but also taking a view of operations compatible with the whole continuum of activity suggested by the going concern concept. The results of past experience may be misstated, but they are not disregarded.

SUMMARY AND CONCLUSIONS

This chapter might have been called "The Rise and Fall of Historical Costing" except that, just as in 1900, accounting behavior remains rooted in conservatism, acquisition cost valuation, and all their subsidiary doctrines and methods. This unresponsiveness of practice to theory is a striking aspect of the valuation question during this century. Concepts have developed logically and coherently during the last seventy years, but practitioners have hardly been affected by them. Instead, the reasons for change have been largely external: inflation, taxation, the growing complexity of businesses, the increasing importance of stockholders as compared to creditors, the threat of government interference, and the codification of accounting methods. This is partly because asset valuation presented quite *different* problems to accounting practitioners, theorists, and corporate managers. It may also be that the present asset valuation methods, centered around conservatism and practically indefensible theoretically, have proved so durable precisely because they are only conventions rather than logically derived principles which interact with the rest of accounting theory. As in 1900 they survive largely because of accountants' failure to agree on workable alternatives.

A weak accounting profession permitted arbitrary asset writeups during the 1920s and was later blamed for the results. Today's public criticisms of accountants more often center around their rigid adherence to cost prices, the unrealistic figures this produces in published statements, and the reluctance of practitioners to approve writeups to current values. It now seems likely that basic improvements in accounting theory will begin with changes in asset valuation procedure. Already theoretical emphasis has shifted from acquisition costs to current values in measuring financial position, and from income realization at the point of sale to the determination of profits as soon as objective measurements can be made. G. Edward Philips concludes that:

> The accounting theory revolution consists essentially of an attempt to overthrow the traditional emphasis on costs in accounting theory and to replace it with a logical structure centered on values. It is hoped that this will provide a basis for resolving major theory controversies and for narrowing the present diversity of accepted practice.[59]

FOOTNOTES

1. Henry Rand Hatfield, "Some Variations in Accounting Practice in England, France, Germany, and the United States." *Journal of Accounting Research* 4 (Autumn, 1966), 169-82.
2. George O. May, *Memoirs and Accounting Thought of George O. May*, Paul Grady, ed. (New York: Ronald Press, 1962), 23.
3. R.H. Parker, "Lower of Cost or Market in Britain and the United States: An Historical Survey," *Abacus* 1 (December, 1965), 158-59.
4. S. Paul Garner, *Evolution of Cost Accounting to 1925* (Alabama: University of Alabama Press, 1954), 321.
5. Reed K. Storey, "Revenue Realization, Going Concern, and Measurement of Income," *The Accounting Review* 34 (April, 1959), 236-37.

6. Richard P. Brief, "Nineteenth Century Accounting Error," *Journal of Accounting Research* 3 (Spring, 1965), 12-31.
7. Storey, *op. cit.*, 233-34; D.A. Litherland, "Fixed Asset Replacement a Half Century Ago," *Accounting Review* 26 (October, 1951), 475-80.
8. May, *op. cit.*, 233.
9. Lawrence R. Dicksee, *Auditing*, 5th ed. (London: Gee, 1902), 180-81.
10. Lawrence R. Dicksee, *Advanced Accounting* (London: Gee, 1903), 5.
11. Storey, *op. cit.*, 237-38.
12. Henry Rand Hatfield, *Modern Accounting*, (New York: D. Appleton-Century Company, 1909), 81.
13. Henry Rand Hatfield, *Accounting, Its Principles and Problems*, (New York: D. Appleton-Century Company, 1927), 152.
14. Storey, *op. cit.*, 236-38.
15. William A. Paton, *Accounting Theory* (New York: Ronald Press, 1922), 293.
16. Stephen A. Zeff, "Episodes in the Progression of Price-Level Accounting in the United States," *Accountants' Magazine* 68 (April, 1964), 304.
17. John B. Canning, *The Economics of Accountancy*, (New York: Ronald Press, 1929), 12-13.
18. *Ibid.*, 227.
19. J.D. Edwards and R.F. Salmonson, eds., *Contributions of Four Accounting Pioneers* (East Lansing: Michigan State University Business Studies, 1961), 46, 53-56.
20. A.C. Littleton, "Prestige for Historical Cost," in M. Chatfield, ed., *Contemporary Studies in the Evolution of Accounting Thought*, (Belmont, Cal.: Dickenson Publishing Company, 1968), 308.
21. May, *op. cit.*, 314.
22. Storey, *op. cit.*, 238.
23. Robert R. Sterling, "Conservatism: The Fundamental Principle of Valuation in Traditional Accounting," *Abacus* 3 (December, 1967), 110.
24. Lawrence L. Vance, "Authority of History in Inventory Valuation," *Accounting Review* 18 (July, 1943), 219-27; A.C. Littleton, "Geneology for Cost or Market," *Accounting Review* 16 (June, 1941), 161-67.
25. Eldon S. Hendriksen, *Accounting Theory*, rev. ed. (Homewood, Ill.: Richard D. Irwin, 1970), 278-79.
26. May, *op. cit.*, 67.
27. *Ibid.*, 235-36.
28. *Ibid.*, 64.
29. Committee on Terminology, American Institute of Certified Public Accountants, "Review and Resumé," *Accounting Terminology Bulletin No. 1*. (New York: AICPA, 1953), 16.
30. Thomas Henry Sanders, Henry Rand Hatfield and Underhill Moore, *A Statement of Accounting Principles*, (New York: American Institute of Accountants, 1938), 114-15.
31. Executive Committe of the American Accounting Association, "A Tentative Statement of Accounting Principles Underlying Corporate Financial Statements," *Accounting Review* 11 (June, 1936), 188.
32. W.A. Paton and A.C. Littleton, *An Introduction to Corporate Accounting Standards*, American Accounting Association Monograph No. 3 (New York: American Accounting Association, 1940), 10.
33. *Ibid.*, 14.
34. *Ibid.*, 80-81, 126-29.
35. See Germain Boer, "Replacement Cost: A Historical Look," *Accounting Review* 41 (January, 1966), 92-97.
36. "Cost Versus Value," *The Journal of Accountancy* 45 (September, 1927), 200-1.
37. Solomon Fabricant, "Revaluations of Fixed Assets, 1925-34." *National Bureau of Economic Research, Bulletin No. 62* (December 7, 1936), 5.
38. Research and Service Department: National Association of Cost Accountants, "Report on a Survey of the Revaluation of Plant Assets," *N.A.C.A. Bulletin* (March 15, 1933), 1039.

39. Henry T. Chamberlain, "Adjustments of Fixed Assets," in *Papers on Accounting Principles and Procedures* (New York: American Institute of Accountants, 1938), 8-12.
40. Henry W. Sweeney, *Stabilized Accounting.*(New York: Harper and Brothers, 1936), 24.
41. Henry W. Sweeney, "'Reporting the Financial Effects of Price-Level Changes,' A Critique," *Accounting Review* 39 (October, 1964), 1100.
42. Kenneth MacNeal, *Truth in Accounting* (Philadelphia: University of Pennsylvania Press, 1939), 84.
43. Edward Wilcox, "Fluctuating Price Levels in Relation to Accounts," in *Handbook of Modern Accounting Theory*, Morton Backer, ed. (Englewood Cliffs, N.J. Prentice-Hall, 1955), 255.
44. *Ibid.*, 257-58; Stewart Y. McMullen, "Depreciation and High Costs: The Emerging Pattern," *Journal of Accountancy* 88 (October, 1949), 302-4.
45. *Accounting Research Bulletin No. 29*, "Inventory Pricing" (New York: AICPA, 1947), 235-42.
46. Accounting Research Bulletin No. 43, "Restatement and Revision of Accounting Research Bulletins" (New York: AICPA, 1953), 28.
47. See Chapter Fifteen.
48. Maurice Moonitz, "The Case Against LIFO as an Inventory Pricing Formula," *Journal of Accountancy* 95 (June, 1953), 682-83.
49. "Price Level Changes and Financial Statements," *Accounting Review* 26 (October, 1951), 468-71.
50. American Accounting Association Committee on Accounting Concepts and Standards, *Accounting and Reporting Standards for Corporate Financial Statements and Preceding Statements and Supplements* (Columbus, Ohio: American Accounting Association, 1957), 6.
51. American Institute of Certified Public Accountants, "Reporting the Financial Effects of Price-Level Changes," *Accounting Research Study No. 6* (New York: AICPA, 1963), 53.
52. Samuel S.O. Lee, "Korean Accounting Revaluation Laws," *Accounting Review* 40 (July, 1965), 622.
53. Zeff, *op. cit.*, 303-4.
54. Robert T. Sprouse and Maurice Moonitz, "A Tentative Set of Broad Accounting Principles for Business Enterprises," *Accounting Research Study No. 3* (New York: AICPA, 1962), 20.
55. *Ibid.*, 34.
56. Edgar O. Edwards and Philip W. Bell, *The Theory and Measurement of Business Income* (Berkeley and Los Angeles: University of California Press, 1961), 284.
57. Raymond J. Chambers, *Accounting, Evaluation and Economic Behavior* (Englewood Cliffs, N.J.: Prentice-Hall, 1966), 91-92.
58. *Ibid.*, 92.
59. G. Edward Philips, "The Revolution in Accounting Theory," *Accounting Review* 38 (October, 1963), 707.

SELECTED BIBLIOGRAPHY

American Accounting Association, Committee on Concepts and Standards–Long-Lived Assets. "Accounting for Land, Buildings, and Equipment." Supplementary Statement No. 1. *Accounting Review* 34 (July, 1964), 693-99.

American Accounting Association, Committee on Concepts and Standards–Inventory Measurement. "A Discussion of Various Approaches to Inventory Measurement," Supplementary Statement No. 2. *Accounting Review* 34 (July, 1964), 700-14.

American Institute of Certified Public Accountants. "Reporting the Financial Effects of Price-Level Changes." *Accounting Research Study No. 6.* New York: AICPA, 1963.

Boer, Germain, "Replacement Cost: A Historical Look." *Accounting Review* 41 (January, 1966), 92-97.

Brief, Richard P. "The Origin and Evolution of Nineteenth-Century Asset Accounting." *Business History Review* 40 (1966), 1-22.

———. ed. *The Late Nineteenth Century Debate Over Depreciation, Capital and Income.* New York: Arno Press, 1976.

Canning, John B. *The Economics of Accountancy.* New York: Ronald Press, 1929, chaps. one and two.

Chambers, Raymond J. *Accounting, Evaluation and Economic Behavior.* Englewood Cliffs, N.J.: Prentice-Hall, 1966. Reprinted by Scholars Book Company, Houston, 1975. Especially 91-93, 103-123.

———. "The Development of the Theory of Continuously Contemporary Accounting." *Academy of Accounting Historians Working Paper No. 13.* University, Alabama: Academy of Accounting Historians, 1975.

——— "Second Thoughts on Continuously Contemporary Accounting." *Abacus* 6 (September, 1970), 39-55.

Devine, Carl T. "The Rule of Conservatism Reexamined." *Journal of Accounting Research* 1 (Autumn, 1963), 127-38.

Dicksee, Lawrence R. *Advanced Accounting.* London: Gee, 1903. Reprinted by Arno Press, New York, 1976.

———. *Auditing.* London: Gee, 1892. Reprinted by Arno Press, New York, 1976.

———. *Depreciation, Reserves, and Reserve Funds.* London, 1903. Reprinted by Arno Press, New York, 1976.

———. *Goodwill and its Treatment in Accounts.* London: 1906. Reprinted by Arno Press, New York, 1976.

Edwards, Edgar O., and Bell, Phillip W. *The Theory and Measurement of Business Income.* Berkeley and Los Angeles: University of California Press, 1961, chaps. six through nine.

Elvik, K.O. "Acquisition Cost Versus Revaluation: a Historical Perspective." *International Journal of Accounting* 9 (Spring, 1974), 155-67.

Hatfield, Henry Rand. "Some Variations in Accounting Practice in England, France, Germany, and the United States." *Journal of Accounting Research* 4 (Autumn, 1966), 169-82.

———. *Modern Accounting.* New York: D. Appleton-Century Company, 1909. Reprinted by Arno Press, New York, 1976.

Hendriksen, Eldon S. *Accounting Theory*, rev. ed. Homewood Ill.: Richard D. Irwin, 1970, chaps. nine through fourteen.

Horn, C.A. "Changing Attitudes to Obsolescence and Depreciation." *Accountant* 158 (May 11, 1968), 619-622.

Ijiri, Yuji. *The Foundation of Accounting Measurement.* Englewood Cliffs, N.J.: Prentice-Hall, 1967, especially 64-67.

Iselin, Errol R. "Chambers on Accounting Theory." *Accounting Review* 43 (April, 1968), 231-38.

Kitchen, J. "Lawrence Dicksee, Depreciation, and the Double-Account System." In Harold Edey and B.S. Yamey, eds. *Debits, Credits, Finance and Profits.* London: Sweet and Maxwell, 1974, 109-130.

Leake, P.D. *Depreciation and Wasting Assets and their Treatment in Assessing Annual Profit and Loss*. London: 1912. Reprinted by Arno Press, New York, 1976.

Littleton, A.C. "Geneology for Cost or Market." *Accounting Review* 16 (June, 1941), 161-67.

_____ "Prestige for Historical Cost." In M. Chatfield, ed., *Contemporary Studies in the Evolution of Accounting Thought*. Belmont, Cal.: Dickenson Publishing Company, 1968, 307-12.

Littleton, A.C., and Zimmerman, V.K. *Accounting Theory: Continuity and Change*. Englewood Cliffs, N.J.: Prentice-Hall, 1962, chaps. seven and eight.

Litherland, D.A. "Fixed Asset Replacement a Half Century Ago." *Accounting Review* 26 (October, 1951), 475-80.

MacNeal, Kenneth, "What's Wrong with Accounting?" In W.T. Baxter and Sidney Davidson, eds. *Studies in Accounting Theory*. Homewood, Ill.: Richard D. Irwin, 1962, 56-69.

_____. *Truth in Accounting*. Philadelphia: University of Pennsylvania Press, 1939. Reprinted by Scholars Book Company, Lawrence, Kansas, 1970.

Matheson, Ewing. *The Depreciation of Factories, Mines and Industrial Undertakings and their Valuation*. London and New York: 1893. Reprinted by Arno Press, New York, 1976.

Mathews, R.L. "Price-Level Changes and Useless Information." *Journal of Accounting Research* 3 (Spring, 1965), 133-55.

May, George O. "Comment on 'Prestige for Historical Cost.'" In M. Chatfield, ed. *Contemporary Studies in the Evolution of Accounting Thought*. Belmont, Cal.: Dickenson Publishing Company, 1968, 313-15.

Moonitz, Maurice. "The Case Against LIFO as an Inventory Pricing Formula." *Journal of Accountancy* 95 (June, 1953), 682-90.

Mueller, Gerhard G. "Valuing Inventories at Other than Historical Costs—Some International Differences." *Journal of Accounting Research* 2 (Autumn, 1964), 148-57.

Parker, R.H. "Lower of Cost or Market in Britain and the United States: An Historical Survey." *Abacus* 1 (December, 1965), 156-72.

Paton, W.A., and Littleton, A.C. *An Introduction to Corporate Accounting Standards*. American Accounting Association Monograph No. 3. New York: American Accounting Association, 1940, chaps. two and three.

Securities and Exchange Commission. *Accounting Series Release No. 190*. Washington, D.C.: Securities and Exchange Commission, March 23, 1976.

Solomons, David. "Economic And Accounting Concepts of Cost and Value." In Morton Backer, ed., *Modern Accounting Theory*. Englewood Cliffs, N.J.: Prentice-Hall, 1966, 117-140.

Sprouse, Robert T. "Historical Costs and Current Assets—Traditional and Treacherous." *Accounting Review* 38 (October, 1963), 687-95.

Sprouse, Robert T., and Moonitz, Maurice. "A Tentative Set of Broad Accounting Principles for Business Enterprises." *Accounting Research Study No. 3*. New York: AICPA, 1962, chaps. three and four.

Sterling, Robert R. "Conservatism: The Fundamental Principle of Valuation in Traditional Accounting." *Abacus* 3 (December, 1967), 109-32.

_____. "The Going Concern: An Examination." *Accounting Review* 43 (July, 1968), 481-502.

_____. ed. *Asset Valuation and Income Determination*. Houston: Scholars Book Company, 1973.

Storey, Reed K. "Revenue Realization, Going Concern, and Measurement of Income." *Accounting Review* 34 (April, 1959), 233-38.

Sweeney, Henry W. *Stabilized Accounting*. New York: Harper and Brothers, 1936. Reprinted by Holt, Rinehart and Winston, New York, 1964.

Thomas, Arthur L. "The Allocation Problem in Financial Accounting Theory." *American Accounting Association Studies in Accounting Research, No. 3*. Menasha, Wisc.: George Banta Company, Inc., 1969.

Tritschler, Charles A. "A Sociological Perspective on Accounting Innovation." *International Journal of Accounting* 5 (Spring, 1970), 39-67.

Vance, Lawrence L. "The Authority of History in Inventory Valuation." *Accounting Review* 18 (July, 1943), 219-27.

Vangermeersch, Richard. "Historical Overview of Depreciation: U.S. Steel, 1902-1970." *Mississippi Valley Journal of Business and Economics* 8 (Winter, 1971-1972), 56-74.

————. "Management Behavior on Original Valuation of Tangible and Intangible Fixed Assets," and "The Significance of Writeups of Tangible Fixed Assets in the 1920's." *Academy of Accounting Historians Working Paper No. 15*. University, Alabama: Academy of Accounting Historians, 1975.

Zeff, Stephen A. "Episodes in the Progression of Price-Level Accounting in the United States." In M. Chatfield, ed. *Contemporary Studies in the Evolution of Accounting Thought*. Belmont, Cal.: Dickenson Publishing Company, 1968, 316-35.

————. ed. *Asset Appreciation, Business Income and Price-Level Accounting: 1918-1935*. New York: Arno Press, 1976.

Chapter 18

REALIZATION AND INCOME MEASUREMENT

INCOME FINDING BEFORE 1900

Modern concepts of business income, like our notions of asset valuation, are most easily understood as an amalgam of earlier views. Pre-double entry bookeeping was primarily concerned with resources rather than profits. Stewards kept accounts not for the entity's sake but for their own, to control assets for which they were responsible. There was no clear distinction between capital and income, no cost accounting to build up asset values by components, and no tradition of precise income measurement to impose a discipline on asset valuation and amortization. The systems in use did not favor data accumulation, nor did they normally involve futurity. The modern reasons for income finding hardly existed.

When Renaissance merchants felt the need to summarize the results of their trading judgments, income calculation replaced accountability as the major bookkeeping problem and the double entry system evolved. "It must be concluded that income determination by matching cost and revenue has, for 500 years, been the central feature of double entry."[1] The unique aspect of this new system, and the one which distinguished it from earlier attempts to measure income, was the integration of real and nominal accounts which allowed the results of many transactions to be expressed as the balance of a single profit and loss account. Double entry provided the mechanism to replace subjective views of income with a quantitative, uniform calculation which made gross profit essentially the difference between buying and selling prices.

256

But this income finding potential was scarcely used before the seventeenth century. Because of the piecemeal nature of venture trading, and the fact that different voyages had very different profit margins, merchants preferred to open a separate account for each consignment of goods and leave it open until everything was sold. At that time the venture account was ruled and its balance transferred to profit and loss, which at longer intervals was closed to capital. In each case profit was considered earned when the venture was liquidated. Overall income determination was at best a by-product of the closing process. Each "adventurer" could calculate his earnings just by substracting his original investment from his final proceeds.

Operating continuity and the advent of the corporation required periodic reckonings as a prelude to dividend payments. Attempts to measure the income earned during a particular time period led naturally to a system of accruals and deferrals. It was now the use of goods and services, not merely their purchase, which created expense, and sales rather than cash collections which signalled that income had been earned.

During the nineteenth century a series of court decisions, reinforced by statutes, required that dividends could be declared only from current and retained earnings. To make the necessary distinction between capital and income, industrial corporations developed sophisticated asset valuation and depreciation methods. Yet income measurement was nearly always subsidiary to asset valuation. Profits were calculated as the increase in net assets during a period, either through a policy of replacement accounting or by way of periodic asset appraisals. These methods were hard to standardize, and in 1900 there was still very little precision or consistency in profit calculations. Still, it had become accepted that the computation of annual income available for dividends was a primary accounting task. The profit figure was also widely accepted as an indicator of managerial efficiency, as a predictor of future operating results, as a basis for taxation, and as a guide to government regulatory policies.

THE LEGAL VIEW OF REALIZATION

The accounting concept of profit as an increase in net assets was undermined by English and American income tax laws.[2] For tax purposes there had to be an objective, legally authorized way to determine a year's income. The tax was on income, not wealth, and it was simply not feasible to make assessments on the basis of annual balance sheet revaluations. By defining taxable income as the excess of cash receipts over cash payments, these early tax laws made it necessary to measure income separately from the capital which generated it. So from the first a realization rule was an integral part of the tax code. Any increase in wealth had to be confirmed by some event or transaction, normally the receipt of money, before profit came into existence. This principle of realization through cash receipt prevailed throughout the administration of the Civil War tax laws (1862–1873), and was probably strengthened by the fact that the 1909 corporate income tax was enacted in the guise of an excise tax.

The Revenue Acts which followed passage of the Sixteenth Amendment began a process of convergence between tax and accounting income, in which each had an immediate and permanent influence on the other. Most larger corporations kept their books on an accrual basis, and it proved impractical to make them determine taxable income in a radically different way (which was also less accurate and consistent). Almost at once the courts made accrual accounting discretionary with the taxpayer. In 1916 taxpayers were given the option of computing income either on the statutory cash basis or according to their usual bookkeeping method, if the latter in the Commissioner's opinion correctly reflected taxable income. The 1918 Revenue Act specifically allowed accrual methods, and the tax code was virtually rewritten to conform to financial accounting procedures, on the premise that calculating business income was a commercial, not a legal problem.

If financial accounting affected taxation, the reverse was also true. Many if not most of the rules used today by accountants in determining business income emerged from tax cases decided between 1913 and 1920. Treasury Decision 2090, in 1913, stated that a sale and the existence of a valid account receivable were sufficient tests of realization. The Supreme Court ruled that only the gain from sales is income, and that the cost of goods sold and operating expenses needed to produce revenues may be deducted without express statutory permission.[3] Court decisions supported the idea that assets should be carried at historical cost until realized. The courts held that the *right* to receive money might be equivalent to actual receipt in measuring earned income, and that the government could tax profits which had not yet been collected in cash.

Asked to define income as the term was used in the Sixteenth Amendment, the Supreme Court identified its sources and emphasized that it was entirely different and distinct from capital.[4] In later decisions the courts ruled that gains resulting from the sale of capital assets were taxable as income. A much more critical question concerned the taxability of holding gains. In *Towne v. Eisner* (1918) and *Eisner v. Macomber* (1920), the Supreme Court held that receipt of common stock dividends did not constitute effective realization and was therefore not taxable income to the recipient, because such dividends took nothing from the property of the corporation and added nothing to that of the investor. In his opinion on the latter case, Justice Charles Evans Hughes stressed that income could not arise without (1) an effective addition to the wealth of the recipient, and (2) a "severance" of gain from capital. A man may grow rich from owning assets which increase in value, but he incurs no tax liability until he sells them.

The *Eisner v. Macomber* decision became a precedent for almost every subsequent court test of realization. Its thesis that income requires a separation from capital by way of an exchange transaction remains the general rule in law and accounting today. But tax decisions since 1920 have gradually extended the scope of realization to include events other than the receipt of cash or the creation of a receivable.[5] Taxable income may now be realized when a change occurs in the legal status of property. Realization may also coincide with the "final enjoyment of income," whatever form this may take. In certain cases the intent of the parties is considered decisive in determining whether or not income has been earned. The courts have even amended *Eisner v. Macomber* to the extent of ruling that leasehold income can arise without a separation of the gain from capital. However, the legal view of realization is still that income comes into existence only when certain conditions have been met in connection with an asset value increase. The gain or increase must be objectively measurable, it must be definite and irrevocable, and it must be confirmed by some transaction or event such as the receipt of money or property, relief from liability, or a change in the nature of legal rights.[6]

REALIZATION IN ACCOUNTING THEORY

There were certain points of contact between accounting theory and the emerging legal concept of realization. By a different line of reasoning, Lawrence Dicksee and several other early theorists had reached rather similar conclusions about income measurement. Dicksee's assumption of indefinite life for the corporation ruled out the use of liquidation prices in its balance sheet, just as the need for objectivity ruled out their use in tax reporting. If a business must maintain its fixed assets permanently, it seemed illogical to determine profits by annual appraisals based on current resale values. There being no intention to sell such assets, fluctuations in their market prices cannot be considered gains or losses. Long term assets should be booked at historical cost; income is realized on them only when they are sold. Dicksee felt that in general profits should not be anticipated. He considered that, though there might be exceptions, manufacturing profit should be recognized only when production is completed, and trading income only at the time of sale.[7]

The logic of business continuity required that current assets be priced at net realizable value, with holding gains as well as losses carried to profit and loss. This conflicted with tax regulations and accounting conservatism. It is probable that the realization rule was superimposed on the going concern concept because the latter was too radical and subjective in its implications for current asset writeups above cost. "The failure to carry the going concern assumption to its logical conclusion left a gap in accounting theory which was filled by the realization convention."[8] The realization rule required only that all assets be valued at historical cost prior to sale. But its popularization meant that "Asset valuation and income measurement were based on an incomplete application of the going concern convention tempered by conservatism."[9]

George O. May states that before World War I the notion that value equals cost was virtually unquestioned, the continuity principle was gaining acceptance, and the realization rule was not accepted at all. He adds that:

> A review of accounting, legal, and economic writing suggests that . . .
> in 1913 leading authorities in all these fields in England and America
> seemed to agree on the "increase in net worth" concept of income.[10]

This last suggests more agreement than in fact existed. Practice before 1933 was a mixture of methods based mainly, but not entirely, on the going concern concept. There was no single dominant or "generally accepted" theory of income determination. The first authoritative use of the word realization seems to have occurred in the 1932 correspondence between the American Institute's Special Committee on Cooperation with Stock Exchanges, and the Stock List Committee of the New York Stock Exchange.[11] The Institute Committee supported the realization test of income and rejected the asset appraisal methods, on the grounds that in any large company the real value of assets is collective and depends mainly on the firm's earning power.[12]

With the transition from "increased net worth" to realization at sale, it became common to speak of income finding as a process of matching related costs and revenues. This approach was actively promoted by the American Institute and the SEC during the 1930s because its results were objective and verifiable. At that stage in accounting development, uniformity was considered more important than precision. The profession's bad experiences with appraisal writeups during the preceding decades gave an air of reform to techniques which minimized the possibility of manipulation. In realization and matching the Institute offered its membership the protection of easily standardized procedures which were also explicable to the investing public. Both methods conformed to a tradition of accrual accounting, objectivity, and conservatism, and were flexible enough to allow for such exceptions as cost-or-market writedowns and deferred realization on installment sales. Widespread acceptance of the income statement as an expression of the matching process closely followed a corporate shift from debt to equity financing, and coincided with the advent of progressive taxation. It soon became common for theoretical and practical improvements to be promoted as attempts to refine income measurement. Even innovations such as LIFO, accelerated depreciation, interperiod tax allocations, and the percentage of completion method were justified on the grounds that they improved cost and revenue matching.

THE CRITICAL RESPONSE

While admitting the need for methods which reduced income finding to a routine, many accounting theorists of the interwar period were highly critical of realization-matching. This was due less to the system's obvious faults and inconsistencies than to the very constricted view it afforded of operating results, and to the near impossibility of defending it *as a theory*.

Henry Rand Hatfield and William Paton expressed dissatisfaction with the realization rule before it had even become established. Hatfield criticized as simplistic the notion that "profits existed only when the increase in wealth is realized" rather than when assets appreciated in value.[13] In the preface to *Accounting Theory* (1922), Paton adopted "without argument" . . .

> The liberal view that, ideally, all bona fide value changes in either direction, from whatever cause, should be reflected in the accounts. . . . To show that all possible types of situations and transactions can be handled in a rational manner . . . is a chief reason for this attitude. At the same time the writer believes that this logical position is the proper one for the professional accountant, at least as a starting point.[14]

Asserting that periodic income measurement even under the best conditions is "no more than a good guess," Paton reasoned:

> The argument that recognizing appreciation would call for recording "unrealized profits" is not correct, since all accruals are based on the "unrealized" transactions in the same sense. Furthermore, appreciation can in many instances be estimated more accurately than depreciation or decline in value due to deterioration or handling.[15]

Besides calling for a more broadly based measurement of business income, critics deplored the fact that the accountant's profit finding was guided by a series of arbitrary rules rather than a coherent theory. In *The Economics of Accountancy* (1929), John Canning saw the need for a transfusion of ideas from other disciplines:

> A diligent search of the literature of accounting discloses an astonishing lack of discussion of the nature of income. One could hardly expect that the profession which, above others, is most constantly engaged in the statistical treatment of income should have found almost nothing at all to say about the nature of the thing they measure so carefully.[16]

Not only was there no accounting theory of income, but even in the late 1930s there was no agreement as to just how the realization rule should be applied. Canning had suggested that income is realized when three conditions are fulfilled: (1) the receipt of money within a year has become highly probable, (2) the amount to be received is known or can be accurately estimated, as can (3) the expenses incurred or to be incurred in producing the revenues.[17] But in *Accounting Concepts of Profit* (1939), Stephen Gilman considered that realization does not take place until cash or some extremely liquid asset has actually been received:

> In any specific instance the test for realization is found in the question: Will the relinquishment of merchandise result in cash or in the creation of an asset which, in the normal course of events, will be converted into cash, i.e., does any further selling have to take place in order to obtain cash?[18]

In 1940 Paton and Littleton reflected an equally mechanistic position, but emphasized conversion more than collectability:

> Revenue is realized, according to the dominant view, when it is evidenced by cash receipts or receivables, or other new liquid assets. Implicit here are two tests: (1) conversion through liquid sale or similar process; (2) validation through the acquisition of liquid assets.[19]

But such minor disagreements hardly affected practice. The Institute's revamping of accounting during the 1930s had concentrated on matching and realization, and by 1940 the latter rule was almost universally applied. Without being quite sure what it *was,* accountants understood perfectly what it *did.* Realization occurs when income has become definite and measurable enough to deserve recognition in the accounts. This is nearly always at the time of sale, when the earning process is almost complete, current assets and working capital increase, title passes, and there has been an objective, verifiable transaction with outsiders. The consequences of realization were equally well understood. Costs accrue as time passes, but income from sales appears all at once. Unrealized gains are irrelevant and can be ignored, but losses must be anticipated by means of asset writedowns. Accounting is essentially a process of matching related costs and revenues. Once these are known in total the problem is to apportion them between present and future accounting periods. Expenses assigned to the present period are closed to profit and loss; the rest, and all assets generally, are simply deferred costs of future revenues. Because it synchronizes this matching process, the realization test is "the most important convention in the determination of income and the valuation of assets at the present time."[20]

Theorists might object that the realization rule actually frustrated matching by deferring recognition of holding gains until years after the costs of producing them had been recorded. But income finding depended on a series of interlocking assumptions which included historical cost, continuity, conservatism, and periodicity as well as matching and realization. These were made compatible by the ascendency which income measurement had attained over asset valuation, and by the fairly stable prewar price structure. If not exactly elegant, they generally corresponded to perceived reality as reflected in the periodical literature. It would prove very difficult to alter any one of them without changing their conglomerate effect. Those who accepted these assumptions confronted a closed and self-justifying system which, like the laws of Newtonian physics at the turn of the century, seemed to leave little to be discovered. After World War II, inflation would create an environment in which most of these conventions would be challenged and in which the classical notions of realization and income, though continuing to prevail in practice, would become theoretically disreputable.

ECONOMISTS' VIEWS OF BUSINESS INCOME

In its formative period, the accounting concept of realization was dominated by the legal view that income does not exist until certain events have occurred to make it objectively measurable. In contrast, economists generally consider that income comes into being with any increase in the present value of future services. Postwar changes in technology and in price levels, the general upgrading of accounting theory, and the higher expectations of report readers have created major differences among accountants as to what business income is and how it should be measured. Since the 1950s theorists have tried to reconcile economic and accounting ideas of income finding, not only to give the latter a new conceptual basis but to make accounting techniques consistent with what is now considered good theory.

The realization-at-sale rule was never an accounting principle in the true sense, but rather "a statistical generalization" which could "be applied or not, depending on whether it fits the situation under review."[21] Its value depended entirely on its specific applications. In the prewar environment this may even have been an advantage, but when inflation undermined the concept of income measured in historical dollars, the inability of accountants to abstract from the realization test became a serious handicap. The stewardship assumptions on which asset valuation and income measurement had traditionally rested no longer reflected the real motives of large manufacturing corporations or the primary interests of their stockholders. By making income recognition so dependent on decisions to take or not take particular actions, the realization rule permitted and encouraged the manipulation of periodic income figures. By focusing attention entirely on the *current* realization of assets while excluding or ignoring all other value changes, it produced at best a partial picture of operating results and managerial effectiveness. The "events test" of income recognition left investors and financial analysts to make the subjective interpretations which accountants had avoided.

During the last 200 years accounting and economic concepts of business income have developed in precisely opposite directions.[22] Accounting income was originally the result of asset appraisals on the balance sheet but now is almost always measured on the income statement as the excess of realized sales revenues over the costs incurred in producing them. Eighteenth century economists conceived of business income as the difference between the gross revenues and expenses needed to maintain fixed and circulating capital intact, and Adam Smith's doctrine that goods yield no profit until they "change masters" could stand as a definition of accounting realization today. But most contemporary economists define income as an increase in the present value of assets. As Sidney Alexander puts it, "A year's income is, fundamentally, the amount of wealth that a person, real or corporate, can dispose of over the course of a year and remain as well off at the end of the year as at the beginning."[23]

The accountant's relationship to his clients and the public prevents this economic definition of income from being wholly applicable to accounting measurement.[24] Not being as vulnerable to third party liability, the economist is less inclined to seek protection in such doctrines as objectivity and conservatism. His analysis also tends to be directly concerned with managerial expectations and much less with financial history or the current costs of past decisions. Accordingly the greatest difference between the accounting and economic approaches to income finding is the economist's willingness to recognize the effects of inflation, holding gains, increments to goodwill, and other value changes *as they accrue.* He would insist that a man is "better off" at the moment when his asset increases in value, not at the time when it is sold. In these terms realization implies a classification of income by sources rather than a test of income recognition. Comparison of economic and accounting concepts of income serves chiefly to suggest the shortcomings of the latter and the major lines of development which accounting theorists have lately tried to follow.

CHALLENGES TO THE REALIZATION RULE

In 1947 the American Institute of Accountants organized the Study Group on Business Income, consisting of over forty participants with a variety of backgrounds, to make a three-year examination of the accounting, legal, and economic aspects of business income. Its main achievements were to publicize the fact that there are *various* feasible approaches to income measurement and to elaborate a number of these viewpoints and possibilities. The Study Group's publications included George O. May's *Business Income and Price Levels, an Accounting Study,* and five monographs on business income by economists, one of which was Sidney Alexander's "Income Measurement in a Dynamic Economy." Alexander proposed:

> ... to analyze the income concept from a purely theoretical point of view and to compare the results of that analysis with income as conventionally measured by accountants. The object of the analysis will be to clarify what happens to income as actually measured in periods of changing prices or changing prospects.[25]

His theoretical measurement of business income called for periodic determinations of the present value of all future income streams. May's paper proposed that railroads and public utilities be required to supplement their depreciation charges to reflect the matching of current revenues with costs incurred in dollars of greater purchasing power, and that unregulated industrial companies be encouraged to do the same. As co-author of the Study Group's 1952 report,[26] May recommended a gradual transition to financial statements adjusted for price level changes.

Most prewar accountants seem to have considered the realization test part of the definition of income. That is, the events signalling realization must occur before income even exists. Opposed to this is the view that income, in the form of value increases, can exist and be *recognized* before it is formally *realized.* In 1957 the American Accounting Association's Committee on Concepts and Standards offered this definition:

> The essential meaning of realization is that a change in an asset or liability has become sufficiently definite and objective to warrant recognition in the accounts. This recognition may rest on an exchange transaction between independent parties, or on established trade practices, or on the terms of a contract performance of which is considered to be virtually certain. It may depend on the stability of a banking system, the enforceability of commercial agreements, or the ability of a highly organized market to facilitate the conversion of an asset into another form.[27]

This definition refers only to "definite and objective" changes rather than to the receipt of cash or other liquid assets. It includes changes in liabilities as well as assets, carrying the implication that realization might apply to various types of value changes. Much more than earlier definitions it bases income measurement on the use of estimates and the exercise of judgment. The Committee's report concluded that the realization rule should assist "the use by investors of published financial statements in making investment decisions and in exercising control over management."[28] It recommended that holding gains be recorded in the accounts, but shown on the income statement below the net income figure, to disclose value changes while maintaining the distinction between realized and unrealized profits.

In place of the assumption that profit is earned entirely at the moment of sale, G. Edward Phillips proposed an accretion concept of income, under which some portion of profit would be considered earned during each phase of a company's operating cycle.[29] While not going this far, several authors favored recording manufacturing income, not at any particular point in the operating cycle, but whenever it became obviously determinable. In a 1959 article,[30] John H. Myers concluded that apportioning income to each phase of the cycle is probably more trouble than it is worth. Besides, income is the joint product of efforts which are hard to subdivide, the value added at each stage depending on the whole continuum of planning, investment, production, selling, collection, and perhaps even product warranty after sale. Myers proposed that income should be reported at the moment of making the most critical decision or performing the most critical task in the operating cycle. This would not radically alter current practice, since the "critical event" is generally the sale, but it would substitute a general principle of revenue recognition for the existing series of rules which only cover particular situations.

In their "Principles" research study, Sprouse and Moonitz agreed that:

> ... revenues should be identified with the period during which the major economic activities necessary to the creation and disposition of

> goods and services have been accomplished, provided objective measure-
> ments of the results of those activities are available. These two conditions,
> i.e., accomplishment of major economic activity and objectivity of mea-
> surement, are fulfilled at different stages of activity in different cases,
> sometimes as late as time of delivery of product or the performance of a
> service, in other cases, at an earlier point of time.[31]

Sprouse and Moonitz stressed not only the timely recognition of profits but the
need to improve financial statement comparisons and interpretations by separating operating income, holding gains, and the effects of price level changes.[32]
This separation would apparently be achieved by isolating changes in asset
values rather than by applying the realization rule, which "lacks analytical
precision" and might better be abandoned entirely than amended.

To test the validity of the realization rule, Arthur Thomas considered
whether certain gains and losses from speculation in currency should be recognized in determining income. He found that:

> The realization rule itself is not suitable for reporting the results of
> speculation to investors. . . . Since there are few cases in which we might
> wish to use the realization rule that do *not* involve speculation, this is
> tantamount to rejecting that rule for most financial accounting purposes.[33]

The 1964 American Accounting Association Committee on the Realization
Concept issued a report designed to amend and expand on the 1957 Statement.[34] It proposed that a market transaction should remain the basic test for
realization, but that measurability rather than liquidity should be the prime
consideration in judging the quality of assets received, and that the test of
rendering services to customers should be supplanted by a policy of recognizing revenue after the addition of economic value to products or following the
crucial event in the earning process. The Committee agreed unanimously that
verifiable changes in asset values should be recorded in the accounts, though
a majority felt that they should be shown on the income statement below the
net income line, and on the balance sheet as a separate item in the retained
earnings section. In this way the advantages of matching current costs with
revenues and showing the "current economic significance" of assets could be
combined with disclosure of the fact that realized and unrealized profit figures
were based on a different quality of evidence. In effect the realization rule
would be used not only to determine the timing of income recognition, but also
to subdivide net worth increases by source.

Edwards and Bell may be seen as successors to Canning, Gilman, and
Alexander in favoring adoption by accountants of economic concepts of income. But while these earlier writers confined themselves almost entirely to
theoretical comparisons, Edwards and Bell set out to show how the different
types of equity increase can be segregated and reported by accounting prac-
tioners. In doing so they retain the realization rule and even extend its scope
to include cost savings. Realizable gains are divided into three categories: those

realized through direct sale, those realized through use in production which is then sold, and those not yet realized. Holding gains may be realized either through direct sale of an asset which has risen in price (capital gains), or through price increases following the acquisition of assets used in producing goods which were later sold (cost savings). The authors emphasize that *any* sophisticated analysis of income requires the inclusion of unrealized as well as realized holding gains and their classification by source. Not recording holding gains as they accrue results in a failure of disclosure in the current period and a later mismatching of revenues with unrelated costs when assets are sold. On the other hand, lumping together operating income and holding gains diminishes the predictive power of the income statement, because they normally result from quite different types of managerial decisions and have different patterns of recurrence.

Edwards and Bell demonstrate how, with only slight changes in present accounting methods, four types of income can be isolated in the accounts. They define *current operating profit* as the excess of sales revenues over the current cost of inputs used in production and sold. *Realizable cost savings* are increases in the prices of assets held during the period. *Realized cost saving* is the difference between historical costs and current purchase prices of goods sold. *Realized capital gains* are the excess of sales proceeds over historical costs on the disposal of long-term assets.[35] The total of these increments offers investors a measure of their relative "well-offness" and a rational starting point for detailed analysis of company operating results and comparative financial position.

In "How Should We Interpret the Realization Concept?" (1965), Charles Horngren summarizes the position of accountants who wish to move closer to an economic theory of income while preserving the distinction between realized and unrealized profits. Horngren argues that the pure economic view that recognition of value increases *is* realization has no chance of adoption in accounting practice. The need is to find some workable compromise position. So while agreeing that "the reporting process should be broadened to encompass value changes that can be supported by objective, verifiable evidence,"[36] he believes that accountants should not discard the realization rule simply because they could measure asset value increases earlier than they now do. The realization test is valuable because (1) it indicates relative degrees of objectivity, and (2) it preserves the distinction between types of events which interested parties may view and weigh differently. Aiming at a balance between objectivity and disclosure, Horngren proposes to combine a liberal "recognition rule" for value changes with a strict realization test governing earned income. This middle ground between the present "too stark alternatives" would offer investors the simultaneous use of economic and accounting concepts of income and might permit more interaction between the two disciplines. The accounting test of realization would get another chance to adapt and prove itself in competition with economic ideas. If it could not do so, and some variant of economic income finally displaced it, this compromise position could help smooth what promises to be a difficult transitional period.

REALIZATION AND INCOME MEASUREMENT

Realization as a formal accounting rule governing the timing of revenue recognition developed early in the twentieth century. It had antecedents in law and economics, and its application has fluctuated between a concern for definiteness and objectivity on the one hand, and for precise measurements of net worth increases on the other. So long as accounting uniformity was a major problem and inflation was not, the legal view prevailed in theory as well as practice. But since World War II, economic concepts of income have dominated theoretical discussions of accounting realization. Such controversies over the timing of income recognition do not, as some think, prove anything about the intrinsic importance of profit measurement. Since the seventeenth century, nations and business firms have taken the income figure as an index of their competitive strength. It has not been established that this is less true today, or that the gloomy predictions of the early 1960s (" ... the next twenty-five years may subsequently be seen to have been the twilight of income measurement.")[37] are being borne out in practice. Rather there is a sense of transition. The old methods have been discredited, but no consensus has emerged as to what will replace them. Accountants are still working to construct a unified theory of income which will conform more closely to economic doctrines, yet will be objective and procedurally uniform. The recent literature seems to reflect a gradual shift from the traditional accounting position toward an economic view of income, favoring retention of the realization test as long as it remains useful.

FOOTNOTES

1. A.C. Littleton, *The Structure of Accounting Theory* (Iowa City: American Accounting Association, 1953), 27.
2. See Chapter Fifteen for a background discussion of the tax laws.
3. In *Doyle v. Mitchell Brothers Company*, 247 U.S. 17.
4. Defining it as the "gain derived from capital, from labor, or from both combined."
5. Floyd W. Windal, *The Accounting Concept of Realization*, Occasional Paper No. 5 (East Lansing: Bureau of Business and Economic Research, Michigan State University, 1961), 28-29.
6. *Ibid.*, 34.
7. Lawrence R. Dicksee, *Advanced Accounting* (London: Gee, 1903), 5.
8. Reed K. Storey, "Revenue Realization, Going Concern, and Measurement of Income." *Accounting Review* 34 (April, 1959), 236-37.
9. *Ibid.*, 236.
10. George O. May, "Business Income," *The Accountant* 123 (September 30, 1950), 316.
11. Samuel J. Broad, "Cost: Is It a Binding Principle or Just a Means to an End?" *Journal of Accountancy* 97 (May, 1954), 583.
12. *Audits of Corporate Accounts: Correspondence with New York Stock Exchange* (New York: The American Institute of Accountants, 1934), 5-7 ff.
13. Henry Rand Hatfield, *Accounting, Its Principles and Problems*, (New York: D. Appleton-Century Company, 1927), 251.

14. William A. Paton, *Accounting Theory* (New York: Ronald Press Company, 1922), vii.
15. William A. Paton, "The Significance and Treatment of Appreciation in the Accounts," *Twentieth Annual Report of the Michigan Academy of Science* (1918), 35-49; summarized in J.D. Edwards and Roland F. Salmonson, *Contributions of Four Accounting Pioneers* (East Lansing: Michigan State University, 1961), 176.
16. John B. Canning, *The Economics of Accountancy* (New York: Ronald Press Company, 1929), 5.
17. *Ibid.*, 102-5.
18. Stephen Gilman, *Accounting Concepts of Profit* (New York: Ronald Press Company, 1939), 102.
19. William A. Paton and A.C. Littleton, *An Introduction to Corporate Accounting Standards* (Columbus, Ohio: American Accounting Association, 1940), 49.
20. Storey, *op. cit.*, 238.
21. Robert T. Sprouse and Maurice Moonitz, *A Tentative Set of Broad Accounting Principles for Business Enterprises*, Accounting Research Study No. 3 (New York: AICPA, 1962), 14.
22. Emily Chen Chang, "Business Income in Accounting and Economics," *Accounting Review* 37 (October, 1962), 637-38.
23. Sidney S. Alexander, "Income Measurement in a Dynamic Economy," as revised by David Solomons and reprinted in W. T. Baxter and Sidney Davidson, eds., *Studies in Accounting Theory* (Homewood, Ill.: Richard D. Irwin, 1962), 127.
24. See Keith Schwayder, "A Critique of Economic Income as an Accounting Concept." *Abacus* 3 (August, 1967), 23-35.
25. Alexander, *op. cit.*, 132.
26. Study Group on Business Income of the American Institute of Accountants, *Changing Concepts of Business Income* (New York: Macmillan, 1952).
27. American Accounting Association, *Accounting and Reporting Standards for Corporate Financial Statements and Preceding Statements and Supplements* (Columbus, Ohio: American Accounting Association, 1957), 3.
28. American Accounting Association, Committee on Concepts and Standards." Accounting and Reporting Standards for Corporate Financial Statements–1957 Revision," *Accounting Review* 32 (October, 1957), 542.
29. G. Edward Phillips, "The Accretion Concept of Income," *Accounting Review* 38 (January, 1963), 14.
30. John H. Myers, "The Critical Event and Recognition of Net Profit," *Accounting Review* 34 (October, 1954), 528-32.
31. Sprouse and Moonitz, *op. cit.*, 47.
32. *Ibid.*, 51.
33. Arthur L. Thomas, *Revenue Recognition* (Ann Arbor: University of Michigan Press, 1966), 2.
34. American Accounting Association 1964 Concepts and Standards Research Committee–The Realization Concept. "The Realization Concept," *Accounting Review* 40 (April, 1965), 312-22.
35. Edgar O. Edwards and Philip W. Bell, *The Theory and Measurement of Business Income* (Berkeley and Los Angeles: University of California Press, 1961), 111.
36. Charles T. Horngren, "How Should We Interpret the Realization Concept?" *Accounting Review* 40 (April, 1965), 327.
37. David Solomons, "Economic and Accounting Concepts of Income," *Accounting Review* 36 (July, 1961), 383.

SELECTED BIBLIOGRAPHY

Alexander, Sidney S. "Income Measurement in a Dynamic Economy," As revised by David Solomons and reprinted in W.T. Baxter and Sidney Davidson, ed., *Studies in Accounting Theory*. Homewood, Ill.: Richard D. Irwin, 1962, 126-200.
_____. et al. *Five Monographs on Business Income.* New York: 1950. Reprinted by Scholars Book Company, Lawrence, Kansas, 1973.

American Accounting Association 1964 Concepts and Standards Research Study Com-
mittee–The Matching Concept. "The Matching Concept." *Accounting Review* 40
(April, 1965), 368-72.
American Accounting Association 1964 Concepts and Standards Research Study Com-
mittee–The Realization Concept. "The Realization Concept." *Accounting Review*
40 (April, 1965), 312-22.
Backer, Morton, and Bell, Philip W. "The Measurement of Business Income," In Morton
Backer, ed, *Modern Accounting Theory*. Englewood Cliffs, N.J.: Prentice-Hall, 1966,
68-98.
Bedford, Norton M. *Income Determination Theory: An Accounting Framework*. Reading,
Mass.: Addison-Wesley, 1965, chap. six.
Brown, Clifford D. *The Emergence of Income Reporting: An Historical Study*. East Lansing:
Michigan State University Business Studies, 1971.
———. "The Emergence of Income Reporting." *International Journal of Accounting* 10
(Spring, 1975), 85-107.
Chang, Emily Chen. "Business Income in Accounting and Economics." *Accounting Review*
37 (October, 1962), 636-44.
Davidson, Sidney, "The Realization Concept." In Morton Backer, ed., *Modern Accounting
Theory*. Englewood Cliffs, N.J.: Prentice-Hall, 1966, 99-116.
———. Green, D., Horngren, C.T., and Sorter, G.H. *An Income Approach to Accounting
Theory: Readings and Questions*. Englewood Cliffs, N.J.: Prentice-Hall, 1964.
Edwards, Edgar O., and Bell, Philip W. *The Theory and Measurement of Business Income*.
Berkeley and Los Angeles,: University of California Press, 1961, especially the last
chapter.
Gilman, Stephen. *Accounting Concepts of Profit*. New York: Ronald Press Company,
1939, chap. eight.
Hansen, Palle. *The Accounting Concept of Profit: An Analysis and Evaluation in the Light
of the Economic Theory of Income and Capital*. Amsterdam: North-Holland Pub-
lishing Co., 1962.
Hendriksen, Eldon S. *Accounting Theory*, rev. ed. Homewood, Ill.: Richard D. Irwin, 1970,
chaps. five and six.
Horngren, Charles T. "How Should We Interpret the Realization Concept?" *Accounting
Review* 40 (April, 1965), 323-33.
Ijiri, Yuji. *The Foundations of Accounting Measurement*. Englewood Cliffs, N.J.: Prentice-
Hall, 1967, chap. two.
Kehl, Donald. *Corporate Dividends*. New York: Ronald Press Company, 1941. Reprinted
by Arno Press, New York, 1976.
Lee, Geoffrey, A. "The Concept of Profit in British Accounting, 1760-1900." *Business
History Review* 49 (Spring, 1975), 6-36.
Littleton, A.C. "Variety in the Concept of Income." In M. Chatfield, ed., *Contemporary
Studies in the Evolution of Accounting Thought*. Belmont, Cal.: Dickenson Pub-
lishing Company, 1968, 289-96.
Mattessich, Richard. *Accounting and Analytical Methods*. Homewood, Ill.: Richard D.
Irwin, 1964, chap. five.
May, George O. "Business Income." *The Accountant* 123 (September 30, 1950), 315-23.
———. "Taxable Income and Accounting Bases for Determining It." *Journal of Accoun-
tancy* 41 (October, 1925), 248-66.
Moonitz, Maurice. "Should We Discard the Income Concept?" *Accounting Review* 37
(April, 1962), 173-80.
Myers, John J. "The Critical Event and Recognition of Net Profit." *Accounting Review* 34
(October, 1954), 528-32.
Oddy, D.J. "Ealing Business History Seminar: Accounting in the Nineteenth Century."
Business History 16 (July, 1974), 175-182.
Parker, R.H. ed. *Readings in the Concept and Measurement of Income*. London: Cambridge
University Press, 1969.
Philips, G. Edward. "The Accretion Concept of Income." *Accounting Review* 38 (January,
1963), 14-25.

Reiter, Prosper. *Profits, Dividends, and the Law*. New York: Ronald Press Company, 1926. Reprinted by Arno Press, New York, 1976.

Shwayder, Keith. "A Critique of Economic Income as an Accounting Concept." *Abacus* 3 (August, 1967), 23-35.

Solomons, David. "Economic and Accounting Concepts of Income." *Accounting Review* 36 (July, 1961), 374-83.

Sprouse, Robert T. "Observations Concerning the Realization Concept." *Accounting Review* 40 (July, 1965), 522-26.

Sterling, Robert R. *Theory of the Measurement of Enterprise Income*. Lawrence, Kansas: The University Press of Kansas, 1970, especially chaps. eleven and twelve.

Storey, Reed K. "Revenue Realization, Going Concern, and Measurement of Income." *Accounting Review* 34 (April, 1959), 232-38.

Study Group on Business Income of the American Institute of Accountants. *Changing Concepts of Business Income*. New York: Macmillan, 1952. Reprinted by Scholars Book Company, Houston, 1975.

Thomas, Arthur L. *Revenue Recognition*. Ann Arbor: University of Michigan Press, 1966.

Walker, L.M., Mueller, G.G., and Dimian, F.G. "Significant Events in the Development of the Realization Concept in the United States." *Accountant's Magazine* 74 (August, 1970), 357-360.

Windal, Floyd. *The Accounting Concept of Realization*. Occasional Paper No. 5. East Lansing: Bureau of Business and Economic Research, Michigan State University, 1961.

_____. "The Accounting Concept of Realization." *Accounting Review* 36 (April, 1961), 249-58.

Chapter 19

DISCLOSURE IN PUBLISHED REPORTS

CORPORATE DISCLOSURE BEFORE 1900

The efforts of British accountants to secure passage of compulsory audit and disclosure laws have been described. The English companies acts had their counterparts in European commercial codes which were intended to protect investors, creditors, and the public by requiring distribution of audited financial statements. Before 1900 several European countries went farther than England by compelling corporate directors to furnish stockholders with income statements as well as balance sheets.[1] In France and Germany the forerunners of uniform accounting codes even specified the types of account books to be kept and in some cases the accounting methods to be used.

In contrast, the amount of financial data revealed by American manufacturing corporations was left almost entirely to the discretion of management. They presented whatever information they wished, and arranged it as they pleased. Some firms issued reports irregularly or long after the end of their fiscal year. Many others told their stockholders nothing at all.[2] Since there was no tradition of accompanying published statements with an independent auditor's certificate, even the meager information given was colored by management's viewpoint. Certain industries were notoriously secretive. The smaller closely held corporations were among the worst in this respect, but so were many of the largest monopolistic "trusts."[3] Companies heavily dependent on outside sources of capital, and those whose securities were listed on the stock exchanges, often published detailed accounting reports. But very few managements considered financial disclosure a good policy.

This attitude was largely a holdover from the formative period of American industrial development, when most manufacturing firms were small, closely held, and served local markets.[4] This era produced no tradition of corporate publicity, for no one would have thought of asking individual proprietors, partners, or the owners of family businesses to divulge financial information. Later the same ingrained fear of aiding competitors provided a motive for suppressing sales and profit figures of publicly held companies. Until the 1880s, when large industrial corporations began to be formed, American business did not draw much capital from the public sale of stocks.[5] The commoner practice of short-term bank borrowing had never involved communication with the general public. It seemed just as natural to consider the sale of securities a private matter between corporation and investor.

Corporate charters were often silent on the question of management's financial reporting responsibility. By 1900 corporation acts in about half the states provided for some kind of report to stockholders, but seldom specified its contents or required that it be mailed to shareholders who were unable to attend the company's annual meeting.[6] Accountants might deplore the results of this system, but without a strong professional organization or a body of doctrine they were in no position to challenge their clients' desire for secrecy. They repeatedly tried and failed to obtain federal disclosure legislation.[7] Nor were they able to impose standards of practice. The choice of accounting methods was left entirely to management. Public opinion, which supported the regulation of railroads and banks, seemed generally indifferent to legislation affecting industrial corporations. Buyers of new securities relied more on the prestige of the investment bankers who handled the sale than on the prospectus of the issuing company.

MANAGEMENT AND ITS CRITICS, 1900–1933

The dominant economic role played by industrial corporations after 1900, and the rapid increase in the number of their shareholders,[8] produced for the first time a widespread feeling that corporate secrecy was antisocial and that the general public as well as individual investors required the protection of financial publicity. Without abandoning their preference for nondisclosure, American manufacturers gradually improved their reporting practices. By 1930 balance sheets had become more standardized, a brief income statement was typically included in annual reports to stockholders, and certification by independent auditors was the rule rather than the exception.[9] U.S. Steel and a few other enlightened companies became voluntary proponents of a full disclosure policy.[10] But most industrial managers did not consider financial reporting a matter of great importance, and there were still major corporations which published no accounting reports of any kind. There were few external constraints on management's financial disclosure policies. The reporting provisions of most state corporation acts had hardly changed since the nineteenth

century, and federal law remained silent on the question. In general, managements felt secure enough to ignore unwelcome criticisms.

During the 1920s J. M. B. Hoxsey and William Z. Ripley repeatedly expressed concern about the quality of financial information available to stockholders. After making a survey of annual reports, Ripley was particularly
disturbed by "enigmatic" accounting practices which allowed companies to
manipulate their reported results almost at will.[11] Taking Ripley's work as a
point of departure, Adolph A. Berle, Jr. and Gardiner C. Means produced the
first scholarly and authoritative analysis of the modern corporation, its position in society, and its relation to shareholders. *The Modern Corporation and
Private Property* (1933)[12] has been called a blueprint for the Securities Acts,
and certainly it expressed the philosophy underlying them, as well as increasing the pressure for legislation to protect investors.

Berle and Means' thesis was that the modern corporation had revolutionized
the American economy, and that solutions to the problems it had created
required equally radical changes in public policy. They pointed out that in
1930 the 200 largest nonbanking corporations controlled nearly half the nonbanking corporate wealth of the nation, and almost a fourth of the total
national wealth. Half the anthracite coal was mined by four companies; a
fourth of the steel industry was in the hands of two companies; aluminum and
nickel production were virtual monopolies. Three corporate groups controlled
more than half of the electric power industry; two companies made nearly
two-thirds of the cars; three controlled 70 percent of cigarette manufacturing;
one company made half the agricultural machinery. Berle and Means calculated that in 1932 65 percent of American manufacturing assets were owned
by about 600 corporations, which meant that the 2000 active directors of these
corporations virtually controlled American economic life. If the current rate
of industrial concentration were to continue, by 1950 70 percent of the nation's
corporate activity would be conducted by just 200 businesses.[13]

Oligopoly was no longer the exception, but rather the norm and the trend.
The competitive "trading market" described by Adam Smith had given way
to an "administered market" dominated by a few large corporations. The
latter, by bringing so much of the nation's economic life within their administrative control, had decisively altered the nature of the economy. As fixed
markups replaced competitive prices, the market no longer had the same
tendency toward equilibrium. In the classical model, an excess of supply over
demand would cause a fall in *prices* until demand caught up, but an excess
supply in an administered market was apt to cause a fall in *production* while
prices were maintained. This in fact tended to happen during the 1930s.

Large corporations also had become much too powerful in relation to the
individual employees, customers, and investors with whom they dealt. The
diffusion of stock ownership gave management almost complete control over
corporate finances and the distribution of accounting information to investors.
The mass of "owners" were effectively disenfranchised; their only options were

to hold their stock or sell it at the market price. Corporate managers were not mainly interested in paying dividends to stockholders. Their companies were becoming social institutions, influencing cultural values, contending for political as well as economic power.

In such circumstances much depended on responsible business leadership. But the business community, Berle and Means wrote, was still characterized by "seizure of power without recognition of responsibility—ambition without courage." Industrial directors recognized few obligations to their communities, their customers, or labor. They deliberately misled stockholders by withholding financial information and by misusing accounting alternatives. They also lacked cohesion, quarreling among themselves. The managerial class might in time mature and build a "technocracy," a "collectivism without communism." In the meantime, the federal government had to create the socioeconomic environment appropriate to an advanced industrial society. This would include programs of unemployment, sickness, and retirement insurance. There must be immediate government spending programs to stimulate demand. The banking system must be centralized, the stock market reorganized, and the marketing of securities issues brought under federal control. The antitrust laws should be revised to permit further corporate consolidation and even monopoly, which was after all a fact of American life. But the public welfare required detailed regulation of all such concentrated industries.

EFFORTS AT REFORM

Here it is important to distinguish between opinions and conduct. The critics of big business eventually prevailed, but in most cases their immediate influence was slight. They were powerless to force higher reporting standards on industrial management or, in the absence of widespread public sympathy, to translate their ideas into legislation. The public appeal of their proposals fluctuated, being low throughout the 1920s and rising sharply after the stock market crash. But even before the securities acts of 1933–34, three organizations outside the government made systematic efforts to improve the quality of financial reporting.

To take the least of them first, the Investment Bankers Association of America issued a series of reports (1920–1927) in which they set forth minimum standards of disclosure for use in prospectuses and other statements involving industrial securities. The Association wished not only to standardize the information given investors, but also to protect legitimate investment bankers from growing public resentment against sales of fraudulent stocks, and thereby to forestall securities regulation by the state and federal governments. They suggested the use of consolidated financial statements, summaries of earnings by years, and standard methods of reporting inventories, working capital, and depreciation.[14] Few of these recommendations were ever put into effect by investment bankers or corporations. Partly this lack of support reflected the old attitude that the reputation of the investment banker was the stockholder's best protection. In other cases investment bankers relied on nondisclosure to hide weaknesses in the securities they offered for sale.

The major influence for improved disclosure during this period was the New York Stock Exchange. The Exchange had a long history of opposition to corporate secrecy.[15] As early as 1866 it had tried to collect financial statements from listed companies. By 1900 all corporations applying for listing had to agree to publish annual balance sheets and income statements, though this rule was not always enforced. In 1910 the Exchange abolished its Unlisted Department, which traded stocks of companies that were not required to furnish the Committee on Stock List with accounting data. Beginning in 1922 it collected information on the financial condition of each of its member firms of stockbrokers, and required that all listed corporations file with it copies of their regular financial statements. By 1926 90 percent of all industrial stocks listed on the exchange were audited annually,[16] and each listed company was required to publish and submit to stockholders at least fifteen days before the annual meeting, a report containing the company's financial statements. Holding companies had to prepare either consolidated statements or separate statements for the parent and each majority-owned subsidiary. In addition, listed companies were requested to publish semiannual or quarterly income statements. In 1930 the Exchange began its famous correspondence with the American Institute of Accountants, intended to settle the problems of audit scope and responsibility, and establish approved methods of financial reporting.

The Exchanges's dilemma was that it could only regulate the companies which sought to list securities, and by setting higher reporting standards, it tended to drive away precisely those who most needed improvement. Higher standards also put it at a competitive disadvantage with provincial exchanges and over-the-counter dealers whose disclosure requirements were much less stringent. This resulted in a certain reluctance to enforce inconvenient reporting requirements. There was a tendency to apply new rules to all *future* registrants but not to the securities of corporations already listed. The Exchange was also hesitant to strike violators from its list, taking the view that this penalized the stockholder seeking information, without punishing the corporate insiders who were really at fault.[17]

THE ACCOUNTING PROFESSION

The accounting profession became an essential part of American economic life during the years 1900–1933, mainly as a result of the income tax and the dependence of businesses on outside sources of capital. During this period agitation for better financial disclosure came from accounting educators, individual practitioners, and from the American Institute of Accountants. A number of leading CPAs, such as George O. May, were English and felt that disclosure provisions like those included in the British companies acts should be adopted by American corporations.

Accounting efforts to improve disclosure took two forms: attempts to formulate theoretical doctrines suited to the activities of large corporations, and
collaboration with enforcement agencies, especially the New York Stock Exchange.

Theoretical emphasis first shifted from reporting a firm's ability to pay
current debts as they matured, to reporting on company directors' stewardship
of the assets entrusted to them.[18] Investor interest in periodic net earnings as
a measure of managerial performance then led to the assumption that current
income is an important predictor of a firm's future earning ability, and that
a company's value lies mainly in such future earning power, not in the liquidation prices of its assets. The accountant's going concern principle is based on
this premise, which implied a further shift in emphasis from balance sheet to
income statement. The entity theory of accounts stressed the corporation's
separateness from its stockholders. The concept of conservatism, once associated with liquidity and credit granting, evolved into the "fairness doctrine."
—the idea that financial statement presentations should be fair to all users.[19]
But what was fair (or conservative) for credit granters might not be for stockholders. The implementation of conservatism in its corporate context required
specifying the financial statement audience, which the doctrine itself was not
helpful in doing. For this and other reasons conservatism began to receive fairly
rough treatment in the accounting literature.

The first nationwide society of American accountants was formed in 1886,
but not till thirty years later did the profession seriously attempt to standardize
reporting practices. Prepared by the American Institute of Accountants and
sponsored by the Federal Trade Commission and the Federal Reserve Board,
Uniform Accounting (1917), as the title suggests, was intended to improve
financial communication by promoting accounting uniformity. However, its
proposals had little immediate effect on published reports, mainly because
bankers, fearful of antagonizing their clientele, would not insist on audited
statements from loan applicants.[20] In addition many businessmen felt that the
model financial statements outlined in *Uniform Accounting* required too
much disclosure and might be used to their detriment by competitors.

Until 1930 all the Institute's pronouncements on disclosure were aimed at
small and medium-sized firms preparing statements for credit purposes. In that
year its special Committee for Cooperation with Stock Exchanges, and the
New York Exchange's Stock List Committee, commenced a joint study of
corporate accounting and reporting practices. The Institute's report, published
in 1934 as *Audits of Corporate Accounts,* proposed that the Exchange work:
(1) to publicize the fact that balance sheets were not meant to show the current
values of assets and liabilities, and to encourage financial statement disclosure
of the valuation methods which were being used; (2) to emphasize the importance of the income statement; and (3) to require that listed corporations
adhere to certain broad accounting principles which had won fairly general
acceptance. It also contained the Exchange's announcement that after July 1,
1933, financial statements submitted with listing applications must include the

audit certificate of an independent public accountant, together with an agreement that future reports to stockholders would be accompanied by similar certificates. No longer was management to be the sole arbiter of the contents of published reports.

It is doubtful whether collaboration between the Institute and the Stock Exchange could have enforced reporting standards throughout American industry. Investors were not corporately aware of their interests. Managers had shown a preference for selective disclosure based on a wide choice of accounting options. The Institute at that time had only a few thousand members, and very limited resources with which to combat the nation's largest corporations. Accountants had never achieved effective control over the contents of published reports. Not much had been done to develop technical accounting standards, and those which existed had no support in law. Being established pragmatically, accounting techniques always seemed to be a step behind the latest corporate developments. There was no agreed-on conceptual framework within which specific problems could be solved, and lacking this, practitioners could not easily reach a consensus on controversial issues. In any case, within six months the Institute's disclosure program was preempted by the federal government. The election of Franklin Roosevelt and the passage of the Securities Acts resulted in financial reporting practices being subjected to a degree of control that would have seemed impossible a few years earlier.

THE SECURITIES ACTS

The government's task was not only to upgrade the quality of published reports, but also to make the results of a rather technical accounting process intelligible to ordinary people, and to convince investors that such reports were worth relying on in judging the value of securities. These goals were based on the assumptions that the public's willingness to invest depends partly on a study of and confidence in financial statements, that this confidence had been damaged by the events of 1929, and that the national interest required that it be restored. The Securities Act of 1933 was concerned primarily with the information given original purchasers.[21] It required registration with the Federal Trade Commission of new issues sold in interstate markets, and this registration had to include a certificate from an independent public accountant regarding the issuing company's financial condition. The Securities Exchange Act of 1934, which created the SEC to administer both laws, required information directed toward the owners and traders of securities already listed on the stock exchanges. A 1964 amendment extended annual reporting requirements to over-the-counter corporations with a million dollars in assets and 500 or more shareholders, and specified that any differences between their reports to stockholders and the annual 10K statement filed with the SEC must be noted and in effect reconciled in reporting to the Commission.

It was understandable that laws intended to protect investors should heavily penalize errors and fraud on the part of those responsible for financial disclosure. Its advocates liked to compare the Securities Act with the English companies acts, but the American law proposed to regulate the accounting procedures used by corporations as well as their published reports. Section 11 of the 1933 Act drastically increased the auditor's third party liability and placed the burden of proof on the defendant accountant rather than on the stockholder who claimed to have been misled. An honest oversight or misstatement by a CPA or his subordinate could result in the same penalty as deliberate fraud. Section 19 authorized the Federal Trade Commission to define the accounting terms and prescribe the accounting methods to be followed by corporations subject to its jurisdiction in preparing reports for the Commission. At this pivotal moment in accounting development, Congress had in effect given a governmental agency the power to introduce a uniform system of corporate accounts.

Why was this power held in abeyance? First, because the SEC did not have, and expected never to have, sufficient resources to supervise directly the accounting practices of the nation's publicly owned corporations.[22] Also, because previous efforts at self-regulation within the securities industry, particularly the Exchange's requirement of annual audits, had been effective enough so that their continuation seemed a feasible alternative to direct government control.[23] The SEC standardized the formats of the 10K and other reports submitted to it, but generally refrained from detailed regulation of financial statements distributed to the public. Within somewhat narrower limits than before, corporate managers still had their choice of accounting methods. Certification of published reports remained in the hands of the accounting profession, which was encouraged by the SEC to develop auditing standards and accounting principles.

In trying to narrow the areas of difference in reporting on similar events, the SEC had the advantage of being able to quickly impose minimum standards on all its registrants. Few hesitated to discard a procedure which had been rejected by the Commission. But in reacting against the financial abuses of the 1920s, the SEC heavily emphasized objectivity, consistency, and historical cost valuations—concepts many accountants of the postwar era would wish to modify or supersede entirely. It chose to promote uniformity by encouraging the old accounting bias toward conservatism, with its implications of understatement and concealment. Registrants were discouraged from giving investors price level adjusted data, estimates of future earnings, or appraisals of almost any kind.[24] The final result of these activities was to enforce a situation of mutual dependence between the Commission and the accounting profession on the one hand, and between accountants and their corporate clients on the other. Regardless of differences in philosophy or actual influence, each was now compelled to deal with the others on terms prescribed by law.

DISCLOSURE SINCE THE SECURITIES ACTS

Efforts to standardize financial reporting soon produced a body of doctrine. In 1936 the American Institute of Accountants revised *Verification of Financial Statements* (1929), to emphasize reports to stockholders rather than those prepared for credit purposes. The Institute's case-by-case approach to reporting problems corresponded to that of the SEC, whose *Accounting Series Releases* generally took positions similar to the Institute's *Accounting Research Bulletins.* So many of the latter were concerned with financial statement disclosure that in 1948 the Institute's Research Department published a list of its earlier bulletins on the subject.[25] The American Accounting Association's 1954 Committee on Accounting Concepts and Standards made a broader survey of the adequacy of published reports in *Supplementary Statement Number 8.*[26] Beginning in 1966 the Institute required disclosure of all material departures by audited statements from procedures specified in *Accounting Research Bulletins* and APB *Opinions.* Instead of resulting in conflicting sources of authority, these pronouncements and publications largely reinforced each other. All of them agreed that stockholders of large corporations were now the principal group at which financial statements should be aimed.

The financial statements published today by American industrial corporations are the most detailed and comprehensive in the world.[27] The latest disclosure laws in several countries consciously imitate American practice.[28] Both *Accounting Trends and Techniques,* and the *Financial Executive's* annual survey of 600 companies, indicate a constant tendency to add to the background data being reported. Footnotes, supplementary schedules, and historical summaries proliferate, and items such as backlog and divisional results are increasingly included. The formerly sharp dividing line between secretive and progressive corporations is rapidly disappearing.

Still, it is possible to note similarities in the events and attitudes of the early 1900s, the late 1940s, and the present. Then as now, the government was concerned about the quality of published reports, but reluctant to interfere directly. Then as now, investors complained that financial statements did not provide the data they needed to evaluate management's direction of the firm or to compare meaningfully the earnings prospects of different companies. Then as now, the accounting profession's response to these problems lagged behind the pace of change in corporate life. Of course many current financial reporting problems are peripheral to the basic issues attacked by the SEC and the American Institute during the 1930s. Criteria have been developed to help practitioners decide when disclosure is necessary and what forms it should take. But there is ample evidence that some of the original problems remain essentially unsolved.

One of these, discussed at length in the chapter on American auditing, is that many reporting procedures "generally accepted" by accountants are not generally understood by the public. Articles in accounting and business journals, surveys made by the profession itself and by allied groups such as the Financial Executive's Institute, and lawsuits against corporations and their auditors for false or misleading financial disclosure, all make it clear that the public still misunderstands the accountant's role in financial reporting and attestation. The popular impression is that the CPA's authority over the contents of financial statements and his responsibility for financial disclosure are much greater than is actually the case. At the extreme, this view makes the auditor responsible for evaluating management's actions as well as the company's operating results and financial condition.

A second perennial disclosure problem results from management's wide choice of accounting options. The existence of alternative methods which give different results poses a constant temptation to create an appearance of earnings and growth without actually improving performance. Because the SEC and the AICPA have not specified accounting procedures in enough detail to make the reports of different companies comparable, mere financial statement disclosure of the methods used by each firm may be of little help to the ordinary investor. There is evident need to eliminate alternatives which prevent comparability, to simplify and standardize terminology and account classifications, and to define rigorously the accounting principles on which reporting practices are based.

THE EFFICIENT MARKET HYPOTHESIS

Efforts to reduce the number of accounting options and to refine financial statement disclosure are valid only to the extent that they help investors and others who must make decisions about companies. Accountants have always assumed that financial statement analysis can improve investor performance in securities markets. Given this assumption, the problem becomes one of selecting appropriate accounting and reporting methods for particular firms, or of choosing comparable methods for different companies whose operations are similar. When inappropriate accounting methods are used, investors may be misled and resources may be misallocated in capital markets. Certain securities could become overpriced compared to others, and some corporations might be able to raise capital more cheaply than others, even if the only difference between them was their accounting and reporting procedures. If financial statements are resource allocation devices, the misuse of competing accounting methods could cause an inefficient distribution of invested capital throughout the economy.

But much empirical evidence[29] suggests that capital markets are capable of absorbing and adjusting for financial information regardless of how it is reported. The semi-strong form of the efficient market hypothesis states that *all* publicly available information about a corporation will immediately be reflected in the market prices of its securities. If capital markets are efficient, no investment strategy based on financial statement analysis will allow an investor in publicly traded securities to earn an above average return on his portfolio, because the information in those financial statements has already been discounted by the securities markets.

What implications has the efficient market hypothesis for accounting? It does not imply that financial statement disclosure is unimportant, or that investors cannot use accounting data in assessing the risk of individual security investments. On the contrary, failure to disclose accounting information may result in speculative profits for insiders at the expense of other investors and the public. Moreover, accounting data is useful for internal reporting and for such non-investment purposes as obtaining credit and reporting to tax and government regulatory agencies. The efficient market hypothesis does suggest that the *manner* in which financial statement information is made public may not be as important as accountants have supposed. A contingent liability which is disclosed only in a footnote, or perhaps in a 10-K report to the SEC, should be reflected in securities prices just as surely as if it were reported as a line item in the balance sheet. Also, attempts to standardize disclosure in published reports by eliminating accounting options may be less rewarding than accountants have thought, especially if the choice of options does not affect actual operating results. A change from FIFO to LIFO inventory valuation for reporting purposes only does not alter a corporation's economic condition and therefore should not influence the prices of its securities.

SUMMARY AND CONCLUSIONS

The problem of full disclosure has confronted American accountants since the profession's beginnings in this country. But it developed slowly, and for many years disclosure seemed to be a concept outside the scope of accounting responsibility. Until 1933 most companies favored a policy of secrecy, and agitation for improved corporate publicity came mainly from people outside the managerial group—critics of big business, individual accountants, and officials of the New York Stock Exchange. Throughout this period managements had almost complete control over the selection of financial information distributed in published reports.

Changes in public attitudes after 1929, and the fact that so many companies had not adapted their reporting practices to the needs of stockholders, led to federal intervention in the form of the Securities Acts of 1933–34. The SEC and the American Institute of Accountants, taking a case-by-case approach, developed a series of accounting and reporting guidelines which dramatically raised the average quality of corporate financial statements. Yet since World War II, improvements in accounting standards and managerial reporting practices have again lagged behind the pace of corporate development and investor demands for more comprehensive, detailed, and comparable financial information.

It is now likely that unless accountants and their corporate clients take the initiative in reducing the number of acceptable accounting practices, financial disclosure will become much more a matter of law. There seems to be increasing pressure to limit the diversity of accounting methods by establishing an arbitrary set of rules, and increasing belief that only the federal government can do this successfully. Whichever approach prevails, it is apparent from the recent history of financial reporting that efforts will be made to meet the public's demands. If the accounting profession does not do so, "its position of eminence may be lost to those who seize the larger opportunity."[30]

FOOTNOTES

1. Henry Rand Hatfield, "Some Variations in Accounting Practice in England, France, Germany, and the United States," *Journal of Accounting Research*, 4 (Autumn, 1966), 174.
2. David F. Hawkins, "The Development of Modern Financial Reporting Practices Among American Manufacturing Corporations," *Business History Review* 37 (Autumn, 1963), 135.
3. *Ibid.*, 138.
4. *Ibid.*, 137.
5. A.C. Littleton and V.K. Zimmerman, *Accounting Theory: Continuity and Change* (Englewood Cliffs, N.J.: Prentice-Hall, 1962), 109-12.
6. Hawkins, *op. cit.*, 142-43.
7. John L. Carey, *The Rise of the Accounting Profession*, in 2 vols. (New York: AICPA, 1969-1970), vol. 1, 57-58.
8. The number of American stockholders increased from about half a million in 1900, to two million in 1920, to an estimated ten million in 1930, and thirty million in 1970.
9. Hawkins, *op. cit.*, 160.
10. R.S. Claire, "Evolution of Corporate Reports," *Journal of Accountancy* 79 (January, 1945), 39-51.
11. William Z. Ripley, *Main Street and Wall Street* (Boston: Little, Brown & Company, 1927), chap. six.
12. Adolf A. Berle, Jr., and Gardiner C. Means, *The Modern Corporation and Private Property* (New York: Macmillan, 1933).
13. See Carl Kaysen, "The Corporation: How Much Power? What Scope?" Chap. five of E.S. Mason, ed., *The Corporation in Modern Society* (Cambridge, Mass.: Harvard University Press, 1960).
14. Hawkins, *op. cit.*, 151-52.
15. See James Don Edwards, *History of Public Accounting in the United States* (East Lansing: Michigan State University, 1961), 6.
16. George O. May, *Twenty-Five Years of Accounting Responsiblity*, in 2 vols. (Rahway, N.J.: Quinn and Boden Company, 1936), vol. 2, 54.
17. Hawkins, *op. cit.*, 153.
18. Eldon S. Hendriksen, *Accounting Theory*, rev. ed. (Homewood, Ill.: Richard D. Irwin, 1970), 58.
19. Carl T. Devine, "The Rule of Conservatism Reexamined," *Journal of Accounting Research* 1 (Autumn, 1963), 129-30.
20. Hawkins, *op. cit.*, 156.
21. Provisions of the Securities Acts are described at greater length in Chapter Ten.
22. William W. Werntz, *William W. Werntz, His Accounting Thought* (New York: AICPA, 1966), 509.
23. Richard W. Jennings, "Self-Regulation Within the Security Industry," in *Law and Contemporary Problems* (Duke University School of Law, 1964), vol. 29, 1-14.
24. George J. Benston, "The Value of the SEC's Accounting Disclosure Requirements," *Accounting Review* 44 (July, 1969), 526.

25. American Institute of Accountants Research Department, "Disclosure in Financial Statements—Code of Institute Pronouncements," *Journal of Accountancy* 86 (August, 1948), 112.
26. American Accounting Association, Committee on Accounting Concepts and Standards, "Supplementary Statement Number Eight," *Accounting Review* 30 (July, 1955), 400-6.
27. Gerhard G. Mueller, *International Accounting* (New York: Macmillan, 1967), 149.
28. *Ibid.*
29. William H. Beaver, "The Behavior of Security Prices and Its Implications for Accounting Research (Methods)," in Robert R. Sterling, ed., *Research Methodology in Accounting* (Lawrence, Kansas: Scholars Book Company, 1972), 9-37.
30. Robert K. Mautz and Hussein A. Sharaf, *The Philosophy of Auditing.* American Accounting Association Monograph Number Six. (Menasha, Wisc.: American Accounting Association, 1961), 200.

SELECTED BIBLIOGRAPHY

Ameiss, A.P. "Two Decades of Change in Foreign Subsidiary Accounting and United States Consolidation Practices." *International Journal of Accounting* 7 (Spring, 1972), 1-22.

American Institute of Certified Public Accountants. *Objectives of Financial Statements.* New York: AICPA, 1973.

Aranya, Nissim. "The Influence of Pressure Groups on Financial Statements in Britain." *Abacus* 10 (June, 1974), 3-12.

Backer, Morton. "Comments on 'The Value of the SEC's Accounting Disclosure Requirements.'" *Accounting Review* 44 (July, 1969), 533-38.

Barr, Andrew. "Changing Financial Reporting: Yesterday, Today and Tomorrow." *California CPA Quarterly* (June, 1968), 15-19.

Benston, George J. "The Value of the SEC's Accounting Disclosure Requirements." *Accounting Review* 44 (July, 1969), 515-32.

Berle, Adolf A., and Means, Gardiner C. *The Modern Corporation and Private Property.* New York: Macmillan, 1933.

Birkett, W.P., and Walker, R.G. "Response of the Australian Accounting Profession to Company Failures in the 1960's." *Abacus* 7 (December, 1971), 97-136.

Brundage, Percival F. "Influence of Government Regulation on Development of Today's Accounting Practices." *Journal of Accountancy* 90 (November, 1950), 384-91.

Buttimer, Harry. "The Evolution of Stated Capital." *Accounting Review* 37 (October, 1962), 746-52.

Carey, John L. *The Rise of the Accounting Profession*, in 2 vols. New York: AICPA, 1969-1970.

Chatov, Robert. *Corporate Financial Reporting: Public or Private Control?* New York: Free Press, 1975.

Chen, Rosita. *The Behavioral Implications of the Stewardship Concept and Its effects on Financial Reporting.* Unpublished Ph.D Dissertation, University of Illinois at Urbana, 1973, University Microfilms, Ann Arbor, Michigan.

Chetkovich, Michael N. "Standards of Disclosure and Their Development." *Journal of Accountancy* 50 (December, 1955), 48-52.

Claire, R.S. "Evolution of Corporate Reports." *Journal of Accountancy* 79 (January, 1945), 39-51.

Dyckman, T.J., Downes, D.H., and Magee, R.P. *Efficient Capital Markets and Accounting: A Critical Analysis.* Englewood Cliffs, N.J.: Prentice-Hall, 1975.

Evans, E.J. *Prospectuses and Annual Reports: An Historical Look at Rule Development.* Armidale, N.S.W.: New England Accounting Research Study No. 3, 1974.

Gibson, Robert W. *Disclosure by Australian Companies.* Melbourne: Melbourne University Press, 1971.

Greidinger, B. Bernard. *Preparation and Certification of Financial Statements.* New York: Ronald Press Company, 1950, chap. one.

Hatfield, Henry Rand. "Some Variations in Accounting Practice in England, France, Germany, and the United States." *Journal of Accounting Research* 4 (Autumn, 1966), 169-82.

Hawkins, David F. "The Development of Modern Financial Reporting Practices Among American Manufacturing Corporations." In M. Chatfield, ed. *Contemporary Studies in the Evolution of Accounting Thought.* Belmont, Cal.: Dickenson Publishing Company, 1968, 247-79.

Hendriksen, Eldon S. *Accounting Theory*, rev. ed. Homewood, Ill.: Richard D. Irwin, 1970, chap. nineteen.

Johnson, Hans V. "Evidential Matter Pertaining to the Historical Development of the Concept of Disclosure and its Uses as a Teaching Aid." *Academy of Accounting Historians Working Paper No. 17.* University, Alabama: Academy of Accounting Historians, 1975.

Kitchen, J. "The Accounts of British Holding Company Groups: Development of Attitudes to Disclosure in the Early Years." *Accounting and Business Research* 2 (1972), 114-136.

_____. "Consolidated Accounts and Disclosure: Retrospect and Prospect." *Accountancy* 83 (January, 1973), 14-17.

Littleton, A.C., and Zimmerman, V.K. *Accounting Theory: Continuity and Change.* Englewood Cliffs, N.J.: Prentice-Hall, 1962, chap. four.

Mautz, Robert K., and Sharaf, Hussein A. *The Philosophy of Auditing.* American Accounting Association Monograph Number Six. Menasha, Wisc.: American Accounting Association, 1961, chap. seven.

May, George O. *Financial Accounting: A Distillation of Experience.* New York: Macmillan, 1953. Reprinted by Scholars Book Company, Lawrence, Kansas, 1972. Chapter twenty-six.

McLaren, Norman. *Annual Reports to Stockholders.* New York: Ronald Press Company, 1947, chap. one.

Mueller, Gerhard G. "An International View of Accounting and Disclosure." *International Journal of Accounting* 8 (Fall, 1972), 117-134.

Parrish, Michael E. *Securities Regulation and the New Deal.* New Haven: Yale University Press, 1970, especially 179-232.

Rappaport, Louis H. *SEC Accounting Practice and Procedure*, 2d ed. New York: Ronald Press Company, 1963.

Rayburn, Frank R. "The Evolution of Pooling of Interests Accounting: 1945-1970." *Academy of Accounting Historians Working Paper No. 19.* University, Alabama: Academy of Accounting Historians, 1976.

Ripley, William Z. *Main Street and Wall Street.* New York: Little, Brown and Company, 1927. Reprinted by Scholars Book Company, Lawrence, Kansas, 1972. Chapter six.

Scott, D.R. *The Cultural Significance of Accounts.* Columbia, Mo.: Lucas Brothers, 1927. Reprinted by Scholars Book Company, Lawrence, Kansas, 1973.

Skousen, K. Fred. "Chronicle of Events Surrounding the Segment Reporting Issue." *Journal of Accounting Research* 8 (Autumn, 1970), 293-99.

Chapter 20

POSTULATES AND PRINCIPLES

American accountancy seems to be following in the footsteps of older professions which have found it necessary to go beyond doctrines based on experience. Initially theory is distilled from practice and consists of explanations of things done by individuals who improvised and preserved the ideas that proved useful. The resulting generalizations may solve particular problems, but when conditions change rapidly or novel situations arise, the profession relying solely on inference has difficulty. At this point an explicit set of concepts is needed to supplement literal descriptions of reality. Logically derived principles allow accumulated knowledge to be applied to a changing environment. They provide a frame of reference within which the adequacy of specific methods can be judged, offering rational explanations as to why some are better than others. Integrating individual procedures into a coherent accounting framework should narrow areas of difference in reporting on similar events and reduce the number of inferior methods in use. It should also free accountants from the need to exercise judgment on frequently recurring problems and permit them to concentrate attention on less routine issues.

This road to accounting sophistication is not uniquely American, but only in the United States have principles been the *chief* criteria for accounting improvement. So it is appropriate that this last chapter should trace the attempts to codify these concepts which have so largely determined American accounting development.

AMERICAN CODIFICATIONS TO 1940

There were many forerunner attempts to justify accounting methods by reference to principles.[1] American accountants of the early twentieth century, with no legal code or uniform chart of accounts to guide them, tended more than others to judge procedures by reference to general concepts. Even at that time two distinct schools of thought were evident. William Paton, author of the first comprehensive discussion of accounting principles (1922), took the majority position that such generalizations were rarely capable of complete demonstration and that "Accounting is a highly purposive field and any assumption, principle, or procedure is accordingly justified if it adequately serves the end in view. . . ."[2] Only a few early writers argued that principles might be discovered rather than invented, and that accounting methods should be deduced from principles rather than *vice versa*. In introducing *The Philosophy of Accounts* (1913) Charles E. Sprague wrote that, "As a branch of mathematical and classificatory science, the principles of accountancy may be determined by *a priori* reasoning, and do not depend upon the customs and traditions which surround the art."[3]

Yet at the end of the 1920s there was still no authoritative statement of essential principles which could be used to determine the soundness of procedures. Auditors were asked to certify financial statements when no satisfactory criteria for their correctness had been agreed on. The shift in emphasis from debt to equity financing, the growing separation of ownership and managerial control, the income tax laws, and the increasing interdependence of company activities and national interests all had extended the responsibility and influence of accountants. In normal times the profession might have adjusted gradually to these changes, but after the 1929 stock market crash the need was urgently felt for a codified body of theory to support and discipline practice.

Reed Storey identifies three periods of intense interest in accounting principles. The first (1932–1940) and most fruitful was marked by individual attempts to define principles and by the inception of research programs on the part of the major accounting societies, though no "generally accepted" list of principles emerged. The second period (1946–53) was characterized by institutional derivations of principles, chiefly by the American Institute of Accountants and the American Accounting Association. The third, beginning in 1956 and extending into the early 1960s, was dominated by the Accounting Principles Board and its effort to combine the Institute's pragmatic approach with the Association's attempt to formulate logically rigorous principles. During all three periods of peak interest, the periodical literature was highly critical of financial accounting and reporting practices, emphasizing that a reduction in

the number of permitted methods was desirable and that specifying accounting
principles could help accomplish this.[4]

THE AIA–STOCK EXCHANGE COMMITTEE

The first important effort to codify accounting principles was made in 1932
by the American Institute's Special Committee on Cooperation with Stock
Exchanges, chaired by George O. May. The New York Stock Exchange had
expressed concern about the wide variety of accounting and reporting methods
used by companies whose securities it listed. On the Institute's side there was
uncertainty over the precise wording of the audit certificate and the responsibility it imposed on CPAs. The Committee was appointed to formulate improved accounting standards which might then be enforced through the Stock
Exchange's listing requirements.

In May's view, the Committee had two specific tasks: to educate the public
as to why a variety of accounting methods was necessary, and to suggest ways
to curtail that variety and gradually make the better methods universal:

> In considering ways of improving the existing situation two alternatives
> suggest themselves. The first is the selection by competent authority out
> of the body of acceptable methods in vogue today a detailed set of rules
> which would become binding on all corporations of a given class . . . . The
> arguments against any attempt to apply this alternative to industrial cor-
> porations are, however, overwhelming.
>
> The more practical alternative would be to leave every corporation free
> to choose its own methods of accounting within the very broad limits to
> which reference has been made, but require disclosure of the methods
> employed and consistency in their application from year to year.[5]

In choosing a methodology based on accounting principles, May was guided
by his British auditing background and his personal outlook. Both are worth
describing, since as the dominant figure of the Committee he changed the
course of American accountancy more than any other individual, before or
since.

Never was a revolution made by a more cautious man. To him "Conservatism is still the first virtue of accounting" and consistency the second.[6] After
the abuses of the 1920s, he viewed the historical cost doctrine and the realization
rule as aspirations. But while emphasizing the historical nature of accounting
reports, he also believed the income statement more useful than the balance
sheet because the value of a going concern's assets depends mainly on its future
earning power. And he realized that stockholders had become the main consumers of reported data and that their options seldom include replacing management. Usually statements were valuable to them only insofar as they helped
them decide whether to hold, sell, or increase their investments.

For May principles were conventions. "The rules of accounting, even more than those of the law, are the product of experience rather than logic."[7] A code of principles should aim, at different levels, to achieve both flexibility and a reasonable uniformity in practice. Principles should be widely applicable, and accounting rules which derive from them should not only be sound but should *seem* reasonable to the intelligent user of accounts.

May's intention was to give American investors the same protection which English stockholders had enjoyed for almost 100 years under the companies acts. We have seen that the British system required accounting disclosure in exchange for the privilege of incorporation with limited liability. Corporate managements had to publish audited balance sheets, file copies of their Articles of Association, and give the government annual statements of capital and lists of shareholders and directors.

In proposing an extension of English practice to fit the American situation, May could expect no statutory assistance. Aside from the Exchange's listing rules, success would depend on the integrity and cooperation of company officials and on the competence of CPAs. He believed most business managers were honest, most financial statements adequate, and most accountants capable.[8] So it was all to be done without disturbing managerial prerogatives, "and with no compulsion except that of educated opinion."

The Committee's final report contained five recommendations:

1. To promote consistency, corporations listing their stock on the Exchange were asked to adhere to certain broad accounting principles. Within this framework, each firm could adopt whatever accounting methods it preferred.
2. Each listed company would prepare a summary of accounting methods used in its statements. This summary would be formally approved by the firm's board of directors, would be filed with the Exchange, and would be available on request to any stockholder.
3. The procedures listed in this summary would be consistently followed from year to year and would not be changed without prior notice to the Stock Exchange and to the company's investors.
4. Financial statements were to be the representations of management. The auditor's task was to inform stockholders whether the methods adopted by each company were actually being used, whether they were compatible with "generally accepted" principles of accounting, and whether they were being applied consistently.
5. The Committee suggested that a qualified group of accountants, lawyers, and corporate officials draw up an authoritative list of accounting principles to help corporations in preparing their own lists of procedures.[9]

However, the American Institute's Committee on Accounting Procedure (also headed by George O. May) accepted only two of these recommendations. It retained the provision that, subject only to the restraint imposed by accounting principles, each company might choose the methods most suitable for its own operations. The Committee also specified that an auditor was responsible only for his opinion, not for the contents of financial statements. To help make these decisions operative, in 1933 the standard audit certificate was revised to include the phrase "accepted principles of accounting," which later was changed to "generally accepted accounting principles."

But the recommendation that corporations be required to disclose their accounting procedures was never put into effect. Virtually no summaries of methods were filed with the stock exchange or sent to shareholders. Nor was a statement of generally accepted accounting principles forthcoming. Instead, the Institute opted for a case-by-case treatment of accounting issues as they arose.

The Committee's positive contribution was to set the direction of principles development which has been followed ever since. Out of this initial effort came the *Accounting Research Bulletins* and the Institute's later codifications. But without disclosure of the methods to be used by each firm, and with no statement of accepted principles on which the CPA could base his conclusions, there was still no reference for the auditor's opinion, and no safeguard but his individual judgment in each audit situation. Managers still had great freedom in choosing accounting procedures. Inappropriate ones were often adopted, and the ultimate result was a proliferation of acceptable methods. May's committee had failed in the sense that it remained difficult for even a sophisticated reader of financial statements to determine the methods used by a company and their effects on reported results.

The Securities Act of 1933 and the Securities and Exchange Act of 1934 transferred to the SEC much of the listing authority formerly held by the stock exchanges. Ironically, the SEC took up several of the recommendations so recently rejected by the American Institute. Like the British companies acts, the SEC's intention was to protect investors by enforcing disclosure and consistency and by requiring the periodic filing of audited financial statements. Its ultimate goal was to remedy a situation in which insiders knew much more than ordinary stockholders about the details of corporate activities. To achieve this the SEC could either prescribe accounting rules for every situation— which it had the power to do—or work through and reinforce the accounting profession's principles program. In 1938 it chose the latter policy.[10] Since then its influence on accounting theory has depended largely on accountants' knowledge that they could limit the extension of SEC regulation by improving the effectiveness of accounting principles, with the implied threat that if they did not, the government would.

ESSAYS IN CODIFICATION

There remained the task of defining those principles under which the Institute's program was to operate. In 1936 the American Accounting Association published "A Tentative Statement of Accounting Principles Underlying Corporate Financial Statements."[11] Its list of twenty "principles" was really a mixture of rules and standards, including definitions of particular account titles, instructions concerning the form of financial statements and the correct handling of asset writeups and depreciation, attempts to distinguish precisely between paid in capital and retained earnings, and between normal and extraordinary income, and a series of preferred methods in other areas where abuses had occurred. As a comprehensive statement of accounting concepts it had two major faults: it mixed broad principles with procedural rules, and it had no single derivation, either in logic or in practice.

The first codification of principles which we would recognize as such was proposed by Gilbert Byrne in a prizewinning essay on the occasion of the fiftieth anniversary celebration of the American Institute in 1937.[12] Beginning with a definition of principles as fundamental truths, he followed with a list of eight, including historical cost valuation, the proper matching of costs and revenues, the taking of depreciation, realization at the point of sale, conservatism, the distinction between paid in capital and earned surplus, and the need for accounting consistency.

In 1938 the Haskins and Sells Foundation commissioned three educators, T. H. Sanders (Harvard), H. R. Hatfield (Berkeley), and Underhill Moore (Yale Law School) "to formulate a code of accounting principles which would be useful in the clarification and improvement of corporate accounting and of financial reports issued to the public."[13] In preparing *A Statement of Accounting Principles* they interviewed both makers and users of accounting data, reviewed the periodical literature, and studied laws, court decisions, and current corporate reports.

Their method of analysis had the effect of a public opinion survey, producing a catalogue of doctrines then in use. This placed its authors in a trap: their principles were derived almost solely from the methods they sought to improve. And by condoning bad practices so long as they were widely used, the authors left accountants in an essentially passive role. At a time when the profession was striving to have its independence recognized, they assumed it was management's duty to decide what data should be included in financial statements and how it should be presented. However, this study was "the first relatively complete statement of accounting principles,"[14] and as such influenced the form of later efforts.

A common weakness of all codifications up to this time was the lack of precise terminology. Discrimination between levels of accounting concepts was difficult because each writer used terms such as "principle," "doctrine," "convention," and "rule" just as he pleased, or even interchangably. In chapters Twelve through Sixteen of *Accounting Concepts of Profit,* (1939) Stephan Gilman attempted to define rigorously the terms used in codifying accounting principles. Starting with dictionary definitions, he set out to distinguish between four levels of accounting thought and to reclassify accordingly the concepts formerly called principles.

He defined *conventions* as the basic premises underlying accounting theory and cited four as examples—the entity convention, the valuation convention, the period convention, and the convention of debit and credit.[15] *Doctrines* were accounting practices which were held as articles of faith or matters of policy. For instance, conservatism, consistency, disclosure, and materiality were doctrines of reporting which were justified by convenience rather than logic.[16] *Rules* were "prescribed guides for conduct or action," and this term had for Gilman the same connotative meaning we give it. As in the natural sciences, *principles* were fundamental truths from which rules might be derived. They differed from doctrines and conventions in remaining the same regardless of new laws, court decisions, or rulings by government bodies. They did not vary between industries, nor were they affected by changes in the form of business ownership. Gilman found no true principles of accounting.[17]

In seeking specific relationships between broad and narrower accounting formulations, Gilman attacked the largest remaining obstacle to making principles operative. While his four tier approach was not followed by later writers, it had two advantages over the methodology which finally developed. Gilman made the accounting meanings of terms conform to the general usage, and his proposed terminology was more precise than the one now in use.[18]

The next step was the application of principles to discipline rules, and this also was aided by a fresh approach. In 1938 A. C. Littleton published two articles on the development of accounting concepts.[19] Like Gilman he began with the terminology problem. "Each book usually contains a mixture of axioms, conventions, generalizations, methods, rules, postulates, practices, procedures, principles and standards. These terms cannot all be synonymous."[20] So his first task was "to distinguish unchanging truths from variable practices." Rules are a basis for conformity, whereas principles are gauges to measure departures from the norm. He accepted Byrne's thesis that principles embody a "coercive or compelling force which carries a penalty for violation,"[21] and Gilman's idea that, whereas rules are influenced by the diversity of business conditions, accounting principles express fundamental truths. It follows that principles derived wholly from experience are inadequate. Generalizing from practice to improve practice is in effect asking the profession to lift itself by its own bootstraps. A successful approach must combine inductive reasoning with deductive logic. Setting standards above the level of current practice need not embarrass the profession. The problem is not simply to formulate principles but also to apply them, associating particular accounting goals with specific means of attainment.

These ideas permeated Paton and Littleton's *An Introduction to Corporate Accounting Standards* (1940), the most coherent statement of principles to emerge from this period, and still probably the best exposition of cost-based accounting theory. It was the first codification of accounting principles to be developed mainly deductively rather than from practice. It emphasized theory at a higher level than previous statements and subordinated operative rules to concepts. Doctrines such as conservatism and the lower of cost or market rule were either not supported or not even discussed. This was the first codification which not only elaborated a list of principles but showed their specific interactions with accounting methods. It foreshadowed the development of a complete framework of accounting doctrine from which preferred practices might be deduced before problems became acute.

All the codifications of the 1930s were harshly criticized.[22] None achieved wide professional acceptance or noticeably influenced accounting practice at the time. Yet never before or since have the ablest academic accountants had such influence on the accounting societies' official pronouncements. At no other time during this century has the discussion of accounting theory combined a comparable range and intensity. In *The Search for Accounting Principles* Reed Storey summarizes this remarkable era:

> Accounting, as it is practiced today, probably owes more to the decade of the thirties than to any other period after the development of double-entry bookkeeping. During this period both the American Institute of CPAs and the American Accounting Association formalized their respective machinery for the promulgation of accounting principles. ... The basic form of financial accounting as a process of cost allocation based on the matching of revenues and expenses crystalized during this period. The concept of accounting principles developed in the late thirties has dominated accounting thinking for more than twenty years. So have the prevailing ideas as to how principles are formulated.[23]

THE ACCOUNTING SOCIETIES DEVELOP PRINCIPLES

The second peak of interest in accounting principles began just after World War II. By this time emphasis in the literature had shifted from defining principles toward applying them to solve immediate problems of practice. The worst methods of the 1930s had been eliminated, to be replaced by a superabundance of "generally accepted" alternatives. The profession's new problem was one of finesse. Taking note of the real differences between firms and reporting situations, it had to reduce the variations in practice, but without producing a detailed accounting code, provoking government interference, or putting undue pressure on client managements.

The search for accounting principles was stimulated by criticisms of accounting and accountants. Surveys indicated widespread public ignorance and mistrust of financial statements, the corporations which issued them, and the auditors who certified them.[24] These critics divided roughly into two groups. The first argued that inflation makes certain accounting principles inoperative and reported results obviously wrong. They singled out the historical cost and conservatism doctrines as preventing published reports from describing business events realistically, and favored their replacement by more flexible concepts which permitted price level adjustments. Other critics emphasized the social responsibilities of accountants and advocated a broader approach to the reporting problem. They suggested that (1) the concept of accountant's independence should be enlarged to make him the protector of the public interest, not just of investors' interests; (2) accounting services should be expanded to meet the information needs of employees, consumers, and the general public; (3) financial statement comparability should be improved by reducing the number of alternative methods of handling similar transactions. Both lines of criticism led, in the early 1950s, to a shift of interest from the codification of principles to direct consideration of the price level problem.[25]

Most progress during this period resulted from the efforts of the accounting societies. While the existence of multiple sources of authority has obvious disadvantages, attempts by the American Institute and the American Accounting Association to codify accounting principles were mutually supportive. Both emphasized the historical aspect of accounting, both viewed financial accounting as a process of cost allocation, and both had the goal of improving published reports by restricting the use of alternative methods. They differed mainly in their approach to formulating accounting principles. The Institute regarded principles as conventions created and altered by changing patterns of general acceptance. Such principles were a distillation of experience to be subjected constantly to the test of usefulness. The Association called principles "standards" and regarded them as ideals. It tried to create a general framework of standards which could be refined and updated by successive comparisons with practice. Whereas the authors of Association monographs tended to be guided by their examination of the literature, most Institute bulletins codified the judgments of practitioners regarding preferred methods of dealing with situations encountered in practice.

THE AMERICAN INSTITUTE OF CPAs

Between 1939 and 1959 the Institute's Committee on Accounting Procedure issued fifty-one *Accounting Research Bulletins.* These covered most aspects of financial accounting and became the mechanism for promoting specific reforms in practice. The Committee was composed of twenty-one members and required two-thirds approval to enact a bulletin. But such approval did not mean that all CPAs would use the sanctioned procedures. The bulletins' influence depended almost entirely on their "general acceptance" by accounting practitioners and their clients. Thus popularity was crucial. The Committee's aim was to issue statements which improved practice and to which there was no serious objection, thereby placing the burden of proof on any CPA who failed to enforce compliance with the authorized methods.

The accomplishments of this approach are well known; its limitations bear more on present accounting problems. Some of these were self-imposed or were inherent in the Institute's situation. CPAs needed immediate guidance in solving particular problems. The bulletins responded by considering specific issues as they became urgent and by recommending one or several possible solutions as superior to others. An area received attention only when problems became evident, and each such problem was viewed in isolation. The bulletins were not arranged in any related order nor were the positions taken always mutually consistent. The decisions emerging from such a piecemeal approach tended to support established ideas of valuation, matching, realization, and disclosure. As one result of the failure to define principles before attacking practical problems, certain procedural questions (such as the merits of LIFO) were discussed at too high a level. Bulletins were sometimes based on the Committee's opinion of what practitioners and the public thought about an issue. Others took arbitrary and indefensible positions which ignored legal precedents and economic realities. These *ad hoc* solutions rarely proved definitive, and the Committee found itself continually reconsidering basic questions of asset valuation, depreciation, inventory pricing, and corporate consolidation.

Other weaknesses of the Institute's approach can only be called political. In making rules for its membership, any association of practitioners must be influenced by possible client reactions. There was a tendency to drop rulings which seriously inconvenienced clients.[26] The requirement of a two-thirds Committee majority for passage sometimes prevented the issuance of bulletins on controversial subjects. More typically, the Committee failed to come to grips with such problems. Compromises extended acceptance to several methods where one would have sufficed. This not only proliferated "generally accepted" procedures but created certain allowed alternatives which were markedly inferior to others. Much of the resulting theory was contrived and still exists for the auditor's convenience or for the convenience of management.

THE AMERICAN ACCOUNTING ASSOCIATION

In December 1935, the American Association of University Instructors in Accounting changed its name to the American Accounting Association and announced an expanded research program. The Association's Executive Comitee believed accounting practice could best be improved by "perfecting the framework within which the accountant operates." It wanted, not rules requiring universal observance, but standards by which existing methods might be judged. The ideal was that "a corporation's periodic financial statement should be continuously in accord with a single, coordinated body of accounting theory."[27] The Association foresaw the difficulties of this approach ("It must inevitably embody some conflict with existing accounting practice, since accounting practice is in conflict with itself at a hundred points."),[28] and expected a gradual overall improvement rather than immediate results in particular areas. Having less ability to quickly influence practice was in some ways an advantage to the academic accountants. It allowed them to take a broader view of issues and to make recommendations that were theoretically correct even though they might be temporarily impolitic.

The Association's parallel effort to the *Accounting Research Bulletins* centered around four statements of accounting principles:

1936 *A Tentative Statement of Accounting Principles Underlying Corporate Financial Statements*
1941 *Accounting Principles Underlying Corporate Financial Reports*
1948 *Accounting Concepts and Standards Underlying Corporate Financial Statements*
1957 *Accounting and Reporting Standards for Corporate Financial Statements*

The 1936 statement was a mixture of principles and methods, and attacked basic problems apparent at the time. Noting deficiencies in three areas—costs and values, income measurement, and accounting for capital—it attempted to correct malpractices of the 1920s and particularly to establish as generally accepted the historical cost doctrine and the idea that accounting is a process of allocating such costs.

Three major revisions and eight supplementary statements amplified this first list of principles into a comprehensive theoretical catalogue. But the basic approach and ideas of the 1936 statement—the emphasis on historical costs, matching, and the income statement—changed very little. The 1941 revision was divided into four sections (Cost, Value, Income, and Capital) rather than the three of 1936. In the 1948 Revision "Concepts and Standards" replaced "Principles" in the title, and the statement itself became predominantly theoretical. The 1957 Statement was even more conceptual than its predecessors but its proposals were less rigidly rooted in theory. Reference was made to "conventions derived from experience."[29]

The Association's *A Statement of Basic Accounting Theory* (1966) was a departure from past pronouncements in that it was not limited to external reporting problems. It was also less concerned with specific issues of current practice than earlier bulletins had been. The intention was a more basic, general theory based on four criteria: relevance, verifiability, freedom from bias, and measureability. It proposed that any data which met these standards should be reported. It also recommended that both historical and current costs be shown in separate columns in the income statement and balance sheet.

ASOBAT's critics objected less to these conclusions than to the manner of their derivation.[30] The gist of such criticisms was that the AAA committee had not followed out the implications of its own deductive method. The four postulates were loosely defined and coordinated, their relation to lower level criteria was not specified, nor did the committee show how to implement these standards in judging accounting practice. The scope of the theory was not clearly indicated. And in general it seemed that principles extracted from the accounting environment by a kind of authoritarian intuition, so useful in codifying practice during the preceding two decades, had by the mid-1960s taken the profession as far as they could.

SUMMARY: AAA AND AICPA

Analysis of Institute and Association statements shows remarkable similarity between the topics covered by each and their stated recommendations.[31] But neither the conceptual nor the pragmatic approaches solved the underlying problems which had produced demands for accounting principles in the first place. The Institute could claim that a majority of practitioners adhered to its *Accounting Research Bulletins* and could point to many instances where these had visibly changed practice. In fact they had no real competition. The Association not only lacked sanctions to impose its ideas but failed to communicate effectively with practitioners, since its statements offered little help in solving the CPA's immediate problems. But the AICPA's goal of adequate financial statement disclosure was not attained either. Practice was to some extent standardized and the worse abuses of the 1920s were eliminated. But in accomplishing this, the ARBs actually increased the number of acceptable alternatives, especially in such vital areas as depreciation and inventory valuation, because of the Committee's inability to make firm choices and its reluctance to disallow widely used practices even when they conflicted with its recommendations. General acceptance became a minimal test which many inferior methods were able to pass, and the resulting diversity of reporting practices obstructed statement comparability. Probably this defect was inherent in an approach which emphasized disclosure and consistency rather than the application of specific principles.[32]

THE ACCOUNTING PRINCIPLES BOARD

There were obvious advantages in combining the practitioner's approach with that of the academic accountant. The third phase of intense interest in accounting principles centered around the Institute's attempts to find a balance between deductive and pragmatic research efforts.

In 1957 the Institute's newly installed president, Alvin R. Jennings, called for a reexamination of accounting concepts and a shift in emphasis from applied to basic research.[33] The problem was no longer that of the 1930s—a lack of standards—but rather the need to refine existing rules. Treating individual cases had become less important than identifying and gaining acceptance of a unified body of accounting theory. This required research which led rather than followed practice, and a long-range program instead of one aimed at producing immediate improvements. In 1959, just twenty years after publication of *Accounting Research Bulletin No. 1,* the Institute's research program was reorganized to facilitate this new approach to accounting principles.

The Accounting Principles Board and the Accounting Research Division were established as successors to the Committee on Accounting Procedure and the Accounting Research Department. The Board was to consist mainly of practitioners; the Research Division mainly of academics. A permanent staff was organized to aid in preparing specialized *Accounting Research Studies.* These were not official pronouncements of the AICPA, but were published under authority of the Director of Accounting Research and given wide circulation before being acted on by the Accounting Principles Board. The APB would then consider the research study and accept or reject it. Both the *Research Studies* and the Accounting Principles Board *Opinions* would include a detailed statement of the reasoning behind proposed practices, something the *Accounting Research Bulletins* had notoriously lacked. The new program received added impetus when the AICPA Council recommended that after 1965 all material departures from *Accounting Research Bulletins* and APB *Opinions* must be disclosed in footnotes to the financial statements or in the audit opinion. This made CPAs and their clients directly responsible for relating accounting practices to established principles. Weldon Powell, Chairman of the Institute's Accounting Principles Board, described the Institute's new research program:

> We visualize the broad problem of financial accounting as requiring attention at four levels: first, postulates; second, principles; third, rules or other guides for the application of principles in specific situations; and fourth, research.
>
> Postulates we understand to be the basic assumptions on which principles rest. We are going to try to make clear our own understanding and interpretation of what they are, to provide a meaningful foundation for the formulation of principles.
>
> We also are going to try to formulate a fairly broad set of coordinated accounting principles on the basis of the postulates, probably similar in scope to the statements on accounting and reporting standards issued by the American Accounting Association.
>
> We plan then to try to develop rules or other guides for the application of accounting principles in specific situations, in relation to the postulates previously expressed. Statements of these probably will be comparable as to subject matter with the present accounting research bulletins. They are to have reasonable flexibility.
>
> Adequate accounting research, we believe, is necessary in all the foregoing. We plan that our pronouncements on accounting matters will be based on thoroughgoing, independent study of the matters in question, during which consideration is given to all points of view.[34]

The groundwork of this new program was to consist of two research studies, *ARS No. 1* "The Basic Postulates of Accounting" (1961), and *ARS No. 3,* "A Tentative Set of Broad Accounting Principles for Business Enterprises" (1962). Broad principles would be deduced from a previously established set of postulates, which would in turn become guidelines for research in specific areas. From these it was hoped that better practices "would emerge as almost inescapable conclusions."

Moonitz's "Postulates" were the result of a search for "self-evident propositions" about the accounting environment which all would agree were both
valid and meaningful. They were inferences which had held true for several
centuries over a wide geographical area, and as such gave the Institute's
program a foundation and a certain impetus. They were also intended to
suggest needed theoretical changes, while the "Principles" outlined revisions
in practice.[35] Since the proposed theory changes were modest, most of the
postulates were not controversial or widely criticized.

In contrast, nearly every member of the Project Advisory Committee criticized Sprouse and Moonitz's "Principles."[36] First, because the approach was
not truly rigorous or deductive: the "Postulates" did not *have* to produce the
particular principles listed in *ARS No. 3.* Nor were the two statements really
compatible. For instance, exchange values were stressed in the "Postulates";
present values of future benefits in the "Principles." Even more important, the
principles in *ARS No. 3* suggested rules which went far beyond existing
practice and which would require radical changes that practitioners were
unwilling to make. Doctrines which offered CPAs legal protection—objectivity, consistency, historical cost, and conservatism—were rejected or largely
ignored. The realization rule was set aside in favor of an essentially accretion
concept of income. Assets were defined as future service potentials but no
measurement criteria were specified. Not only were their concepts of matching, realization, and asset valuation hard to relate to present practice, but the
authors offered no basis for transition to the proposed methods. In April 1962,
the Accounting Principles Board rejected the "Postulates" and "Principles"
as being "too radically different from present generally accepted accounting
principles for acceptance at this time."

A new study was commissioned. Paul Grady's "Inventory of Generally
Accepted Accounting Principles for Business Enterprises" (*ARS No. 7*) was
an attempt, like the Sanders, Hatfield and Moore monograph of thirty years
before, to compile a catalogue of generalizations from current practice. His ten
principles included: (1) a society honoring private property rights, (2) specific
business entities, (3) continuity, (4) monetary expression in the accounts, (5)
consistency, (6) diversity between business entities, (7) conservatism, (8) de-
pendability of data through internal control, (9) materiality, and (10) timeliness of reporting requires estimates. Grady saw his task as one of identification,
not discovery. His attention was limited to the existing accounting environment. Methods not generally used were excluded.

Partly as a result of this reversion to the inductive and pragmatic derivation
of principles from practice, the APB *Opinions* were not basically different
from the *Accounting Research Bulletins* which preceded them. In particular
the cases of consolidations (APB *Opinion No. 16*) and the investment credit
(APB *Opinions Nos. 2 and 4*) showed the Principles Board in the position of
the old Committee on Accounting Procedure. *Accounting Research Studies*
received more exposure prior to official adoption and contained more discus-

sion of the reasons for choosing the course of action taken. But the studies themselves were a series of independent analyses in which each author was left to determine his own treatments and provide his own justifications for the conclusions reached. ARS recommendations were not always followed in the *Opinions*, nor did research solve the old problem of proliferating "generally accepted" alternatives in practice.

The evident lack of professional and public confidence in the *Opinions* finally led the AICPA to broaden its rule making to include participation by nonaccountants. Following the recommendations of the Wheat Committee Report, the Institute in March 1973 replaced the Accounting Principles Board with a Financial Accounting Standards Board (FASB), to be appointed by nine trustees of an independent Financial Accounting Federation. In contrast to the eighteen part-time, unpaid members of the APB (all were CPAs; fourteen were affiliated with major CPA firms), the FASB consists of seven full-time, highly paid members serving five-year terms. Only four are CPAs in public practice. The other three can be nonaccountants with broad experience in the financial reporting field.

TWO THEORIES OF ACCOUNTING

The dilemma of those who formulate accounting principles is evident. If their codifications are derived from practice they cannot improve it in any major way or anticipate new developments. If they are ahead of practice they fail to win professional acceptance.

In retrospect it is clear that Sprouse and Moonitz's "Principles" was premature in more ways than one. Underlying the *ARS No. 3* controversy was an increasingly strident methodological debate which had by no means been settled in favor of the Institute's approach. That is, while some critics of *ARS No. 3* opposed its particular content, others opposed the whole idea of improving practice through deduced principles, feeling that a radically different solution was needed.[37] Specific disputes arose between those who merely wanted consistency in accounting practice, and those who wanted rules to be established in such detail that similar transactions would *always* be handled similarly in the accounts. Another faction considered that the particular situation should be decisive in determining how assets were valued, income measured, and so on. The need to generalize about accounting practice could also be minimized by making separate statements for each major party at interest.[38]

Even before the reorganization of the AICPA's research program and the appearance of *ARS 1* and *3*, Richard Mattessich[39] and R. J. Chambers[40] had tried to create integrated structures of accounting theory based on postulates and principles of greater cohesiveness and applicability than any previously developed. Their search was not just for accounting principles but for a complete and articulated system of thought by reference to which every accounting action could be evaluated. As preambles to their own formulations, Chambers and Mattessich criticized existing ones on three main counts: (1) they were not *logically coherent,* (2) they were not sufficiently *pervasive,* and (3) their conclusions were not *testable.*

First, they consider it essential that a system of accounting propositions should "hang together."[41] The set of doctrines must be systematic, and postulates and principles must be mutually consistent. In this way the accounting superstructure may be both rigorously derived from and supported by a substructure of valid premises. Even postulates which are essentially value judgments gain validity from a closely reasoned "understructure of justification."[42] Here methodology is important, because great care must be taken in discriminating between propositions of different levels of generality.

The validity of an accounting concept seems to depend not only on the rigor with which it is derived, but also on the "extent of its domain." An effective theory should not only fix postulates and principles in relation to each other, but should spell out their relationship to the whole range of existing accounting methods. Only when this is done can the decision to use one method rather than another be based on sound theoretical evaluation. Many accounting systems—financial, cost, managerial, governmental—derive from similar underlying postulates and principles, but present models fail to tie them together, or even to describe all of accounting practice. Yet we can properly understand and evaluate accounting choices only if we look at the field as an entity.[43] The continuing fragmentation of accounting practice makes this doubly necessary. Accountancy is now too broad a subject to approach by way of observing particular cases, or by learning the practical alternatives of all its aspects. Instead, accountants must adopt a theory which can abstract far enough from these specifics to incorporate them into one comprehensive framework.

Finally, Chambers and Mattessich urge that accounting formulations be open to refutation; that is, criteria for their acceptance or rejection must exist, and they should be capable of being rigorously tested by others than the propounder of the theory.[44] Or at least testable hypotheses should be distinguished from value judgments and definitions. But even the latter gain in validity if they can be tested. Different tests may be required for accounting propositions of different degrees of abstraction, but in general testing means seeing that the formulation is compatible with all its possible consequences. A postulate must not be refuted by even one of the whole gamut of principles and rules underlying it. Every principle must be in conformity with all the postulates, and with each rule to which it pertains. Rules may be tested against each other by determining that the long-run net benefit of using one model is greater than its operating cost, and no less than the benefit of using the next best competing model.[45]

INTERNATIONAL ACCOUNTING PRINCIPLES

For other countries to repeat independently the American experience of developing practices from principles would be evidence of its universality, just as deliberate imitations would be tributes to its feasibility. To date those nations

HISTORY OF ACCOUNTING THEORY

which regulate accounting practice through uniform charts of accounts have shown little interest in theory. On the other hand, countries which have legally regulated accountancy *via* companies acts have often felt the need for statements of preferred methods similar to the *Accounting Research Bulletins*. These have usually taken the form of procedural recommendations issued by accounting societies or government units, and do not in themselves represent attempts to reason from general principles. But practitioners complain of gaps between the statutory provisions and the rules contained in these bulletins. In nations as diverse as Japan and Mexico, accountants have attempted to codify principles as a means of narrowing the number of alternatives in practice.[46] Authors in several countries suggest that accounting principles be made uniform between nations to facilitate international trade and investment.[47]

American practitioners show many signs of impatience with accounting theory. After forty years of discussion there is still no comprehensive, integrated statement of concepts on which accountants and statement readers can agree and rely. There is still no consensus as to the exact meaning of the standard audit opinion that financial statements present the results of operations "fairly" in accordance with "generally accepted accounting principles." One result is that accounting methods have changed much more slowly than has the accounting environment. And the profession has not solved its basic problems of disclosure, consistency, and statement comparability.

American accounting today is an art simultaneously at different stages of development. The periodical literature is divided between scholars who still use the deductive principles approach to determine and defend their choice of accounting techniques, and many others who are making empirical studies of accounting methods without reference to accounting theory.

But in no other country have practicing accountants as a group committed themselves to the principles approach as they have in the United States. Elsewhere, accounting codification is considered too important a matter to be left to accountants. Basic rule making is nearly always a government prerogative. And this may be inevitable. Maurice Moonitz believes that a professional accounting body, acting by itself, can never agree on a set of accounting principles, much less enforce it in practice.[48] It is now evident that the first generation of American theorists badly underestimated both the conceptual and practical difficulties involved in principles formulation and codification.

1. With remarkable prescience, Angelo Pietra in 1586 supported practical bookkeeping advice with an analysis of such doctrines as historical cost, separate entities, conservatism, and periodicity. See Edward Peragallo, "A Commentary on Vigano's Historical Development of Ledger Balancing Procedures, Adjustments and Financial Statements During the Fifteenth, Sixteenth, and Seventeenth Centuries." *Accounting Review* 46 (July, 1971), 531-34.
2. William A. Paton, *Accounting Theory* (New York: Ronald Press Company, 1922), 472.

3. Charles E. Sprague, *The Philosophy of Accounts* (New York: Ronald Press Company, 1913), iii.
4. Reed K. Storey, *The Search for Accounting Principles* (New York: AICPA, 1964), 3.
5. *Audits of Corporate Accounts, Correspondence with New York Stock Exchange* (New York: American Institute of Accountants, 1934), 9.
6. George O. May, *Financial Accounting—A Distillation of Experience* (New York: Macmillan, 1946), 44-48.
7. *Ibid.*, viii.
8. For example, see George O. May, *Twenty-Five Years of Accounting Responsibility, 1911-1936* (New York: American Institute Publishing Co., 1936), 53-59.
9. *Audits of Corporate Accounts, op. cit.*, 13-14.
10. Carman G. Blough, "Development of Accounting Principles in the United States," *Berkeley Symposium on the Foundations of Financial Accounting* (Berkeley: School of Business Administration, University of California, 1967), 5.
11. See "A Tentative Statement of Accounting Principles," *Accounting Review* 11 (June, 1936), 187-91.
12. Gilbert Byrne, "To What Extent Can the Practice of Accounting be Reduced to Rules and Standards?" *Journal of Accountancy* 44 (November, 1937), 364-79.
13. Thomas Henry Sanders, Henry Rand Hatfield, and Underhill Moore, *A Statement of Accounting Principles* (New York: American Institute of Accountants, 1938), xiii.
14. Storey, *op. cit.*, 31.
15. Stephen Gilman, *Accounting Concepts of Profit* (New York: Ronald Press Company, 1939), 245.
16. *Ibid.*, 231-44.
17. *Ibid.*, 251-57.
18. Storey, *op. cit.*, 24.
19. A.C. Littleton, "Tests for Principles," *Accounting Review* 13 (March, 1938), 16-24; "High Standards for Accounting," *Journal of Accountancy* 66 (August, 1938), 99-104.
20. A.C. Littleton, "Tests for Principles," *op. cit.*, 16.
21. Byrne, *op. cit.*, 371.
22. Storey, *op. cit.*, 19-31.
23. *Ibid.*, 19.
24. *Ibid.*, 36-37.
25. *Ibid.*, 37-38.
26. For example, in the *ARB No. 43* revision of *ARB No. 40* on business combinations, the requirement that consolidated firms be similar in nature was quietly dropped, to the advantage of clients who wished to account for such mergers as poolings rather than purchases. *APB Opinion No. 16* was similarly emasculated.
27. "A Tentative Statement of Accounting Principles," *op. cit.*, 188.
28. American Accounting Association, *A Tentative Statement of Accounting Principles Underlying Corporate Financial Statements* (New York: American Accounting Association, 1936), 3.
29. American Accounting Association, *Accounting and Reporting Standards for Corporate Financial Statements*, (New York: American Accounting Association, 1957), 1.
30. See John W. Buckley, Paul Kircher, and Russell L. Mathews, "Methodology in Accounting Theory," *Accounting Review* 43 (April, 1968), 274-83.
31. A.C. Littleton, "The Search for Accounting Principles," *New York Certified Public Accountant* 28 (April, 1958), 250; Storey, *op. cit.*, 40-48.
32 Storey, *op. cit.*, 49.
33. Alvin R. Jennings, "Present-Day Challenges in Financial Reporting," *Journal of Accountancy* 105 (January, 1958), 28-34.
34. Weldon Powell, "Report of the Accounting Research Activities of the American Institute of Certified Public Accountants," *Accounting Review* 37 (January, 1962), 26.
35. Arthur M. Cannon, "Discussion Notes on 'The Basic Postulates of Accounting,'" *Journal of Accountancy* 113 (February, 1962), 42-53.
36. Robert T. Sprouse and Maurice Moonitz, "A Tentative Set of Broad Accounting Principles for Business Enterprises," *Accounting Research Study No. 3* (New York: AICPA, 1962), 60-83.

37. See "Comments of Leonard Spacek," in Maurice Moonitz, "The Basic Postulates of Accounting," *Accounting Research Study No. 1* (New York: AICPA, 1961), 56. Also Leonard Spacek, "The Need for an Accounting Court," *Accounting Review* 33 (July, 1958), 368-79.
38. For a methodological survey, see Eldon S. Hendriksen, *Accounting Theory*, rev. ed. (Homewood, Ill.: Richard D. Irwin, 1970), 1-21.
39. Richard Mattessich, "Toward a General and Axiomatic Foundation of Accountancy," *Accounting Research* 8 (October, 1957), 328-56.
40. R.J. Chambers, "Blueprint for a Theory of Accounting," *Accounting Research* 6 (January, 1955), 17-25.
41. R.J. Chambers, *Accounting, Evaluation and Economic Behavior* (Englewood Cliffs, N.J.: Prentice-Hall, 1966), 4.
42. Richard Mattessich, "Some Thoughts on the Epistemology of Accounting," a paper presented at the Second International Conference of Accounting Education, London, 1967.
43. Richard Mattessich, *Accounting and Analytical Methods* (Homewood, Ill.: Richard D. Irwin, 1964), 8-15.
44. *Ibid.*, 19; R.J. Chambers, *Accounting, Evaluation and Economic Behavior, op. cit.*, 7.
45. Richard Mattessich, *Accounting and Analytical Methods, op. cit.*, 232-41.
46. See Stephen A. Zeff, *Forging Accounting Principles in Five Countries: A History and Analysis of Trends*, (Champaign, Ill.: Stipes Publishing Company, 1972).
47. T.K. Cowan, "The International Harmonization of Accounting Principles," *The Accountant's Journal* (New Zealand), (February, 1968), 206-10; Jacob Kraayenhof, "International Challenges for Accounting," *Journal of Accountancy* 109 (January, 1960), 34-38.
48. Maurice Moonitz, *Obtaining Agreement on Standards in the Accounting Profession*, (Sarasota, Florida: American Accounting Association, Studies in Accounting Research No. 8, 1974).

SELECTED BIBLIOGRAPHY

Abel, Rein. "The Impact of Environment on Accounting Practices: Germany in the Thirties." *International Journal of Accounting* 7 (Fall, 1971), 29-47.

American Accounting Association. *A Statement of Basic Accounting Theory*. Evanston, Ill.: AAA, 1966.

American Institute of Certified Public Accountants. "Restatement and Revision of Accounting Research Bulletins." *Accounting Research Bulletin No. 43*. New York: AICPA, 1953.

American Institute of Certified Public Accountants. *APB Statement No. 4: Basic Concepts and Accounting Principles Underlying Financial Statements of Business Enterprises*. New York: AICPA, 1970.

American Institute of Certified Public Accountants, Study Group on the Establishment of Accounting Principles. *Establishing Financial Accounting Standards*. New York: AICPA, 1972.

Benson, Sir Henry. "The Story of International Accounting Standards." *Accountancy* 87 (July, 1976), 34-39.

Blough, Carman G. "Development of Accounting Principles in the United States." *Berkeley Symposium on the Foundations of Financial Accounting*. Berkeley: School of Business Administration, University of California, 1967, 1-25.

Bray, F. Sewell. "Accounting Postulates and Principles." In Morton Backer, ed. *Modern Accounting Theory*. Englewood Cliffs, N.J.: Prentice-Hall, 1966, 28-47.

Buckley, John W., Kircher, Paul, and Mathews, Russell L. "Methodology in Accounting Theory." *Accounting Review* 43 (April, 1966), 274-83.

Burns, Thomas J. *Accounting in Transition: Oral Histories of Recent U.S. Experience*. Columbus, Ohio: College of Administrative Science, Ohio State University, 1974.

Chambers, R.J. *Accounting, Evaluation and Economic Behavior*. Englewood Cliffs, N.J.: Prentice-Hall, 1966, 341-63.
_____. "Blueprint for a Theory of Accounting." *Accounting Research* 6 (January, 1955), 17-25.
_____. "Detail for a Blueprint." *Accounting Review* 32 (April, 1957), 206-15.
_____. "Why Bother with Postulates?" *Journal of Accounting Research* 1 (Spring, 1963), 3-15.
Davidson, Sidney, and Kohlmeier, John M. "A Measure of the Impact of Some Foreign Accounting Principles." *Journal of Accounting Research* 4 (Autumn, 1966), 183-212.
Devine, Carl T. "Research Methodology and Accounting Theory Formation." *Accounting Review* 35 (July, 1960), 387-99.
Gilman, Stephen. *Accounting Concepts of Profit*. New York: Ronald Press Company, 1939, chaps. twelve through sixteen.
Gordon, Myron. "Postulates, Principles and Research in Accounting." *Accounting Review* 39 (April, 1964), 251-63.
Gorelik, George. "Notes on the Development and Problems of Soviet Uniform Accounting." *International Journal of Accounting* 9 (Fall, 1973), 135-148.
Grady, Paul. "The Quest for Accounting Principles." *Journal of Accountancy* 113 (May, 1962), 45-50.
Hendriksen, Eldon S. *Accounting Theory*, rev. ed. Homewood, Ill.: Richard D. Irwin, 1970, especially chaps. one, three, and four.
_____. "Toward Greater Comparability Through Uniformity of Accounting Principles." *New York Certified Public Accountant* 37 (February, 1967), 105-15.
Ijiri, Yuji. *The Foundations of Accounting Measurement*. Englewood Cliffs, N.J.: Prentice-Hall, 1967, especially chap. three.
Imke, Frank J. "Relationships in Accounting Theory." *Accounting Review* 41 (April, 1966), 318-22.
Littleton, A.C. *The Structure of Accounting Theory*. Menasha, Wisc.: George Banta Company, 1961.
Littleton, A.C., and Zimmerman, V.K. *Accounting Theory: Continuity and Change*. Englewood Cliffs, N.J.: Prentice-Hall, 1962, chap. six.
Mattessich, Richard. *Accounting and Analytical Methods*. Homewood, Ill.: Richard D. Irwin, 1964, especially chap. two.
_____. "Toward a General and Axiomatic Foundation of Accountancy." *Accounting Research* 8 (October, 1957), 328-56.
Mautz, Robert K. "The Place of Postulates in Accounting." *Journal of Accountancy* 119 (January, 1965), 46-49.
_____. "Accounting Principles—How Can They Be Made More Authoritative?" *CPA Journal* (March, 1973), 185-190.
May, George O. *Financial Accounting: A Distillation of Experience*. New York: Macmillan, 1953. Reprinted by Scholars Book Company, Lawrence, Kansas, 1972. First six chapters.
Metcalf, Richard W. "The Basic Postulates in Perspective." *Accounting Review* 39 (January, 1964), 16-21.
Moonitz, Maurice. "The Basic Postulates of Accounting." *Accounting Research Study No. 1*. New York: AICPA, 1961.
_____. "Accounting Principles—Some Lessons from the American Experience." *Journal of Business Finance* 2 (1970), 51-64.
_____. *Obtaining Agreement on Standards in the Accounting Profession*. Sarasota, Florida: American Accounting Association, Studies in Accounting Research No. 8, 1974.
_____. "Three Contributions to the Development of Accounting Principles Prior to 1930." *Journal of Accounting Research* 8 (Spring, 1970), 145-155.
_____. "Why Do We Need 'Postulates' and 'Principles'?" *Journal of Accountancy* 96 (December, 1963), 42-46.
Newman, Maurice S. "Historical Development of Early Accounting Concepts and Their Relation to Certain Economic Concepts." *Academy of Accounting Historians Working Paper No. 11*. University, Alabama: Academy of Accounting Historians, 1975.

Paton, William A. *Accounting Theory*. New York: Ronald Press Company, 1922. Reprinted by Accounting Studies Press, Chicago, 1962, and by Scholars Book Company, Lawrence, Kansas, 1972. Chapter twenty.

Paton, W.A., and Littleton, A.C. *An Introduction to Corporate Accounting Standards*. American Accounting Association Monograph No. 3. New York: AAA, 1940.

Powell, Weldon. "Inventory of Generally Accepted Accounting Principles." *Journal of Accountancy* 119 (March, 1965), 29-35.

Sanders, T.H., Hatfield, H.R., and Moore, U. *A Statement of Accounting Principles*. New York: American Institute of Accountants, 1938. Reprinted by American Accounting Association, Columbus, Ohio, 1959.

Savoie, Leonard. "Accounting Attitudes." *Financial Executive* (October, 1973), 78-84.

Schmalenbach, Eugen. *Dynamic Accounting*. London: Gee, 1959.

Spacek, Leonard. "A Suggested Solution to the Principles Dilemma." *Accounting Review* 39 (April, 1964), 275-84.

_____. "The Need for an Accounting Court." *Accounting Review* 33 (July, 1958), 368-79.

Sprouse, Robert T., and Moonitz, Maurice. "A Tentative Set of Broad Accounting Principles for Business Enterprises." *Accounting Research Study No. 3*. New York: AICPA, 1962.

Storey, Reed K. "Accounting Principles: AAA and AICPA." *Journal of Accountancy* 117 (June, 1964), 47-55.

_____. *The Search for Accounting Principles*. New York: AICPA, 1964.

Vatter, William J. "Postulates and Principles." *Journal of Accounting Research* 1 (Autumn, 1963), 179-97.

Zeff, Stephen A. *Forging Accounting Principles in Five Countries: A History and Analysis of Trends*. Champaign, Ill.: Stipes Publishing Company, 1972.

_____ "Chronology of Significant Events in the Establishment of Accounting Principles in the United States, 1926-1972." *Journal of Accounting Research* 10 (Autumn, 1972), 217-227. Reprinted in Burns, *op. cit.*, 1-15.

Index

316